D1601180

THE AGE OF EDWARD III

The Age of Edward III

Edited by
J. S. Bothwell

THE UNIVERSITY *of York*

YORK MEDIEVAL PRESS

First published 2001

A York Medieval Press publication
in association with The Boydell Press
an imprint of Boydell & Brewer Ltd
PO Box 9   Woodbridge   Suffolk IP12 3DF   UK
and of Boydell & Brewer Inc.
PO Box 41026   Rochester   NY 14604–4126   USA
website: http://www.boydell.co.uk
and with the
Centre for Medieval Studies, University of York

ISBN 1 903153 06 9

A catalogue record for this book is available
from the British Library

Library of Congress Cataloging-in-Publication Data
The age of Edward III/edited by J. S. Bothwell.
   p. cm.
A York Medieval Press publication in association with the Boydell Press.
Includes bibliographical references and index.
ISBN 1–903153–06–9 (hardback: alk. paper)
   1. Great Britain – History – Edward III, 1327–1377.   2. Edward III,
King of England, 1312–1377.   I. Bothwell, James.
DA233 A36 2001
941.03′7–dc21   2001023539

This publication is printed on acid-free paper

Typeset by Joshua Associates Ltd, Oxford
Printed in Great Britain by
St Edmundsbury Press Ltd, Bury St Edmunds, Suffolk

CONTENTS

LIST OF ABBREVIATIONS

BIHR   *Bulletin of the Institute of Historical Research*
BL   British Library
BPR   *Register of Edward, the Black Prince*, ed. M. Dawes, 4 vols. (London, 1930–3)
CCharR *Calendar of Charter Rolls* 1226–1516 6 vols. (London, 1903–27)
CCR   *Calendar of Close Rolls* 1272–1485 45 vols. (London, 1892–1954)
CFR   *Calendar of Fine Rolls* 1272–1509 22 vols. (London, 1911–62)
CIM   *Calendar of Inquisitions Miscellaneous* Henry III–Henry V 7 vols. (London, 1916–68)
CIPM   *Calendar of Inquisitions Post Mortem*, 15 vols. (London, 1904–70)
CP   *The Complete Peerage*, 13 vols. in 12 (London, 1910–59)
CPR   *Calendar of Patent Rolls* 1232–1509 52 vols. (London, 1891–1916)
EcHR   *Economic History Review*
EHR   *English Historical Review*
EMDP   *English Medieval Diplomatic Practice*, ed. P. Chaplais, 2 parts in 3 vols. (London, 1975–82)
Foedera *Foedera, conventiones, literae, et cuiuscunque generis acta publica*, ed. T. Rymer (edition as cited in text)
HR   *Historical Research*
PP   *Past and Present*
PRO   Public Record Office
RDP   *Report from the Lords' Committees for all Matters Touching the Dignity of a Peer*, 4 vols. (London, 1820–9)
RP   *Rotuli Parliamentorum*, 6 vols. (London, 1783)
RS   Rolls Series
SR   *Statutes of the Realm*, 11 vols. (London, 1810–28)
TRHS   *Transactions of the Royal Historical Society*
YB   *Year Book*

Unless otherwise stated, all unpublished documents are in London, Public Record Office.

Introduction

CHRIS GIVEN-WILSON AND MICHAEL PRESTWICH

The conference at which the eleven papers included in this volume were delivered, which was organized by Dr James Bothwell and Professor Mark Ormrod, and held in July 1999 at the Centre for Medieval Studies, University of York, was a very good conference – and for no-one more so than for the man upon whom its proceedings were focused, namely, King Edward III. For, although the subjects covered by these papers vary widely, on one point at least the contributors exhibit virtual unanimity: namely, that Edward's style of kingship, whatever the epithets by which one might choose to characterize it, was successful kingship, and that the man himself, whatever quibbles or reservations might be allowed in relation to specific policies or actions, deserves the praise which, for the most part, his contemporaries heaped upon him. This is, of course, in many ways far from surprising: Edward's reputation has been rising steadily during the second half of the twentieth century, and the evidence presented here will do nothing to reverse that trend. Not that there is any lack of revisionism in this volume – indeed several of the papers included here quite explicitly challenge ideas put forward by earlier historians – but it is revisionism of the kind that results, not in our questioning of Edward's abilities, but in a readjustment of our perception of the ways in which his success was achieved. Several of the contributors, for example, emphasize the king's bent for what we now call spin-doctoring, while others stress his concern for the maintenance of law and order – an often overlooked, and sometimes frankly discountenanced, facet of his kingship. Yet there is an unmistakable impression that, above all, for Edward III, everything came back to the war, and it is war, therefore, accompanied as ever by its faithful shadow, diplomacy, which underlies many of these papers.

Of those contributors who take Edward's wars as their principal theme, the one who addresses the subject most directly is Andrew Ayton. His subject, or at any rate his starting-point, is the military career of Sir Thomas Ughtred, who fought at Bannockburn, acted as sub-marshal of the English army at Crécy, and, shortly before his death in 1365, was admitted to the Order of the Garter. Yet this is much more than a study of one Yorkshire knight's exploits, for, as the title of Ayton's paper implies, his real subject is

1

not so much Thomas Ughtred as the 'Edwardian Military Revolution', and his aim is to use Ughtred's career to spotlight the factors that made the English army the most feared military machine in Europe in the mid-fourteenth century. In terms of tactics, what lay at the heart of this military revolution was 'the replacement of retinues of heavy cavalry and companies of arrayed infantry, recruited and functioning as separate contingents, by wholly mounted, "mixed" retinues composed of men-at-arms and archers'. Yet, as Ayton demonstrates, what may have been just as important for the establishment of England's military superiority was the experience and continuity of service built up by members of the gentry and nobility during half a century and more of near-continuous war with France and Scotland. What we witness, therefore, from the 1290s onwards, is the 'militarization' of the English gentry, resulting in the formation of a military élite with 'abundant collective experience and a powerful shared mentality', accompanied by the increasing stabilization of military retinues. Revolutions, as Ayton points out, are commonly associated with 'new blood'; in this case, however, it may well be that the more important role was played by the 'old blood', veterans like Ughtred, 'whose careers spanned the period of crucial change from Bannockburn to Crécy and beyond'.

If Thomas Ughtred's life was dedicated largely to warfare, so too, manifestly, was that of Edward the Black Prince: as David Green points out at the beginning of his paper, 'there were few, if any, aspects of his life which were not shaped by the Anglo-French conflict'. Whether it follows from this that the prince 'was not a political animal' is perhaps more questionable. It would surely have been difficult for the heir to the throne *not* to be a political animal: one thinks, for example, of the way in which Edward III had to intervene to curb his eldest son's 'insensitive expansionist designs' in the Welsh March during the 1340s and 1350s,[1] or of the prince's forceful attempts to make the church contribute more to the war effort in the early 1370s.[2] Nevertheless, a study of the prince's retinue – the principal concern of Green's paper – seems to reveal significant differences to the much more exhaustively studied retinue of his younger brother, John of Gaunt, and these apparent differences may be explicable in terms of their differing political aims: 'Gaunt', as Green points out, 'sought a crown elsewhere, and his affinity was shaped with that object in mind.' One of the most striking differences between the two brothers was in their use of life indentures to recruit men to their service. Whereas Gaunt, as is well known, used them extensively (173 men are recorded as indentured with him for life in 1382), the Black Prince is only known to have sealed twenty-

---

[1] The quotation is from R. R. Davies, *Lordship and Society in the March of Wales, 1282–1400* (Oxford, 1978), p. 273.
[2] G. A. Holmes, *The Good Parliament* (Oxford, 1975), p. 17; J. I. Catto, 'An Alleged Great Council of 1374', *EHR* 82 (1967), 764–71.

one life indentures with his followers; and, although he made rather greater use of life annuities, most of those who served the prince in war did so on short-term military contracts. Arguments *ex silentio* must of course always be treated with some degree of caution, and it may be that there are other ways to explain these differences: is it simply a question of the survival (or not) of evidence? Were life indentures simply more accepted in the 1380s and 1390s than they had been in the 1350s and 1360s? The evidence of the royal affinity in the fourteenth century, or of Henry of Grosmont's affinity in the 1340s and 1350s, might suggest this. There is, at any rate, plenty of evidence for an inner core of trusted 'bachelors' and close friends at the heart of the prince's retinue (most notably, James Audley and John Chandos, the prince's right-hand men on the Poitiers campaign, according to Chandos Herald),[3] and such men must have provided the same kind of continuity and experience in the prince's retinue as men like Thomas Ughtred did in Edward III's armies. Indeed, one of the reasons why England's military fortunes suffered such a dramatic reversal in the 1370s may well have been because, within the space of the half a dozen years between Ughtred's death in 1365 and the Black Prince's retirement on health grounds in 1371, virtually an entire generation of English war-captains seems to have passed from the scene: five Knights of the Garter, for example (Audley, Chandos, Warwick, Suffolk and Burghersh) died in 1369 alone, the year that saw the renewal of the French war. It was 'new blood' that was obliged to pick up the torch in the 1370s.

Although Clifford Rogers' and Craig Taylor's papers are focused more on diplomacy than on war, both naturally have significant implications for the conduct of the 'war on the ground' as well. Clifford Rogers' paper is the most explicitly revisionist in the volume. Taking as his starting-point John Le Patourel's widely-accepted belief that it was the 'failure' of Edward III's Reims campaign of 1359–60 that forced him to settle, at Brétigny in May 1360, for considerably less than he really wanted or might plausibly have achieved, Rogers argues, through detailed examination of the texts of the various draft treaties of 1354–9, that in fact Brétigny was a 'triumph' for Edward, since it gave him 'de facto what he had gone to war for in 1337 – a free hand in Scotland, an end to French interference in Gascony, and restoration of the lands promised to him in 1329'. The arguments upon which this conclusion is based are numerous and detailed: it was the French, not the English, according to Rogers, who in the end refused to ratify the Treaty of Guînes of 1354; contrary to what Le Patourel thought, the First Treaty of London (1358) was not simply a 'ransom treaty', but a full draft peace; the Second Treaty of London, although it did indeed substantially raise the stakes, was not nearly as 'preposterous' as has sometimes been suggested; and the Reims campaign, far from being a failure, was in fact what finally forced the French

---

[3] 'Cils deuz eurent grant renomée/Et furent ordeignez au frayne/Du prince. . . .': *La Vie du Prince Noir by Chandos Herald*, ed. D. B. Tyson (Tübingen, 1975), p. 64 (l. 574).

to concede what they had twice before (in 1354 and 1358) agreed to but failed to implement. All this undoubtedly has much to recommend it, and may well become the new orthodoxy. What does still require some explanation, however, is why, if the campaign of 1359–60 was a military success, Edward felt obliged in May 1360 to step back from the terms which he had attempted to force upon the French a year earlier in the Second Treaty of London. The answer, according to Rogers, may lie in a 'religious experience' which Edward underwent as a result of the 'Black Monday' hailstorm which struck his army on 13 April 1360 (just three weeks before peace was made at Brétigny), the effects of which were so severe that, so Froissart tells us, Edward promptly vowed to the Virgin that he would now make peace. That may be. On the other hand, habitual Froissart-watchers will doubtless instantly recognize the kind of story, and the kind of explanation for human motivation, that litter the great chronicler's works, and might perhaps be more cautious before asserting that 'there is no reason to doubt the chronicler's testimony'. This is not to deny that 'Black Monday' probably did extensive damage both to the morale and the military effectiveness of Edward's army – enough damage, possibly, to force him into a settlement. Alternatively, however, might it not have been the French who – given the alleged success of Edward's campaign – now indicated that they were prepared to accept Edward's terms and make peace? Why, in other words, is it necessary to postulate a 'religious experience' on Edward's behalf, when in fact Edward was getting almost exactly what he had previously shown that he was prepared to settle for?

However, this is really just a quibble. More significant for our under-standing of Edward's diplomatic and military strategy is the fundamental assertion by Rogers that the English king 'began his war with France with three basic aims', and that the assumption of the French throne was simply 'a means to achieving his initial ends'. Craig Taylor, working from quite different evidence and covering a rather longer period, reaches the same conclusion: the claim to the French throne was, he says, 'in reality . . . a secondary goal for the English during the Hundred Years War'. Indeed, neither Rogers nor Taylor feels it necessary to debate this point, and this in itself is significant: Le Patourel's argument that Edward III really did want to become king of France finds few supporters nowadays, despite the vigour and persuasiveness with which he set it out some forty years ago. Never-theless, as Taylor points out, if Edward was going to advance a claim to the French throne, and if he hoped to employ it to good effect, then he must be seen to be taking it seriously, and this he did. Basing his argument primarily upon a 'dossier' used by English diplomats at the Avignon peace conference of 1344 (parts of which had in fact been written for presentation to Pope Benedict XII in 1340), Taylor shows how a detailed, legal basis was developed for Edward's claim, in response to which the French too developed increas-ingly complex arguments in order to counter it. The Salic Law, however, was *not* apparently one of the arguments used by the French to counter Edward III's claim; despite later French assertions to the contrary, it was not in fact until the early fifteenth century that 'official Valois writers' began to use the Salic Law ('an otiose Frankish law concerning private inheritance that could have no direct bearing on the French succession') as a riposte to the Plantagenet claim to their master's crown.

One of the problems relating to the development of these various arguments is, of course, the question of whom they were intended to impress. According to Taylor, there was little *public* propaganda value to be derived from the often quite technical and legalistic language in which they were couched. They were for debating by lawyers at peace conferences, not for nailing on church doors. Even so, they show clearly Edward's skill in developing different arguments for different audiences, and, as Alison McHardy argues in another paper based upon close study of a specific corpus of texts, Edward also showed a keen awareness of the publicity value of the church door. It has of course long been recognized that Edward made consistent efforts (through the numerous newsletters preserved by chroniclers, for example, or through speeches, usually by proxy, to parliament and convocation) to make sure that his subjects were informed about his successes abroad, about his hopes and aims, and about the perfidy of his enemies. However, what has not been fully understood until now is the care that was taken to ensure that the king's propaganda was disseminated as widely as possible, or the methods by which this was achieved. Yet, as McHardy shows, the evidence to demonstrate this has been readily available, largely in the form of bishops' registers – for it was through the machinery of diocesan administration that the king had the best chance of reaching the widest audience, and Edward was not slow to realize this. Thus writs were regularly sent out by the government to the bishops ordering the saying of prayers and masses, the holding of processions and public thanksgiving ceremonies, and so forth, and the certificates of execution returned by the bishops suggest that they were regularly acted upon. Moreover – and here one gets an even more revealing glimpse of Edward as spin-doctor – these writs were not simply generalized orders to offer prayers, etc.; on the contrary, their wording suggests that they were 'intended to form the basis of sermons or homilies which would be preached on these occasions', sermons which were 'strongly political in character'. As to the target audience, McHardy makes the interesting suggestion that this might have consisted especially of the old, the underemployed, and those who for other reasons were unable to make an active contribution to the war effort, thus encouraging them too to get caught up in the 'good war'. Yet, however sophisticated Edward III's propagandist tactics might have been, McHardy is suitably cautious as to the efficacy of his methods: certainly, as she points out, to judge from the highly volatile state of the country in 1340–41, Edward's subjects would take a lot more convincing than they had had so far. Whether their apparently greater willingness to contribute to the war over the next two decades was as a consequence of more sophisticated propaganda techniques, or of the psychological boost of a remarkable series of military victories, is difficult to know.

Similar questions are raised by Mark Ormrod's examination of the royal style used by Edward following his formal assumption of the French throne in January 1340, and the consequent creation – in name, at any rate – of his 'double monarchy'. The task facing Edward was 'to make the French claim acceptable and attractive to the domestic political community' – the apparent inference to be drawn from which is that it was not, on the face of it, likely to be either. And so, indeed, it would appear, if one is to judge by the proceedings of the parliament of March–May 1340, in which Edward issued his oft-quoted statute guaranteeing the constitutional separation of the English and French crowns – which, it is worth noting, Henry V was in turn asked by parliament to confirm, following the concession to him at the Treaty of Troyes of his claim to the French throne following Charles VI's death.[4] It may be, as Ormrod argues, that the 1340 statute was not, as has often been assumed, squeezed by a sceptical lords and commons out of a reluctant monarch, but was rather 'offered as a premeditated concession to parliament'. Nevertheless, as he notes, it clearly *was* a concession, and on such a touchy subject the king had to continue to play his hand with some circumspection. One of the ways in which he did this over the remaining years of his reign was, systematically, to vary his royal style in accordance with the audience which he was addressing. To a French audience, he was *rex Francie et Anglie*; to an English audience, however, he was *rex Anglie et Francie* – 'a concerted – and apparently successful – effort on the part of the king to offset both official and unofficial anxieties over the wisdom of his new claim'. When addressing the subjects of other dominions which he either ruled or claimed to rule (Normandy, for example, or Calais), he would again vary his style in order to appeal to regional sympathies. Not surprisingly, his chancery clerks occasionally became confused and inadvertently used the wrong style. For them, the easiest solution would doubtless have been to adopt the address used by one petitioner in 1360, who simply called Edward 'the mightiest king of all the world'. Not that he was the only medieval king of England to be flattered by such terms. Forty years later, in the opening speech to the parliament of 1402, chancellor Edmund Stafford too would remind the assembled commons that the King of the Romans had recently sent a letter to Henry IV 'as if to the most powerful king in the world'.[5] Richard II, who set much store by forms of address,[6] would not have been impressed; there is no record of *him* ever being addressed in such terms.

[4] *RP*, IV, 127.
[5] *RP*, III, 485: '. . . ad escript a notre dit seigneur le Roi come a le plus puissant Roi du monde'.
[6] N. Saul, 'Richard II and the Vocabulary of Kingship', *EHR* 110 (1995), 854–77.

Manipulation of public opinion by Edward III is usually associated with the winning of national support for his wars. Yet, as James Bothwell shows in a paper centring on Edward's celebrated creation of six new earls in March 1337, decisions relating to patronage and promotion were potentially just as controversial as the claiming of the French throne, and here too it was important to cultivate wider support. Moreover, given the traumas and competing claims to land which had torn the nobility apart during the 1320s, not only did Edward have to win support for his 'favourites', but he also had to try to afford them as much legal security as he could for the lands which he granted them. What Bothwell shows us, therefore, is the development by Edward during the first decade of his reign of a 'patronage policy' – a policy based upon the winning of consent for the granting out of lands, careful explanation of the reasons for its redistribution, and the maintenance of the co-operation of the 'old blood' while simultaneously promoting the interests of 'new blood'. To begin with, Edward proceeded cautiously; later, as those whom he favoured were seen to earn their rewards, his confidence grew, until, by 1337, he was ready to make a 'flamboyant and well publicized gesture of backing the "new men" in the hope of making the landed settlement a secure one . . .'. Yet, as Bothwell demonstrates, getting the balance of patronage right was a tricky business, and every new grant, however carefully warranted or securely backed, simultaneously had the effect of creating one more competing claim which might come back to haunt the king in the future. Moreover, however good Edward's publicity machine, there were always going to be some who opposed the king's patronage not merely for personal reasons but as a matter of policy: Sir Thomas Gray, for example, author of the *Scalacronica*, was noticeably underwhelmed by the grants made to the new promotions of 1337, commenting that:

> . . . upon which earls [the 1337 creations] and other good men of his, the king bestowed so liberally of his possessions that he retained for himself scarcely any of the lands appertaining to the crown, but was obliged to subsist upon levies and subsidies, which were a heavy burden to his people.[7]

Such sentiments are a useful reminder that, although it is easy to look back at Edward III's comital creations of 1337 and depict them as a master-stroke of royal policy, it is similarly easy to imagine how things might have turned out rather differently. Even so, it remains surprising how few objections there seem to have been to the actual promotions of 1337, especially given the controversy – and subsequent 'demotions' – which had followed the comital creations of the previous thirty years (Gaveston, the elder Despenser, Harcla, Mortimer). It is this lack of attendant controversy that suggests that Edward's 'patronage policy' had indeed been an effective one.

---

[7] T. Gray, *Scalacronica*, ed. and trans. H. Maxwell (Glasgow, 1907), p. 102.

If the promotions of March 1337 can, with hindsight, be seen as bringing to a successful conclusion the development of royal policy towards the nobility during the first phase of Edward's personal rule, there is no doubt that it was 'the king's secret plan' – the coup at Nottingham castle on the night of 19 October 1330, by which Roger Mortimer and Queen Isabelle were toppled from power – which had marked the opening of that phase. The story of the coup is well-known, as are the king's principal associates: this, indeed, is what gives the coup a good part of its longer-term significance, for it was men such as William Montagu, Robert Ufford and William Clinton, all of whom were promoted to earldoms in 1337, who acted as midwives to Edward's seizure of power. For them, and especially for Montagu, the leader of the band, the night of 19 October 1330 marked the turning-point of their careers. Had they failed, Mortimer would surely have condemned them to the same fate as he had so recently visited upon the king's own uncle, the earl of Kent. In the event, their success meant that they became, for the next generation, Edward's principal advisers and confidants (even before they received their earldoms in 1337, they were already – in the early 1330s – the leading bannerets of Edward's household). Yet, as Caroline Shenton shows, new evidence can sometimes shed a rather different light on our understanding of events even as well-known as this. In this case, the evidence comes partly from royal pardons issued in the aftermath of the coup, and partly from a royal armourer's account of November 1330, which, taken together, reveal the names of more than a dozen further men who were involved in the coup. Moreover, the significance of these discoveries is not limited simply to the fact that they add to our knowledge of the events of 19 October. They also yield clues as to the (long suspected) extent of Henry of Lancaster's involvement in Mortimer's overthrow; indeed, Shenton argues that they set the coup in a rather different context, as 'the last of several attempts to overthrow the regency, orchestrated by Lancaster'. Whether, in the end, it was in fact Lancaster or Montagu – or even the young Edward himself – who masterminded the coup, is a question we shall probably never be able to answer for sure, but the evidence unearthed by Shenton shows that it was undoubtedly the work of more than just a small band of desperadoes.

Yet if uncertainty remains as to the true author of the coup, there is no doubt as to its principal victims. Mortimer's fate is unlikely to have troubled Edward for long: the indignities which he had heaped upon the young king over the past few years had rankled deeply, and he was soon hurried away to London to suffer the ultimate penalty. More problematic was the question of what Edward might do with his own mother. There could clearly be no question of putting *her* to death, not least because she was the daughter of a French king. On the other hand, Isabelle had a well-founded reputation for political intrigue, and, given her behaviour over the previous few years, Edward must have felt distinctly uneasy about allowing her too free a hand. In the event, therefore, she was despatched to Castle Rising in Norfolk, where

8

she spent most of the remaining twenty-eight years of her life in honourable retirement, before dying in August 1358 – or so, at least, it has generally been assumed. Michael Bennett, however, working principally from the evidence of the surviving account-book of Isabelle's household during the last year of her life, suggests that this picture might need some revision. Isabelle, he argues, was not nearly as cut off, either culturally or politically, from her son's court as has usually been thought. Moreover, in the rather unusual circumstances prevailing during the last fifteen months of her life, she may once again have had a useful political role to play, for this, of course, was the period during which the French King Jean and more than a dozen of his leading nobles, captives since the battle of Poitiers in September 1356, were held prisoner in England, and several of them (Marshal d'Audrehem and the comte de Tancarville in particular) made a habit of visiting Isabelle at Hertford castle, where she was now based. Whether, as Bennett speculates, she may have been acting as an intermediary in the Anglo-French negotiations that were going on throughout this period, is difficult to know. The record of her meetings with both French and English dignitaries – meticulously preserved in the margins of her account-book – is certainly suggestive. If not, she was certainly living a very full social life – but this, as Bennett points out, is not impossible, for England was 'the centre of an international court culture' in the late 1350s, and the English court was in celebratory mood following the triumphs of the mid-1350s. Indeed, the courtly festivities of the late 1350s – once termed by the Anglophobe Jules Michelet 'the insolent courtesy of the English' – are a reminder of the close cultural links which, despite twenty years of unrelieved war, still existed between the English and French aristocracies.

The fact that, during the last year of her life, Isabelle may still have been trying to broker the lasting peace between England and France upon which, fifty years earlier, her marriage to Edward II had been intended to set the seal, is symptomatic of the degree to which warfare had dominated her son's reign. Some historians have argued that one unfortunate consequence of this preoccupation with military affairs was that Edward III tended to neglect another of the principal obligations of kingship, the maintenance of law and order. This argument (commonly characterized as war state *versus* law state)[8] is vigorously rejected by other contributors in this volume, Anthony Musson and Richard Partington. Yet, while both of them arrive at the same conclusion on this question, the angles from which they approach it are very different. Musson is concerned with the making of the law – with Edward's record as a 'legal legislator' – and his conclusions, like those of Rogers, are explicitly revisionist. Edward's reign, he argues, far from being a stagnant period in the history of English legislation, was in fact 'a constructive period . . . which

---

[8] For the most comprehensive exposition of this argument, see R. W. Kaeuper, *War, Justice and Public Order: England and France in the Later Middle Ages* (Oxford, 1988).

witnessed decisive enactments in the areas of administrative law', and the king himself 'deserves the accolade "second English Justinian"'. Any such epithet naturally invites comparison with the first 'English Justinian', Edward I, yet there were clear differences between Edward III's legislation and that of his grandfather: it was in the area of procedural rather than substantive law that the significant advances were made during Edward III's reign. The backdrop to this was the growing acceptance of the closely-linked concepts of 'the binding force of statutes' and 'the legislative supremacy of parliament'; the result was a series of enactments many of which are justly famous (for example, the Statute of Treasons, the Ordinance and Statute of Labourers, the Ordinance of the Staple, and the various legislative acts relating to the peace commissions), but for which Edward has never received the credit he deserves – for, Musson argues, Edward never really surrendered the initiative in making legislation to parliament, and the growing authority and precision of statute law during his reign were attributable primarily to the careful work of the king and his justices. There was, however, one sense in which Edward's attitude to the law justifies the label of 'pragmatic opportunist', that is, in his granting of pardons to criminals as a means of recruiting soldiers for his armies. This is, of course, precisely the sort of evidence which historians of the 'war state *versus* law state' persuasion have used extensively in order to demonstrate Edward's lack of concern with the maintenance of law and order, and one suspects that this particular debate still has some distance to run.

Nevertheless, Musson's carefully-argued paper certainly constitutes a well-aimed shot across the bows of those who argue that Edward neglected the law and order question, as does that of Richard Partington. Partington's paper is concerned not with the making of the law, but with its enforcement, and in particular with the 'police function' performed by that hitherto strangely neglected group of royal servants, the king's sergeants-at-arms; and, although it is based primarily on a study of their activities in three counties (Essex, Shropshire and Leicestershire), it has much wider implications than this might suggest. According to Partington, it was in the aftermath of the crisis of 1340–41 that the sergeants-at-arms really came to the fore as the 'enforcers' of the royal will in the localities, and the main reason for this was because one of the lessons which Edward had learned from the crisis was that there were certain people whom he could not trust, whereas the sergeants were men whom he could. Crucial to this was the fact that the sergeants were – at least nominally – attached to the royal household. Their primary duty, in fact, was to act as the king's personal bodyguard, and it was in this capacity that the element of trust between them and the king was developed: 'their authority must have rested in their manifest closeness to the king and his purposes'. The tasks assigned to them were remarkably diverse: they were prominent, for example, in the organization of military campaigns, and some appear to have been specialists in naval affairs; they were frequently used to make arrests (sometimes of persons of much higher social status than themselves), or simply to act as trouble-shooters when reports of disturbances reached the king from the localities. What Partington emphasizes in particular, however, is that the uses to which Edward put them reveal the king's genuine concern to deal with order in the localities – 'to punish corruption, deal with its consequences and prevent its repetition' – and that the king employed them 'not only in support of war but also in support of justice'. Richard II, on the other hand, used his sergeants-at-arms not for the 'common good', but as agents of a very different brand of kingship, and it is this that explains why the sergeants-at-arms have, generally speaking, received such a bad press in the past.

Partington's paper is one of a number in this volume to make either explicit or implicit comparisons between Edward and either his father or his grandson, and, as might be expected, such comparisons almost invariably serve to bring Edward III's talents and triumphs into sharper focus. As has already been pointed out, there is practically nothing in these papers that is likely to diminish or even dent Edward's reputation. Given that the list of contributors to this volume includes some of the leading current historians and brightest young scholars of the reign, such unanimity might not have been expected, and is perhaps worth a moment's consideration. An obvious comparison would be with Henry V. Like Edward III, Henry V has enjoyed remarkable favour with historians during the second half of the twentieth century. The volume of essays edited by Gerald Harriss and published in 1985 under the title *Henry V: The Practice of Kingship* similarly contained barely a hint of criticism of the man whom Bruce McFarlane once called 'the greatest man that ever ruled England' (although in this case the degree of consensus was less remarkable, given that Harriss himself wrote five of the ten chapters in the book).[9] Thus, despite the fact that the current generation of historians is probably more aware than any before of the methods by which both Edward III and Henry V sought to influence the ways in which their deeds were portrayed, and is thus suitably cautious about accepting the praise of contemporaries too readily, in neither case does it seem that a devil's advocate is yet rash enough to poke his or her head more than an inch or two above the parapet. Perhaps this will change in the twenty-first century – and perhaps that would be no bad thing, for dissent and provocation will inevitably stimulate further debate and thereby sharpen understanding. For the moment, however, there can be no doubt that Edward III's reputation rests secure.

---

[9] G. L. Harriss, *Henry V: The Practice of Kingship* (Oxford, 1985); for the quotation, see K. B. McFarlane, *Lancastrian Kings and Lollard Knights* (Oxford, 1972), p. 133.

1

Edward III and the Coup of 1330

CAROLINE SHENTON

Formal announcement of the success of the palace coup which brought Edward III's minority to an end was made to the sheriffs on 20 October 1330 in the following terms:

> Whereas the king's affairs and the affairs of the realm have been directed until now to the damage and dishonour of him and his realm and to the impoverishment of his people, as he has well perceived and as the facts prove, wherefore he has, of his own knowledge and will, caused certain persons to be arrested, to wit the Earl of La Marche, Sir Oliver Ingham, and Sir Simon de Bereford, who have been principal movers of the said affairs, and he wills that all men shall know that he will henceforth govern his people according to right and reason, as befits his royal dignity, and that the affairs that concern him and the estate of the realm shall be directed by the common counsel of the magnates of the realm and in no otherwise: he therefore enjoins the sheriff to cause this his intention to be published through his bailiwick, so that all people may fully understand it.[1]

The writs were confirmation of the success of a hasty, though not altogether unprepared, plot conceived by the king and his closest friends to overthrow the regents, the queen mother, Isabelle, and her ally, Roger Mortimer. While the events themselves are well known, other aspects are not. The identity of six high-profile participants has long been established, yet many more conspirators were involved and their names have only recently come to light.

Under the tutelage of Mortimer and Isabelle, Edward III had suffered a series of indignities between 1326 and 1330 well chronicled at the time. In almost every way possible, Mortimer had compromised and humiliated the king. Edward had been crowned in unique and difficult circumstances in January 1327, following the deposition of his father. Henry of Lancaster, the king's cousin, was appointed head of the regency council, but within a few months, Mortimer was bypassing the council, and quickly became the driving force

---

[1] *CCR 1330–3*, p. 158.

behind Isabelle's policies. The situation in Scotland, in particular, was an utter humiliation. The king's only foray across the border in 1327 ended in disaster when the Scots surrounded the English camp, and took large numbers of English and Hainault soldiers prisoner. James Douglas even managed to break through the watch and advance right up to the royal pavilion, then evade capture, leaving the king behind weeping tears of rage and frustration.[2] The peace which followed, in March 1328, gave Scotland to Bruce and his heirs. Under the terms of the Treaty of Northampton, all English rights in Scotland were renounced, and the border reverted to its position under Alexander III. A marriage was arranged between the king's sister, Joan, and David Bruce, and 20,000 marks were paid to the English as a sweetener. Edward refused to attend the occasion.[3] The settlement money was quickly spent, for no trace of it survived by the end of 1330.[4] Indeed, on Mortimer and Isabelle's fall, the treasury was virtually empty, the regents having stripped it of the estimated £62,000 hoarded by Edward II up to 1326.[5]

Then, sometime in September 1328, with Mortimer's connivance, Thomas Gourney and William Ocle murdered Edward II.[6] Early in 1330, the king's uncle, Edmund earl of Kent, was brutally executed after being inveigled into believing that Edward II was still alive. Alongside this reign of terror, lesser indignities continued unabated. Queen Philippa's coronation was delayed so much that it was only in February 1330 that she was crowned, two years after her marriage to Edward when, presumably, it seemed indecorous for her to be five months pregnant with Edward's first child and yet not officially his queen.[7] Mortimer himself was personally objectionable to the king, and sought to advance his position in the most blatant manner. In 1328 he gave

[2] *John of Fordun's Chronicle of the Scottish Nation*, ed. W. F. Skene (Edinburgh, 1872), p. 344; *Chronicon de Lanercost*, ed. J. Stevenson (Edinburgh, 1839), p. 260; T. Gray, *Scalacronica*, ed. J. Stevenson (Edinburgh, 1836), p. 155; *The Brut*, ed. F. W. D. de Brie, 2 vols. (Oxford, 1908), I, 251.

[3] *Lanercost*, pp. 261–2.

[4] *RP*, II, 53; R. G. Nicholson, *Edward III and the Scots* (Oxford, 1965), p. 50.

[5] N. M. Fryde, *The Tyranny and Fall of Edward II, 1321–1326* (Cambridge, 1979), p. 209. Contemporaries were only too well aware of the depletion of the royal treasure: see also *Croniques de London*, ed. G. J. Aungier (London, 1844), p. 61; *Chronicon Domini Walteri de Hemingburgh*, ed. H. C. Hamilton, 2 vols. (London, 1849), II, 300. The regents may have sought some rather alternative solutions to their cashflow problem because in 1329 they sought out some alchemists who claimed to have made silver out of base metal, presumably for the purpose of augmenting the contents of the Treasury: *Foedera, conventiones, literæ et cujuscunque generis acta publica inter reges Angliæ et alios quosvis imperatores, reges, pontifices, principes vel communitates, ab anno 1101, accurante T. Rymer (R. Sanderson). ab A.D.1066, aucta et multis locis emendata, accurantibus A. Clarke (J. Caley) and F. Holbrooke*. 3 vols [in 7 pt.] (Record Commission, London, 1816–30), II2, 25.

[6] *Chronicon Galfridi le Baker de Swynbroke*, ed. E. M. Thompson (Oxford, 1889), p. 34.

[7] 'Historia Roffensis de William Dene', in *Anglia Sacra*, ed. H. Wharton, 2 vols. (London, 1691), I, 370, noted 'gravida fuit et impraegnata' at her coronation.

himself the novel title of earl of March and expanded his estates enormously.[8] He then married his two daughters extremely advantageously, to the son of the earl Marshal and the heir of Sir John Hastings.[9] The king lived with the embarrassment of his mother's illicit affair with the man behind his father's death, and – worst of all – in the late summer of 1330 a rumour spread abroad that Mortimer intended to overturn the royal bloodline and usurp the throne himself, the implication being that Isabelle was pregnant with his child.[10] By the time parliament was due to sit at Nottingham on 20 October 1330 Mortimer was showing scant respect for the king's status, berating him in public and audaciously walking in front of him in full view of the court.[11] In short, he was guilty of 'provoking the death of Edward II and the annihilation of the position of the king, his consort and his son'.[12]

The king's close friend, Montagu, persuaded Edward to act, saying 'it is better to eat dog than be eaten by the dog'.[13] The king was unlikely to have needed much encouragement. He was approaching his eighteenth birthday and he must have been aware that a man who had engineered the murders of his father and uncle might just countenance disposing of him as well. The existence of the king's heir, Edward of Woodstock, born in June 1330, was an added incentive for Edward to move against Mortimer at the Nottingham parliament, due to be held on 20 October.

Study of the events and personnel involved in the coup is hindered by the covert nature of the plot, declared in Parliament to have been the king's 'secret plan'.[14] Secrecy was a wise move: the first charge against Mortimer at his trial included the accusation that he had placed a man called John Wyard, and others, around the king to spy on his words and deeds.[15] Nevertheless,

---

[8] G. A. Holmes, *The Estates of the Higher Nobility in the Fourteenth Century* (Cambridge, 1957), p. 13.

[9] *Baker*, p. 42.

[10] *Baker*, pp. 45–6. Isabelle was about thirty-four in 1330, so a pregnancy was quite possible: see P. C. Doherty, 'The Date of the Birth of Isabella, Queen of England, 1308–1358', *BIHR* 47 (1975), 246–8 (p. 247). Froissart, writing long after the coup, was convinced that Isabelle was pregnant in October 1330: J. Froissart, *Oeuvres*, ed. Kervyn de Lettenhove, 25 vols. (Brussels, 1867–77), XII, 247; her subsequent retirement to Castle Rising could easily have hidden a miscarriage or birth. Paul Doherty suggests that several times between September 1329 and July 1330 Isabelle nominated Mortimer as her heir in case of her death; only when she had been pregnant with Edward III in 1312 had she made such nominations before, and this is suggestive: P. C. Doherty, 'Isabella, Queen of England 1308–1330' (unpublished D.Phil. dissertation, University of Oxford, 1977), p. 287.

[11] *Baker*, p. 45.

[12] *RP*, II, 53–5.

[13] *Scalacronica*, p. 157: 'qe meutz serroit a mangier de la chien qe chien de eaux'.

[14] *RP*, II, 56.

[15] *RP*, II, 52a, no. 1. See also *Brut*, II, 268: 'some that were of the Kyngus counseil lovede the Mortymer, and tolde him in privitee how that the Kyng and his conseil wer about fram day to day hym forto shende and undo.'

Mortimer was exceptionally uneasy as parliament gathered in Nottingham on 19 October, so he lodged in the castle with Isabelle for their own safety.[16] Isabelle took personal possession of the castle keys.[17] During the day Mortimer, angered by recent rumours put about concerning his involvement in the murder of Edward II, heard advice from his supporters: the queen mother, Henry Burghersh, bishop of Lincoln, Hugh Turplington, steward of the household and Simon Bereford, the escheator south of the Trent.[18] At the same time, the king's supporters – William Montagu, Edward Bohun, Ralph Stafford, Robert Ufford, William Clinton and John Neville de Hornby – went to persuade him to move against Mortimer.[19] The regent heard of the plan through his spies, and the king and his 'covyne' were summoned before Mortimer's council to be interrogated. All remained silent, except Montagu who vigorously denied any knowledge of a plot.[20] The conspirators then left the castle and lodged in the town, afraid that Mortimer was about to strike against them.[21] Montagu arranged with his man on the inside, William Eland, to get inside again that night by a secret subterranean passage opening outside the castle walls but leading directly into the keep.[22]

Once inside the keep, the band mounted the stairs and entered the queen mother's chamber through an open door.[23] Within the chamber a considerable fight took place. Three of Mortimer's supporters were killed. The steward, Hugh de Turplington, was killed by John Neville.[24] An usher, Richard de Crombek, who was presumably guarding the door, and a household squire called Richard de Munimuth were also killed in the fray.[25] Mortimer was arrested with his advisers Bereford and Oliver de

---

[16] *Robert of Avesbury, De Gestis Mirabilis Regis Edwardi Tertii*, ed. E. M. Thompson (RS, 1889), p. 285.

[17] *Brut*, II, 268.

[18] *Brut*, II, 269.

[19] *Scalacronica*, p. 157; *Brut*, II, 269; *Baker*, p. 46. The *Brut* also names Edward Bohun's brothers, Humphrey and William, as conspirators but their names are not found among those pardoned for the murders. Ralph Stafford, mentioned here, was not among those given pardons either.

[20] *Scalacronica*, p. 157.

[21] *Brut*, II, 269.

[22] *Baker*, p. 46; *Brut*, II, 270–1. *Scalacronica*, p. 158, suggests that a postern gate was left open for them on the order of the king but since Isabelle had the castle keys and one of the charges against Mortimer at his trial was that he had commanded that his orders were to be obeyed even when they differed from those of the king, this seems unlikely. The rock on which Nottingham castle was built still contains naturally-formed passages: see C. Drage, 'Nottingham Castle: A Place Full Royal', *Transactions of the Thoroton Society of Nottinghamshire* 93 (1989), 1–151 (pp. 50–1); *The Buildings of England: Nottinghamshire*, ed. N. Pevsner and T. Williamson, 2nd edn (London, 1979), p. 226.

[23] *Baker*, p. 46.

[24] *Brut*, II, 271, says with a mace; *Scalacronica*, p. 158, says with a knife; *Baker*, p. 46, merely says he directed the fatal blow.

[25] *Scalacronica*, p. 158; *CPR 1330–4*, pp. 69 and 90. A livery list for 1328 gives the name

Ingham, the seneschal of Aquitaine.[26] Henry Burghersh apparently tried to escape down the privy, a fact which one monastic chronicler included in his account with some glee.[27] The queen mother ran out of her bed-chamber crying, 'Good son, have pity on noble Mortimer.' The picture painted by chroniclers is one of chaos and confusion. But the conspirators must have made some tactical plans before entry into the chamber, and must have been highly disciplined once inside. It was essential that Mortimer remained uninjured in order that he could be put on trial: a public statement that his tyranny and regime of regicide had been overthrown was vital to the re-establishment of Edward III's position. In order for this to happen, the conspirators must have taken active steps to ensure that Mortimer's person was protected in the fray. Similarly, although it was of the highest importance that Edward was seen to participate in the coup, it was essential that he was not injured or killed in the fray. To prevent harm coming to the king at this most vulnerable of moments, he may have remained out of the way: one chronicler certainly states that Isabelle knew her son was nearby but that she could not see him.[28]

Other questions remain tantalizingly without answer. Why did Mortimer and his companions not hear the approach of a heavily-armed band, which as we shall see later, comprised at least sixteen men, possibly more? Did the conspirators know that there would only be six men with Mortimer at the time, or were they expecting more resistance? Why weren't the conspirators easily overpowered as they emerged individually from the top of the staircase leading into the chamber? Why was the door of the chamber open? Why didn't the castle guards intervene, hearing the sounds of a struggle inside the chamber? And finally, to what extent was the success of the coup the king's or Montagu's?

Nevertheless, the success of the coup was greeted with delight. At dawn on

---

of a Richard de Minemuth among the household squires, who may well be 'Munimuth'. The next surviving list of the household is from 1330: Minemuth does not appear. It certainly dates from after the coup because Mortimer's hench-men, Turplington and Simon Bereford, listed in 1328, are also missing: see *Calendar of the Memoranda Rolls, Michaelmas 1325 to Michaelmas 1326*, ed. R. E. Latham (London, 1968), pp. 373–85. Munimuth had been a supporter of Mortimer for some years: he escaped from the Tower of London in 1323 with Mortimer after their imprisonment there the year before, and was pardoned for this in 1327 by Mortimer: *CPR 1327–30*, p. 14; E. L. G. Stones, 'The Date of Roger Mortimer's Escape from the Tower of London', *EHR* 66 (1951), 97–8. Richard de Crombek's name cannot be found among the lists of members of the household.

[26] *Brut*, II, 271; 'Gesta Edwardi de Carnarvan Auctore Canonico Bridlingtoniensi cum Continuatione ad A. D. 1377', in *Chronicles of the Reigns of Edward I and Edward II*, ed. W. Stubbs, 2 vols. (RS, 1882–3), II, 101.

[27] *Chronica Monasterii de Melsa*, ed. E. A. Bond, 3 vols. (RS, 1869), III, 360.

[28] *Baker*, p. 46.

20 October, Lancaster himself led the hue and cry which announced the fall of Mortimer and his accomplices, and it is perhaps not coincidental that the route chosen to take Mortimer to London was via Loughborough and Leicester, on Lancaster's home territory.[29] An opportunistic thief called James Trumpwyn stole £100 from Mortimer's personal treasure on the day he was arrested, money which the crown was still seeking to reclaim over forty years later.[30] Parliament sat in November to hear the charges, and Mortimer and Bereford were sentenced to be hung, drawn and quartered. Thomas Gourney, who along with William Ocle, another of Edward II's killers, had fled abroad, was captured, though he was killed before he was able to return to England.[31] John Maltravers, accused of the killing of Kent, took flight on a fishing boat from Mousehole in Cornwall to France, staying in exile on the continent for over twenty years.[32] Parliament issued an order for the capture, dead or alive, of Bogo Bayons and John Deveril, the men who deceived Kent about Edward II, but their subsequent fate is unknown.[33] However, Oliver Ingham was pardoned for his adherence to Mortimer because of his long service in Gascony[34] and John Wyard, the spy, was also forgiven and had his lands restored in January 1331.[35] Henry Burghersh was soon back in favour, and continued as bishop of Lincoln.[36] Generous to men he had little reason to spare, the king was yet more generous to his supporters.

Six conspirators mentioned by name in the chronicles are also found among the names of people pardoned for the murders which took place at Nottingham: Montagu and Eland, Edward Bohun, Robert Ufford, William Clinton and John Neville.[37] The conspirators were given a general pardon by parliament, although some took the extra precaution of taking out additional, personal, pardons. All received major rewards from the king.

William Montagu was showered with honours – as was appropriate for the leader of the band. The parliament rolls recorded that in undertaking the arrest of Mortimer and his henchmen, William had acted nobly for the peace and tranquillity of the whole realm.[38] It is likely that he and the king grew up

[29] *Baker*, p. 46.
[30] *Royal Writs Addressed to John Buckingham, Bishop of Lincoln, 1363–1398: Lincoln Register 12B, A Calendar*, ed. A. K. McHardy, Lincoln Record Society 86 (1997), pp. 44 and 52. I am most grateful to Alison McHardy for this fascinating reference.
[31] *Adam Murimuth, Continuatio chronicarum*, ed. E. M. Thompson (RS, 1889), pp. 63–4.
[32] *CPR 1330–4*, p. 144; *CPR 1350–4*, p. 110.
[33] *RP*, II, 53 and 55. John Deveril had connections with Corfe Castle, where Kent believed Edward II was being imprisoned in 1330 (*CPR 1327–30*, p. 557).
[34] *CPR 1330–4*, p. 22 (8 December 1330).
[35] *CPR 1330–4*, p. 53.
[36] *CPR 1330–4*, pp. 16 and 18.
[37] *RP*, II, 60b, no. 24. The names of three further conspirators mentioned in chronicle sources – Ralph Stafford, Humphrey Bohun and William Bohun – are not found among the names of those pardoned (see *Brut*, II, 269).
[38] *RP*, II, 56b, no. 4.

together and he was already highly in favour with Edward before the coup, being a household banneret.[39] Parliament granted him and his heirs land worth £1000 a year, and he was given, with poetic justice, a large proportion of Mortimer's personal property, including the castle, town, manor and honour of Denbigh, the cantreds of Ros, Rhyfiniog and Caermer in Wales, and Sherborne Castle.[40] He was also given the rents of Isabelle's manors of Christchurch, Westover and Ringwood in Hampshire; Crookham in Berkshire; the manor of Catford in Lewisham; the Wiltshire manors of Kingsbury, Somerton and Camel which had escheated to the king on the murder of the earl of Kent; and was made keeper of the royal manor and park of Woodstock with its rent of £100 a year.[41] The process of rewarding him continued apace in the following years. In 1335 he was granted, as a result of war in Scotland, the forest of Selkirk, Ettrick and Peebles. He was made governor of the Channel Islands and constable of the Tower of London.[42] Ultimately Montagu was rewarded with the earldom of Salisbury in March 1337, having accompanied the king on many diplomatic negotiations and military projects, while receiving numerous smaller gifts along the way. Had he lived long enough, Montagu would undoubtedly have been granted the Order of the Garter, which on its foundation comprised many of those whose loyalty to Edward stretched back to the coup; as it was his son took his place as a founder member.[43] On Montagu's death the income from his lands alone was worth £2,400 annually.[44]

William Eland was the man who told Montagu of the secret tunnel into the castle and who guided the conspirators into the keep.[45] All the information about Eland's career to 1330 comes from Baker, who says he had been speculator of the castle for many years and knew the building intimately. Exactly what the post of speculator involved is not entirely clear. It suggests someone who has oversight of the fabric, or who had a surveying function in the castle; this would certainly explain how Eland knew about the secret passages inside the building. Eland was definitely not the constable: this post

---

[39] R. Douch, 'The Career, Lands and Family of William Montagu, Earl of Salisbury (1301–44)', *BIHR* 24 (1951), 85–7 (p. 85); *Memoranda Rolls*, pp. 373 and 377. For a comprehensive analysis of the rewards given to Montagu, Clinton and Ufford, see J. S. Bothwell, below.

[40] *RP*, II, 56b, no. 4.

[41] *CPR 1330–4*, pp. 31 and 53; *CFR 1327–37*, p. 225.

[42] *Dictionary of National Biography*, ed. L. Stephen and S. Lee, 22 vols (reprinted Oxford, 1921–22), XIII, 659.

[43] J. Vale, *Edward III and Chivalry: Chivalric Society and its Context, 1270–1350* (Woodbridge, 1982), p. 89.

[44] Douch, 'Career, Lands and Family', p. 87; Holmes, *Estates of the Higher Nobility*, p. 26.

[45] *Baker*, p. 46 (Baker confused Eland with Robert Holand, constable of Chester castle, and a former retainer of Thomas of Lancaster); Holmes, *Estates of the Higher Nobility*, pp. 72 and 123; J. R. Maddicott, 'Thomas of Lancaster and Sir Robert Holland: A Study in Noble Patronage', *EHR* 86 (1971), 449–72.

was occupied by a Sir Richard de Grey who appears not to have been involved in the coup and was probably not present at all. Whatever his exact position, Eland was rewarded just seven days after his heroic efforts when he was made constable of the castle for life, and given the bailiwick and honour of Peverel.[46] In 1336 this latter grant was converted from life tenure to one inheritable by his heirs.[47] Clearly Eland and his wife were on familiar and trusted terms with Edward. In 1333 the king gave a gift of an overtunic and a mantle to Eland's wife[48] and in 1336 Eland was given custody of the earl of Moray, who was at the time the most sensitive political prisoner in the country.[49]

Edward Bohun was a household banneret of some standing.[50] Edward was implicated in the deaths of Turplington and Munimuth and was granted land worth £400 per annum by parliament.[51] Five days after the take-over he was made constable of England in place of his brother, John, who was too ill to carry on his duties.[52] Edward was clearly an active and energetic man, but he died in 1334 on the Scottish March, drowned while trying to help his man-servant drive away a wild beast.[53] In 1348, William, his twin brother and another close companion of Edward III, became a member of the Order of the Garter. William himself was not present at the coup.

Robert Ufford, a household banneret by summer 1329,[54] was granted £300 worth of land a year by parliament and made keeper of the Forest south of the Trent.[55] He received the manors of Cawston and Fakenham in Norfolk and houses in Cripplegate, London, presumably as part of his parliamentary grant 'for his services at the arrest in Nottingham Castle of certain men who were bringing the business of the realm into ruin and disgrace', and was one of the 'new earls' of 1337, becoming earl of Suffolk.[56] He was made a knight of the Order of the Garter in 1349.

William Clinton, like Montagu, Bohun and Ufford, a banneret of the household,[57] was appointed to the lucrative post of justice of Chester after the coup, as well as being given custody of the castles of Chester, Bechestan, Rhuddlan, and Flint. By the end of the year he was also constable of Dover castle and warden of the Cinque Ports.[58] Clinton was made earl of North-

[46] *CPR 1330–4*, p. 18; C 81/176/4012.
[47] *CFR 1327–37*, p. 493 (26 September 1336). Eland is styled 'king's yeoman'.
[48] E 101/387/1.
[49] SC 8/202/10098; *CCR 1334–8*, p. 617.
[50] *Memoranda Rolls*, pp. 373 and 377; Holmes, *Estates of the Higher Nobility*, p. 22.
[51] *CPR 1330–4*, p. 53; *RP*, II, 57a, no. 15.
[52] *CPR 1330–4*, p. 12.
[53] *Murimuth*, p. 74; *CIPM*, VIII, 428 (inquisition, 14 December 1334).
[54] E 101/384/7, m. 4.
[55] *RP*, II, 57a, no. 15; *CFR 1327–37*, p. 206 (16 December 1330).
[56] *Dictionary of National Biography*, LVIII, 9–13; *CPR 1330–4*, p. 69.
[57] *Memoranda Rolls*, pp. 373 and 377.
[58] *CPR 1330–4*, p. 13 (23 October 1330); *CFR 1327–37*, p. 204 (14 December 1330).

ampton in 1337, along with the other new earls Montagu and Ufford, and was one of Edward's most successful war captains, and, like his fellows, became a member of the Order of the Garter.[59]

John Neville of Hornby was a household knight.[60] He was pardoned for the killing of Turplington and Munimuth at the coup and was granted 'for service at the arrest of Roger Mortimer' three manors in Dorset and Chelrie manor in Buckinghamshire, all of which had belonged to John Maltravers; he also received the manor of Wynterbourne Houton in Dorset which was once a Despenser holding.[61]

Apart from these six men, the names of a further ten, not previously known to have been involved, have been discovered among the royal pardons which followed the take-over. Firstly, associated with Montagu was Thomas West, a household knight; his close connections to Montagu suggest he was one of the latter's own retainers:[62] in particular, he accompanied the king and Montagu on diplomatic missions in May and September 1329.[63] In January 1331 he was named keeper of the castle and manor at Ringwood from which Montagu was receiving the rents as a reward; in February 1331 he was pardoned for the killings at Nottingham, and he was also granted Christ-church Castle, the borough of Westover, Southampton Castle, and the manor of Lyndhurst.[64] He owned lands in Wiltshire and on the south coast, and these were augmented in October 1331 by the grant of Sutton Mandeville manor in Wiltshire.[65] Further evidence of his association with Montagu is provided by a petition and grant to alienate some of his land, stipulating that the chaplains were to pray for Montagu and his wife, Catherine, and for Sir John Molyns and his wife, Egidia.[66] So, it is not surprising to discover that Molyns was also involved in the coup.

Molyns was a household squire by late in 1330, a knight by 1334 and a banneret of the household by 1337.[67] It is therefore probable that his initial entry into household service came directly because of his involvement at Nottingham. He appears not to have been involved in the actual killings at Nottingham, for his pardon concerns armed entry and being present at Mortimer's arrest only.[68] Nevertheless, his rise in the household was rapid, and by 1334 he was Montagu's knight and eventually rose to become steward

---

[59] Holmes, *Estates of the Higher Nobility*, p. 4.
[60] *Memoranda Rolls*, pp. 373 and 377.
[61] *RP*, II, 57a, no. 15; *CPR 1330–4*, pp. 82 and 116.
[62] *Memoranda Rolls*, pp. 373 and 377.
[63] *CPR 1327–30*, pp. 388 and 433.
[64] *CPR 1330–4*, pp. 54 and 82; *CFR 1327–37*, p. 205.
[65] *CPR 1330–4*, p. 174.
[66] SC 8/256/12783; *CPR 1334–8*, p. 77 (31 January 1335).
[67] *Memoranda Rolls*, p. 379; E 101/387/9, mm. 9–11; E 101/388/5, mm. 17–19.
[68] *CPR 1330–4*, p. 110; C 81/180/4500.

of the chamber lands and keeper of the royal stud.[69] However, thuggish behaviour led to his fall from grace in 1340, followed by a return to favour in 1345 and then a final imprisonment for embezzlement with menaces in 1357 at Nottingham Castle, where effectively his career had begun on that October night in 1330.[70] Indeed, the curious fact that he continued to be indulged by the king and queen for so long, in spite of his thoroughly anti-social behaviour, suggests that they had some vestigial sentimental fondness for him dating back to his involvement in the coup. Montagu had obviously hand-picked these two companions from his most trusted retainers. The Montagu-West-Molyns connection continued through the 1330s: they all accompanied the king on the secret mission to do homage to Philip VI at Pont-Ste-Maxence in 1331, disguised as merchants,[71] and Molyns and West witnessed at least one charter of Montagu's together in 1337.[72]

Sir William Latimer was present at the coup with a small group of men he had recruited.[73] Latimer was a household banneret by late 1330, and it may well have been his involvement at Nottingham which won him this position.[74] Along with this profitable promotion he was granted the manor of Islehampstede in Buckinghamshire which had belonged to Simon Bereford: again, one of Mortimer's henchmen. The band he assembled was made up of one Elias de Revede and his son Thomas, and John Maunsell.[75] The Revedes (or Reads) were either retainers of Latimer or locals picked out for the job. Maunsell was a household squire from at least 1328;[76] by April 1335 he had left the household to go into the church, but was not forgotten by the king who gave him twenty shillings in alms at Peterborough to replace his clothes and couch.[77] Another man, Robert Dyggeby, was granted the hundred of Getre in Leicestershire, for his 'good service' at Nottingham in Latimer's company.[78]

Other men who formed part of the band have no apparent connections with either the royal household or with the nobles involved. Robert Walkefare was granted custody of Beaumaris Castle for his efforts in the coup,[79] which included taking Mortimer under arrest from Nottingham to London

[69] N. M. Fryde, 'A Medieval Robber Baron: Sir John Molyns of Stoke Poges', in *Medieval Legal Records*, ed. R. Hunnisett and J. B. Post (London, 1978), pp. 197–221 (p. 200).
[70] Fryde, 'Medieval Robber Baron', p. 207.
[71] *CPR 1330–4*, p. 73 (4 February 1331); *Baker*, p. 48.
[72] *CPR 1334–8*, p. 432.
[73] *CPR 1330–4*, p. 18; C 81/176/4031.
[74] *Memoranda Rolls*, p. 377.
[75] *CPR 1330–4*, p. 18 (3 November 1330).
[76] *Memoranda Rolls*, pp. 375 and 379.
[77] E 101/387/9, mem. 5. 'Johanni Maunsell nuper scutiferi hospicii Regis de elemosina ipsius domini Regis ad unam lectum et unam robam sibi emendum . . . xx.s.'
[78] *CFR 1327–37*, p. 211 (28 December 1330).
[79] *CPR 1330–4*, p. 30 (17 December 1330). He was pardoned on 2 October 1331, p. 172; C 81/185/4939 and C 81/185/4940.

via Leicester.[80] William de Carleton Forehaugh, 'king's yeoman', was pardoned for the death of Crombek at the coup. He appears to have been the only one involved in Crombek's death.[81] On 16 October 1331, attempts to get him into a corrody at Boxle Abbey were thwarted by the abbey's claim to hold lands in frank almoin.[82] Sir Thomas de Thornham was pardoned late in 1331 because, due to his involvement in the coup murders, he had been barred from entering the order of St John of Jerusalem.[83]

Besides this band of sixteen, how many more conspirators might have been involved? Contemporary retinues were of surprisingly small size. Perhaps between ten and twenty-five participants were all that was required for the exercise of decisive political force on campaign.[84] The 1330 band was simply a rather eccentric manifestation of this model. The *Scalacronica* suggested that twenty-four men met Montagu and Neville outside the walls of Nottingham Castle that October night, but that many more had failed to appear.[85] It is likely that not all those involved bothered to take out an individual pardon for themselves. Latimer was not pardoned separately although his companions were,[86] and the case of Thornham, who only sought a personal pardon when he found himself barred from taking holy orders, suggests some of those involved may have thought the general pardon granted to them by parliament was enough. Thus it is possible that several more men took part as well as those who are mentioned specifically in official records, and the names of a further four men who may just have been involved have come to light in an unexpected place.

The source is a surviving royal armourer's account for November 1330, detailing the costs of seven 'aketons', made for seven men in royal service that month.[87] An aketon was a plain quilted jacket worn between shirt and mail: a protection against the friction caused by the metal links lying close to the

---

[80] SC 8/152/7583.

[81] *CPR 1330–4*, p. 90 (31 March 1331).

[82] *CPR 1330–4*, p. 190.

[83] *CPR 1330–4*, p. 177 (7 October 1331); C 81/184/4843. Thornham was also known as Thomas Wyneman of Thornham and Thomas, son of Henry Wyneman.

[84] For example, muster rolls indicate that the earl of Warwick had twelve men with him at Newcastle upon Tyne in May 1337 (E 101/20/7); from June to October 1342 Thomas Lord Wake had 20 men-at-arms with him (E 101/23/25); in 1340 in the Low Countries John Molyns had 23 men (E 101/22/35); in Ireland in 1361–4 Ralph Ferrers had 20 men (E 101/28/30); and the garrison at Dover Castle from 1355–7 comprised Roger earl of March with just seven men-at-arms (E 101/27/2). I am most grateful to Richard Partington for supplying these figures.

[85] *Scalacronica*, p. 157: 'le dit Willam conveyna oue ses coumpaignouns dencountrier dedenz la nuyt en le park a un certain bussoun qe vindrent touz, mais ils faillerent le lour triste, hors pris le dit Willam de Mountagow et Johan de Nevyl oue xxiiii homs, qi tyndrent bien lour signal'.

[86] *CPR 1330–4*, p. 13.

[87] E 101/384/17: transcribed in Appendix, below.

skin.[88] The internal evidence of the document suggests that it is likely that these jackets were made as a reward for some of the men involved in the coup. How can we be sure that the aketons were not made for livery or some martial occasion such as a tournament? The answer lies in a number of unusual features about the account. Firstly, the aketons were quite out of the ordinary for livery given to retainers. Livery, even of the most costly kind assigned to household bannerets, was usually a length of fine woollen cloth and furs, or a cash payment in lieu of such material. Alternatively, plain robes, made up of a number of garments, were distributed.[89] The 1330 aketons were, in contrast to the norm, splendid garments: made variously of green and purple velvet and silk, all lined with red linen and embroidered with gold and silver thread, they cost between thirty-five and ninety shillings each. In addition, the costs of making up the aketons were meticulously noted in the surviving account, whereas ordinary livery accounts usually group similar liveries given to individuals together under a general description.

Another reason for believing that the aketons were something out of the ordinary is the identities of the recipients. Three of the jackets were made for John Neville, William Clinton and Robert Ufford, all men we know definitely to have been involved in the coup. Four other men are named: Maurice Berkeley, Thomas Bradeston, a 'Master Pantis', and the Bishop of Salisbury. All men moved in the same circles at court. Berkeley, Ufford and Clinton were household bannerets. Bradeston and Neville were household knights.[90] 'Master Pantis' was Pancio de Controne, the king's physician,[91] and the bishop of Salisbury was Robert Wyville, Queen Isabelle's favourite clerk.[92] It is possible that all of these men were involved in the coup in some way and the jackets were made in recognition of the service they had performed for the king. The jackets are almost certainly not made for members of a tournament team, because the two clerks, Pancio and Wyville, would be most unlikely participants in such an event, and no tournament is known to have taken place in November or December 1330.[93] An even more suggestive fact is that

---

[88] L. Southwick, 'The Armoured Effigy of Prince John of Eltham in Westminster Abbey and Some Closely-Related Military Monuments', *Church Monuments* 2 (1987), 9–12 (p. 9). The word 'aketon' derives from the Arabic for cotton: 'al-qutun', and is a precursor of the word 'jacket'.

[89] For examples of liveries received by the household of Edward III in 1329, see C. Shenton, 'The English Court and the Restoration of Royal Prestige, 1327–1345' (unpublished D.Phil. dissertation, University of Oxford, 1995), pp. 56–9.

[90] *Memoranda Rolls*, p. 377.

[91] *Memoranda Rolls*, pp. 374 and 378. His job is specified in the livery roll for 1334. E 101/387/9, mm. 9–11.

[92] T. F. Tout, *Chapters in the Administrative History of Mediaeval England*, 6 vols. (Manchester, 1920–33), III, 34.

[93] See Vale, *Edward III and Chivalry*, appendix 12, for a list of tournaments up to 1348. The latest tournament took place in Dunstable in October 1329, and the next tournament after the coup was in May 1331, although there was certainly a joust after the birth of Edward of Woodstock in July 1330. Interestingly, the enrolled

two similar jackets had been made a few months before, for the king, and a 'William' whose surname is damaged in the roll. This 'William' was almost certainly William Montagu. It was not unusual for the king and his favourite to wear matching outfits, and there is substantial evidence that the king and his close companions at court in the 1330s dressed in similar outfits on a number of other occasions.[94] It would therefore seem that an initial plan was to make matching jackets for the king and Montagu in the summer of 1330, and following the coup, this project was extended to include seven more men, holding household positions close to the king, who had been involved in some way at Nottingham. In the same way as a tournament team wore matching outfits to distinguish members of the same side in a melée, and just as the Garter robes in 1348 picked out the king's men in blue and gold, these jackets, if worn at court simultaneously by the coup participants (as they were surely meant to be), would have made a very obvious statement about these men being a 'team' of loyal supporters who had played a major role in the liberation of the king from the tyranny of Mortimer.

There is no explicit record that Bradeston, Pancio, Berkeley and Wyville were involved, but Juliet Vale's research into Bradeston's career has indicated that he, at least, is a strong contender for inclusion in a list of conspirators. She finds the pardon given to Bradeston in April 1339 suggestive: 'in part recompense of his labours and charges in service of the king from his early years in constant attendance at his side'.[95] Bradeston was a retainer of Maurice Berkeley, and this provides more weight for the argument that the tailor's account concerned rewards for the coup. Just four months before the coup, Berkeley agreed to his life-long retainership by the king, and was given the farm of Andover and the rent of Kirkstall priory.[96] In May 1331 Berkeley was given Mortimer's old

household account sent to the Exchequer for auditing (E 361/3 rot. 16d, m.1) describes the jackets thus: 'ii. Aketoni cum retibus de serico pro Rege et Willelmo de MonteAcuto, iii. Aketonari cum retibus de serico pro Johanne de Eltham comite cornubiae, Willelmo Clynton et Mauricio de Berkeley, i. Aketoneri cum i. rete de serico et i. hernes' pro just' pro Thoma de Bradeston, quatuor Aketoner pro Roberto de Ufford, Johanne de Neville, Episcopo Sarum et Magistro Pauncio de Controne'. The account contains items pertaining to jousts mixed in with the aketons, but it is clear that this is just the way the tailor's account has been summarized. The pertinent fact here is that an aketon was also made for the king's younger brother, John of Eltham, who was aged about fourteen at the time: however, it is impossible to tell whether he also played some part in the coup, or whether he was simply included in the 'team' at court by virtue of being a royal prince.

[94] For details of co-ordinated outfits worn at court see Shenton, 'The English Court', pp. 193–5. There is also mention of matching clothes made in the early 1330s for John of Eltham, the king's younger brother, Montagu, the Bohun twins, Ufford and Ralph Neville in PRO E 361/3, rot. 24d, m.1.

[95] Vale, *Edward III and Chivalry*, p. 61; *CPR 1338–40*, p. 381.

[96] N. Saul, *Knights and Esquires: The Gloucestershire Gentry in the Fourteenth Century* (Oxford, 1981), pp. 75–8; J. Smyth, *The Berkeley Manuscripts: Lives of the Berkeleys 1066–1618*, ed. J. MacLean (Gloucester, 1883), I, 282–5; *CPR 1327–30*, p. 530.

manors of Mawardyn and Wynforton in Herefordshire; it is tempting to interpret this as a reward, especially as it has already been shown that other conspirators received the escheated estates of Mortimer and his supporters.[97] The inclusion of Pancio de Controne in a list of conspirators is not difficult to explain. The struggle in Isabelle's chamber was a violent one and a physician would have been needed, afterwards at least, to tend the injured, and to confirm that Turplington, Crombek and Munimuth were dead.

Wyville's role is altogether more obscure. The chronicler Murimuth described him as Isabelle's personal secretary, though he remained unimpressed by his learning.[98] He was a prominent figure in Mortimer's council, yet also appears to have been close to the king, and had been appointed bishop of Salisbury in June 1330.[99] It is impossible to tell how much support the bishop may have secretly given the king towards the end of Isabelle and Mortimer's regime, but the fact that Wyville retired happily to Salisbury after the coup, and immediately gained several valuable concessions for the dean and chapter of Salisbury, suggests that he was especially in favour with the king for some reason.[100] It would fit a pattern of some dissident clerical support for Edward III during the minority, as we know of at least one other clerical supporter who gave moral backing of this kind. Richard de Bury's secret negotiations on behalf of the king behind Mortimer's back by means of coded letter to the pope is well known.[101] After the coup this former tutor of the king continued in his post of keeper of the privy seal, and was given the bishopric of Durham in 1335.

One final conspirator – the twenty-second – remains to be identified. The role played in the coup by Henry of Lancaster is a shadowy one, but has long been suspected, and his was probably the most important of all, despite his incipient blindness.[102] Once the regency council headed by him had become little more than a cipher, the earl began a series of attempts to overthrow the rule of Isabelle and Mortimer.

[97] *CPR 1330–4*, p. 145.

[98] *Murimuth*, p. 60.

[99] See, for example, the writ of September 1330 recalling Nicholas de Ludlow from abroad because of his slanderous comments to the pope about Wyville (*CCR 1330– 3*, p. 156).

[100] *CPR 1330–4*, pp. 81–2; he managed to get permission to use the masonry from Old Sarum Cathedral for the new cathedral church and obtained an exemption from purveyance and seizure of cathedral accommodation when the royal household visited.

[101] C. G. Crump, 'The Arrest of Roger Mortimer and Queen Isabel', *EHR* 26 (1911), 331–2.

[102] For example, Stubbs thought that Lancaster's motivation came from seeing his cousin, the earl of Kent, beheaded: W. Stubbs, *Constitutional History of England*, 2nd edn (Oxford, 1877), II, 372. Stubbs provides no evidence for this. Others have also followed this unsubstantiated line of thought, claiming that Lancaster recruited Montagu and Bury to his cause: see Crump, 'Arrest of Roger Mortimer', pp. 331–2; M. McKisack, *The Fourteenth Century* (Oxford, 1959), pp. 100–101; K. Fowler, *The*

Lancaster's opposition is best known through his rebellion of 1328–9, when he gathered troops in Winchester, leading to armed conflict with royal troops in Warwickshire and Leicestershire, and ending with the earl's surrender at Bedford.[103] But he seized at least five other opportunities to express his antipathy towards the regents. Firstly, early in the minority, Lancaster sent the bishop of Winchester and Thomas Wake to the city of London to complain about the 'aliens and evil counsellors' who surrounded the king, and of the heavy debts and unpaid bills which followed the royal court.[104] Secondly, taking advantage of the anti-Mortimer riots in Bury St Edmunds in 1327, a mercenary employed by Lancaster called John of Bedford led four of the men under his command in a follow-up raid on the London lodgings of the Abbot.[105] Most compellingly of all, Lancaster was involved in the three other conspiracies (besides his rebellion) which threatened to unseat the regents during the minority. The earl of Kent was linked to them all and lost his life as a result, but Lancaster was far more circumspect, and kept his head.[106] However, a letter survives which indicates that he was behind, or at least, certainly knew of, the earl of Kent's plot to spring the supposedly still-living Edward II from prison in 1330, and he is known to have stood surety for a murderer implicated in the second, failed, Dunheved plot.[107] Griffin de la Pole, ringleader of a third, Welsh-based plot, was a former retainer of Thomas of Lancaster.[108] Henry of Lancaster was in self-imposed exile from the court from July 1329 to June 1330, when he suddenly made a short appearance followed by attendance for a week in July, but his next visit was on 16 October, just three days before the coup.[109] It is more than likely that his arrival at court was to recontact the king, following the birth of Edward of Woodstock, an event which had shifted the regents' hold on power significantly. Mortimer remained highly suspicious of Lancaster. On the very day of the coup he had ordered Henry to lodge himself and his household outside the city walls, chaperoned by John de Bohun, the constable of England.[110]

This fifth conspiracy against the regents was successful. Knowing the names of a possible twenty-one conspirators reveals the full extent of

King's Lieutenant: Henry of Grosmont, First Duke of Lancaster 1310–1361 (London, 1969), p. 25.

[103] G. A. Holmes, 'The Rebellion of the Earl of Lancaster, 1328–9', *BIHR* 28 (1955), 84–9.
[104] V. B. Redstone, 'Some Mercenaries of Henry of Lancaster, 1327–1330', *TRHS* 3rd ser. 7 (1913), 151–66 (p. 162).
[105] Redstone, 'Some Mercenaries of Henry of Lancaster', pp. 152–4.
[106] For Kent's involvement in the two Dunheved plots, the conspiracy of Griffin de la Pole and the earl of Lancaster's rebellion, see Doherty, 'Isabella, Queen of England, 1309–1330', pp. 208–11.
[107] Redstone, 'Some Mercenaries of Henry of Lancaster', p. 166 and appendix B.
[108] J. R. Maddicott, *Thomas of Lancaster 1307–1322: A Study in the Reign of Edward II* (Oxford, 1970), p. 54.
[109] Fryde, *Tyranny and Fall*, p. 224.
[110] *Baker*, p. 45.

Henry of Lancaster's opposition to Mortimer throughout the regency, because we can now see a number of the men concerned in the 1330 coup had significant connections with Henry of Lancaster or with his brother. Humphrey Bohun, earl of Hereford and father of Edward and William, was Thomas of Lancaster's most powerful supporter and died at Boroughbridge in 1322.[111] William Latimer's father, also called William, was a Lancastrian retainer, so the four men he brought with him to the coup may well have been of that persuasion too.[112] Robert Walkefare was described as Lancaster's 'consanguineus' and 'affinis', and in addition, had been Humphrey Bohun's steward, and was also associated with Maurice Berkeley (d.1326), father of another of our conspirators.[113] The Berkeley connection also spread, as we have seen, to Thomas Bradeston. Thomas de Thornham had been involved in Henry of Lancaster's rebellion, and was imprisoned, but escaped.[114] William Clinton had acted as one of Henry's envoys to treat with Mortimer during the earl's rebellion in December 1328.[115]

Why Henry of Lancaster wished to involve himself in the coup in this way is complex, for in several ways, Lancaster did well out of the minority. His brother's lands were restored to him, almost in full, and he acquired the title of earl. Following his surrender to Mortimer in 1329, his lands and title remained intact, so the restoration of his estates cannot have been his main motivation. After his rebellion he was fined £11,000, but this remained unpaid, without, it seems, any penalty.[116] However, there were a number of compelling reasons why he wished for the overthrow of Mortimer. Firstly, as a member of the royal family, and as the leading magnate of the realm, he was no doubt deeply resentful and scandalized at the personal behaviour of an upstart such as Mortimer compromising the king's position. The position which Mortimer held as regent had been rightfully his, and Mortimer was draining the wealth of the crown for his own ends. After the deaths of Edward II and Kent, he must have felt that his own position was extremely precarious, and that he was lucky to have survived his own rebellion. Most importantly of all was the way in which his own affinity had suffered under Mortimer, particularly in Scotland. Thomas Wake, his son-in-law, was one of the most prominent 'Disinherited' lords driven out in 1328. After his rebellion, some supporters, like Henry Ferrers, Hugh d'Audley and the earl of Atholl made large recognizances, but those supporters who remained

---

[111] Holmes, *Estates of the Higher Nobility*, pp. 20–1 and 140; Maddicott, *Thomas of Lancaster*, pp. 307–10.

[112] Maddicott, *Thomas of Lancaster*, pp. 41–8.

[113] Maddicott, *Thomas of Lancaster*, pp. 263–4; Holmes, *Estates of the Higher Nobility*, p. 73; Smyth, *Lives of the Berkeleys*, pp. 246–7.

[114] He was helped to escape from Norwich Castle after imprisonment for allegiance to Henry of Lancaster by a Roger Freng: *CPR 1330–4*, p. 97.

[115] Holmes, 'Rebellion of the Earl of Lancaster, 1328–9', p. 85.

[116] *Dictionary of National Biography*, IX, 552.

unreconciled to Mortimer fled abroad. Often they were also prominent members of the Disinherited and included Wake, Henry Beaumont, William Trussel, Thomas Rocelyn, the earl of Arundel's heir, Griffin de la Pole, Fulk Fitzwarin and Thomas Wyther.[117] All returned to England as soon as Mortimer fell, restoring Lancaster's party to its former strength. All were pardoned at Mortimer's trial for their rebellion and for the recognizances due.[118] It is notable that high up the list of accusations against Mortimer are two which mention Lancaster by name. The third accusation is that Mortimer had taken over the Regency Council and control of the Great Seal, which was rightfully Lancaster's, and had put Lancaster and others in peril of their lives. The fourth accusation is that Mortimer's deeds caused Lancaster and others to rise against the king in his own best interests.[119] These accusations echo parts of the declaration made by Edward III on 20 October 1330 to the sheriffs – and perhaps bear the stamp of Lancaster's hand – particularly in the declaration's insistence that the royal dignity would be restored and that the king would in future govern with the common consent of all the magnates.

The coup of 1330 remains an extraordinary and unique event. Other minorities in medieval England came to an end more or less by agreement or by the gradual, often late, handover of power to the adult king. But desperate measures were required in 1330, and they proved to be the last of several attempts to overthrow the regency, orchestrated by Lancaster. The effects of the 1330 coup were felt for many years afterwards at court. It had utilized existing networks within the royal household; all the household men and the two clerics involved advanced significantly in their careers as a result. Indeed, these men formed the core of favourites around the king for the next fifteen years. Contemporary criticism of the 'new men' at court which emerged towards the end of the 1330s was linked to the promotion of Montagu, Clinton, Ufford and William Bohun: all but the last were partici- pants in the coup. The new earldoms of 1337 followed the depletion of the court party because of the premature deaths of the erstwhile conspirators Edward Bohun, John Neville and William Latimer, in the mid-1330s.[120] But by the mid-1340s, the most significant conspirators were also dead: Montagu died in 1344 from internal injuries sustained in a tournament, while both Bury and Lancaster died in 1345. These deaths profoundly changed the personnel around the king. As much as any other event of the mid-1340s these changes mark out the beginning of a new phase of Edward's reign: Edward's links to his youthful past had been brutally severed, and he had to build up new networks of support as he approached middle age.

---

[117] 'Gesta Edwardi de Carnarvon auctore canonico Bridlingtoniensi cum continuatone ad AD 1377', in *Chronicles of the Reign of Edward I and Edward II*, ed. W. Stubbs, 2 vols (RS, 1882–3), ii, p. 99; *Lanercost*, p. 266.

[118] *RP*, II, 54; *CPR 1330–4*, pp. 26–8, 33 and 35.

[119] *RP*, II, 53.

[120] *Murimuth*, p. 74; *CIPM*, VIII, 428, 467 and 475.

APPENDIX

Particulars of Account of John of Cologne, King's Armourer, 4 Edward III

London, Public Record Office E 101/384/17[1]

Main roll

m. 1.

[Details of Harnesses made for the King for the Queen's Churching, 1 July 1330]

m. 2.

[Details of Harnesses and Banners]

m. 3.

Pro Rege. Emptiones.[2]

Item pro Aketona Regis.

Antolino de Bache mercatori Londoniensi pro j. ulna et j. quarta velveti de Pourpee ab eodem empta pro Aketona domini Regis xj die Julii anno quarto per preceptum Regis . . . xvj.s.viij.d.

Eidem pro una quarta velveti rubei pro predicta Aketona Regis . . . iij.s.iiij.d.

Johanni de Knopworth mercatori Londoniensi pro iij. ulnis cindonis viridis ab eodem emptis pro predicta Aketona . . . ij.s.iij.d.

Eidem pro una ulna et dimidita de taffeta ab eodem empta pro predicta Aketona Regis . . . lxvj.s.viij.d.

Johanni Somer pro viij. unciis auri ab eodem emptis pro predicta Aketona Regis . . . xxiv.s.

Alicie Prince pro [filacione] auri . . . v.s.

Johanni de Cauxton mercatori Londoniensi pro lapide Dubletto[3] ab eodem empto pro predicta Aketona Regis . . . x.s.

Gerardi de Alston mercatori Londoniensi pro ponderis septem denariis de perlis pro predicta Aketona Regis . . . iiij.s.viij.d.

Eidem pro vij. unciis serici diversis coloribus pro predicta Aketona . . . [damaged]

Item pro tribus B[uc]helibus cum iij. mordantibus et ix. barris argenti pro predicta Aketona . . . [damaged]

---

[1] Crown copyright material in the Public Record Office is reproduced by permission of the controller of The Stationery Office.

[2] Marginal entry.

[3] Doublet stones were sandwiches of coloured glass used as decorations. See E. W. Safford, 'An Account of the Expenses of Eleanor, Sister of Edward III, on the Occasion of her Marriage', *Archaeologia* 76 (1927), 111–40 (pp. 114–15).

Item cuidam Aurifabro . . . pro predictis inde faciendo . . . [damaged].s.
In una libra de Tyssens a Sion[4] idem opus . . . xxj.s.
Summa . . . vij.li.iijs.ij.d.

[Damaged section containing details of at least seven embroiderers working between 23 July and 9 August 1330]
m. 4.
[Damaged section containing details of an item of clothing for 'the said William']
[Damaged section containing details of embroiderers' wages, 'operanti super eadem Aketon' ipsius domini Willelmi']
m. 5.
[More clothes for king: 10 August 1330]
[Wages for embroiderers' work on these clothes]
[Details of Aketon made for John of Cornwall: 1 Sept. 1330]

Loose rotulet A
m. 1.
[Account for harness for Thomas Bradeston, newly knighted]
[Embroiderers' wages 26 August – 7 Sept. 1330 for work on this]
[Account for pennants, with details of wages for embroiderers]
[Account for covering two plates of thigh armour for the King]
[Account for Russet bought for the King at Daventry]

Aketona pro Episcopo Sarum.[5]

Quarto die Novembris anno eodem. In una ulna et quarta velveti viridis empta Johanni de Cauxton mercatori Londoniensi pro Episcopo Sarum per preceptum Regis . . . xij.s. vj.d.
Eidem pro iiij. ulnis de Aylesome rubeo pro eadem Aketona . . . xij.d.
Eidem pro iij. ulnis Cindonis viridis pro eandem Aketona . . . ij.s. vj.d.
Eidem pro vij. unciis serici diversis coloribus pro eadem Aketona . . . viij.s. ij.d.
Eidem pro tribus unciis auri pro eadem Aketona . . . ix.s.
In viij. libris Candelae emptae pro predicto opere . . . xvj.d.
Item pro filacium predicti auri et argenti[6] . . . iiij.d.
Summa . . . xlvij.s. vj.d

[Wages of embroiderers for work on the aketon totalling 23s. 9d.]
Loose rotulet B
m. 1.
Aketona pro magistro Pancio per preceptum Regis.[7]

[4] Superscript.
[5] Marginal entry.
[6] Gold thread was made by winding strips of beaten gold leaf around several threads of silk.
[7] Marginal entry.

Quarto die Novembris. In una ulna et dimidia de camaca purpurea empta pro Aketona magistri Pancii per preceptum domini Regis . . . ix.s.
Cuidam mercatori de Londoni pro ij. ulnis Cindonis rubro pro eadem . . . xx.d.
Eidem pro iiij. ulnis de Aylesome pro eadem Aketona . . . xij.s.
Eidem pro iij. unciis auri ad eamdem Aketonam . . . ix.s.
Eidem pro iij. unciis serici ab eodem emptis pro predicta Aketona . . . iij.s.vj.d.
In vj. libris candelae emptis . . . xij.d.
Summa . . . xxv.s.ij.d.

[Wages of six embroiderers working for a total of thirty-six days; costs of creating gold thread; drink money; total: 10s. 3½d.]
m. 2.
Aketonara pro Roberto de Ufford

Undecimo die Novembris anno presento iiijto. In j. ulna j. quarta velveti purpurei empta pro j. Aketonara facta ad opus domini Roberti de Ufford per preceptum domini Regis . . . xij.s.vj.d.
Johanni de Causton pro iij. ulnis Cindonis emptis ad idem . . . iij.s.
Eidem eodem die pro iiij. ulnis Ayleshami rubeo ad idem Aketonara . . . xvj.d.
Ricardo le Goldbetere pro vij. unciis auri emptis ad idem. . . . xxj.s.
Predicto Johanni de Causton pro vij. unciis serici diversis coloribus pro eodem Aketonara. . . . viij.s.ij.d.
Item Alicie Prince pro filacio predictas vij. uncias auri . . . iv.s.viij.d.
Item in vj. libris candelae emptis pro eodem opere de nocte operando . . . xij.d.
Summa . . . lj.s.viij.d

[Wages of fourteen tailors, cutters and embroiderers working for a total of sixty-five days between 11th and 17th November, plus their drink money: 27s. 7d.]

Aketonara pro Mauricio de Berkeley.[8]

Item xvij. die Novembris anno eodem. In j. ulna j. quarta velveti empta pro uno Aketonara facienda pro domino Mauricio de Berkeley per preceptum domini Regis. . . . xij.s.vj.d.
Item cuidam mercatori Londoniensi pro j. Rete de serico ad imponendum in eodem Aketonara empto ibidem. . . . xxxiij.s.iij.d.
Eidem pro iiij. ulnis de Ayleshami tynctis . . . [damaged]
Ricardo le Goldbeter pro iiij. unciis auri emptis ad idem. . . . xij.s.
Eidem pro ij. unciis argenti . . . emptis ab eo ibidem eodem die . . . vj.s.
Alicia Prince pro filacio predicti auri et argenti . . . iiij.d
Predicto J[ohanno]. de Causton pro vj. unciis serici diversis coloribus . . . vij.s.
Item in vj. libris candelae emptis pro eodem opere . . . xij.d.
Summa . . . lxxix.s.iiij.d.

[8] Marginal entry.

[Wages of five embroiderers working for a total of 30 days: total 11s.]

Pro ij. Aketonaris ad opus dominorum Johanni de Neville et Thome de Bradeston, militum.

Item xxiij. Novembris anno presento quarto. Johanni de Causton pro ij. ulnis et dimidi velveti pro ij. Aketonaris facientis per preceptum domini Regis ad opus dominorum Johanni de Neville et Thome de Bradestan . . . xxv.s.

Item in vj. ulnis Cindonis emptis pro eisdem Aketonaris . . . v.s.

Item in viij. ulnis Aylesham. . . . ij.s.

Item Ricardo le Goldbetere pro viij. unciis auri emptis pro eisdem Aketonaris. . . . xxiiij.d.

Eidem pro iiij. unciis argenti pro eisdem Aketonaris . . . xiij.s.

Et pro filacio predicti auri et argenti dando . . . viij.s.

Item pro viij. unciis serici diversis coloribus pro eisdem Aketonaris . . . ix.s.iiij.d.

Item in xij. libris candlae emptis pro eodem opere . . . ij.s.

Summa . . . v.li.viij.d.

De quibus pro Bradestan . . . lxxvij.s

Et pro J. Neville . . . xliij.s.viij.d.

[Details of 16 embroiderers working on Neville's jacket from 23 November onwards; total cost damaged]

Loose rotulet C

m. 1

[Details of 17 embroiderers working on Bradeston's jacket for a total of 79 days from 23 November onwards: 25s. 10½d.]

Aketona pro Willelmo de Clynton, milite

Item Johanni de Causton mercenari Londoniensi pro j. ulna j. quarta velveti purpurei pro j. Aketonarae inde facienda per preceptum domini Regis ad opus domini Willelmi de Clynton empta ab eo London' xxix. die Novembris anno presento quarto . . . xij.s.vj.d.

Item In quo Rete serici empto ad idem . . . xl.s.

Item In iii. ulnis sindonis. . . . iij.s.

Item In iiij. ulnis de Aylesham' rubro optimo . . . xvj.d.

Item In v. unciis auri emptis pro eodem . . . xv.s.

Item In ij. unciis Argenti . . . emptis ad idem . . . vj.s.

Item pro filacio predicti auri et argenti dandorum . . . iiij.s.viij.d.

Item In dimidia libra cotoni ad idem . . . ij.d.obulum.

Item In vj. libras candelae . . . xij.d.

Summa . . . iiij.li.viij.s.iiij.d.obulum.

[Details of 16 embroiderers working on Clinton's jacket for a total of 71 days beginning on 29 November: cost of wages and drink money 27s. 9d.]

33

[Details of a harness made for the King]
[Wages for the above]
[Details of a crest made for the King]
[Wages for the above]
[Details of a hood for John of Eltham]

2

Edward III, The English Peerage, and the 1337 Earls: Estate Redistribution in Fourteenth-Century England

J. S. BOTHWELL

The period between 1326 and 1330 had many important implications for fourteenth-century history, not the least of which was its impact upon the pattern of noble landholding in the realm. Due to the run of events in these years, substantial amounts of land were in – or had returned to – the king's possession upon Edward III's assumption of independent power in late October 1330.[1] These properties can be divided into two main groups. Firstly, there were those connected with the events surrounding the downfall of Edward II in 1327. These lands were brought in during late 1326 and early 1327, resulting primarily from the summary execution of Hugh Despenser the elder at Bristol and of Hugh the younger at Hereford – who had themselves amassed considerable estates after the defeat of the 'Contrariants' at Borough-bridge in 1322.[2] Such properties had two fates under the minority regime: either they were re-granted by Mortimer and Isabelle, under the aegis of the young Edward III, to themselves, their friends and supporters;[3] or, somewhat less often, they were kept under the control of the crown – in effect being placed in a 'temporary royal demesne'.[4] Secondly, there were the estates returned into the king's hands resulting from the coup at Nottingham Castle in October 1330. Of the central players in the minority regime of 1327–30, Roger Mortimer, the earl of March, was executed and declared forfeit, and Queen Isabelle pardoned – though forced to give up many of the lands she held.[5] With their demise came in not only large portions of the above-mentioned

---

[1] For more about the 1330 coup, and those who participated, see C. Shenton, above.
[2] N. Fryde, *The Tyranny and Fall of Edward II 1321–26* (Cambridge, 1979), chap. 6 and 8.
[3] Fryde, *Tyranny and Fall*, pp. 208–9; W. M. Ormrod, *The Reign of Edward III: Crown and Political Society in England 1327–1377* (New Haven and London, 1990), p. 4; B. P. Wolffe, *The Royal Demesne in English History* (London, 1971), Appendix Ai; C 49/45/16.
[4] See H. M. Jewell, *English Local Administration in the Middle Ages* (Newton Abbott, 1972), pp. 75–80 and 99–102.
[5] G. A. Holmes, *The Estates of the Higher Nobility in Fourteenth-Century England*

Despenser estates but also lands which they held of their own right, either the result of inheritance or independent acquisition – whether through purchase or other means. These properties, as well as those of the supporters of the minority regime such as Simon Bereford and John Maltravers, were to play a crucial role in Edward III's re-assertion of monarchical position and power with respect to the nobility in the decade after the Nottingham coup, culminating in the earldom creations of 1337.

For the first couple of months after the coup, Edward III was relatively cautious in the way in which he dealt with these estates. When he did re-grant these lands,[6] he tended to distribute them piecemeal to less contro-versial members of the established nobility. For instance, on 1 December 1330, six weeks after the coup, Richard Grey of Codnor, who managed to stay clear of most of the problems of the previous decade,[7] was granted 'for the good service of him and his ancestors', the manor of Overstone (Northants.), which John Maltravers, a henchman of the minority regime often connected with the death of Edward II, had held for life by the king's grant. This was initially granted, on the petition of council, to Grey during royal pleasure in return for a rent to be paid at the exchequer[8] – though later, in November of 1331, it was granted for a set period of seven years, and at a rent of £35 12s. 11¾d. per annum.[9] On 17 December 1330, William Latimer of Corby was granted the manor of Iselhampstede (Bucks.) in fee, which had been of the estate of Simon Bereford, another servant of the minority regime also implicated in the death of Edward II.[10] Similarly, on 22 January 1331 John Ros of Watton, likewise a fairly solid member of the establishment,[11] was granted 'during pleasure' the keeping of lands in Ketton and Kilthorp (Rutland), again of the estate of Simon Bereford 'which came as an escheat to the king's hands by his forfeiture'.[12] The only notable exception to this early cautious land redistribu-tion policy on the part of Edward III was the extensive entailed grant to his own brother, John of Eltham, earl of Cornwall, on 4 December 1330 of a block of lands, including the manor of Haughley, the castle and manor of Eye (Suffolk), the town of Rockingham (Northants.), the castle and town of Berkhamsted with

---

(Cambridge, 1957), pp. 7–40; H. Johnstone, 'The Queen's Household', in *The English Government at Work, 1327–1336*, ed. J. F. Willard et al., 3 vols. (Cambridge, Mass., 1940–50), I, 257–60. She was also granted, on her petition, £3,000 per annum in 1331, increased to £4,500 in 1337. P. C. Doherty, 'Isabella Queen of England 1296–1330' (unpublished D. Phil. dissertation, University of Oxford, 1977), p. 325; SC 1/38/77; E 163/4/30.
[6] Other parts of these estates were granted to a variety of members of the adminis-tration, church, etc. See *CPR 1330–4*, passim; *CFR 1327–37*, passim.
[7] See *CP*, VI, 124–5.
[8] *CFR 1327–37*, p. 219.
[9] *CFR 1327–37*, p. 287.
[10] *CPR 1330–4*, p. 31; *RP*, II, 41.
[11] See *CP*, XI, 122–3.
[12] *CFR 1327–37*, p. 224; E 199/38/2 (Rutland).

the honour (Herts.), the manors of Princes Risborough and Cippenham (Bucks.), and the castle and town of Wallingford (Oxon.), all of which Queen Isabelle had been forced to surrender the previous November.[13] Later, in October of 1331, Cornwall was granted more of the king mother's properties, including the castle, borough and manor of Tintagel, the castle and manor of Restormel, the castle and manor of Trematon, the castle and manor of Launceston, the manor of Helston-in-Trigg (Cornwall), as well as the manor of Watlington (Oxon.), and the castle and manor of Mere (Wilts.).[14]

 Nonetheless, this was an exceptional case, brought about no doubt largely because John of Eltham was the king's brother. However, as time went on Edward III had a growing tendency to broaden the scope of those nobles – or sires of nobles – to whom he granted confiscated lands as well as the amount of land he was granting out to them. In February of 1331, Ebulo Strange was made an entailed grant of the manor of Overton (Wales), the castle and manor of Ellesmere and the hamlets of Colemere and Hampton (Salop.), all of which were held by Queen Isabelle in 1330.[15] Moreover, in 1333 and 1336, the earl of Arundel received two parts of the forfeited Mortimer estate – the castle, manor and lands of Chirk in Wales, which after the coup had initially been annexed to the crown 'for ever',[16] and the manor of Church Stretton (Salop.)[17] – both of which ended up being granted in fee to Arundel. Even some of the sires of the problematic families of the 1320s were gradually being granted limited patronage from this source. In November 1333, Hugh, the son of Hugh Despenser the Younger, an individual who was slowly to regain the monarch's favour over the course of the 1330s, was granted the manor of *Fritheby* (Frisby?) (Leics.), again part of the Bereford estate confiscated in 1330.[18] The latter was initially granted for a limited term, but it was shifted to an 'in fee' grant later in the 1330s[19] – evidence of Edward's growing confidence in the young Hugh.[20]

Such patronage helped increase Edward III's support within established noble families. Through these grants, Edward can be seen as not only reaffirming the king's interest in those solid, generally uncontroversial members of the nobility who tended to follow the royalist line whoever was actually in charge, but also showing at least limited faith in the next generation of those families who had caused problems in the 1320s. Indeed,

[13] *CCharR 1327–41*, p. 198.
[14] *CCharR 1327–41*, p. 233; E 199/5/9.
[15] *CCharR 1327–41*, pp. 213–14.
[16] *CPR 1330–4*, p. 109; *CFR 1327–37*, pp. 373–4; *CCharR 1327–41*, pp. 318–19; *CPR 1334–8*, p. 519; SC 8/242/12085.
[17] *CCharR 1327–41*, p. 353.
[18] *CPR 1330–4*, pp. 241 and 267.
[19] *CPR 1334–8*, p. 462.
[20] As witness the 1337 grant to him of a number of his father's manors and lands in Devon, Hampshire, Leicestershire, Surrey, Sussex and Wiltshire. *CPR 1334–8*, pp. 461–2.

acts of favour to these families were usually the first indication that, at some point in the future, rehabilitation was on the way.[21] But equally, or arguably more, importantly the estates which came into Edward III's hands as a result of the events of 1326–30 played a crucial first part in his attempts to raise a number of supporters to estates befitting peers, and in some instances, earldoms – or to make those already promoted by him secure therein. A number of these men had been key secondary figures in the events of the 1320s, but were of families who had not previously been called to parliament. Nonetheless, because of their obvious importance, Edward decided it was necessary to bring them into the parliamentary peerage during the 1330s as well as to grant them various confiscated estates. Gilbert Talbot, a 'Contrariant',[22] and thus on the losing side at Boroughbridge, later became a favoured servant of the minority regime. In 1327, he was forgiven the bond for good behaviour he had been forced to acquiesce to after Boroughbridge,[23] and in addition was made royal chamberlain by 1328.[24] Elevated to the peerage by Edward III in 1332,[25] he was granted for life the manor of *Wheatley* by Doncaster (Yorks.), free of any rent payment, an estate which had previously been held by Queen Isabelle.[26] John Darcy, another favourite of the minority regime and individually summoned to parliament from 1332–4,[27] gained from both Despenser and Mortimer estates. First, there was the manor of Marston Meysey (Wilts.), a Despenser 'acquisition' of the 1320s, which on 20 August 1331 was granted to John Darcy during pleasure.[28] It was re-granted on 25 March 1332, for his better maintenance and in recompense for other lands taken out of his control, along with the manor of Wyke-Valors by Marston Meysey, both properties once held by the elder Despenser, to hold for life, rent free.[29] Darcy, moreover, was to gain

---

[21] As discussed below.

[22] *Calendar of the Memoranda Rolls, Michaelmas 1325 to Michaelmas 1326*, ed. R. E. Latham (London, 1968), p. 54. The first evidence I have been able to find of Talbot's opposition to Edward II comes in December of 1321 when the king ordered the sheriff of Gloucester to take his estate, along with those of a number of others, into royal possession. *CFR 1319–27*, p. 84. After Boroughbridge, some of his estate went to Simon Dryby, Gilbert Ash, Adam Orleton, bishop of Hereford, and some to Hugh Despenser the Younger. Fryde, *Tyranny and Fall*, p. 72; *CFR 1319–27*, pp. 96, 98–9 and 191; *CPR 1321–4*, pp. 17 and 191; *CCR 1318–23*, p. 433; R. M. Haines, *The Church and Politics in Fourteenth-Century England: The Career of Adam Orleton c.1275–1345* (Cambridge, 1978), p. 145.

[23] *CFR 1319–27*, p. 170.

[24] J. E. Powell and K. Wallis, *The House of Lords in the Middle Ages* (London, 1968), p. 314; Fryde, *Tyranny and Fall*, p. 187; *RP* II, 427b and 428a; *CCharR 1327–41*, p. 81.

[25] *CP*, XII1, 610–12.

[26] *CPR 1330–4*, p. 479.

[27] See R. H. R. Mortimer, 'Lordship and Patronage: John Darcy and the Dublin Administration 1324–47' (unpublished M.A. dissertation, University of Durham, 1990), esp. Part 1.

[28] *CPR 1330–4*, p. 165.

[29] In February of 1338 it was granted that the manor should remain to John Darcy 'le

from the fall of the minority regime as well. In April of 1335, he was granted *in tail male* the manors of Rathwer and Kildalk, late of the earl of March's Irish estates, which March himself had gained hold of as a result of the forfeitures of Walter and Almaricus Lacy, who had allied themselves with the Scots.[30]

Indeed, whatever their previous histories, lands taken in as a result of the events of 1326–30 were a useful source for Edward III for patronizing those he decided, for one reason or another, to promote into the parliamentary peerage. One of Edward's future promotions, Roger Swynnerton, a minor player in major events since early in Edward II's reign,[31] was made a series of grants of Despenser lands – in this case a continuation of a policy of patronage of Mortimer and Isabelle.[32] In 1331, he was granted all the knights' fees and advowsons of churches belonging to his lands, often originally of the Despenser estate, in Staffordshire and Cheshire.[33] In December of 1333, he was further granted, during royal pleasure, the manor of Little Barrow (Cheshire), late of Hugh Despenser the younger,[34] and in July of 1334 the earl of Winchester's manor of Barrow (Cheshire) and Despenser lands and rents in Rushton, Corneford, Alstonfield and Caldon (Staffs.) were given to him in fee.[35] Ending this series of grants, on 25 September 1334, Swynnerton was given the manor of Little Barrow in fee, without payment of any rent.[36]

John Maltravers, as we have seen, also had all his lands forfeited on Edward's assumption of personal rule in 1330.[37] For the next twenty years, these lands, spread throughout southern England and Wales, were to be a constant source of patronage for Edward III – though much of it also went to

---

fitz' for life after the death of Darcy. *CPR 1330–4*, pp. 165 and 268; *CPR 1338–40*, p. 16.

[30] This grant also included the reversion of the grange connected with Rathwer upon the death of Herbert Sutton. *CPR 1334–8*, p. 94.

[31] Pardoned for his part in the death of Gaveston in 1312. *CPR 1313–17*, p. 25.

[32] *CFR 1327–37*, pp. 7–8; *CPR 1327–30*, p. 33.

[33] C 81/178/4290; *CPR 1330–4*, p. 56.

[34] *CFR 1327–37*, p. 381.

[35] E 142/33/9; *CPR 1330–4*, p. 569. This, along with all the other lands of Hugh Despenser the Elder in Stafford and Cheshire, he had originally been granted *during pleasure* in 1327. The grant of the manor of Barrow, at least, seems to have been changed to a life grant later on in the minority. *CPR 1327–30*, p. 331; *CFR 1327–37*, pp. 7–8; E 357/2/10/1; *CPR 1330–4*, pp. 50 and 569.

[36] *CPR 1334–8*, p. 21. For a history of this manor in the 1320s, see KB 27/301/48 ff.; C 47/10/34.

[37] *CFR 1327–37*, p. 207; E 199/13/5 (Gloucs.); E 199/15/10 (Hants); E 199/29/15 (Norf. and Suff.); E 199/31/12 (Northants.); E 199/38/23 (Salop and Staffs.); E 199/47/10 (Wilts.); E 199/46/23 (Worcs.). However, his wife, Agnes, did manage to get back a number of lands, primarily her own through inheritance and two previous marriages, over the course of the 1330s – sometimes through petition to Queen Philippa, sometimes through the courts. *CPR 1330–4*, pp. 84, 89–90, 106 and 120; KB 27/286/107; KB 27/293/112; KB 27/294/22v; KB 27/295/100; KB 27/297/66v; KB 27/299/81.

lesser members of the administration.[38] Nonetheless, Robert Ufford was granted a house of the Maltravers estate called *le Bas court* by Cripplegate in London.[39] More importantly, John Wilington, an older individual elevated to the peerage during the reign,[40] was granted the castle of Carreg Cennen together with the commote of Is Cennen in 1337,[41] a substantial lordship in Wales which would later find its way into the hands of Henry of Grosmont, earl of Derby, in 1340.[42]

By far, though, the most important beneficiaries of the events of 1326–30 were those individuals who took part in the overthrow of Isabelle and Mortimer's minority government in 1330 and/or helped Edward III consolidate his hold on the kingdom thereafter: namely William Bohun, William Clinton, William Montagu, and Robert Ufford, four of the six men elevated to earldoms in 1337. Indeed, the majority, and the most important, of the estates taken into the king's possession as a result of the events of the previous decade which went out to the nobility tended to go to these men in a series of grants spread over the first half of the 1330s. However, probably due to the quantity and often controversial identity of the lands being granted out and the relatively low birth of most of the men involved, Edward III apparently thought that more authorization, as well as explanation, was needed in presenting these grants to the polity as a whole. First, Edward seemed to feel, as he had with some of the larger grants to new members of the lesser peerage, such as that to Reginald Cobham in 1337,[43] that parliamentary sanction was needed. Regular forms of authorization – by privy seal, king and/or council – were not seen to be enough in such circumstances.[44] Rather, variations on the phrase 'with the assent of the present parliament at Westminster' were used in the grants and orders to the most important of the new men, such as in grants to William Montagu and Robert Ufford in 1331 of confiscated properties of Mortimer and Isabelle.[45] Moreover, even after they had been promoted to their respective earldoms, references to the new men in official documents often still mentioned the

---

[38] E.g. *CFR 1327–37*, pp. 224, 233 and 287.

[39] *CPR 1330–4*, pp. 73 and 106; *CPR 1340–3*, p. 201.

[40] See *CP*, XII2, 646–8.

[41] *CPR 1334–8*, p. 561.

[42] R. Somerville, *History of the Duchy of Lancaster I* (London, 1953), p. 38; *CPR 1338–40*, p. 549; K. Fowler, *The King's Lieutenant: Henry of Grosmont, First Duke of Lancaster 1310–61* (London, 1969), p. 172.

[43] *CPR 1334–8*, p. 401.

[44] A. L. Brown, *The Governance of Late Medieval England* (London, 1989), p. 47; A. L. Brown, 'The Authorization of Letters under the Great Seal', *BIHR* (1964), 125–56; e.g. *CFR 1327–37*, pp. 219, 224, 243 and 287.

[45] *CCharR 1327–41*, pp. 199 and 210–11; for another version of this phrase, also see E 208/2/42 (concerning William Montagu). Though this was also obviously part of the fulfilling of a promise by Edward III after 1330 to 'consult the magnates concerning the state of the realm'. W. Morris, 'Introduction' in *English Government at Work*, I, 23.

parliamentary assent for the elevations, at times both in the text of the order and at the end.[46]

If the authorizations for the large number of confiscated land grants to these four men were more substantial than for grants to the other individuals discussed, so too were the explanations given. For run of the mill grants of confiscated land in this period to a less favoured member of Edward's nobility, either no explanation was given or some brief general statement, usually in the form of a reference to good service in the past or future by the grantee.[47] However, the 1331 grant to Montagu, mentioned above, was granted:

> to have due regard to the honour of William de Montagu, to whom the king revealed his secret design touching the arrest of Roger de Mortuo Mari, late earl of March, and his accomplices, and who was strenuous therein and preserved the peace and tranquillity of the realm.[48]

Similarly, Ufford was made his grant:

> in consideration of the good service rendered by Robert de Ufford, and especially of the danger incurred by him in the castle of Nottingham in arresting certain persons at the king's command, who were causing loss and dishonour to the king and the realm.[49]

Most famously, according to an often cited charter elevating William Clinton to the earldom of Huntingdon and read out in the parliament held in March of 1337, the background reasoning for the promotion was as follows:

> Among the signs of royalty we considered it to be the most important that, through a suitable distribution of ranks, dignities and offices, the position (vallatum) is sustained by the wise counsels and protected by the many powers of formidable men. Yet, the hereditary ranks in our kingdom, both through hereditary descent to coheirs and coparceners according to the law of the kingdom and through a failure of issue and various other events, having returned into the hand of the king, this realm has experienced for a long time a substantial loss in the names, honours and ranks of dignity.[50]

The need felt for explaining royal patronage in the latter passage in particular was the result not only of the number of earls that Edward III was creating later in the decade, but more than likely the way he had been endowing them throughout the 1330s: namely, not only through annuities, wardships and

---

[46] E.g. E 208/3/62 and E 208/3/63 (concerning William Bohun); E 208/3/96 (concerning William Clinton).

[47] E.g. *CFR 1327–37*, p. 219; *CPR 1330–4*, p. 268.

[48] *CCharR 1327–41*, p. 210.

[49] *CCharR 1327–41*, pp. 210–11.

[50] Repeated in three of the charters creating new earls in 1337. *RDP*, V, 28–32.

marriages which others might have, and indeed did, feel to be their right, but also through a considerable use of the confiscated estates which the young king found at his disposal after the Nottingham coup.

Equally important, though, was the fact that Edward III could also justify his re-grant of the lands taken in by his choice of the right sort of individual in the first place. Bohun, Clinton, Montagu and Ufford, it was clear, were patronized by the king with these lands, as well as other forms of patronage, to a considerable extent because of their exemplary service to Edward III and the kingdom as a whole during the early part of the reign.[51] It was the evidence of loyal royal service, sometimes dating back to the 1320s, but mostly during the period of Edward's independent rule starting in late 1330,[52] which made these individuals appear acceptable as recipients of otherwise controversial grants of forfeited lands. All these men had certainly shown good service to Edward III prior to 1337.[53] Not only had they often taken very real, sometimes dangerous parts in the events of 1330,[54] but they also had proved themselves in wars against the Scots as well as in the administrative offices of the kingdom.[55] For instance, in late 1330, William Clinton was charged with two offices, justice of Chester and the Constable of Dover Castle and warden of the Cinque Ports, as well as the custody of the castles of Chester, Becherston, Rhuddlan, and Flint.[56] In the following years, up until the outbreak of war with France in 1337, he was a constant companion of the king on his Scottish campaigns, made Admiral of the West in 1333, and used continually in high level diplomatic missions, especially concerning the status of the duchy of Aquitaine.[57] William Bohun likewise spent a large part of the early 1330s either being of personal service to Edward III,[58] or being on campaign in Scotland, including an

---

[51] For a more detailed look at the activities of these men, see J. M. Parker, 'Patronage and Service: The Careers of William Montagu, earl of Salisbury, William Clinton, earl of Huntingdon, Robert Ufford, earl of Suffolk, and William Bohun, earl of Northampton' (unpublished M.A. dissertation, University of Durham, 1986).

[52] Notably, all four men were household bannerets from at least 1330. See C. Shenton, 'The English Court and the Restoration of Royal Prestige, 1327–1345' (unpublished D. Phil. dissertation, University of Oxford, 1995), Appendix 2.

[53] See also A. Ayton, 'Edward III and the English Aristocracy at the Beginning of the Hundred Years' War', in Armies, Chivalry and Warfare in Medieval Britain and France, ed. M. Strickland (Stamford, 1998), pp. 173–206 (pp. 188–90). My thanks to Dr Ayton for sending me a copy of this article.

[54] See Shenton, above.

[55] Parker, 'Patronage and Service', chap. 3, 4, and 5.

[56] CPR 1330–4, p. 13.

[57] E.g. CPR 1330–4, pp. 273, 466, 467 and 532; CPR 1334–8, pp. 30 and 423. As early as 1327, he was being appointed to delicate tasks, such as conducting his future queen to Edward III. CPR 1327–30, p. 190.

[58] Considering the events of the previous couple of months, there is a rather touching writ of aid for 21 December 1330 listing Bohun as one of those 'sent to bring Queen Isabelle from Berkhamsted to spend Christmas at Windsor'. CPR 1330–4, p. 36.

attempt to treat for peace with the Scots.[59] A banneret as early as 1328,[60] and a clear favourite of the king during his minority,[61] William Montagu was also sent on missions to the continent on the king's service.[62] Moreover, in February of 1333, he was granted 200 marks from the tenth and fifteenth of York, Lincoln, Nottingham, Derby, Lancaster, Cumberland, Westmorland, and Northumberland, presumably to help him in his expenses whilst he was laying siege to Berwick, which fell in July of the same year.[63] Finally, most of Robert Ufford's energies also seem to have been spent in the service of king and kingdom during the 1330s. A household banneret in 1330,[64] in December of that year he was made keeper of the forest south of Trent,[65] and in January 1331 he was given the same office in Wiltshire.[66] These appointments, as well as many to the eyre, oyer and terminer, commissions of the peace and other justice commissions,[67] appear to have kept him out of court for at least two years running.[68] In November of 1335, he was appointed a member of an embassy to treat with the Scots and, that having failed, served against them and was made warden of Bothwell Castle. He was made steward of the household from March 1336 to March 1337,[69] as well as holding the office of Admiral of the Northern Fleet between January and August of 1337.

The redistribution of estates to Bohun, Clinton, Montagu and Ufford throughout the 1330s, then, all had some justification aside from their authorization – whether by parliament or otherwise – or the reasons stated in the texts of the grants. In one way or another these individuals can be seen to be deserving of grants of lands, rents and rights through their past service, even if these grants had come at the expense of others. A large portion of the properties taken in as a result of the events of 1326–30 which were destined

---

[59] In September of 1336 the sheriff of Oxford was ordered not to go after Bohun until Midsummer for the payment of reliefs, farms, and other debts, because the latter was on the king's service in Scotland. *CCR 1333–7*, p. 714.

[60] *Memoranda Rolls*, p. 373.

[61] See Shenton, above.

[62] *CPR 1330–4*, pp. 223–4 and 532; E 401/320 (9 April 1334).

[63] *CCR 1333–7*, p. 7. In connection with this, the king made Montagu a grant 'in consideration of the great place which he holds in the direction of the affairs of the realm'. *CPR 1330–4*, p. 462. And again, in May of 1336, a royal grant was made for Montagu's 'fruitful and laudable service in the management of the king's affairs and those of the realm, and in consideration of the dangers to which he has exposed himself in the preservation of the king's honour and the defence of his rights'. *CCharR 1327–41*, p. 359.

[64] *Memoranda Rolls*, p. 377.

[65] *CFR 1327–37*, p. 206.

[66] *CPR 1330–4*, p. 66.

[67] *CPR 1330–4*, pp. 63, 66, 69, 144, 329 and 572.

[68] See C. Given-Wilson, 'Royal Charter Witness Lists: 1327–1399', *Medieval Prosopography* 12 (1991), 35–94 (p. 63).

[69] T. F. Tout, *Chapters in the Administrative History of Mediaeval England*, 6 vols. (Manchester, 1920–33), III, 37.

43

for the nobility, then, went to these men over the first half of the decade. Some were indirect holdovers from the Despenser estate. On 9 September 1332, William Bohun was the recipient of a grant for his good service to the king of the manors of Hinton and Speen (Berks.), Haseley, Ascot, Deddington, Pyrton, and Kirtlington (Oxon.), the town and manor of Wycombe (Bucks.), the manors of Long Bennington (Lincs.), Kneesall (Notts.), Newnham (Gloucs.), Wix (Essex), and a farm of £42 from the manor of Bosham (Sussex), to hold for himself and the heirs of his body.[70] These lands had come into royal possession through the surrender of the king's uncle, Thomas, earl of Norfolk – who, though something of a favourite of the previous regime, did not seem to have been forced to give up the lands involved.[71] They were, however, originally from the forfeited Despenser estate which, in 1327, had been granted to Norfolk.[72]

The properties which Isabelle was forced to give up in 1330, including those which she had taken from the Despensers at the beginning of the reign, were obviously a more important part of the land redistribution to these men throughout the decade.[73] Some of them were granted out under limited terms. On 2 January 1331, William Montagu was allowed the keeping of the royal manor of Woodstock (Oxon.), at a fixed farm of £100 per annum, and the manor of Hanborough (Oxon.) at £27 16s. 6d., both of which had come in as a result of Isabelle's forced return of large parts of the estate which she had built up over the course of the minority.[74] Similarly, on 8 February 1331, Robert Ufford was granted the manors of Cawston and Fakenham (Norfolk), again controlled by Isabelle in 1330, 'until he obtain the manor of Costeleye [Norfolk]'.[75] Most, however, were granted out under longer terms. Some of it went, on account of his part in the coup, to Robert Ufford. On 24 January 1331, he was granted the manors of Gravesend (Kent) and Burgh (Norfolk) in tail male.[76] Later in the same month, William Montagu also received grants of confiscated properties, namely the manors of Christchurch Twynham, Westover and Ringwood (Hants), Crookham (Berks.) and Catford in Levesham (Kent), all previously held by Isabelle.[77] It is notable that a number of these

---

[70] *CFR 1327–37*, pp. 323–4.

[71] C 266/8/60.

[72] *CCharR 1327–41*, pp. 3–4. There was no reason given for the surrender, though Holmes has found evidence that it was with Norfolk's approval. Holmes, *Estates of the Higher Nobility*, p. 23, n. 1. Prestwich and Given-Wilson, however, see Thomas of Brotherton as being somewhat out of favour by the early 1330s. M. Prestwich, *The Three Edwards* (London, 1980), p. 157; C. Given-Wilson, *English Nobility in the Late Middle Ages* (London, 1987), p. 34.

[73] Aside from those lands granted to Isabelle. Wolffe, *Royal Demesne*, p. 56.

[74] *CFR 1327–37*, p. 215. See also *CFR 1319–27*, p. 318.

[75] *CPR 1330–4*, p. 69.

[76] *CPR 1327–30*, p. 67.

[77] *CCharR 1327–41*, p. 210; C 81/178/4285; *CPR 1330–34*, p. 54; *Victoria History of the Counties of England: Hampshire and the Isle of Wight* (London, 1911), IV, 608; V, 92.

manors had once been in the hands of the Despensers, and had been granted to Isabelle just after the Deposition.[78] Indeed, Isabelle's estate would continue to be of importance throughout the 1330s as a source of patronage for the king, though later it was through the use of reversionary rights on her life estate. In 1337, in order to sustain the rank of earl of Huntingdon, William Clinton was granted, among other properties, in expectancy the manors of Holme and Glatton (Hunts.), both of which were previously controlled by Hugh Despenser the Younger and were taken over by Queen Isabelle after 1326.[79]

Also important for endowment of those later to be promoted to earldoms was the fall of Roger Mortimer, earl of March.[80] Though many of the lands of the earl of March tended, according to Holmes, to remain either in the king's hands or be leased out, some were nonetheless granted away as semi-permanent or permanent patronage during the first half of the reign.[81] Most notably, in 1331 William Montagu was granted one of the most important parts of the Mortimer estate, the lordship of Denbigh, and the cantreds of Ros, Rhyfiniog, Carmarthen, and the commote of Dinmael in Wales.[82] Worth over 1000 marks per annum to Montagu, this lordship was forfeited by Lancaster in 1322, then granted to Hugh Despenser the elder, who in turn forfeited it in 1326 when it came into Mortimer's hands.[83] But, for the nobility as a whole, and those who were to become the new titled nobility in particular, the Mortimer estate also was of importance because of the knock-on effects of the events of 1326–30 – especially the premature death of Roger Mortimer's son, Edmund, in 1331. Indeed, the way in which the estate was used was primarily connected with the guardianship of the Mortimer heir. Of the lesser new men, on 30 April 1334, Thomas Bradeston, one of the new generation of men who were to be ennobled, had been granted the keeping of the manor of Kingsland (Hereford.), until the lawful age of the heir of Edmund Mortimer, at a yearly rent of £47 19s.[84] More importantly, part of this estate was granted to William Bohun, later to be raised to the earldom of Northampton in 1337. Probably in connection with his wife's affiliation with the Mortimer family, in April of 1336 Bohun was given control of part of the wardship of the heir to the estate, which included the manors of Cleobury Mortimer and Earnwood (Salop.), the reversion of the manor of Arley (Staffs.), and the manor of Bisley (Gloucs.).[85] In

---

[78] See Wolffe, *Royal Demesne*, pp. 232–4.

[79] E 142/33/5; *CPR 1334–8*, p. 415.

[80] E 199/15/6 (Hants); E 199/15/10 (Hants); E 199/25/6 (London and Middlesex); E 199/38/23 (Salop and Staffs.); E 199/39/10 (Soms. and Dors.); C 257/16.

[81] Holmes, *Estates of the Higher Nobility*, pp. 14–18.

[82] *CCharR 1327–41*, pp. 199 and 210; *CCR 1330–3*, p. 115.

[83] *An Inventory of the Ancient Monuments in Wales and Monmouthshire IV: County of Denbigh* (1914), p. 39; *Survey of the Honour of Denbigh: 1334*, ed. P. Vinogradoff and F. Morgan (1914), pp. xii–xiv.

[84] *CFR 1327–37*, p. 407.

[85] *CPR 1334–8*, p. 252.

September of the same year, he also gained control in a similar way of the castle of Wigmore, the ancient home of the Mortimers.[86] William Montagu was likewise to gain from the Mortimer estate. In June of 1336, for 1000 marks to the exchequer, Montagu obtained control of the custody of the body of the Mortimer heir, and in order to be able to sustain the latter, he was given the wardship of the Mortimer manors of Bromsgrove (Worcs.) and Worthy Mortimer (Hants).[87]

Similarly, the estate of the underage heir of Edmund, earl of Kent, who had been executed in 1330 on the orders of Roger Mortimer and whose son had died within a few months of being restored to his father's lands in 1331, was also of use for grants of lands in wardship to two of the men who Edward III was to elevate to earldoms. William Bohun was granted lands of the earl of Kent in Hampshire in November of 1331, the grant comprising the farm of the town of Basingstoke (worth £80 16s. a year) and £20 of rent payable by the prior of Bath to the barton in the town.[88] Similarly, though on a larger scale, William Montagu was given the wardship of the earl of Kent's manor of Camel, the manor and town of Somerton with the hundred, the warren and pasture of Kingsmore, the manor of Kingbury Regis with the rent of assize of Melbourneport, the hundred of Horethorne, and a rent of £20 payable by the prior and convent of Bath for the town of Bath and its Barton, all in Somerset.[89]

The success of Edward III's use of the estates which had come into his hands either as a direct or indirect result of the events of 1326–30 is clear. Firstly, it helped break up the potentially dangerous power blocks of the latter part of the 1320s, and placed the estates of these individuals in the hands of men Edward knew to be loyal to him.[90] As a result of confiscations and connected minorities, the Despenser and Mortimer estates, as well as those of henchmen such as Maltravers and Bereford, were divided up into a series of grants. Though these often returned to the rightful heirs later in the reign, as will be discussed below, at least for the years immediately following the coup, they were usually safely away from any members of the families who might want to cause problems for the young king. Indeed, in the short term, such a policy was crucial if Edward did not want the descendants of the troublemakers of the previous decade to have immediate access to the power which larger estates conferred.

---

[86] On 23 September 1336, Hugh, bishop of Lincoln was ordered to give up keeping of the castle of Wigmore. *CFR 1327–37*, p. 495.

[87] *CFR 1327–37*, pp. 488–9.

[88] *CPR 1330–4*, p. 217; *CCR 1330–3*, p. 459.

[89] *CPR 1330–4*, pp. 113–14.

[90] A similar policy seems to have been used by Edward III when it came to wardships and marriages of problematic members of the 1320s nobility. See J. S. Bothwell, '"Escheat with Heir": Guardianship, Upward Mobility and Political Reconciliation in the Reign of Edward III', *Canadian Journal of History* 35 (2000), pp. 242–73.

Secondly, this redistribution of estates after 1330 – those which were not retained in the hands of keepers or granted to minor royal officials[91] – helped give the established nobility some stake in the new landed settlement. Grants to families such as the Greys, Ros's and Latimers, as relatively uncontroversial members of that group, were an integral part in the redistribution of these estates. However, it was clear that they were not intended to be the main beneficiaries of the post 1330 settlement. Although the earl of Cornwall received sizeable chunks of Isabelle's estate, this was the only large grant of the confiscated lands which went to members of the pre-1330 nobility. Rather, from examining the pattern of property redistribution, it becomes obvious that, at least in the case of the estates of the major players of the 1320s, Edward III had little set policy of even-handed redistribution.[92] Instead, Edward used these confiscations to begin the build-up of a solid power base in the nobility of 'new men' loyal to him – helping him to elevate individuals to estates befitting peers in parliament. This estate redistribution, then, was crucial in helping create support both within the rank and file of the parliamentary peerage and, more importantly, the titled nobility – the place where problems had usually begun in previous decades.

Indeed, Edward III's favour with the confiscated lands does not, on the whole, tend to be misplaced. Most of the men who benefited from the land settlement after 1330 proved to be of great utility in the Hundred Years War.[93] Though the earl of Huntingdon, and even the earls of Salisbury and Northampton,[94] appear to have caused Edward problems briefly during the crisis of 1340–1, for the most part those favoured in the post 1330 settlement served the king well in the decades to come. Take the example of the earl of Northampton: after his elevation to an earldom in 1337, William Bohun was constantly on commissions to the Continent during the first phase of the Hundred Years War.[95] In October 1337 he was appointed to 'punish disturbances, if any arise, among the knights, esquires, and men-at-arms going beyond the seas on the king's service in the present fleet'.[96] Moreover, he took part in Sluys and the siege of Tournay,[97] as well as acting on various

[91] For example, grants to Robert Wodehous and Robert Bullok. See *CFR 1327–37*, pp. 224 and 233.

[92] To be discussed in a monograph under preparation by the editor of this volume on Edward III's relations with the English parliamentary peerage.

[93] It was these men, along with more established members of the English nobility, 'who in the autumn of 1339 were responsible for breaking the "thread of silk" which, according to the cardinals, surrounded France'. Ayton, 'Edward III and the English Aristocracy', p. 206.

[94] B. Wilkinson, 'The Protest of the Earls of Arundel and Surrey in the Crisis of 1341', *EHR* 46 (1931), 177–93 (p. 181).

[95] *CPR 1334–8*, p. 530; *CCR 1337–9*, p. 515; *CCR 1339–41*, pp. 223 and 225; *CPR 1338–40*, pp. 371, 374, 385, and 397; *Treaty Rolls 1337–9* (London, 1972), passim.

[96] *CPR 1334–8*, p. 576.

[97] *CCR 1339–41*, p. 482.

occasions throughout the 1340s and 1350s both as surety for royal war debts – to the point of going to prison for them[98] – and agent in the king's wool credit schemes.[99] In 1341, for part of the year at least, Bohun was serving in Scotland. Later in the same year, he was made the king's lieutenant and captain general in Brittany, and, as such, relieved Brest in August, defeated the French at Morlaix in September, took La Roche Darrien by assault, and was sent to besiege Nantes in November. By June of 1345, he was again in France, initially in charge of an expedition in Brittany,[100] and present at both the battle of Crécy in 1346 and the siege of Calais the next year. Thereafter, he remained in France for most of the next two years involved in royal negotiations.[101] It was in this period that he was made a knight of the Garter,[102] Warden of the Scottish Marches (1350), and Admiral of the Northern Fleet (1351). He also took part in the naval battle with the Spanish off Winchelsea in 1350, and was made Essex and Hertfordshire's commissioner of array in 1352 to oppose a potential landing of the French. In 1355, he was listed as going on the French campaign in Artois,[103] though by January 1356, in his role as warden and lieutenant of the March, he was commissioned to negotiate with the Scots concerning the ransoming of David Bruce.[104]

Overall, then, estates taken into custody as a result of the events of 1326–30 were well used by Edward III in order to give the individuals he favoured the economic status to uphold their ranks and to function as men of account in the king's service. There were, however, some complaints and court action as a result of this redistribution of estates. The bannerets often seem to have had the most trouble holding on to lands granted from this source. On 26 July 1333, Thomas Bradeston was granted the manor of Knolle by Bristol, held by William Dovyll, in expectancy. This was originally granted as a result of the forfeiture of Thomas Gournay, a servant of the

[98] G. L. Harriss, *King, Parliament, and Public Finance in Medieval England to 1369* (Oxford, 1975), p. 281.
[99] E.g. E 208/3/62; *CPR 1338–40*, pp. 371, 372 and 391; *CCR 1339–41*, 532, 533 and 556; *CPR 1340–3*, p. 189; E 403/322 (25 January 1342); E 401/375 (11 February 1344); *CPR 1345–8*, p. 539; *CPR 1354–8*, p. 469; Harriss, *King, Parliament, and Public Finance*, p. 350. On the shift towards royal indebtedness to the nobility after the outbreak of war, see E. B. Fryde, 'Magnate Debts to Edward I and Edward III: A Study of Common Problems and Contrasting Royal Reactions to Them', *National Library of Wales Journal* 27 (1991–2), 249–87 (pp. 272–80).
[100] Harriss, *King, Parliament, and Public Finance*, p. 324.
[101] *CP*, IX, 667.
[102] Though, notably, neither he nor Suffolk were original members of the Order. See H. Collins, *The Order of the Garter 1348–61: Chivalry and Politics in Late Medieval England* (Oxford, 2000), p. 289.
[103] *CPR 1354–8*, p. 255.
[104] For more about the earl of Northampton's varied and numerous wartime activities, see A. Ayton, *Knights and Warhorses: Military Service and the English Aristocracy under Edward III* (Woodbridge, 1994), passim.

minority regime.[105] However, later in the decade, the widow of Gournay, Joan, won back the manor from Bradeston, and the king had to grant him other lands in its stead.[106] Grants from lands involuntarily surrendered were indeed sometimes hotly contested, not only by the original owners or their descendants, but also by any others who had claims upon the properties involved. The manor of Marston Meysey (Wilts.), mentioned previously, is an illustration of this point.[107] Originally held by John Meysy in the reign of Edward I,[108] Hugh Despenser the elder forcibly disseised him from the manor and apparently imprisoned him until he signed it over.[109] Meysy then sought a writ of *novel disseisin* against Despenser, which he pursued without success, except insofar as to get Despenser angry enough to name Meysy as one of the 1322 rebels. As a result, Meysy abjured the realm, but appears to have come back after Despenser's fall and regained hold of the manor.[110] In 1330, he granted the manor to a group of feoffees who then granted it back to him, with remainder to Peter le Veel and Cecily, his wife, 'the heirs of their bodies, and the right heirs of Peter'.[111] This continued to be the situation until 5 May 1331 when it was taken back into the king's possession as part of the forfeiture of Despenser,[112] and granted to John Darcy, first as a simple appointment during royal pleasure, then for his life, and in 1338 for the life of his son.[113] There appears to have been no major dispute concerning the manor in Darcy's lifetime, but after his death, an action was started in October of 1350 by the designated heir of John Meysy, the son of Peter Veel, who claimed his right through the aforementioned fine which gave him control of the manor after the death of Meysy.[114] Similarly, another example of the confusion over ownership caused by the forfeiture and redistribution of the Despenser estate was Adam Moldworth's suit to regain control of the manor of Little Barrow (Cheshire), which Edward III had granted to Roger Swynnerton but which Moldworth claimed was his through an agreement with Hugh Despenser the elder.[115]

Perhaps the most famous reversal of fortune when it came to the grants of estates taken in as a result of the events of 1326–30, however, came in connection with the honour of Denbigh. Denbigh was one of the lordships

---

[105] *CPR 1330–4*, p. 457; *CCharR 1327–41*, p. 305.

[106] *CPR 1334–8*, p. 562.

[107] Except where noted, the following is from CP 40/360/94 ff.

[108] C 260/61/10.

[109] For a summary of the events in the 1320s, see *CCR 1327–30*, pp. 495–6; CP 40/360/94ff; C 260/61/10.

[110] *CCR 1327–30*, pp. 495–6.

[111] C. R. Elrington, *Abstracts of Feet of Fines Relating to Wiltshire for the Reign of Edward III* (Wiltshire Record Society, vol. 29, 1973), p. 23.

[112] E 357/2/7/1v.

[113] *CPR 1330–4*, pp. 165 and 268; *CPR 1338–40*, p. 16.

[114] CP 40/360/94 ff.

[115] KB 27/301/48; C 47/10/34.

conquered by Edward I in the early 1280s, being originally granted to Henry Lacy, earl of Lincoln.[116] It was held by the Lacy family until 1311 when the male line failed. Alice, the daughter of Henry, earl of Lincoln, then married Thomas, earl of Lancaster, and the lands passed into the Lancastrian estate. However, in 1322, the lordship came into the king's hands as a result of Lancaster's forfeiture, and threats by the Despensers against Lancaster's wife further diverted it into the elder Despenser's possession.[117] After Despenser's fall, it was granted to Mortimer, who in turn held it until he forfeited in 1330. As has been noted, it was then granted to William Montagu in 1331 as a sign of favour for his aid in the overthrow of Mortimer.[118] However, in order to secure the title, he ended up having to pay substantial sums to members of those families who had held the lands over the last half century – most notably to Alice Lacy, countess of Lincoln, to the son of Hugh Despenser the younger and to Hugh the elder's widow, Eleanor, and her husband, William de la Zouche.[119] As Davies notes, this, along with further purchases in the area including the reversion of the Montalt inheritance from the queen mother, made Montagu into one of the more substantial Marcher lords.[120] However, as has often been observed, a king's preference for a man did not necessarily extend to his offspring, so that when the 1330 judgement against Roger Mortimer was reversed in the autumn of 1354,[121] his estate was again open season for his heirs. Roger Mortimer, the second earl of March, asserted in the Hilary session of King's Bench in 1354 that William Montagu, the second earl of Salisbury, had illegally entered into the lordship of Denbigh and unjustly held it.[122] Both men then showed up to court in person, emphasizing the importance of the case. The earl of Salisbury did not recognize the hold of the earl of March and said that his father had been granted Denbigh and connected lands by the king. March, however, claimed that since the disinheritance of his grandfather was erroneous, he should be reseised. The latter, probably as a result of his growing favour with Edward III, won the case, though there is evidence that Salisbury was still trying to win back the lordship in 1359, 1377–80 and even as late as 1397.[123]

[116] R. R. Davies, *Lordship and Society in the March of Wales, 1282–1400* (Oxford, 1978), p. 27.

[117] Fryde, *Tyranny and Fall*, p. 113.

[118] Mortimer's widow also tried to get some of his lands back. C 47/10/19(6).

[119] C 47/10/35(8); Davies, *Lordship and Society*, p. 50.

[120] Davies, *Lordship and Society*, p. 50.

[121] See J. G. Bellamy, *The Law of Treason in England in the Later Middle Ages* (Cambridge, 1970), pp. 83–5.

[122] KB 27/376/21; SC 1/40/122; J. G. Edwards, *Calendar of Ancient Correspondence concerning Wales*, Board of Celtic Studies History Law Series 2 (Cardiff, 1935), pp. 190–1; see also London, British Library, Egerton Roll 8725.

[123] C 47/10/33(8); SC 1/38/106; *RP*, III, 7 and 58–9; see also Holmes, *Estates of the Higher Nobility*, p. 19, n. 3. Others who gained from Mortimer's fall had similar

Despite such cases, Edward III continuously exploited forfeited lands en masse as a source of royal endowment throughout the first half of his reign. However, the use of these confiscations – for the sake of elevating 'new men' to peerages and revived earldoms – meant that the redistribution of these estates had to be protected to a large degree by the reputation or status of many of the individuals involved. Indeed, it is notable that some of the most significant parts of the lands, wardships and marriages of the most important of the estates involved – the Despensers and the Mortimers – were granted to those individuals closest to the king, namely many of those raised to earldoms in 1337. This was not simply to show favour. It could also help protect the post-1330 land settlement against potential legal challenges. Indeed, Edward ensured through his land redistribution that the people to whom he granted the most substantial properties had enough position to defend themselves in court should any dispute arise over rights to the land. However, in the longer run, Edward III also covered himself with respect to his use of the estates forfeited in 1330 by rarely allowing these lands to be alienated from families permanently.[124] Through the granting out of most of these confiscated lands under conditional terms – life, tail male or entailed – a way was left open so that those problematic families who had lost lands were not seen to be disinherited permanently, but perhaps only until the animosities between such families and the monarchy had died down. The rehabilitations of most of the major families during the reign were thus not made as difficult, or as shocking, as they might have been had the lands been granted out in perpetuity.

Nonetheless, due to the controversial nature of the land redistribution, Edward III needed the spectacle of the elevation of those most favoured with these properties to earldoms in 1337, an act which used men who were clearly loyal to him, but who would also, through their position both as earls and leaders of the government on the home and war front, be able to defend the settlement both in the courts and on the public stage for years to come. Moreover, the 1337 elevations were the clearest affirmation possible by Edward III of his intention to stick by the land redistribution resulting from the events of 1326–30. Since these estates in themselves were made up of lands often acquired by various questionable means, both for the sake of the 1337 earls, and for the sake of the other members of the nobility who had gained from the new tenurial settlement, Edward III needed a flamboyant and well publicized gesture of backing the 'new men' in the hope of making the landed settlement a secure one, at least until the animosities of

experiences, such as John Beauchamp and the Berkeley family. See KB 27/375/71, KB 27/376/20.

[124] Part and parcel of his treatment of royal patronage as a whole to his 'new nobility' during the reign. See J. S. Bothwell, 'Edward III and the New Nobility: Largesse and Limitation in Fourteenth-Century England', *EHR* 112 (1997), 1111–40 (pp. 1127–32).

the 1320s and early 1330s subsided. Thus though the 1337 elevations were about the coming French war and the need for competent, well backed administrators and generals – as has often been remarked –[125] they can also be seen as publicly reaffirming Edward III's tenurial settlement as a whole after 1330.

[125] For example, see K. B. McFarlane, *The Nobility of Later Medieval England* (Oxford, 1973), pp. 156–64; A. Tuck, *Crown and Nobility 1272–1461: Political Conflict in Late Medieval England* (London, 1985), pp. 118–19; Given-Wilson, *English Nobility*, pp. 33–42; and, most recently, Ayton, 'Edward III and the English Aristocracy', pp. 188–90.

3

Politics and Service with Edward the Black Prince

DAVID S. GREEN

The Black Prince was born to a military inheritance. There were few, if any, aspects of his life which were not shaped by the Anglo-French conflict, and the administration of his estates and the complement of his retinue were governed by such concerns. The life story of the man who died on Trinity Sunday (the feast-day for which he had particular reverence) in 1376 is well known. On that day, in the midst of the political crisis of the Good Parliament, the prince was lauded and mourned despite his (partial) responsibility for the loss of the principality of Aquitaine and much of the territory acquired by the English from the opening of hostilities in 1337 to the treaty of Brétigny (1360). This was the man who, as a boy of sixteen, had won his spurs fighting in the vanguard at Crécy. Ten years later his reputation reached its height when, outside Poitiers, he captured the king of France in battle. The consequence of that victory, despite the failure of the Reims expedition to enforce the demands of the treaties of London, was a prin- cipality for Edward of Woodstock. It was from there that the Black Prince launched his last campaign when he became involved in the Castilian civil war. Disaster followed victory at Nájera (1367) and the prince returned to Bordeaux, bankrupt and broken with the illness that would eventually claim his life. The Gascon rebellion, probably engendered by Charles V and Louis of Anjou, as much as by the haughtiness of the prince and his predominately English officers, was further encouraged, perhaps even excused, by the 1367 *fouage* and war soon followed.[1] It was to be a war in which the prince could play almost no part.

The military aspects of the prince's career are well known and their ramifications influenced every other facet of his life, but such matters were not his only concern and this was demonstrated in the composition of his household and retinue. Men were drawn to the prince's service because of

[1] R. Delachenal, *Charles V*, 5 vols. (Paris, 1909–31), IV, 74–5 and 77–8; F. Autrand, *Charles V* (Paris, 1994), p. 547.

the potential financial rewards and his military reputation. Furthermore, he was the heir apparent and as such, his influence at court was considerable and could be used to bring his servants and retainers to the attention of that greatest of all patrons, the king – an office and dignity that would, in time, be held by Edward of Woodstock. This not only made the Black Prince an attractive employer but it dictated the composition of his retinue and was evident in the manner by which he recruited and rewarded its members.

The nature of the prince's demesne also influenced the complement of his retinue. Wales, Cheshire and Cornwall were not areas rich in highly influential members of the aristocracy who could bring their own followings within a greater affinity. Therefore, although the prince did recruit heavily within his own demesne, the retinue was not exclusively made up of those from the west. Perhaps surprisingly, a significant number of prominent individuals came from or had close connections in East Anglia, particularly Norfolk. The region certainly did not have the military, indeed the aggressive, reputation of Cheshire or Wales but it was there that the Black Prince found some of his most loyal (and indeed militarily active) servants.[2]

The purpose of this retinue was primarily military. It was created in the preparations for the Crécy campaign, developed through Edward's appointment as prince of Wales, lieutenant of Gascony and finally prince of Aquitaine and given impetus by the 1355 *chevauchée* and the triumph at Poitiers. It goes without saying that an army was expensive, that it needed supplies, food, horses, arms, armour and wages. Although the prince was supported in all his campaigns except the Spanish expedition by the royal exchequer, a very considerable bill had to be met through his own resources. These resources needed to be exploited, collected and maximized, all of which were tasks of the retinue. Such efforts were not always adequate for the prince's needs and despite the ransoms and booty taken at Poitiers, in preparation for the Reims campaign of 1359, he had to take out loans of at least £21,350. His creditors included Richard FitzAlan, earl of Arundel,[3] the

---

[2] The prince's only tenurial interests in the county were at Castle Rising though he also had rights to the tollbooth at Lynn. These were valued at £116 13s. 4d. in 1376 (C 47/9/57). After his marriage to Joan, the prince did acquire some additional property in Norfolk, such as Ormsby manor. Members of the retinue with Norfolk connections included Thomas Felton, William Elmham, Stephen Hales, Thomas Gissing and Nicholas Dagworth. Robert Ufford and Robert Knolles also had interests in the county.

[3] £2,000 was advanced by Arundel on the security of a crown and a jewelled star taken from the king of France at Poitiers, 24 July 1359 (*BPR*, IV, 302 and 333). The chamberlain of Chester was ordered to levy funds on 20 May 1360 to repay FitzAlan (*BPR*, III, 381). On 21 May, John Delves, lieutenant of the justices of north Wales and Cheshire, was notified that he was to receive £1,000 and then deliver it to the prince. Delves was also to inform the chamberlains of Chester (John Brunham) and north Wales that they were also to bring/send all available funds to London (*BPR*, III, 354). See also 27 July, *BPR*, III, 355. Delves received £3 expenses in connection with this transaction at Holt castle and the transportation costs. *BPR*, III, 364.

Malabayala family,[4] assorted members of the lay and episcopal aristocracy[5] and members of the London merchant community.[6] Of this sum, 20,000 marks was negotiated by Sir John Wingfield, governor of the prince's business.[7]

Therefore, violence or the capacity for violence, the prowess of the knight, the skill at arms of the infantryman or archer was not the only criterion by which the prince recruited. Wingfield was a knight and fought with the prince in 1355 and at Poitiers but his value was far greater as an administrator and financier than on campaign. Matters of policy that were most clearly expressed through the *chevauchée* or on the battlefields of France were underpinned by political action in England. That action could take place on many stages and in many forms, not only in parliament – in opposition to or in concert with the increasing influence of the commons – but through the diplomatic and propaganda services provided by the church and through the manipulation of the chivalric ethic, most particularly in the creation of the Order of the Garter. Such practice served to bind together the military community in its widest form in support of Edward III's war in France. In this, the Black Prince and his retinue were highly significant.

The recruitment of that retinue is something of a 'grey area'. It is uncertain how or if individuals were approached or if they directly sought the prince's patronage. The means by which they were retained, however, provides a clear distinction between the retinue of the Black Prince and other contemporary and near-contemporary associations, such as the Lancastrian affinities of Henry of Grosmont and John of Gaunt and the royal affinities of Edward III and Richard II. Although the prince's retinue did not conform in scale and expense to the unusual model of Gaunt's affinity, there are analogies as well as distinctions with his Lancastrian predecessor. However, both chronologically and in other ways, the fairest comparison may well be with Grosmont since the military and political conditions under which he

---

[4] Antony 'Maubaille', merchant of Ast and Hugh Provane, merchant of Carignano, loaned 1,000 marks. *BPR*, III, 319.

[5] 500 marks were provided by Humphrey Bohun, earl of Hereford and Essex, 30 July 1359 (*BPR*, IV, 304). Ralph Nevill and the bishop of Lincoln each loaned 500 marks and the bishop of Winchester, 1,000 marks. *BPR*, IV, 319 and 327.

[6] John Peche borrowed £1,000 from various London merchants on the prince's behalf and repaid 250 marks to William de la Pole for him. Peche was appointed the prince's attorney for the transfer of certain jewels from the sire de Lesparre and Sir Petiton de Curton and also received the crown which had been pledged as security for Arundel's loan (*BPR*, IV, 321, 327 and 333). £100 was borrowed from both Henry Pickard and Adam Franceys. *BPR*, IV, 327.

[7] *BPR*, IV, 326. Wingfield, another East Anglian in the retinue, held this office until his death in 1360 in addition to being the prince's attorney, steward of his lands and chief of the council. He received wages of 10s. a day. Delves replaced him until his own death in 1369. M. Sharpe, 'The Administrative Chancery of the Black Prince Before 1362', in *Essays in Medieval History Presented to T. F. Tout*, ed. A. G. Little and F. M. Powicke (Manchester, 1925), pp. 321–33 (p. 331).

operated at the height of his authority coincided with the expansion of the prince's retinue in the aftermath of the Crécy campaign. The structure and forms of retaining and patronage also bear more comparison with the first duke of Lancaster than the second. Both made sparing use of life indentures. Only five men are known to have drawn up indentures with Grosmont and one, Richard Felstede, was a London carpenter.[8] Evidence for the Black Prince reveals only twenty-one life indentures,[9] compared with Gaunt's 173 in 1382. Kenneth Fowler, through an analysis of certain associates, annuitants, those who regularly fought with Grosmont on campaign, the witnesses to charters and household and estate officials, noted that the small nucleus of his *comitiva* who were donees provided a core around which temporary servants could collect. Among both retinues the distinctions between forms of service and the areas in which that service might take place were blurred – household and administrative tasks and estate duties were often undertaken by military men. On the basis of these criteria, the prince's retinue appears to have much in common with Grosmont's entourage. However, the prince's retinue was significantly larger than that of the first duke of Lancaster, with over four times as many indentured retainers and many more annuitants. The Black Prince maintained a household and retinue that was, in size, closer to Gaunt's than Grosmont's.[10] It is in the methods of patronage and retaining that the significant difference arises between the sons of Edward III.

It should be remembered that as the future king, the retinue of the prince of Wales and Aquitaine was not the final product. On his accession it would be augmented with the royal household of his father. It is partly a consequence of this that while many of the retinue, particularly administrators, served with Edward for long periods, the military retinue was a constantly evolving institution which was reshaped to meet changing conditions, often on an ad hoc basis and with little vision of the long-term future.

It may be as a consequence of such uncertainties that the prince made far greater use of life annuities than his brother, at the expense of indentures of retainer. It may be that an annuitant could be relied upon across a range of duties, whereas an indentured retainer was constrained, at least theoretically,

---

[8] K. Fowler, *The King's Lieutenant: Henry of Grosmont, First Duke of Lancaster 1310–1361* (London, 1959), p. 181.

[9] Henry Eam was retained on 28 January 1348, Nigel Loryng on 13 March 1349, Edmund Manchester in May 1351, William Aubigny on 31 July 1352, John Sully on 27 January 1353, Baldwin Frevill on 8 August 1358, William Greneway and Richard Mascy on 1 March 1365, Geoffrey Warburton on on 6 June 1365. Aubrey Vere, Gerard Braybrook, William Thorpe, John Golofre, Robert Roos, Baldwin Bereford and Richard Abberbury were all retained between 1 October and 6 November 1367. William Wasteneys and Thomas Guysing were retained on 5 October 1371, John Mascy and Nicholas Vernon in March and May 1373 respectively, and Ralph Davenport on 8 June 1373.

[10] For comparative figures see S. Walker, *The Lancastrian Affinity 1361–1399* (Oxford, 1990), p. 22.

by certain conditions of employment. The annuity was a more generous grant since it was, to quote J. M. W. Bean, 'absolute in law for the life of the recipient and not even his open disobedience or disloyalty could justify the termination of a payment, a fact that did not apply to an indenture of retinue'.[11] However, in practice, it was most unlikely that an individual would bring litigation against the prince. Furthermore, the conditions by which annuities were granted were often expressed in terms reminiscent of later letters of indenture. Thus, the prince granted very generous sums giving him a highly flexible retinue without the necessity for the constraints of an indenture but with a number of the safeguards. James Audley received famously £400 a year as a reward for his services at Poitiers and although such largesse was unusual, annuities in excess of £100 were not.[12] Of £2,538 received in Cheshire in 1369–70, annuities accounted for £1,537 7s. 6d. (over 60%), although these were not only grants made for military service.[13] Such annuities were paid from at least twenty-five sources including manors, lordships and central reserves. The bulk of the burden fell on Cornwall, Chester, the receiver-general and, to a lesser extent, the manor of Wallingford.

Why then did the prince recruit indentured retainers at all? Two early examples – Henry Eam, a Flemish knight and founder member of the Order of the Garter,[14] and Edmund Manchester, a bachelor of the household – indicate that early in his career the prince experimented with a different practice of recruitment and retaining. Eam was, in essence, a life retainer without an indenture, and Manchester was retained during pleasure, not for life. This example corresponds to that of William Greneway in 1365 but this may have been because he was only of yeoman status whereas Manchester had a rather colourful past and had been involved in a number of crimes and misdemeanours.[15] The intention may have been to give the prince flexibility and lessen his responsibilities although these are exceptional cases and the majority of contracts followed more typical practice. The retainers, as suggested by Bean, were, in part, to be the military nucleus of the prince's wider retinue and expeditionary forces.[16] However, the small number and the occasions when these contracts were made suggest that this cannot be the whole story.

The most significant block of indentures, in terms of number and purpose,

---

[11] J. M. W. Bean, *From Lord to Patron* (Manchester, 1989), pp. 14 and 17. For examples of the termination of short-term indentures between the prince and John Arundel and John Trevaignon because of behaviour 'so outrageous and offensive', see *BPR*, II, 9–10.

[12] SC 6/772/5 (Edmund Wauncy); *BPR*, IV, 178–9 and 555 (Stephen Cosington); *CPR 1377–81*, p. 375 (Nicholas Bonde).

[13] SC 6/772/5.

[14] G. F. Beltz, *Memorials of the Most Noble Order of the Garter* (London, 1841), pp. 86–9.

[15] *CPR 1345–8*, pp. 310–11, 319–20, 379, 384–5 and 460; *CPR 1348–50*, p. 33.

[16] Bean, *Lord to Patron*, p. 58.

was that made early in the winter of 1367. In addition to wishing to reward a number of those who were with him in Spain, the prince may have had more prescient concerns. He returned to Bordeaux from Castile early in September. The first tranche of the recalculated sum owed by Pedro for Anglo-Gascon assistance in the (temporary) deposition of Enrique of Trastamara was due to be paid on 6 September. The treaty of Aigues-Mortes between Enrique and Louis of Anjou had been concluded on 13 August, giving the following March as the date for the resumption of the war. Furthermore, the disintegrating situation in Aquitaine required the prince to have a body of soldiers on stand-by for rebellion or to respond to French incursions. It may be that he did not feel he could rely on many of those who had campaigned with him in Spain and had not been paid. The use of indentures on this occasion was probably for very specific reasons and the conditions of the contracts, which specified that there would be no war payment additional to the fee, presumably reflects the unusually penurious position in which the prince found himself. In almost every other instance, the granting of an indenture of retainer seems to have little direct military motivation, the exception being the case of Baldwin Frevill, retained in advance of the Reims campaign.[17]

It may be that the contrast between Gaunt and his brother was the product of an administrative evolution. To quote Bean once more, 'It is reasonable to assume that the Black Prince's attitude towards the making of indentures . . . did not change after 1361 and the indentures that have survived for . . . John of Gaunt, belong to a different generation.'[18] However, only six individuals were retained before 1361 and more specifically before 1365. In the next eight years fifteen received indentures. Changing political conditions, the acquisition (and defence) of the principality of Aquitaine and the aftermath of the Castilian campaign may have necessitated the recruitment of specifically military assistance. In many cases, these men had fought with the prince in the past and were known and trusted. The purpose of a number of indentures made in 1371 and 1373 is less certain. The prince may have been seeking to augment a household depleted after the return from Aquitaine or it may be that these men were recruited for a particular purpose. Financial concerns may again have played a part. A life annuity would have to be paid for many years, an indenture would only remain legally binding for the prince's own lifetime. However, since Edward granted large numbers of annuities in his last years and Richard confirmed many, if not all, of them, including the annuities linked to indentured retainers, this also seems unlikely.[19]

The bulk of military activity was undertaken by men in the service of the

[17] University of Nottingham, Middleton Deeds, Mi F 10/8; *BPR*, IV, 80 and 259.
[18] Bean, *Lord to Patron*, p. 59.
[19] For example, *CPR 1377–81*, pp. 160, 199, 201, 246 and 248. For further comments see D. S. Green, 'The Later Retinue of Edward the Black Prince', *Nottingham Medieval Studies* 44 (2000), 141–151.

Black Prince recruited on short-term contracts, either for a year or the duration of a campaign. This is particularly evident prior to the Reims expedition. The few campaigns in which the prince was involved and the long periods of time between them precluded there being a large body of regular support from identifiable individuals. Retaining with solely military factors in mind would have been, perhaps even for the prince, an unnecessary expense. Recruitment was never a problem; the general factors that encouraged participation in the French wars in most military companies, mercenary and otherwise, were brought into sharp relief in his case. As Bean suggests, 'his retaining practices may embody relics of a time when such arrangements were looser and the indenture of retinue had not evolved into its conventional form'.[20] What might be called the *familia principis* was a military household and it fulfilled that role in the campaigns of 1355 and thereafter. The size of the prince's household, the number of his bachelors and other attendants, meant that he did not need to retain to ensure a more than adequate following.

The role of the prince's bachelors is shrouded by the scarcity of household accounts. They were conspicuous among his military servants, often annuitants and many of them were involved in a number of campaigns with the prince and/or accompanied him to Aquitaine in 1363 or were part of the 1369 Northampton muster, the only such event for which evidence remains.[21] They also numbered among them the most important administrative and estate officials, such as John Chandos, Thomas Felton, Richard Stafford and Edmund Wauncy. The prince maintained a much larger group of bachelors than the great majority of his contemporaries and his household and retinue in this regard draws comparison with a royal rather than a noble model. Gaunt's register for 1372–6 noted twenty-one bachelors, and the 1379–83 register included twenty-seven. The Black Prince's register gives the title to seventy-two individuals which closely equates to the average of seventy knights of the royal household in the first half of the fourteenth century.[22] These were not always military figures, as in the case of William Shareshull, although it may indicate why the royal justice and chief baron of the exchequer was not in receipt of an annuity or was retained in any other way. He may simply have received the privileges of a bachelor in the prince's household. However much it was ignored, it was, after all, illegal to retain a judge.

Such legal considerations may also be responsible for the inconsistencies and differences between the entourages recruited by these two sons of Edward III. The reign of Richard II witnessed the outlawing of retaining other than for life and, in any case, the Lancastrian affinity was exceptional.

[20] Bean, *Lord to Patron*, p. 62.
[21] BL Cotton Julius C IV fols. 288–91; PRO E 101/29/24.
[22] C. Given-Wilson, *The Royal Household and the King's Affinity: Service, Politics and Finance in England, 1360–1413* (New Haven and London, 1986), p. 211.

In Thomas of Woodstock's proposed Irish expeditionary force, there was apparently only one life retainer and such small numbers were common in many of the retinues of the great nobility.[23] The Black Prince's retinue does not conform to either the Lancastrian models of Henry of Grosmont, or that of John of Gaunt. Can a comparison be drawn with the royal household, if, as has been suggested, this was for what the Black Prince himself and his retinue were preparing?

The expectation that the prince would assume the throne was, of course, natural and shared among contemporaries. He was often referred to as Edward IV and his impending coronation and reign were thought 'destined' to be glorious. According to Thomas Walsingham, the Black Prince rediscovered the holy oil presented to St Thomas by the Virgin for use in the coronation ceremony.[24] This had great significance for his putative reign. Nonetheless, the structure of the prince's household and retinue is not immediately apparent as a court in waiting. There is no real evidence of a cadre of chamber knights or esquires, although Thomas Wales was described as 'one of the bachelors of the prince's chamber'[25] and John Sully was retained to be a part of the prince's 'especial retinue'.[26] If they were the only knights so designated, presumably certain bachelors and others fulfilled a similar function to the royal knights of the chamber, without the title. The lack of central and household accounts and loss of the Gascon register prevent anything more than supposition on this matter. It may be significant that a large proportion of Richard's chamber knights and esquires had previously seen service with his father and therefore may have undertaken similar duties. Furthermore, at the royal level, the transformation from knights of the household to knights of the chamber happened gradually in the period 1350–65 and a comparable situation may not have occurred in the prince's retinue until the transfer to Aquitaine in 1363. The scarcity of evidence that followed again does not allow for more than speculation. It is possible that the role of these bachelors compared, in some cases, with that of the 'king's knight' during the reign of Richard II, individuals not part of the household but nonetheless closely associated with the king.

Despite differences in retaining practice, it is possible to see the prince's retinue as forming a core and model among the great bastard feudal associations of the day. The inter-relationships between the royal household under Edward III and Richard II, the Lancastrian affinities of both Grosmont and Gaunt, and the Black Prince's retinue, show the fluidity of service between these institutions. This is in no way surprising, especially if the prince is viewed as the future Edward IV. However, while the retinue of the

---

[23] K. B. McFarlane, *The Nobility of Later Medieval England* (Oxford, 1973), pp. 103–4.
[24] Noted by J. R. Lander, *The Limitations of the English Monarchy in the Later Middle Ages* (Toronto, 1989), pp. 41–2.
[25] *BPR*, IV, 136.
[26] E 36/280/31v; *BPR*, II, 45.

Black Prince may best be described as the king's household in waiting, there were many who stayed resolutely in one camp, royal, Lancastrian or that of the heir apparent. It must be remembered that the knightly community was small and closely connected on a number of levels and through a variety of vertical and horizontal associations. If, as can be supposed, recruitment was a matter of 'word of mouth', local influence, nepotism and military and administrative experience, then the opportunities for overlapping military and administrative service among the great affinities and retinues of the day were very great.

The prince's retinue also provided a bridge to the household and government in the minority rule of his son. This was also achieved through the role of Princess Joan, who acted as a steadying political influence,[27] and '. . . there seems to have been a personal movement on the part of the King's mother to secure her influence in the government by bringing into office dependants of the King's father, the late prince of Wales . . . as a counterpoise to the influence of her brother-in-law'.[28] Cobham, Richard Stafford, Richard Fitz-Alan, John Devereux, Hugh Segrave, John Knyvet and Hugh, earl of Stafford, all had links to the prince, some closer than others, and all served in the early minority councils of Richard II. John Harewell, bishop of Bath and Wells, William Ufford, the son of the prince's companion-in-arms, and Aubrey Vere were drafted into the council in October 1378.[29]

There is also in this regard a question of terminology and definition. Did the prince have an affinity? Can it be said that his influence was widespread but not so overtly political as his brother's? Was a large retinue and luxurious household sufficient for his needs and inclinations, knowing that an affinity would come with the crown? Perhaps, but it was also true that the nature of the prince's demesne ensured that a significant element in any affinity would be limited. Wales, Cornwall and Cheshire were not overly endowed with significant members of the nobility and, therefore, the prince's tenants were not, on the whole, of the same standing as those who comprised the affinities of other great men. Equally, the changing nature of feudal obligations meant that less reliance was placed on a lord's tenants as other sanctions and forms of encouragement came into play. Certainly land as a reward for service was not a common arrangement in the prince's circle and he may have preferred his servants to be dependent on him for a considerable proportion of their income.[30] Without wishing to become involved in the debate concerning the

---

[27] N. Saul, *Richard II* (London, 1997), p. 11.

[28] N. B. Lewis, 'The Continual Council in the Early Years of Richard II, 1377–80', *EHR* 41 (1926), 246–51 (p. 249).

[29] Lewis, 'Continual Council', 247–8 and 250–1. For details of careers and links to the Black Prince see D. S. Green, 'The Household and Military Retinue of Edward the Black Prince' (unpublished Ph.D. dissertation, University of Nottingham, 1998), Appendix.

[30] He may have been following a policy which, it has been suggested, his father

nature of 'feudalism'[31] (suffice to suggest that it indicates a good case for the legitimization of its 'natural' offspring), discussions of bastard feudal associations have, to a greater or lesser extent, bypassed the retinue of the Black Prince. Perhaps this is due to the somewhat anomalous, even anachronistic, place in which his retinue stands in the feudal evolution and perhaps this is as it should be. 'From the beginning, from a kind of primordial soup of property, rights and influence, ephemeral structures formed and dissolved: "feudal" relationships, "affinities", clientèles. What has to be seized upon is what is essential in each of these structures, service in return for reward.'[32]

The rise and development of the prince's retinue mirrored the successes of the English in France and the retinue was a chivalric and military order not a political organization, in so far as they can be distinguished from one another. Parliaments at the time tended to be compliant and supportive and there was little need to exert influence in the commons beyond the natural authority of the royal family and the lords. The prince's political life and the concerns of his retinue involved matters of personal lordship and the control of local society, the extraction of revenue and provision of military support. This was not so for Gaunt whose power-base was moulded by his political concerns at home and dynastic ambitions abroad. The Black Prince believed that one day he would be king and on his coronation his retinue would be augmented with his father's retainers, officials and servants. The retinue was a dynamic association, constantly changing to meet the military demands the prince placed on it and absorbing members from the estates to which the prince was given title. Gaunt sought a crown elsewhere, and his affinity was shaped with that object in mind. The changing fortunes of war and increasing independence of the commons also shaped the Lancastrian affinity. These were forces to which the prince's retinue was only briefly exposed. However, whether it was a direct concern of the prince himself, of his ruling council or merely coincidence and a consequence of the prince's standing and that of his retainers, he and his followers wielded considerable political authority not only in the localities and at court but also in parliament.

A prime concern of the prince, as one of the major figures in his father's hostile foreign policy, was taxation. The increasing importance of the commons was based on the increasing dependence of the crown for financial

---

adopted. See J. S. Bothwell, 'Edward III and the "New Nobility": Largesse and Limitation in Fourteenth Century England', *EHR* 113 (1997), 1111–40; J. S. Bothwell, '"Until he Receive the Equivalent in Land and Rent": The Use of Annuities as Endowment Patronage in the Reign of Edward III', *HR* 70 (1997), 146–69.

[31] S. Reynolds, *Fiefs and Vassals: The Medieval Evidence Reinterpreted* (Oxford, 1994).

[32] P. S. Lewis, 'Reflections on the Role of Royal Clientèles in the Construction of the French Monarchy (mid-xivth/end xvth centuries)', in *L'état ou le roi: Les fondations de la modernité monarchique en France (xive–xviie siècles)*, ed. N. Bulst, R. Descimon and A. Guerreau (Paris, 1996), p. 56.

support of its military escapades. The influence of magnates through their retainers in parliament has often been queried and the same question may be asked of the retinue of Edward of Woodstock. A number of its members sat as MPs, but there is little evidence to suggest that the prince was following a deliberate policy comparable to that of which Gaunt was accused, namely trying to pack the commons for certain votes. Those claiming the prince's support in the Good Parliament only numbered six. In three sessions in 1358, 1365 and 1369, seven members of the retinue sat in the commons. There do not appear to have been any sessions from 1344 until his death that did not contain at least one member of the retinue,[33] although some of these men sat in parliament before they had a firm association with the prince. It is true to say that those sessions when he was best represented were tax granting parliaments,[34] but beyond this, membership of the commons does not seem to have been a major factor in recruitment to the retinue. It may have been the case that the prince's authority and that of his friends and his father's supporters was sufficient to influence the commons as they wished.

A comparison with 'Lancastrian' MPs in this instance is somewhat disingenuous due to the atypical parliamentary positions of Cheshire and Wales where the prince's authority was strongest. His 'tenurial' influence over the composition of the commons was restricted to lands held of the duchy of Cornwall. If the prince did wish to have influence in parliament, it would be achieved through the greater authority that he wielded in the later years of his life and through having influence over individuals representing areas where he himself had little land.

A survey of parliamentary members in the retinue throughout the prince's adult life reveals thirty-six or thirty-seven individuals who sat in the commons, of whom three represented two different constituencies.[35] This is a very considerable number but still fails to answer the question of a

[33] MPs in Gaunt's affinity were concentrated in a handful of counties, whereas those in the prince's retinue represented at least twenty-one of the thirty-six counties that returned members. Gaunt had as few as three and as many as thirteen MPs in every parliament from 1372 to 1397 (five or six in the 1370s, seven or eight in the 1380s and ten to twelve in the 1390s). Walker, *Lancastrian Affinity*, pp. 238–9. Clark suggests that in the eleven parliaments from 1386 to 1397, Gaunt's representatives in the commons averaged a dozen and rose on occasion to seventeen. L. Clark, 'Magnates and their Affinities in the Parliaments of 1386–1421', in *The McFarlane Legacy: Studies in Late Medieval Politics and Society*, ed. R. H. Britnell and A. J. Pollard (Stroud, 1995), pp. 126–53 (p. 139).

[34] W. M. Ormrod, *The Reign of Edward III: Crown and Political Society in England, 1327–1377* (New Haven and London, 1990), pp. 208–9.

[35] The relationship of Matthew Dabernon, who represented the borough of Lostwithiel, with the prince is uncertain. The role of John Dabernon as sheriff and steward of Cornwall in his appointment may have been influential. Matthew was mentioned in John's will. Devon Record Office (Exeter) 158M/T3; M. Webster, 'John Dabernon and his Will (1368)', *Devon and Cornwall Notes and Queries* 36 (1989), 176–84.

deliberate 'Westminster' policy.[36] The presence of a number of members of his retinue in parliament may not have been the consequence of a calculated strategy. The prince recruited widely and among men of high calibre; it is of no surprise that a number of these sat in parliament. In accordance with the geographical character of the retinue, the prince retained or had links to men who sat in constituencies throughout the country. He does not appear to have 'swamped' any particular regions with his familiars, although Norfolk, Herefordshire and Cornwall tended to return members who can be associated with the prince on a fairly regular basis. The majority although by no means all the appointments were dated to the last decade of the prince's life. This may indicate an increasing interest in domestic politics but there is little evidence to corroborate this. More probably, these years marked a period in which the members in question were older, more respected in county society, less militarily active and thus more likely to take up seats in the commons. However, if the prince was trying to develop parliamentary influence, it is probable that this would have occurred after his return from Aquitaine in 1371. Prior to this '. . . neither king nor particular magnates tried to have their own men returned to parliament with any regularity . . . Evidence of politically motivated meddling in elections . . . begins to appear only in the 1370s.'[37] It is unlikely, both as a consequence of his state of health and the intransigence of county communities, that the prince could exercise his will freely or arbitrarily over parliamentary elections. Gaunt does not appear to have had a great deal of influence over the choice of parliamentary representatives even in Lancashire, although he may have been able to sway matters at particular times of crisis. As in the prince's retinue, the size of the Lancastrian affinity made it inevitable that a large number of parliamentary members would have links to the duke.[38]

It remains difficult to judge if the prince gained active support through his retinue in parliament or if others were encouraged to become MPs. The declining use of petitions and the fact that they might have been presented orally has resulted in a paucity of evidence, not helped by the fact that the parliament rolls for the period 1357–61 have been lost.[39] Petitions tended to focus on purveyance and military obligations, trade regulations and matters

---

[36] For comparison, fourteen of the MPs sitting for Westmorland between 1386 and 1421 were associated with the Clifford family and fourteen members of Richard, earl of Worcester's affinity represented that county between 1404 and 1421. Clark, 'Magnates and their Affinities', pp. 129–30.

[37] J. R. Maddicott, 'Parliament and the Constituencies, 1272–1377', in *The English Parliament in the Middle Ages*, ed. R. G. Davies and J. H. Denton (Manchester, 1981), pp. 61–87 (p. 74). The first unambiguous evidence of a magnate interfering in an election concerns the bishop of Rochester in Kent in 1429. Clark, 'Magnates and their Affinities', p. 132.

[38] *RP*, II, 136, 238, 257, 277, 286 and 333; Walker, *Lancastrian Affinity*, pp. 148–9 and 196.

[39] Maddicott, 'Parliament and the Constituencies', pp. 71–2 and 76–7.

of local government, particularly law and order. Complaints were often heard regarding the maintaining and retaining of royal justices, the partiality of oyer and terminer commissions and the ready issue of pardons to criminals.[40] In all these respects, the Black Prince was a leading example of bad practice. He was unlikely to be brought to account, however, as he was influential among those appointed to try the petitions.[41] In the 1352 parliament, Shareshull, Roger Hillary and Richard Willoughby were selected to try the English petitions and Shareshull, Richard Talbot, Thomas Bradeston and Ralph Stafford dealt with foreign matters. They were joined by Henry Green in 1354.[42] All had links to the prince. For example, Bradeston was justice of south Wales, fought at Poitiers and at a tournament in Lichfield in 1348 the prince had competed under his banner.[43] Green was a king's justice and member of the prince's council.[44]

The potential for parliamentary authority was certainly there. More questionable is the use or desire to use that latent influence, and in addition, whether the prince had any political agenda on top of or contrary to his father's and other than preparing for his own accession. His most famous political role, in the Good Parliament of 1376, has almost certainly been exaggerated. He was very ill by that time and if his support was implied by a number of the knights of the shires, it was not given expressly.[45] Corroborative evidence for the prince's support is only supplied by Walsingham, not the most reliable source in matters relating to John of Gaunt.[46] It is Walsingham's account that lies at the root of the exaggerated role ascribed to the prince in the Good Parliament and the supposed hostility between himself and his younger brother. Wilkinson stated that ill feeling developed after Gaunt had

[40] G. L. Harriss, 'The Formation of Parliament, 1272–1377', in *The English Parliament in the Middle Ages*, ed. Davies and Denton, pp. 29–60 (pp. 50–1).

[41] H. G. Richardson and G. O. Sayles, 'The Parliaments of Edward III, pt. 2', *BIHR* 9 (1931), 1–18 (pp. 3–4).

[42] *RP*, II, 236 and 254. On the role of receivers and auditors of petitions see H. G. Richardson and G. O. Sayles, 'The King's Ministers in Parliament', *EHR* 47 (1932), 377–97 (pp. 381–2). They suggest that the receivers were given 'an honorary office to ensure their presence in parliament'.

[43] R. A. Griffiths, *The Principality of Wales in the Later Middle Ages. The Structure and Personnel of Government, I: South Wales, 1277–1536* (Cardiff, 1972), p. 106; J. E. Powell and K. Wallis, *The House of Lords in the Middle Ages* (London, 1968), p. 355; *CIM 1348–77*, p. 24, no. 63; R. Barber, *Edward, Prince of Wales and Aquitaine* (Woodbridge, 1978), p. 93.

[44] *BPR*, IV, 152 (4 September 1355); C. Given-Wilson, *The English Nobility in the Late Middle Ages* (London, 1987), p. 99. He had served the prince in previous years including the 1353 sessions for which he was paid £20. *BPR*, III, 136–7 (3 December 1353). On 4 September 1358 he was given twelve oaks. *BPR*, IV, 261.

[45] G. Holmes, *The Good Parliament* (Oxford, 1975), pp. 134–5 and 137–8.

[46] '. . . exctincto Principe exctinctus est cum eo profecto Parliamenti praesentis effectus. Nam communes, cum quibus ipse tenebat, dicti Parliamenti sorti non sunt talem exitum qualem pro meliori habuisse sperabant.' T. Walsingham, *Historia Anglicana*, ed. H. T. Riley, 2 vols. (RS, 1863–4), I, 321.

superseded the prince in Aquitaine.[47] While the prince certainly mishandled his Gascon subjects, he was in no condition to deal with the situation which developed in Aquitaine after his return from Spain and apparently handed over the reins of power to Gaunt out of necessity if not relief. Indeed, it is difficult to find evidence at any point of hostility between the king's eldest sons.[48] It has been suggested that even if relations between the brothers did not break down, there is evidence of animosity and antagonism between a 'clerical' party nominally led by the prince and a 'court' party led by Gaunt.[49] In 1376, there were indications of co-operation between a group of sympathetic lords and the commons, and '[u]ndoubtedly the knights who presented the accusations depended on certain lords for political support'.[50] Perhaps the prince and Gaunt were amongst those providing such support.

The prince may also have exercised influence over the lower clergy, which has been shown to have been active in parliament for much longer than was previously thought.[51] Particularly in Wales, the prince had considerable authority over the appointment of clerical representatives from vacant dioceses.[52] Such influence would only have been limited, as attendance by the lower clergy in parliament never reached double figures after 1340.[53] However, members of the higher clergy also had a parliamentary role and the prince's influence in parliament may have been extended through such individuals who became increasingly numerous among his acquaintances throughout his life.

That the prince was associated with a large proportion of the House of Lords and a smaller, though still a significant number of the commons is to be expected. Many of the lords were closely linked to the prince and served with him on campaign, often on more than one occasion, and some were in receipt of annuities from him or undertook administrative offices. It is uncertain if the prince used his authority in the lords to influence attitudes throughout

---

[47] B. Wilkinson, *The Chancery under Edward III* (Manchester, 1929), p. 125.

[48] The brothers exchanged gifts on several occasions after the dissolution of the principality (23 November 1372, 24 December 1372, 13 April 1373 and on 8 January 1375). The prince was given 'le couvercle ove un pomel esnamillez de noir ove plume d'esterych'. *John of Gaunt's Register, 1371–75*, ed. S. Armitage Smith (Camden Society, 3rd Series, 20), pp. 96, 112–13, 191–3 and 278.

[49] J. Dahmus, *William Courtenay, Archbishop of Canterbury, 1381–1396* (Philadelphia, 1966), p. 23.

[50] Harriss, 'Formation of Parliament', p. 58.

[51] See A. K. McHardy, 'The Representation of the English Lower Clergy in Parliament During the Later Fourteenth Century', *Studies in Church History* 10 (1973), 97–107; J. H. Denton and J. P. Dooley, *Representatives of the Lower Clergy in Parliament, 1295–1340* (Woodbridge, 1987).

[52] For example, Bangor returned representatives from 1344–57, PRO SC 10/24/1169, 1191; 25/1237; 26/1296; 27/1323. It was without a bishop and under the prince's control in 1357, 1366, 1375–6, A. Hamilton Thompson, 'Medieval Welsh Dioceses', *Journal of the Historical Society of the Church in Wales I* (1947), 90–111.

[53] McHardy, 'Representation of the English Lower Clergy', p. 100.

parliament. It is even more uncertain if the prince's influence could be used counter to the wishes of the king. It may be that some personal authority might be brought to bear in the later years of the reign, but there is little to suggest that the prince had any political ambitions of his own beyond assuming the crown himself and later ensuring that it would pass to his son. This, it appears, was a programme much in keeping with Edward III's own. After saying that 'everything in the garden was rosy' between the prince and Gaunt, a small proviso should be made. The recent discovery of the king's entail for Richard to inherit the throne may reveal concerns about Gaunt's ambitions and Edward's fears.[54]

The Black Prince was not a political animal. The war, however, was political and the prince's life was played out against it as a changing but constant backdrop. There were only four major campaigns to speak of in twenty-one years and the role of the retinue was governed by extended periods of peace and truce even as it was shaped by the hostilities. In the 'closed season' some of the retinue fought elsewhere, with Chandos and the captal de Buch in Brittany, some with Du Guesclin in Spain. Others sat on commissions of array, of oyer and terminer, or acted as members of parliament, and as such they cared for their master's interests and those of fellow members of his retinue. Others saw diplomatic service further abroad. Politics and service in the retinue of Edward the Black Prince were within the broad range of central policy and reflected trends and practices evident among other contemporary associations. However, the retinue itself was different; it was anachronistic in its structure yet, by force of circumstance, highly innovative. It was, in a sense, a bastard feudal archetype in its 'artificiality' and its distance from its tenurial roots, and yet it also reflected the practices and traditions of earlier times.

In spite of its size and expense during his militarily active life, the prince did not bequeath a sizeable retinue to his son. The actions of Richard, particularly in the late 1380s and 1390s, reveal his lack of political support. There were a number of important individuals who went on to serve the Black Prince's son, and a significant number of those who sat on the continual councils during Richard's minority had begun their careers with the young king's father. The chamber knights in the first six or seven years of Richard's reign were mainly his father's former servants.[55] Nine out of nineteen of

---

[54] M. Bennett, 'Edward III's Entail and the Succession to the Crown, 1376–1471', *EHR* 113 (1998), 580–607.

[55] They included Richard Abberbury, Baldwin Bereford, Nicholas Bonde, John and Simon Burley, Lewis Clifford, Peter Courtenay, John del Hay, Nicholas Sarnesfield, Aubrey Vere and Bernard van Zedeles. Among the former servants of Edward III who served as chamber knights to his successor, Nicholas Dagworth, Robert Roos and Richard Stury all had dealings with the Black Prince as did the new men William Beauchamp, John Holland and William Neville. Given-Wilson, *Royal Household*, pp. 161–2.

Richard's esquires of the chamber also formerly saw service with the Black Prince.[56] Indeed, it was many of these who were the focus of attack by the Appellants in 1388. Simon Burley suffered execution but a number of others were required to absent themselves from court including Richard Abberbury, Baldwin Bereford, Nicholas Dagworth and Aubrey Vere. Although they were prominent at court, the remnants of the Black Prince's retinue that went on to serve his son were neither popular nor powerful. It is probably unfair to suggest it, but the failure of the Black Prince may not only have been the loss of Aquitaine but also the failure to establish a secure retinue and a body of support for Richard.

[56] John Breton, Roger Coghull, Lambert Fermer, Richard Hampton, John Peytevyn, Adam Ramsey, Philip Walweyn, snr, Richard Wiltshire and William Wyncelowe. E 101/398/8; Given-Wilson, *Royal Household*, p. 306, n. 128.

4

Second 'English Justinian' or Pragmatic Opportunist? A Re-Examination of the Legal Legislation of Edward III's Reign

ANTHONY MUSSON

The title 'English Justinian' was accorded Edward I with the undoubted intention of highlighting the enduring significance of his legislative programme. The epithet was coined, however, not by a contemporary chronicler, but by the early seventeenth-century judge and scholar, Sir Edward Coke,[1] who marvelled at both the substantive content and the sheer volume of entries in the statute book stemming from Edward's reign. When writing in his *Institutes of the Laws of England* concerning the first Statute of Westminster (1275), Coke considered:

> . . . all other [of] the statutes made in the reign of this king may be styled by the name of establishments, because they are more constant, standing and durable laws than have been made ever since: so as king E. I . . . may well be called our Justinian.[2]

If Coke's comment was to some extent an exaggeration, it probably says as much about Coke and his own agenda as it testifies to the merits of Edward I's legislation. The retrospective reference clearly reflected a desire on Coke's part that the English should have a legislative icon in the same way that the sixth-century Roman Emperor Justinian was hailed for the 'law code' that became the foundation of Roman civil law. By naming his own work (intended to be a comprehensive guide to the national laws of England) after Justinian's *Institutes*, Coke essentially wanted to emphasize the sense of past tradition as well as to identify the architect behind his native law:[3] a motive that was endorsed by the nineteenth-century constitutional historian

---

[1] Chief justice of the court of common pleas (1606–13) and chief justice of the court of king's bench (1613–16).

[2] E. Coke, *The Second Part of the Institutes of the Laws of England*, 2 vols. (London, 1809), I, 156.

[3] C. D. Bowen, *The Lion and the Throne: The Life and Times of Sir Edward Coke, 1552–1634* (London, 1957), pp. 52 and 438–9.

Bishop William Stubbs and the great lawyer and historian Sir William Holdsworth.[4]

In suggesting that Edward III should be dubbed 'second English Justinian', there is tacit acknowledgement of the epithet's validity as applied to Edward I within the framework of English legislative initiatives.[5] My main purpose here, though, is not to justify Edward I's posthumous title, nor dispute his legislative achievements, but to ascertain whether Edward III's enactments can be considered as part of a programme of legislation that laid decisive foundations warranting historical acclaim or whether his laws were essentially short-termist in character, being driven primarily by political concerns and his own dynastic ambitions.

Historians have tended to look upon Edward III's contribution to the law with a mixture of cynicism and ambivalence, contrasting his measures unfavourably with Edward I's ('a series of repetitive and ill-digested statutes that offer such a marked contrast to the legislation of the first Edward')[6] and emphasising the apparent subordination of legal concerns to the demands of the military machine.[7] W. M. Ormrod, who has done so much to rehabilitate Edward III's reign, considers that his (legislative) policies were 'a good deal more coherent and consistent than has usually been suggested', but nevertheless concludes his personal portrait of the king with the opinion that 'Edward was far too much of an opportunist to resist short-term compromises or vote-winning concessions.'[8]

The problem is one of focus and perspective. Are commentators being entirely fair and accurate in their judgments on Edward III's reign by comparing his legislation with Edward I's or in taking his tenure in isolation, unduly magnifying any hiatus or disjunctive element in the legislative programme? Even if there is some justification in allegations of opportunism with regard to Edward III's attitude towards governance, does it necessarily

---

[4] W. Stubbs, *The Constitutional History of England*, 4th edn, 3 vols. (Oxford, 1906), I, 109; W. Holdsworth, *Some Makers of English Law* (Cambridge, 1938), p. 25.

[5] It is significant that while contemporary English commentators did not offer accolades to the Plantagenet kings, the French legists in the court of late Capetian and Valois monarchs did in fact encourage comparison with Justinian: J. Krynen, *L'empire du roi: idées et croyances politiques en France, XIIIe–XVe siècles* (Paris, 1993); A. Gouron, 'Royal Ordonnances in Medieval France', in *Legislation and Justice*, ed. A. Padoa-Schioppa (Oxford, 1997), pp. 57–71. I am grateful to Craig Taylor for this information.

[6] H. G. Richardson and G. O. Sayles, *The English Parliament in the Later Middle Ages* (London, 1981), chap. XXI, p. 13.

[7] R. W. Kaeuper, *War, Justice and Public Order: England and France in the Later Middle Ages* (Oxford, 1988), p. 291: '. . . the strains of governing England while fighting France and Scotland were too great; the efforts to control public order from Westminster were largely given up. . . . The same trend is evident in legislation, which came to be based on petitions from the commons.'

[8] W. M. Ormrod, *The Reign of Edward III: Crown and Political Society in England, 1327–1377* (New Haven and London, 1990), p. 68.

follow that this trait inhibited developments in the law? This essay suggests that we should examine the relevance of his legal legislation in purely legal terms and assess the extent to which it offered any long-term benefits for the judicial system.

How should we go about judging the legal 'productivity' of Edward's fifty-year period as king? Coke emphasized constancy and durability as the pre-eminent qualities he admired. This, however, would appear to be a rather narrow definition of 'establishments'. Therefore, in addition to assessing whether the legislative activities of Edward's reign were influential in the longer term or achieved any degree of permanence, we should also take account of the extent of innovation in his statute law and identify underlying consistencies in policy. It is important that such initiatives are perceived within the general context of fourteenth-century law-making. This will inevitably involve looking closely at the formal statements on the statute roll, but a fuller picture can be gained (where records of parliamentary business survive) from comparing finalized statutes with parliamentary petitions and government responses to those petitions. The attitudes presented in judicial pronounce-ments will also be incorporated into the equation, and to a certain extent I shall need to delve into matters of concern in contemporary politics and society to assess the influence of what one might call the extraneous or 'environmental' factors affecting the promulgation of legislation.

Our revised perception of Edward III's legislation must first involve a consideration of the historical context of his reign in terms of how events both preceding his accession and during his reign may have affected the king's attitude towards law-giving, and with regard to the role played by parliament in the legislative process. I shall emphasize, secondly, the new authority and esteem that was accorded statute law by the political community, litigants and the legal profession, which in turn contributed to a special focus not only on its status as law but also on the requirements for its legitimacy and binding effect. Thirdly, there will be an assessment of the influences on the bulk of statutes and of the nature and extent of control exerted by the commons over the legislative process. Finally, I shall re-examine statutory provisions with important substantive or procedural implications, highlighting their signific-ance in terms of their content, effect and durability. My re-assessment stresses the need to see the reign as a constructive period, one which, it is argued, witnessed decisive enactments in the areas of administrative law against a background of political and social redefinition.

The historical context

Edward III's attitude towards the law was determined by a combination of his education as king, his own ambitions and experiences, and the position of the crown at the start of the reign. His perception of the role of the monarch was based mainly on the templates provided by past generations of kings as well as his more mythical ancestors. It is clear that his imagination and admiration were captured by Henry II and Edward I and that he tried to follow their expansionist foreign policies.[9] I would suggest that his reign also emulated theirs in concern for the workings of the law. This does not mean that he was personally involved in legislative detail, but that he demonstrated some personal interest in justice and presided over a council that not only took his lead, but itself possessed the vision, aptitude and motivation to create good and workable laws (see below). The king's personal involvement in the dispensing of justice was noted when he sat with the court of king's bench and heard the trial of one of the notorious Folville brothers in 1332.[10] He frequently gave audience to petitions brought by those with little or no political influence, and he took an active role in judicial matters during the 1340s and 1350s. In 1343, for instance, he expressed concern over the state of the country following his recent absence and issued a command for the lords and commons to discuss how the law should be better kept.[11] The 'hands on' approach was in keeping with the personal involvement of previous monarchs and not of course (nor should it have been) a continuous thing; but enough to provide an example and give impetus to judicial campaigns.

Edward III has been described as being very image conscious: he wanted people to think well of him.[12] As with many kings, much of his success and popularity stemmed from his military prowess. This duty to lead in war is depicted on one side of the great seal, an icon of the king's will: the king is armed and on horseback. The obverse side, however, shows the king sitting in justice, symbolising his duty to the law.[13] I would argue that these were not mutual exclusives under Edward III. Indeed, the king's record on law keeping and the provision of measures smoothing the path of litigants was just as much a determinant and barometer of public opinion as success in war. Although concessions might be made, the legal system generally did not stop entirely just because there was a war on. If anything, it generated more work: arrangements for internal peace were required and various calls to litigation might arise from the establishing of uses (akin to trusts) over land or as a result of the deaths of holders of landed estates. Above all, it was in the king's interest to ensure that confidence was maintained in the legal processes, whether he was at home or abroad. Some of the legislative provisions may have been enacted out of necessity or pragmatism, but the focused attention produced by war could have a beneficial effect. More

[9] Ormrod, *Reign of Edward III*, p. 44.
[10] E. L. G. Stones, 'The Folvilles of Ashby-Folville, Leicestershire and their Associates in Crime, 1326–1347', *TRHS* 5th ser. 7 (1957), 117–36 (pp. 125–7).
[11] Ormrod, *Reign of Edward III*, pp. 54–8; *RP*, II, 136(10).
[12] Ormrod, *Reign of Edward III*, p. 45.
[13] M. T. Clanchy, *From Memory to Written Record, England 1066–1307*, 2nd edn (Oxford, 1993), pp. 311–12; Kaeuper, *War, Justice and Public Order*, p. 384.

importantly, war did not necessarily mean that judicial concern had totally evaporated or that advances had broken down when the king's attention was momentarily removed. There was continuity provided in the personnel of the higher judiciary and a natural sense in which the law (as a body of rules and processes) maintained its own course, irrespective of the more volatile aspects of judicial administration.[14]

Edward's coronation oath bound him to do justice equally and properly to all his subjects. The ineptitude shown by his father (one of the articles of deposition cited Edward II's failure to abide by his coronation oath and uphold the law) and the lack of harmony within the ruling elite was a scar that ran deep in the political community. The minority regime led by Edward III's mother, Queen Isabelle, and her paramour, Roger Mortimer, though not indicted for its policies on law and order, nevertheless further eroded respect for the crown and undermined consensus. It was a priority for Edward to nurture respect for himself as a person, to rebuild public confidence in the government and to re-establish law and order in a society which had witnessed both tyrannical misuse of the law and several bouts of upheaval and disunity. Edward's assumption of personal control was marked by a renewed insistence upon his responsiveness to the twin issues of good order and justice.[15]

Adjunct to this commitment to law and order, we also have to consider the evolving role of parliament.[16] Edward I had originally encouraged petitioning in parliament as a way of providing redress for individuals and as a means of facilitating royal government in the shires. Under Edward II, the knights and burgesses attending parliament to assent to taxation had begun to articulate specific grievances and draw up lists of demands. As a result, petitions containing matters deemed to be of common interest to the realm (in that their contents concerned the law of the land or the welfare of people) came to be an established part of parliamentary procedure. While parliament continued to function as a court of appeal, as a tribunal for the resolution of difficult cases, and as a venue for state trials, by Edward III's reign it had become predominantly a fiscal and political institution with the commons using their control over taxation to extract concessions from the crown. The adoption of the complaints and remedies outlined in the common petitions as a basis for the formulation of legislation in turn transformed the nature and

---

[14] A. Musson and W. M. Ormrod, *The Evolution of English Justice: Law, Politics and Society in the Fourteenth Century* (Basingstoke, 1999), pp. 80–5 and 157–9.

[15] Ormrod, *Reign of Edward III*, pp. xi, 7, and 11–12; A. J. Verduyn, 'The Attitude of the Parliamentary Commons to Law and Order under Edward III' (unpublished D.Phil. dissertation, University of Oxford, 1991), pp. 14–15 and 29.

[16] For the following paragraph see G. L. Harriss, 'The Formation of Parliament, 1272–1377', and J. R. Maddicott, 'Parliament and the Constituencies', in *The English Parliament in the Middle Ages*, ed. R. G. Davies and J. H. Denton (Manchester, 1981), pp. 29–60 and 61–87; W. M. Ormrod, 'Agenda for Legislation, 1322–c.1340', *EHR* 105 (1990), 1–33; Ormrod, *Reign of Edward III*, pp. 60–2.

content of statutes. Edward III's reign therefore marked a fundamental change in the character of statute law.

A new status for statutes

The new method for the formulation of statutes gave rise to opinions as to the inherent qualities of statute law and a perceptual differentiation from the common law. This in turn contributed directly or indirectly to parliamentary legislation being given a new legal footing in that it was regarded as a directly enforceable body of rules adjunct to the common law. At the beginning of Edward I's reign it was well understood that a judicial decision could 'make a law throughout the land'. With the promulgation of Edward I's new statutory legislation (much of it technically a codification of existing common law) there appears initially to have been no strict delineation between judicial decisions and statutes. Nevertheless, it is apparent from the late thirteenth century that, as a written body of provisions, the legislative corpus of Edward I was gradually set apart in conceptual terms from the ordinary common law. Just as common law was distinguished from 'the usage of the country' (customary law), so statutory law, referred to as *ley especial* or *novel ley*,[17] had come to be seen as distinct from the *auncien ley*.[18] By the beginning of Edward II's reign, it was recognized that a statute could defeat the common law;[19] and by his son's time there was a realization that there could be a considerable difference between the two types.[20] Indeed, in Edward III's reign the common law was contrasted with 'the law now in force'.[21]

Given such an acknowledgement in open court and the increasing number of statutes being passed, it is not surprising that the relationship between judicial decisions and statutes received re-consideration by leading lawyers, among them Geoffrey Scrope and William Bereford. The former advocated that, when seeking to understand a statute, one should not step outside the bounds of its wording;[22] while the latter declared from the bench that, in cases where statute law was applicable, the latter provided the authority and no contrary averment could be accepted.[23] Following the political and judicial crisis of 1340-1, it is surely no coincidence that various judges again urged that a strict line was to be taken when interpreting statutory provisions.

[17] For example: *YB 1 Edward II*, p. 31; *YB 2 & 3 Edward II*, p. 168.
[18] T. F. T. Plucknett, *Statutes and their Interpretation in the First Half of the Fourteenth Century* (Cambridge, 1922), pp. 22–31 and 165–6.
[19] *YB 3 & 4 Edward II*, p. 162.
[20] *YB 11–12 Edward III*, p. 142.
[21] *YB 13 & 14 Edward III*, p. 24.
[22] *YB 5 Edward II*, p. 46.
[23] *YB 6 & 7 Edward II*, pp. 148–50.

Indeed, during the years 1342–3 the maxim *statuta sunt stricta juris* was coined by Robert Thorpe,[24] and later endorsed by William Shareshull, who echoed the words of Scrope when he said of a case that 'we cannot take the statute further than the words of it say'.[25] This was not a theory developed merely to protect their professional reputations from accusations of leniency or bias. It represented an acceptance of the authority of statute law and provides an indication of the power that a form of words (framed as such for a reason) could invoke. Indeed, it was also around this period (in 1338) that a principle of interpretation which still holds good in modern times, the *eiusdem generis* rule,[26] was enunciated by John Stowford, a serjeant in the court of common pleas, namely that general words placed at the end of a statute do not extend its application, but are governed by the preceding special words of limitation.[27]

Although such fine distinctions and technical considerations may have inhabited the higher echelons of the judicial world, they were nevertheless symptomatic of an awareness among ordinary people that new laws were regularly being passed and that this occurrence itself possessed some significance.[28] Information on the legislative canon was regularly conveyed directly to the shires: fresh parliamentary statutes were read out every month in the county courts and proclaimed in fairs, markets and other public places. Moreover, it is clear that during Edward III's reign the government took an interest in the success of its programme of dissemination since the sheriff was at times required to provide for chancery a record of when and where such proclamations had taken place.[29] The public consciousness of statute legislation can be gauged by the growing tendency over the course of the fourteenth century for statutes to be cited back at the crown, not just by members of the political community, but by private parties, concerned that the courts should be more consistent in the enforcement of legislation and anxious about the crown's failure to stick to its own laws in certain respects. A particularly striking example of this phenomenon is the quotation of statutes before royal judges in court.[30]

The perception of statute legislation as a second tier of law to be enforced in addition to the existing and evolving common law was matched by a

---

[24] *YB 17 Edward III*, p. 142; *YB 17 & 18 Edward III*, p. 446; *YB 18 Edward III*, p. 131.

[25] *YB 20 Edward III*, II, 198.

[26] J. A. Holland and J. S. Webb, *Learning Legal Rules* 2nd edn (London, 1991), pp. 195–6.

[27] *YB 12 Edward III*, pp. cxviii–cxx and 50.

[28] It is uncertain whether legislation was proclaimed in its entirety and thus whether direct information of the exact content of all statutes reached the shires.

[29] J. R. Maddicott, 'The County Community and the Making of Public Opinion in Fourteenth Century England', *TRHS* 5th ser. 28 (1978), 27–43 (p. 34); J. A. Doig, 'Political Propaganda and Royal Proclamations in Late Medieval England', *HR* 71 (1998), 253–80 (pp. 258–9).

[30] Maddicott, 'County Community', pp. 36–7; Musson and Ormrod, *Evolution*, pp. 165–6, and see pp. 234–5 nn. 12–15 for extensive references.

growing acceptance of a necessary relationship between parliament and statute legislation. In Richard II's reign, it could satisfactorily be declared that 'The law of the land is made in parliament by the king and the lords . . . and the commonalty of the realm.'[31] Such constitutional formulae had their precedents earlier in the century. As early as 1318 it was perceived that a full parliament was where adjustments to the law of the land should be deliberated and then declared, while in 1322 emphasis was placed on parliament as the forum in which the business of the kingdom 'shall be treated, accorded and established' and on these undertakings requiring the consent of the representatives of the whole political community.[32]

In Edward III's reign, the royal judges appear to have been particularly instrumental in articulating ideas on the relationship between the law and parliament, including voicing opinions on how laws were passed and the effect of their enactment. In 1348, for instance, Chief Justice William Thorpe (giving judgment on a case in parliament) underlined the idea that the power of the king was the necessary enacting force in parliament when he stated that 'the king makes laws with the assent of the peers and the commons and not through the instrumentality of the peers and the commons'.[33] The new role afforded to parliament in the promulgation of legislation was also highlighted and confirmed in a judgment by Chief Justice Robert Thorpe in 1365. In a far-reaching statement that stressed the overriding nature and binding force of statute law, he declared that 'as soon as parliament concludes any matter, the law presumes that every person has cognisance of it, for parliament represents the body of the whole realm and for this reason proclamation is unnecessary since the statute takes effect immediately'.[34]

The notion that parliament was the guardian of legislative enactments was raised again in a petition from early 1377, right at the end of Edward III's reign, which requested that statutes should not be repealed without the assent of parliament.[35] While the text of this petition carries the implication of a concern about the style of Edward III's government, especially some suggestion here of an opportunistic approach on the part of the crown to enforcement of its statutes,[36] it essentially represents perhaps a reminder to the king of the pivotal position of parliament (especially with regard to the position of the commons in parliament) and the importance of consensual politics.[37]

The concept of the binding force of statutes which was emerging in the

---

[31] *RP*, II, 243.
[32] Verduyn, 'Attitude of the Parliamentary Commons', p. 6; W. Holdsworth, *A History of English Law*, 4th edn (London, 1936), II, 437.
[33] *YB 22 Edward III*, p. 3 (Hillary pl. 25).
[34] *YB 39 Edward III*, p. 7.
[35] *RP*, II, 311.
[36] Ormrod, *Reign of Edward III*, p. 67.
[37] Disregard for legislation specifying annual parliaments would probably have been at least at the back of the petitioners' minds.

courts combined with an acceptance of the legislative supremacy of parliament to provide a context for the birth and enforcement of legislation. It is from Edward III's reign, therefore, that 'law-giving' in the form of enacted statutes not only gains a new meaning, but itself earns enhanced authority. While this re-definition of 'law' may not have been consciously constructed, it undoubtedly was a by-product of the relationship between Edward III and parliament (both commons and lords) and between the king and his advisors (particularly the judges). In turn it influenced the way legislation was thought about, framed and enforced.

Whose control was it anyway?

Since parliament's relationship with the law had become decidedly 'political' it would be difficult to analyse Edward III's contribution to the statute book without some form of reference to the immediate context of legislation. As is well known, common petitions were advanced in return for taxation. But what did this mean for initiatives in and the enactment of legislation? To what extent did this tie the hands of the crown? Should capitulation to commons' demands be taken as evidence of pragmatic opportunism?

While there was sometimes a reluctance on the part of the king to have recourse to parliament, it was in Edward III's reign that parliament came to be seen as the appropriate forum for legislative activity. This does not mean, however, that the king was forced to grant the petitions 'on the nod' or that statutes were dependent upon or forthcoming only after an influx of common petitions.[38] Grants of taxation were frequently coincident with bursts of legislative activity (see below) and it is often difficult to divorce the two. Yet some caution should be used in the way the process is described: the bargaining aspect in particular should not be over-emphasized. Dispensation of justice in parliament was, after all, part of the monarch's duty.[39]

Seen from another perspective, the commons' petitions were a useful way for the crown to obtain information on or have brought to its attention problems in the running of the country. The giving of concessions in the form of statutes could also be advantageous to the king in that the process enabled the crown to put forward its own programme of regulation and reform through adjustments and amendments to new or existing statutes. Indeed, it is now reasonably well established that the legislative process was far from being dominated by the knights and burgesses and that the crown was able to promote legislation 'off its own bat', thus pre-empting the petitioning

---

[38] Around 140 common petitions were submitted to the Good Parliament in 1376, yet no statutes were issued: Verduyn, 'Attitude of the Parliamentary Commons', pp. 171–2.

[39] G. Dodd, 'Crown, Magnates and Gentry: The English Parliament, 1369–1421' (unpublished D.Phil. dissertation, University of York, 1998), pp. 34–5.

process.[40] In 1351, for instance, the only petition connected with the Statute of Labourers simply recommended that the profits of the labour sessions be used to relieve the burden of a new direct tax granted in this assembly.[41] Similarly, in the parliament of 1352, although the commons submitted a long series of petitions, it is significant that the only mention of the issue of treason came in a request for definition (and an implied limitation) of the scope of this offence. The resulting statute was entirely the work of the king's council, whose legal experts would have been aware of the more flexible and inclusive notions of treason applied by the king's bench in the previous decade.[42]

A presumption of pragmatic opportunism denies that there was any force to the wishes of the royal judges and those on the council who saw that reforms in various areas of the judicial system were either necessary or appropriate. It also negates the crown's ability to reject petitions and amend or repeal legislation and undermines its control over the enforcement of measures.[43] Edward III's revocation of the statute of 1341 may have highlighted his apparent pragmatism in agreeing to its promulgation, but it also underlined the king's overriding power to decide what was good and just for the kingdom. Asserting the royal prerogative, he declared that the statute was 'contrary to the laws and customs of the realm'. He acknowledged, however, that those sections which might be thought 'reasonable and in accordance with law' could be salvaged and, with the advice of the judges, resubmitted at some later date.[44] Moreover, as highlighted above, the commons needed the king to give effect to legislation; but the crown did not require the commons' petitions to form statutes. This does not mean that the two were in competition with each other. Statute legislation was the product of a wide range of different legislative initiatives (that included decisions from court cases and private petitions): the commons' petitioning was merely one facet of this.[45]

Statutes and legislative provisions

Having outlined the constitutional and judicial context to Edward III's legal legislation, I now want to focus on certain specific statutory provisions. These measures are mainly procedural or administrative (though some have

[40] Ormrod, *Reign of Edward III*, pp. 63–8 and 77–80.
[41] *RP*, II, 228 (8); B. H. Putnam, *The Place in Legal History of Sir William Shareshull* (Cambridge, 1950), p. 54.
[42] *RP*, II, 238 (7); J. G. Bellamy, *The Law of Treason in England in the Later Middle Ages* (Cambridge, 1970), pp. 59–101.
[43] H. L. Gray, *The Influence of the Commons on Early Legislation* (Cambridge, Mass., 1932), pp. 224–7 and 255; S. B. Chrimes, *English Constitutional Ideas in the Fifteenth Century* (Cambridge, 1936), pp. 238–43.
[44] 15 Edward III, st. 2 (*SR*, I, 297); *YB 14 & 15 Edward III*, pp. lxi–lxii; Ormrod, *Reign of Edward III*, pp. 16, 48 and 67.
[45] Musson and Ormrod, *Evolution*, pp. 155–6; Dodd, 'English Parliament', pp. 36–43.

substantive content) and, as enactments possessing significance beyond the confines of Edward III's reign, would appear to warrant the title 'establishments'. These acts may not have been wholly innovative, indeed some practices and legislative ideas current in Edward I's reign were carried forward. The royal judges, the framers of fourteenth-century legislation (as habitually practised in many periods), frequently utilized existing concepts or combined new and old to produce some form of hybrid. Arguably, in some cases this creativity may have been in the pursuit of short-term ends, and within the context of a restrictive focus on Edward III's reign, may hitherto have been accorded limited significance. When viewed with the historian's hindsight, however, many of the statutory provisions take on a new creativity – not least because they were attempts to deal with prevailing political, judicial, economic and social problems.

On the surface some of Edward III's legal legislation does appear to have an overtly extra-judicial motive – more often than not a political one. The abolition of the presentment of Englishry in 1340,[46] for instance, neatly coincided with Edward's assumption of the title 'king of France'.[47] The Ordinance of Justices of 1346, which came on the eve of the king's departure to the continent, has been seen by historians as timed to avoid domestic discontent while embarking on the next French campaign rather than displaying a disinterested concern for equity.[48] The Statute of Labourers of 1351 (reinforcing the ordinance of 1349) has been viewed as introducing measures designed to coerce the lower orders into standing by their social obligations in the wake of the economic crisis precipitated by the Black Death.[49] It could be said that the Statute of Treasons of 1352 was a political concession to the lords, many of whom vividly remembered the executions and arbitrary judgments of Edward II's reign.[50] The Ordinance of Staple of 1353 (issued as a statute a year later, though in a slightly amended version)[51] could be regarded as having pragmatic economic designs in that it comprised a raft of concessions to encourage foreign merchants to England to engage in trade in wool and the country's other exports. To these measures can be added the multifarious changes in the powers and composition of the peace commissions during Edward III's reign, which, it has been argued, arose as 'quick-fix' answers to war-time exigencies and (culminating in the statute of

---

[46] 14 Edward III st. 1, c. 4 (*SR*, I, 282).

[47] 14 Edward III st. 3 (*SR*, I, 292).

[48] 20 Edward III (*SR*, I, 303–6); J. R. Maddicott, 'Law and Lordship: Royal Justices as Retainers in Thirteenth- and Fourteenth-Century England', *PP Supplement* 4 (1978), 44 and 84.

[49] B. H. Putnam, *The Enforcement of the Statute of Labourers*, Columbia University Studies in History, Economics and Public Law 32 (New York, 1908); R. C. Palmer, *English Law in the Age of the Black Death, 1348–1381: A Transformation of Governance and Law* (Chapel Hill, NC, 1993).

[50] Ormrod, *Reign of Edward III*, p. 48.

[51] 27 Edward III, st. 2; 28 Edward III, c. 13, c. 25 (*SR*, I, 332–44 and 348–9).

1361) represented the crown's capitulation to the pressure for judicial devolution exerted by the tax-granting commons.[52]

In all of these statutory measures there may be an element of pragmatism or a political, social or economic motive. But it cannot be said that such concerns formed the sole or necessarily pre-eminent reason for the piece of legislation. They may have influenced the *timing* of the particular statutes, but there were usually perfectly valid legal or administrative reasons, even precedent for the measures. Even if they were pragmatic or opportunistic, they may still have been beneficial and enduring and worthy of the acclaim of posterity.

The presentment of Englishry had been in force since its institution after the Norman Conquest. As an article of the eyre, it had been in regular operation up until the suspension of the general eyre in 1294. Thereafter it remained the case that whenever an eyre was held the community were asked specifically whether they had been accustomed and ought to present Englishry and if so in what form. The strength of feeling against the procedure may be inferred from the declarations by counties that they were not under an obligation to present it through some historical immunity or false memory, statements made in the full knowledge that the justices had the necessary records to refute the posturings. Englishry was raised, for instance, in the eyre of Kent (1313–14) and was still a live issue in the Northamptonshire eyre of 1329–30.[53] Edward III's abolition of the duty, though signalling the hypocrisy of maintaining such a procedure when he was claiming to be king of France, also had a deeper administrative purpose. Originally, the state had vicariously prosecuted slayers of Normans because the victim of a homicide may have had no kin in this country to bring a retributive appeal of felony. As well as no longer serving a social purpose because of frequent intermarriage, it was a procedure that was obsolete, as eyres themselves were now more a threat than a reality; equally it was clearly resented and no longer workable.

The Ordinance of Justices has been described as 'one of the most remarkable pieces of legislation in the reign of Edward III'.[54] Apparently in response to 'many complaints' received by the king, it was a groundbreaking piece of legislation in its attempt to set down in statute form a nucleus of provisions to combat the perceived dangers of judicial corruption. Although the two chapters on maintenance drew on the rhetoric of earlier statutes and

---

[52] Kaeuper, *War, Justice and Public Order*, p. 291; B. H. Putnam, 'The Transformation of the Keepers of the Peace into the Justices of the Peace, 1327–1380', *TRHS* 4th ser. 12 (1929), 19–48; B. H. Putnam, 'Shire Officials: Keepers of the Peace and Justices of the Peace', in *The English Government at Work, 1327–1336*, ed. J. F. Willard *et al.*, 3 vols. (Cambridge, Mass., 1940–50), III, 185–217.

[53] *YB 6 & 7 Edward II (Eyre of Kent, 1313–14)*, pp. xxxvi–xxxvii, 11–12, 19–20, 52 and 57; *YB 3–4 Edward III (Eyre of Northamptonshire, 1329–1330)*, I, 21–2, 23 and 242; *YB 14 & 15 Edward III*, pp. xvi–xvii.

[54] Verduyn, 'Attitude of the Parliamentary Commons', p. 94.

the promises exhorted from magnates in 1331,[55] they were effectively consolidated in this strongly worded enactment to form a clear statement of royal intention. This was backed up by severe punishments for failure to observe the ordinance.

The idea of a 'judicial' oath was not in itself a novelty: since the early thirteenth century royal judges had been required to swear an oath defining their conduct upon taking office.[56] The commons, who attached great importance to the taking of oaths as a method of regulating the behaviour of royal justices, had also explicitly suggested the practice in 1341 and 1343.[57] Nor was the content of the 1346 oath markedly different from that habitually sworn by judges in the thirteenth century in its comprehensive promise to abide by certain ethical standards of judicial conduct. The main difference in this version lay in a new move towards impartiality manifest in the onus placed on judges when in office to accept payment and robes from only one source, the crown. Indeed, the crown's provision of robes for the justices twice yearly (summer and winter) was a significant innovation – a tradition that continues today – and symbolically marked them out visually as being the king's judges.[58] The appointment of the assize justices to investigate perversion of the course of justice (especially by local officials) theoretically enabled enforcement of the ordinance on a regular basis, while the setting up of a central tribunal (consisting of the chancellor and treasurer) to hear complaints was designed to ensure that more exalted persons did not escape the net.

While the statute may have been radical and groundbreaking, it is still unclear how truly effective it was, although its teeth were bared in 1350, when Chief Justice William Thorpe fell foul of its provisions.[59] Clearly some people felt it did not go far enough as many of the petitions of the 1348 parliament requested clarification and definition of points, trying to expand the provisions further.[60] While royal response to these requests was fairly non-committal, the interest shown in the act surely demonstrates its widespread reception. Although some royal judges continued to receive pensions from noble and religious houses for legal advice and assistance, it is noticeable that complaints died down over the next two decades, only resurfacing with vigour in the heat of the Peasants' Revolt.[61] The statute was reconfirmed by Richard II in 1384,[62] and it survived in essence until a bout of amendments

---

[55] For example: 1 Edward III st. 2, c. 14; 4 Edward III c. 11 (*SR*, I, 256 and 264); *RP*, II, 62(9).
[56] P. Brand, *The Making of the Common Law* (London, 1992), pp. 149–51.
[57] Verduyn, 'Attitude of the Parliamentary Commons', pp. 86–7 and 93–4.
[58] J. H. Baker, 'A History of English Judges' Robes', *Costume* 12 (1978), 27–39.
[59] *Select Cases in the Court of King's Bench VI*, ed. G. O. Sayles, Selden Society 82 (1965), pp. xxv–xxvi.
[60] Verduyn, 'Attitude of the Parliamentary Commons', pp. 97–8.
[61] Maddicott, 'Law and Lordship', pp. 48, 59 and 83.
[62] 8 Richard II c. 3 (*SR*, II, 37).

in the nineteenth century. The chapters on maintenance were operative until the offence was abolished in 1967.[63]

The Ordinance and Statute of Labourers were enacted as an attempt to stem prices and wages in reaction to the Black Death.[64] The actual legal measures had precedents, however, in the by-laws of the countryside and the existing local jurisdiction over litigation on breach of contract.[65] The alignment with the Black Death and any inherent pragmatism was more in the quick thinking and intelligence of the royal justices who cobbled together the Ordinance in 1349 (essentially based on customary practices) and then, with more time to think, formulated the statute two years later. Two important aspects of the legislation that differed from previous measures were the efforts made at enforcing the provisions and the stricter penalties that were faced by offenders. In its emphasis on obligation and obedience, the labour legislation must have had a tremendous psychological impact.[66] It also opened the way for further bouts of labour legislation and for a vein of social legislation that ran directly to the Statute of Artificers of 1563 and the Tudor Poor Laws.[67]

The Statute of Treasons was the most important substantive definition to proceed from the parliaments of Edward III. The definition and limitation of the offences covered by the allegation of treason was of particular concern to the lords and members of the clergy and was also voiced in commons' petitions of 1348 and 1352. The legislation, the product of the king's legal advisors, drew a clear distinction between treason and other felonies. It also provided a legal definition that differentiated between high treason (against the monarch and the royal family) and petty treason (against husbands and masters) which effectively put an end to arbitrary judgments 'on the king's record' and represented an important safeguard against tyranny. It also established a yardstick by which to measure actions of menace against the king and the royal family and against those in natural positions of authority.[68] This definition provided the basis for all later enactments and in slightly amended form is still in force today.

[63] Criminal Law Act 1967, s. 13.
[64] S. A. C. Penn and C. Dyer, 'Wages and Earnings in Late Medieval England: Evidence from the Enforcement of the Labour Laws', *EcHR*, 2nd s. 43 (1990), 356–76 (p. 357).
[65] W. O. Ault, 'Some Early Village By-laws', *EHR* 45 (1930), 208–31 (pp. 209 and 211–12); E. Clark, 'Medieval Labor Law and English Local Courts', *American Journal of Legal History* 27 (1983), 330–53; A. Musson, 'New Labour Laws, New Remedies? Legal Reaction to the Black Death "Crisis"', in *Fourteenth Century England* I, ed. N. Saul (Woodbridge, 2000).
[66] Palmer, *English Law*, passim; L. R. Poos, 'The Social Context of the Statute of Labourers Enforcement', *Law and History Review* 1 (1983), 27–52 (p. 30).
[67] C. Given-Wilson, 'The Problem of Labour in the Context of English Government, c. 1350–1450', in *The Problem of Labour in Fourteenth-Century England*, ed. J. S. Bothwell, P. J. P. Goldberg, and W. M. Ormrod (York, 2000).
[68] Bellamy, *Law of Treason*, pp. 86–90.

The Ordinance of the Staple may have been motivated by the wool trade, but the use of legislation to attract alien merchants was nothing new. The 1326 ordinance of the home staples, which was accompanied by a repetition of the old grants of privilege, exemption and safe conduct, had the same ends in mind. Similarly, Edward I's Statute of Acton Burnell (1283), aimed to attract merchants from overseas by providing that those suing for debt in England could add to their debt those costs which had been incurred as a result of their time spent litigating for it.[69]

Although Edward III's statute staple was in many respects a reiteration of his grandfather's Statute of Acton Burnell and the Statute of Merchants (1285) in terms of general substantive principles, it was innovative in three particular procedural respects. Firstly, it altered a merchant's liability for his servant's wrongdoing: in the absence of evidence of collusion, the principal's goods would not be forfeited on a servant's default.[70] Second, and more significant administratively, was the creation of new franchises: fifteen specified towns in England, Wales and Ireland were set under the jurisdiction of a mayor of the staple. The mayor (usually a separate person from the mayor of the borough) dealt with debt recovery under a 'statute staple' and could take cognisance of trade and contracts between merchants there under Law Merchant. Royal justices of any sort were expressly excluded from hearing cases pertaining to things within the mayor's jurisdiction.[71] Thirdly, and finally, although it is not clear whether the provisions for recognisances of debts in the 1354 statute applied solely to merchants, the statute of 1362 expressly enabled non-merchants to enjoy the benefits of the system; they could then use the recognisances to register loans and penal bonds as opposed to specifically debts arising from trade.[72] The potential dangers to trading overseas posed by war and piracy actually helped attract more business to the city of London and encouraged merchants to use of the staple courts there rather than provincial ones.[73]

'The juristic importance of 1353 lay not in the invention of new principles

---

[69] The summary nature of the process, however, may have made the provision 'little more than a gesture of extreme solicitude'. *The Staple Court Book of Bristol*, ed. E. E. Rich, Bristol Record Society 5 (1934), p. 43.

[70] Ordinance of the Staple c. 19 (*SR*, I, 340).

[71] Ordinance of the Staple, cc. 1, 5, 7 and 21. Initially, this included felonies (including homicide and robbery) and trespasses committed by or on merchants within the staple, enabling mayors (in association with other suitable persons) to hear and determine such cases until 1362, when their jurisdiction was restricted to foreign merchants. Pleas of land and freehold remained actionable only at common law. 27 Edward III, st. 2, c. 8; 36 Edward III, st. 1, c. 7 (*SR*, I, 332–3, 335–6, 340–1 and 373).

[72] A. Conyers, *Wiltshire Extents for Debts Edward I–Elizabeth I*, Wiltshire Record Society 28 (1973), p. 3; M. Kowaleski, *Local Markets and Regional Trade in Medieval Exeter* (Cambridge, 1995), pp. 212–15.

[73] P. Nightingale, *A Medieval Mercantile Community. The Grocers' Company and the Politics and Trade of London, 1000–1485* (New Haven and London, 1995), pp. 206–7.

or methods of pleading but in the creation of a machinery for applying known principles more easily to limited and privileged groups of men.'[74] The utility and consequent popularity of the statute staple for merchant and non-merchant alike was such that it was almost 170 years before there was any alteration to the system. Even under the act of 1532, the only significant change concerned a redrawing of the distinction between trade debts and those that were private: the mayors were still responsible for the recognisances of genuine merchants, but other debts went before central court justices.[75] The benefit of Edward III's arrangements continued until the eighteenth century and were only finally abolished in the nineteenth.[76]

Much has been written on the development of the peace commission, but the process has tended to be seen piecemeal or viewed outside the context of wider judicial developments. It should be regarded, first, as part of an evolutionary process and, secondly, in relation to the redefinition of the assize circuits that was occurring during the same period. In a general sense, the fiscal imperatives of war influenced the course of and changes in judicial administration and the short-term fortunes of the peace commissions. But the process was not driven by the commons: they possessed no clear idea, consistent pattern, nor agenda on the judicial aspects of peace keeping until the 1340s. Even then the commons' developing agenda sometimes deviated from royal policy on (sometimes fundamental) points of detail. During the 1350s and 1360s there was an atmosphere of co-operation, which is more adequately reflected in the statutes.[77] The legislation of 1361–2 should be regarded as gathering together all the elements of previous policies pursued by the government: including confirmation of determining powers, jurisdiction over weights and measures, application of more stringent laws against offending labourers, and sanctions against those who took bribes. It betrayed a desire to unify and rationalize the powers of the peace commissions that had hitherto developed piecemeal over the previous quarter century and produce a properly codified statutory basis for the justices of the peace. While it was not the final statute in their evolution, the Justices of the Peace Act of 1361 continues to be cited in courts today as authority for magistrates' powers.[78]

---

[74] *Staple Court Book of Bristol*, ed. Rich, p. 49.

[75] 23 Henry VIII c. 6 (*SR*, III, 372–3): during the law term vacations the mayor of Westminster and the recorder of London had jurisdiction over private debts.

[76] C. Stebbings, 'The Relationship between Commercial Associations and Real Property: a Study in Legal History' (unpublished Ph.D. dissertation, University of Exeter, 1982), pp. 209–43.

[77] Verduyn, 'Attitude of the Parliamentary Commons', pp. 1–106; G. L. Harriss, *King, Parliament and Public Finance to 1369* (Oxford, 1975), pp. 354–5; Musson and Ormrod, *Evolution*, pp. 85–9.

[78] 34 Edward III c. 1 (*SR*, I, 364–5); Putnam, *Shareshull*, p. 54; Verduyn, 'Attitude of the Parliamentary Commons', pp. 138–9; see *Crown Prosecution Service v. Speede, R. v. Liverpool JJ., ex parte Collins* [1998] which can be found in 2 Archbold News, 3.

Alongside this fundamental legislation on the justices of the peace, the reign also witnessed the rationalization and standardization of the assize circuits. In the statutes of 1328 and 1330 there were important chapters relating to the assizes and gaol delivery sessions with a concern to return this area of judicial administration to the paths envisaged by Edward I in the Statute of Fines (1299), which had required the assize justices to deliver the gaols of the counties within their circuits.[79] The composition of the circuits was set out in the Statute of Northampton (effectively comprising professionals drawn from the central courts) and although this provision was modified in 1330 it was confirmed again in the statute of 1340, which required justices dealing with *nisi prius* business (usually the assize justices) to be judges of one of the benches or serjeants functioning in the central courts.[80] The duties of the assize justices also became entwined with the peace commissions and from the 1330s they were appointed as standard practice to the peace commissions in each of the counties forming their own assize circuits. Fully integrated into the system of regional justice, the assize circuits maintained a vital administrative link between central and local justice that in effect lasted until the late twentieth century. The twin pillars of the English judicial system, the justices of the peace and the circuit judges, although originating in earlier reigns, were given their lasting statutory authority under Edward III.[81]

In one area at least it is possible to accuse Edward III of almost unequivocal pragmatism in his legislative enactments: the statutes regarding pardons. Edward III followed his grandfather in issuing pardons as a means of recruiting for his armies.[82] The concern of the commons was that on the soldiers' return there would be an increase in lawlessness and any charges would then be swept under the carpet because the perpetrators could produce a charter from the king pardoning their misdeeds. The king responded to petitions with vague assertions, unwilling to commit himself to restrictions when they were a necessary expedient for the war effort. The assurance in various statutes that any issue of pardons would not be inconsistent with the coronation oath, that they would not be granted other than to the honour and profit of the king and his people, rang rather hollow given the numbers involved. Bearing in mind that 'mercy' was an element of the king's prerogative and Edward III was not keen to see his right to act unduly limited, the law governing pardons was thus slow in developing.[83]

---

[79] 27 Edward I c. 3, 2 Edward III c. 2, 4 Edward III c. 2 (*SR*, I, 129–30, 258 and 261–2).

[80] 14 Edward III st. 1, c. 16 (*SR*, I, 286–7).

[81] A. Musson, *Public Order and Law Enforcement: the Local Administration of Criminal Justice, 1294–1350* (Woodbridge, 1996), pp. 107–22. The circuit system and quarter sessions jurisdiction was abolished under the Courts Act 1971 s. 3.

[82] N. D. Hurnard, *The King's Pardon for Homicide before 1307* (Oxford, 1969), pp. 311–26; H. J. Hewitt, *The Organization of War under Edward III* (Manchester, 1966), pp. 29–30.

[83] 2 Edward III c. 2; 4 Edward III c. 13; 10 Edward III st. 1, cc. 2, 3; 14 Edward III st. 1,

Yet it did achieve some advances in procedural terms. In 1353 it was decreed that pardons had to include the reason for the grant and the name of the man at whose suggestion it was made. Justices were empowered to investigate the truth of the assertions when the charter was submitted. If the information was found to be untrue then the pardon became invalid and the trial would continue.[84] Even if there was a lull in the war, suggesting the pragmatism continued, there was clearer intention on the part of the crown to enforce this measure and a corresponding drop in the commons' complaints.[85]

In addition to the major statutes discussed above, taking the reign as a whole, it is possible to piece together elements of Edward III's legislation which demonstrate in legal terms a commitment to reshaping the law and facilitating legal procedure. A key provision in this respect was the decree of 1362 that legal pleadings were to be in English: an important signal towards greater accessibility of the courts and a measure which was obviously of significance in the world of law thereafter.[86] Although it is possible to observe a significant group of provisions concerning ecclesiastical jurisdiction and legal actions against members of the clergy, inheritance matters, and measures for expediting justice and ensuring due process, for reasons of space, I shall consider here only the legislation on juries.[87]

Legislation relating to the jury system was enacted in the 1350s and 1360s and was largely the result of a sustained effort by the commons following some statutes in the early years of Edward III's reign. The statutory measures concerned both presenting and trial juries and covered the process for taking indictments, the composition of panels and remedies in alleged instances of corruption. Although the jury system had been in operation for over a century, the massive expansion in judicial business not only highlighted the importance of the body in the administration of justice, but also the pressures that justice, sheriffs and jurymen worked under. The statutory measures passed under Edward III were effectively the first comprehensive series of regulations on the mechanics of jury service and jury behaviour.[88] In particular it is noticeable over the course of the reign that there was a conscious broadening in the scope of writs of attaint as a means of combatting perjury. This included tightening up on the allowance of absence so that no excuses or protections were allowed in juries of attainder.[89] In 1327 the writ was applied to the principal as well as the damages and four years

---

c. 15 (*SR*, I, 257–8, 264–5, 275 and 286); Ormrod, *Reign of Edward III*, pp. 54–5: Verduyn, 'Attitude of the Parliamentary Commons', pp. 104–5.

[84] 27 Edward III st. 1, c. 2 (*SR*, I, 330).

[85] Verduyn, 'Attitude of the Parliamentary Commons', pp. 132–3.

[86] 36 Edward III st. 1, c. 15 (*SR*, I, 375–6).

[87] For a fuller treatment of these issues see my forthcoming *English Law in the Middle Ages: A Social History*.

[88] E.g., procedure for taking indictments: 1 Edward III st. 2, c. 17; 34 Edward III c. 13; 42 Edward III c. 11 (*SR*, I, 257, 368 and 389–90).

[89] 5 Edward III c. 6 (*SR*, I, 267).

later could be granted for pleas of trespass initiated by bill.[90] In 1354 the restriction on the level of damages was removed and by 1361 juries of attaint were extended to pleas of land as well as personal actions in return for payment at a 'reasonable rate' (and free to the poor).[91] Over the years harsher penalties for embracery were instituted and it was established that anybody who had been convicted of perverting justice was prohibited from undertaking further jury service.[92]

From an historical point of view, the most significant provision relating to the jury was the statutory recognition in 1352 that the trial jury should not contain members of the original panel of indictors.[93] If anyone was challenged as being so, he could be removed. This was in stark contrast to earlier practice where it was considered right and proper to have members of the presenting jury trying the defendant. Expectations of impartiality were such that it was no longer compatible with the jury system; and the ability to challenge members of the jury (and even the whole jury), a safeguard enshrined in common law, was confirmed and given legislative force in this measure.[94] While it is not clear as yet how effective the chapter was in the short-term, the supposed impartiality of the jury and the ability to challenge members of the trial jury remains a fundamental feature of our jury system today.[95]

From this analysis it should be clear that war had not in fact ousted law as the overriding concern of government. In some ways, legal advancements had become part and parcel of and were sometimes inspired by the war effort. In a phrase of Justinian himself (at least nominally attributable to him) Edward III could be *armis decorata – legibus armata* (decorated with arms – armed with laws).[96] In other words, they were integral and complementary areas of concern rather than opposing ones. War may have been the primary point of discussion for parliament when the *Modus tenendi parliamentum* was written,[97] but, by Edward III's reign, parliamentary sessions were correspondingly devoted to legislative concerns. Even if the 'young Edward III had a distinctly opportunistic attitude to the law',[98] the king's personal involvement above and beyond upholding

---

[90] 1 Edward III c. 6; 5 Edward III c. 7 (*SR*, I, 253 and 267).

[91] 28 Edward III c. 8; 34 Edward III c. 7 (*SR*, I, 346 and 366).

[92] 5 Edward III c. 10; 34 Edward III cc. 4, 8; 38 Edward III st. 1, c. 12 (*SR*, I, 267, 365, 366 and 384–5).

[93] 25 Edward III st. 5, c. 3 (*SR*, I, 320).

[94] A. Musson, 'Twelve Good Men and True? The Character of Early Fourteenth-Century Juries', *Law and History Review* 15 (1997), 115–44 (pp. 117 and 130–43).

[95] The defence no longer has a right pre-emptorily to challenge a juror, but it remains able to challenge for cause if there is a probability of bias.

[96] Cited by Kaeuper in *War, Justice and Public Order*, p. 273.

[97] *Parliamentary Texts of the Later Middle Ages*, ed. N. Pronay and J. Taylor (Oxford, 1980), pp. 75 and 88.

[98] Ormrod, *Reign of Edward III*, p. 55.

the law and facilitating the enactment of legislation was not entirely necessary. The legal system also had its own internal dynamic, not least in its team of judicial experts, two of whom in particular, Geoffrey Scrope and William Shareshull, were the architects of some of the most far reaching and durable statutes of any period.[99]

This essay has suggested that we take a long-term view and judge Edward III's legal legislation on its merits rather than as being tied exclusively to the political or social context of its promulgation. Of course the context may have influenced the direction or extent of a measure at that time, but the cumulative effect should equally be considered. Further, we should not view the reign in isolation nor the legislation of a particular year as necessarily the finished product. We need to remember that legislation must adapt to society and therefore is rarely totally frozen in time: judges and legislators can tinker with it to suit the prevailing conditions. Even if the precise details change over time, it is apparent that certain essential provisions can have a lasting significance. In fact the achievements of Edward I's reign throw his grandson's into relief. Edward I's reign was significant for its statutes setting out the substantive law. Edward III's reign witnessed a number of 'establishments' in the area of judicial administration and procedure; statutes which were *just as* important to contemporaries who were experiencing the law in action. As such, and in spite of his prevailing concerns, he deserves the accolade second 'English Justinian'.

[99] Musson and Ormrod, *Evolution*, pp. 152–5.

5

Edward III's Enforcers:
The King's Sergeants-at-Arms in the Localities

RICHARD PARTINGTON

The king's sergeants-at-arms have, by and large, been overlooked by late medieval English historians; what attention they have attracted has focused firstly on their function as the king's bodyguard, and secondly on the infamous role they played in the reign of Richard II.[1] So far as the former is concerned, the Household Ordinance of 1318 prescribed that there should be thirty sergeants, each one armed, equipped with three horses and resident at court. Four of them were to sleep outside the king's chamber at night, and the remainder within earshot in the hall; when the king travelled, all were to precede him on horseback. It is clear from their actions during Richard's reign, however, that in practice their fulfilment of these stipulated duties was compromised by their being sent away from the king into the localities on various commissions. It is their performance of these local commissions that has really brought them to the notice of historians, for it was this that gave rise to their infamy. The deeply unpopular sergeants John Legg and Richard de Imworth, the former a tax-collector and the latter the governor of the Marshalsea prison, were both targets of the Peasants' Revolt in 1381. In 1387 the king used his sergeants in a vain attempt to raise forces against the Appellants, and one of them, Thomas Usk, was consequently executed by the Merciless Parliament. In 1390, 1394 and 1397, Parliament complained that the sergeants, more numerous than hitherto and allegedly extorting money by colour of their office, were oppressing the shires,[2] and during Richard's

---

[1] T. F. Tout, *Chapters in the Administrative History of Mediaeval England*, 6 vols. (Manchester, 1920–33), III, 362–72 and 434; IV, 44; M. McKisack, *The Fourteenth Century* (Oxford, 1959), pp. 407–12 and 458; M. C. Prestwich, *War, Politics and Finance under Edward I* (London, 1972), p. 48; C. Given-Wilson, *The Royal Household and the King's Affinity: Service, Politics and Finance in England 1360–1413* (New Haven and London, 1986), pp. 11, 13, 21–2, 32, 53–5, 60, 213 and 297. I am grateful in particular to Dr Christine Carpenter, Dr Helen Castor and Ms Caroline Burt for their remarks on what follows. All errors are my own.

[2] Under Edward III the sergeants had generally numbered around twenty, but under Richard this average rose to over sixty: Given-Wilson, *Royal Household*, pp. 22 and 54.

tyranny from 1397 the sergeants were, according to Tout, 'ubiquitous' in the localities as agents of the closest royal control, collecting money, requisitioning ships and men, serving on local commissions, 'and in all sorts of ways . . . [interfering] with the course of local administration and justice'.[3] Given-Wilson has shown that in the period before the tyranny one of them at least, Richard de Markly, routinely performed similar functions in the shires.[4]

But without the lure of infamy to draw historians, the sergeants-at-arms' local activities have remained otherwise hidden; in short, where they provoked little complaint we have overlooked them. This essay will make a start at redressing that omission by exploring the role the sergeants played in the rule of Edward III in the counties. While their standing, functions and operation must and will be outlined, there is a limit to the usefulness of such summaries: if we are properly to weigh the part they played in the governance of England we must go further and ask where they fitted into governmental action as a whole. To this end, this essay will consider how and why the crown under Edward used the sergeants either instead of, or in addition to, the other mechanisms it had at its disposal. In this, attention will focus on three shires, Essex, Leicestershire and Shropshire, but where the available evidence leads to other localities it will be followed. Because this is an area of study essentially unexplored, it will first be necessary to delineate, at some length, certain basics: the sergeants' numbers; their tenure of office; their background; their personal capabilities, pay and equipment; the size of their retinues; their relationship with the king; their primary functions in the shires. After that, the development under Edward of their role in our three shires will be examined; finally, we will ask briefly what Edward's use of the sergeants tells us about his rule.

Numbers and tenure

Ordinarily – and we should remember that under Edward III this meant in time of war – there were slightly fewer sergeants than the thirty stipulated by the 1318 Ordinance, typically twenty-five or so;[5] but when demands on government were especially intense – and again we should remember that the crown faced continuous difficulties from the beginning of Edward's rule until the mid 1360s – more sergeants were appointed. Conversely, when those difficulties abated, their numbers fell back. In 1340–1, for example, at the height of Edward's first great governmental purge,[6] there were over sixty sergeants;[7] on the Crécy-Calais campaign in 1346–7 the keeper of the ward-

---

[3] Tout, *Chapters*, IV, 44.
[4] Given-Wilson, *Royal Household*, pp. 54–5.
[5] Given-Wilson, *Royal Household*, p. 22.
[6] See below.
[7] E 101/389/8, fols. 9–10 and 26–7. I am grateful to Dr Caroline Shenton for this information.

robe accounted for some ninety sergeants, of whom thirty, listed by name, seem to have been a core group. In time of peace in the 1360s only a handful of sergeants acted for the crown on the ground, but the renewed outbreak of the Hundred Years War in 1369 saw their resurgence, and in the early 1370s they were again getting on for thirty in number.[8]

There was similar variation in their tenure of office, in which respect they fall into two broad camps: those who were effectively permanent, and those who seem to have been temporary. To take the latter first, we can quickly dismiss as highly transient those sixty men who during the Crécy-Calais campaign temporarily boosted the number of sergeants from thirty to ninety. Arguably slightly less temporary were the men who were appointed sergeants-at-arms while they performed specific tasks in the localities. In 1341 eight sergeants, for instance, were commissioned together to seize wool. Some of them, for example William Bishop, remained sergeants for years, but others – Walter de Lee, Bérard Mérignac, Gaillard Savignac – received no further commissions as sergeants.[9] Similarly, in 1363 four sergeants were appointed to recapture a prisoner who had escaped; of these, three received no further commissions.[10] Other sergeants served for rather longer but still seem essentially to have been passing through; we might think of them as 'semi-permanent', for during their service they performed the same wide-ranging duties as the permanent men. John de Winwick was one, a clergyman and lawyer who entered the king's service in the 1330s as a clerk. In the early 1340s he was moved sideways, being appointed deputy-constable of the Tower of London and a sergeant-at-arms, while, very interestingly, continuing to act as a chancery clerk and an attorney. His career then rejoined a conventional administrative path where he very much prospered, eventually becoming keeper of the privy seal, and at Brétigny in 1360 chief English negotiator and de facto chancellor.[11] To turn to the permanent men, there was a kernel of sergeants who remained in office for many years and who clearly made a career out of being sergeants. Arguably, the most important of these was Walter de Hanley, who served Edward in the localities from the early 1340s until the mid-1370s; William Atwood was another notably trusted man who served from the early 1340s until the early 1360s; John Lestrange and William Walklate did so from the mid-1340s until the late 1350s.[12] Others served for rather shorter periods

[8] *Crécy and Calais from the Public Records*, ed. G. Wrottesley (London, 1898), pp. 202 and 205–19; *CPR 1364–7*, passim; *CPR 1370–4*, passim.

[9] *CPR 1340–3*, p. 145; *CPR 1343–5*, pp. 273–4; *CPR 1345–8*, p. 455; *CPR 1348–50*, pp. 320–1; *CPR 1350–4*, p. 206; *CPR 1354–8*, p. 611.

[10] *CPR 1361–4*, p. 365 and *CPR 1364–7*, passim. The three were David Breville, Henry Traynell and Simon de Chippenham.

[11] *CCR 1333–7*, pp. 338 and 729; *CPR 1338–40*, p. 216; *CPR 1340–3*, pp. 566–7; *CPR 1343–5*, pp. 26, 95, 100, 124, and 280; Tout, *Chapters*, III, 175–6 and 225–30.

[12] E 101/23/40; E 101/30/8–13; E 101/174/15–16; E 101/394/3; E 101/508/20; *CPR 1340–3*, pp. 305 and 388; *1343–5*, p. 92; *CFR 1337–47*, pp. 254–5; *CFR 1347–56*, pp. 302

but were still evidently careerists: Roger Archer, Gruffudd ap Cadwaladr, John de Ellerton, Walter de Harwell, Thomas Staple.[13]

Background and capabilities

The sergeants' personal origins are largely obscure; but, judging by their names – William Atwood, William Bishop, Peter Crab, John Main – it seems that most, especially the permanent and semi-permanent men, came from modest backgrounds in England.[14] Their apparently humble origins certainly explain why they sought to forge careers in the royal household; they stood straightforwardly to gain standing, pay and allowances, but also stood to receive grants of land. These were, presumably, roughly commensurate with their status, so it may be that their status is indicated by the quantity and quality of land they received. Stephen de Butterley, for example, a career sergeant in the 1340s, received a messuage, a carucate of land, three acres of meadow and 115s. in lands and rents in Shropshire, previously confiscated from a rebel.[15] Unsurprisingly, the few sergeants who did leave an easily discernible personal trail in the localities seem to have come from more elevated backgrounds. John de Winwick, the high-powered royal clerk who did a stint as a sergeant in 1343–4, was a younger son of William de Winwick, a lesser landholder in south-west Lancashire.[16] Thomas Staple, a career sergeant up until his death in 1371, left a fine memorial brass at Shopland church in Essex.[17] Of one quite different man we have a fascinating contemporary account, thanks, once again, to notoriety. Hugh de Lavenham was an apparent criminal gang leader who turned approver, appealing nine men of whom seven were convicted by a jury and hanged; the other two he killed in trial by battle. During his appeal of his former confederates he was treated with great favour by the crown, and later became a sergeant.[18] Others again were clearly from outside England: Gruffudd ap Cadwaladr, Guy of Spain, Bérard Mérignac, Gaillard Savignac. It is possible that even at this modest social level royal service attracted an international crowd,[19] but it

and 427; *Foedera*, ed. T. Rymer, Record Commission edn, 3 vols. in 6 parts (London, 1816–30), III1, 176; *Crécy and Calais*, pp. 205–19.

[13] E 101/393/13; *CPR 1343–5*, p. 275; *CPR 1345–8*, pp. 395–6; *CPR 1350–4*, pp. 207 and 448; *CPR 1358–61*, p. 417; *CPR 1361–4*, pp. 168 and 534; *Foedera*, III1, 176; *Crécy and Calais*, pp. 205–19.

[14] *Crécy and Calais*, pp. 205–19.

[15] *CPR 1343–5*, p. 119.

[16] *CPR 1334–8*, p. 421; *CPR 1338–40*, p. 216; *CPR 1340–3*, p. 567; *CPR 1343–5*, pp. 100, 124, and 280.

[17] J. G. Mann, 'Armour in Essex', *Transactions of the Essex Archaeological Society* 12 (1940), 276–98 (p. 283).

[18] J. G. Bellamy, *The Criminal Trial in Later Medieval England* (Stroud, 1998), p. 41.

[19] As it did among the household knights: Given-Wilson, *Royal Household*, pp. 280–90.

seems just as likely that such men were picked up by the crown because they had local knowledge that its purposes required. On the Crécy-Calais campaign, for instance, Cadwaladr captained his fellow Welshmen; since most of them would have had little English, let alone French, his ability to translate their orders into Welsh must have been essential.[20] Guy of Spain, who was evidently based in Gascony, was captured and imprisoned while on a mission to Navarre in 1332.[21] Mérignac and Savignac, commissioners to arrest wool in 1341, may have been Gascons appointed because of their knowledge of Gascon shipping in the Channel.

The sergeants' personal capabilities were manifestly high, and not just as fighting men. While the sorts of tasks they were typically asked to perform in the localities certainly demanded personal toughness, they also demanded intelligence. Toughness was doubtless needed when they dealt with criminals: outlaws, escaped prisoners, pirates and smugglers. Hugh de Lavenham, the approver turned sergeant who killed two of the men he had appealed in trial by battle, was manifestly as hard as nails, and, to judge by his memorial effigy, the highly educated John de Winwick – who, it should be remembered, was primarily a royal clerk – was a man of great physical stature.[22] It would appear that the sergeants killed in the course of their duties: William Walklate and Walter de Hanley, for example, both received pardons for specific homicides, in 1351 and 1372 respectively.[23] Switching from violence to intelligence, literacy and numeracy must have been an absolute requirement in arraying arms and men, purveying goods, making surveys and paying wages. Although the sergeants were sometimes accompanied by royal clerks in the prosecution of such business, more usually they acted alone, and therefore presumably possessed the requisite skills.[24]

Certain sergeants obviously possessed them in spades. Once again, John de Winwick stands out. While he did differ from his fellows in key ways – as a clergyman, a lawyer, and an outstandingly able and successful royal clerk – he was in many respects not so atypical.[25] Other clerks acted as sergeants – Robert de Cayton, for instance, was a sergeant for a spell in the early 1360s – and in any case many of the functions that the sergeants commonly performed for the crown in the shires were also performed by the king's clerks.[26] Winwick was accompanied on one of his missions by his younger

---

[20] *Crécy and Calais*, pp. 205–19.
[21] *Foedera*, II3, 81.
[22] Winwick's effigy is in Huyton parish church on Merseyside.
[23] KB 27/366 Rex fols. 28r–28v; *CPR 1370–4*, p. 346.
[24] E 101/26/37; E 101/27/19; E 101/393/13; E 101/508/20.
[25] *CPR 1343–5*, p. 26; Tout, *Chapters*, III, 175–6 and 225–30; F. Crooks, 'John de Winwick and his Chantry in Huyton Church', *Transactions of the Historic Society of Lancashire and Cheshire* 77 (1926), 26–38.
[26] E 101/19/4; E 101/19/12–13; E 101/21/32; E 101/26/18; *CPR 1358–61*, pp. 143, 479, and 584; *CPR 1361–4*, p. 365.

brother Richard, another cleric.[27] But more importantly, he was commissioned to perform precisely the same local functions as the other, apparently more typical sergeants were, and was sometimes appointed to act with them: in 1343, for example, he was appointed to arrest an escaped prisoner at Gravesend, and in 1344 was ordered, together with Gruffudd ap Cadwaladr, a career sergeant, to arrest men who had broken into Abergavenny Priory.[28]

Although he was unusually long-serving, Walter de Hanley was more obviously typical of the sergeants in general than Winwick, but he too was evidently immensely able. Early on in his career he began to specialize in maritime matters, and by 1345 was playing a pivotal role organising shipping to transport the king's armies overseas.[29] Surviving records from the late 1360s and early 1370s show that he developed great expertise in this area and came to bear crucial responsibility for it on a near-national basis.[30] Overall control over naval organization remained formally in the hands of the admirals of the North and West, who typically were prominent noble captains such as the earl of Pembroke and Guy Lord Brian. However, although Hanley was generally appointed to be their deputy or sub-admiral, in practice he was the one to whom the king assigned control, and whom they were ordered to obey. This is immensely significant, because it suggests that, in naval command at least, the magnate captains may have been a front (a socially acceptable one, perhaps) behind which stood the sergeants, the men truly in command.[31] The marked consistency of Hanley's appointment in this area in the first half of the 1370s supports this hypothesis. He was frequently commissioned in conjunction with other men, not just the admirals but also fellow deputy-admirals, some of whom were politically rather important.[32] What sets him so clearly apart from them, though, is that he remained a constant presence while they came and went with some rapidity. What exactly did he do? In the period 1369–75 he spent the bulk of his time arraying ships and men for royal service. Usually, he was directly accountable to the king and council, instructing the admirals on their behalf and carrying key information back to them from the localities on a regular basis. He was also appointed to various judicial commissions to enforce recruitment and deal with other maritime crimes, and when the forces he had assembled sailed he led the sailors and acted as adviser to their magnate captains, 'for the safe custody of the fleet'. To have been granted such extensive authority, he must have been deemed outstandingly capable.

[27] *CPR 1343–5*, p. 280.
[28] *CPR 1343–5*, pp. 95 and 275.
[29] E 101/24/18; *CPR 1340–3*, p. 439.
[30] He operated on all coasts, including all liberties, west of the Thames estuary and north from there up to Lynn in Norfolk. For this and what follows: E 101/30/8–13.
[31] Hanley was not the only sergeant to play this sort of role in the early 1370s – another was Walter de Woodborough: E 101/30/36.
[32] For example Richard Lyons.

Other sergeants were evidently just as trusted, for, while the breadth of Hanley's responsibility was arguably unusual, its depth was not: in 1360, for instance, the king entrusted John de Ellerton with the conduct of secret negotiations in Normandy.[33]

Pay and equipment

In terms of pay and equipment the sergeants were well provided for. They were entitled through the household to a standard wage of 12d. per day and a robes allowance of £2 6s. 8d. per annum,[34] sums considerably in excess of those received, for example, by the esquires of the household.[35] Later, under Richard II, many of the sergeants apparently went unpaid for long periods;[36] however, under Edward this seems not to have been the case.[37] It is true that Edward's sergeants were paid in arrears, but those arrears were not allowed to mount up for more than a handful of years,[38] and, given the massive financial demands that war made on the crown for so much of the time, it is hardly surprising that some arrears did accrue. It should be noted, moreover, that the sergeants were meanwhile periodically given money to cover the expenses they incurred pursuing their commissions.[39] In addition they sometimes received exceptional pay on top of their regular wages and allowances. In 1360, for instance, John de Ellerton received an extra 2s. per day for negotiating on behalf of the king and council concerning the requisitioning of ships, and an extra 3s. 3d. per day when he acted as Edward's agent in Normandy.[40] Turning to equipment, the 1318 Household Ordinance commanded that each sergeant-at-arms should be armed and equipped with three horses. If Thomas Staple's memorial brass of 1371 is representative, the sergeants wore top-class armour.[41] Three horses seem to have been a minimum: on his mission in Normandy Ellerton had six horses; in 1369 four grooms accompanied John de Haddon when he brought prisoners he had taken at Sandwich to the Tower; in 1370 the king's officials and faithful subjects in the areas where Walter de Hanley was operating were

---

[33] E 101/393/13.
[34] In the summer of 1329 the sergeants' robes were of green, striped cloth and lambskin: E 101/384/7. I am indebted to Dr Caroline Shenton for this information.
[35] E 101/392/2; E 101/392/9; E 101/392/11; E 101/393/13; Given-Wilson, *Royal Household*, pp. 21–2. The household esquires received 7½d. per day in wages and £2 yearly for robes. I am grateful to Professor Clifford Rogers for bringing this comparison to my attention.
[36] Given-Wilson, *Royal Household*, pp. 54–5.
[37] At least, not in the case of those sergeants for whom records survive.
[38] E 101/29/37; E 101/30/8–13; E 101/30/36; E 101/393/13; E101/394/3.
[39] For example E 101/30/8–13; E 101/393/13.
[40] E 101/393/13.
[41] He is depicted in full plate: Mann, 'Armour in Essex', p. 283.

ordered to provide him with horses without delay so he could report back to Edward on a regular basis.[42] A ready supply of mounts would have been vital for the sergeants to operate at speed, which, indeed, they apparently did. In 1357, for example, the king commissioned Michael de Grendon to arrest one Reginald le French at Bristol. It took Grendon four days to travel there, three days to make the arrest, and four days to bring his prisoner back to London.[43]

They commonly acted along with others, frequently being commissioned jointly with other men.[44] Even when they were appointed singly they appear not to have acted alone. It seems to have been quite usual for them to operate with modest retinues: in 1352 Roger Archer was accompanied by three men when requisitioning supplies for Aquitaine; in 1357 Michael de Grendon led a six-man retinue on a commission of arrest in Somerset; in 1370–1 Walter de Woodborough served at sea with two archers; in 1374 John Staple's war retinue consisted of nine men-at-arms, ten armed men and twenty archers; in 1375 Walter de Hanley was accompanied by five men-at-arms and six archers when pursuing his various naval commissions.[45] In addition, they enlisted further support on the ground when they required it, presumably under the authority of the privy seal letters that they carried, which commanded all officials and other faithful men to assist them.[46] Both Ellerton in 1360 and Hanley in the early 1370s recruited local help heavily on their various missions.[47] The sergeants, then, generally led others on the king's business rather than acting as solo operatives.

Relationship with the king and primary functions

The sergeants were clearly close to Edward. Presumably their role as his bodyguard, which probably required them to spend as much time in his company as anyone beyond his family, nurtured trust between them, trust that was then affirmed by their enactment of his business in the shires. In this they were usually commissioned under the privy seal, a sign of the king's personal will.[48] They also reported back to him in person to keep him informed of developments on the ground.[49] That he employed them especially to pursue matters that we know particularly exercised him suggests that he trusted them more than he did other officials, or at least differently. Walter de Hanley's records from the early 1370s certainly evidence the

[42] E 101/29/37; E 101/30/12 fol. 4r; E 101/393/13.
[43] E 101/508/25, fols. 1–3.
[44] See above and below.
[45] E 101/26/22; E 101/30/8 fol. 2r; E 101/68/6/137; E 101/508/25.
[46] E 101/30/11, fols. 1r, 7r, 10r.
[47] E 101/30/8; E 101/393/13.
[48] *CPR*, passim; Tout, *Chapters*, III, 54–5.
[49] E 101/30/12; *CPR 1345–8*, pp. 386–7.

remarkable trust that Edward placed in him. Some of what they show has already been referred to: Hanley's pre-eminence over other officials in the areas where he operated; the constancy of his appointment; his direct representation of, and accountability to, the king and council; the breadth of his responsibilities. Other things should now be mentioned: that he was addressed by the king as 'very dear and well loved'; that he was assigned 'full confidence . . . in all maritime lands . . . faithfully and circumspectly'; that he was 'shown the king's wishes' therein.[50]

We have already seen that the sergeants performed all manner of business for the crown in the shires, but some primary functions clearly stand out.[51] Taking specific tasks first, their most frequent local employment lay in performing the basic police function of arresting suspects and escaped prisoners. Next in frequency came arraying ships and men for military service, and enforcing the collection of wool. Requisitioning victuals for the army and navy was another common task, followed by pursuing pirates and smugglers, seizing forfeited lands, enforcing economic legislation and making surveys. There could be substantial overlap between these areas, for example in the arrest of recalcitrant wool-collectors, or the pursuit of wool-smugglers. It is striking that the sergeants' key local assignments correlated so overwhelmingly with the two fundamental functions of king-ship: defence and the maintenance of order.[52]

If we consider their functions in more general terms, it is clear that the sergeants furnished Edward with enhanced control over the particular tasks that they were allotted. They did this in three connected ways. Firstly, they provided necessary expertise. While the permanent and semi-permanent men usually performed a variety of local duties, they also manifestly specialized in certain fields, in which they presumably had, or gradually developed, skill. Walter de Hanley's specialization in maritime matters and the key role he played therein has already been highlighted. But, although Hanley does stand out, it would be wrong to think of him as atypical. William Bishop, for example, specialized in collecting wool and apprehending those who smuggled it,[53] and Walter Atwood seems to have been expert in collecting victuals in Essex.[54] Secondly, and this was presumably related to the above, the sergeants provided supervision over the men alongside whom they were commissioned. Again, this is amply demonstrated by Hanley, but

---

[50] E 101/30/8 fol. 3r; /30/12 fols. 1r, 9r.
[51] For what follows: E 101/24/18; E 101/26/22; E 101/26/37; E 101/27/19; E 101/29/37; E 101/30/8–13; E 101/30/36; E 101/68/6/137; E 101/174/15–16; E 101/392/2/9; E 101/392/2/11; E 101/393/13; E 101/394/3; E 101/396/3; E 101/508/20; E 101/508/25; *CPR*, passim.
[52] For further remarks on this, see below.
[53] *CPR 1340–3*, pp. 145, 326, 444, and 504–5; *CPR 1343–5*, pp. 273–4; *CPR 1350–4*, p. 514; *CPR 1354–8*, pp. 163 and 613–14.
[54] E 101/174/15–16; *CFR 1347–56*, p. 427.

there are innumerable other examples where it is obvious from the context that the sergeants were effectively being appointed in a supervisory capacity.[55] Thirdly, they provided the king with regular, up-to-date information regarding local developments.[56] All of this – the deployment of expertise and supervision on the ground, and the information that the sergeants supplied to the centre – must have helped Edward to maintain control over his purposes in the localities and keep them firmly on course.

Connected with this, it is noticeable from the incidence with which the sergeants performed certain tasks in the shires that Edward utilized them most where he had particular preoccupations. The most obvious case of this was in his use of them to raise the shipping he required to transport his armies overseas, but there were others. His heavy employment of the sergeants in wool-collection and on related commissions in the early 1340s was essentially about two things: firstly, his firm belief, in the aftermath of the collapse of his campaigns in the Low Countries in 1340, that corruption among officials and merchants at home had robbed him of the money he had needed and been promised to sustain the war effort;[57] and secondly, the pressing need to pay off certain of the enormous debts he had built up.[58] He issued a series of such commissions to William Bishop, for example, initially with the declared objective of raising the funds necessary to release Henry, earl of Derby, from the debtors' prison in Mechelen in which he was then incarcerated.[59] In 1343–4 Edward was particularly exercised about ships that had withdrawn from his Breton campaigns of 1342–3 without permission, and commissioned William Atwood (among others) to deal with these deserters.[60] And in the late 1340s and early 1350s, when he was notably concerned with treason,[61] he employed Bishop and William de Spalding against alleged rebels and traitors.[62] This principle, that the sergeants were used where the king had special concerns, probably applied throughout their utilization in the shires, not merely in the areas just highlighted. To select a more general field of operation, the named individuals whom the sergeants were frequently commissioned to arrest were presumably men who had, for whatever reason, aroused the crown's exceptional ire:[63] because arrests were normally performed by local men.

[55] To cite but a few instances: *CFR 1347–56*, p. 427; *CPR 1340–3*, pp. 216 and 256; *CPR 1343–5*, pp. 282–3; *CPR 1348–50*, pp. 590–1; *CPR 1361–4*, pp. 168 and 534.
[56] See above.
[57] This is dealt with in my as yet uncompleted University of Cambridge Ph.D. dissertation, 'The Governance of Edward III'.
[58] For example *CPR 1340–3*, pp. 95, 216, 305, and 388.
[59] *CPR 1340–3*, pp. 145, 326, 444, and 504–5; *CPR 1343–5*, pp. 273–4.
[60] *CPR 1343–5*, pp. 92 and 281–2.
[61] J. G. Bellamy, *The Law of Treason in England in the Later Middle Ages* (Cambridge, 1970), pp. 61–74.
[62] *CPR 1345–8*, pp. 386–7; *CPR 1348–50*, pp. 590–1.
[63] For example *CPR 1343–5*, pp. 582–3; *CPR 1348–50*, pp. 64–5; *CPR 1354–8*, p. 128.

The sergeants in Essex, Leicestershire and Shropshire

Having set out the fundamentals of the sergeants' operation in the localities under Edward, we now turn to look directly at our three counties, and how the role played by the sergeants there developed within the context of shire rule as a whole.

There can be no doubt that the thing that brought the sergeants into the shires as major governmental players was something that has just been mentioned: the failure of the war effort in 1340 and Edward's consequent conviction that officials and merchants had acted corruptly.[64] In the 1330s, when the crown had been faced by intense local disturbance, the sergeants had played no significant role in royal rule in the shires,[65] but in the early 1340s that changed dramatically. At the root of this change was Edward's utter determination to purge his officialdom at the centre and in the localities and to pursue recalcitrant merchants, both of which he carried out stead-fastly.[66] So far as the local use of the sergeants is concerned, this purge had two essential effects. Firstly, it removed key governmental manpower from the counties, for the officials being purged, who had received the lion's share of local commissions in the 1330s, were now unavailable to fulfil local offices. This manpower had to be replaced. In the medium and long term the purged officials' places were taken by a new generation of royal officials, many of whom were based in the localities and had links with the king's trusted magnates. But it took time for these new men to come through, especially in certain localities, and so in the short term Edward had to turn to those around him, often literally so, at the political centre. These were men whom he felt he could trust and who had not been part of the perceived corruption that he believed had undermined him. Prominent among them were the sergeants. Secondly, the purge itself had to be administered, and this too demanded manpower. Herein the sergeants played a major role, predominantly as the arresting officers of accused officials and suspected merchants. Both of these effects – the removal of established officials from the shires and the demands of pursuing the corrupt – were exacerbated by the aftermath of the king's military failure, which placed immense pressure on the apparatus of government in its own right. Debts had to be cleared and preparations made for new campaigns, starting effectively from scratch. This too drew the sergeants into the counties.

Their arrival on the local scene at this time is exemplified by their extensive use in Essex and Shropshire. This related mainly to the collection of wool, a

---

[64] See above.

[65] *CPR 1330–40*, passim.

[66] For this and what follows: W. R. Jones, *'Rex et Ministri*: English Local Governance and the Crisis of 1341', *Journal of British Studies* 13 (1973), 1–20; Partington, 'Governance of Edward III'.

task that Edward believed had previously been conducted dishonestly, and which for urgent financial reasons had to be pursued vigorously at this time. In September 1340, shortly before the purge proper began, Gerard Ellis had been ordered to search for wool in London, on the Thames and in Essex. In 1341 Roger Power was given similar responsibility, together with seven deputies of local maritime expertise,[67] across the south-east as a whole, and in Shropshire Walter de Hanley received two wool commissions.[68] The first, issued to Hanley alone, was simply to arrest illegally-purchased wool, but the second, issued jointly to Hanley and the sheriff, was much more significant. They were ordered to arrest and bring before the king and council eleven negligent wool-collectors and a former sheriff who had previously failed to arrest them having been commanded so to do. The wool-collectors included Sir Laurence de Ludlow, a powerful merchant and knight, and two men closely linked with Richard, earl of Arundel, the dominant magnate in the region: William de Caynton and Malcolm de Sheynton. In February 1342 Hanley, William Bishop and Richard de Grimsby were commissioned to arrest pirates in Essex, and two days later the former was again ordered into Shropshire, this time to check that the wool-collectors there were not using fraudulent weights and measures. In 1343 William Atwood, together with the Admiral of the West and others, was ordered to arrest naval deserters north of the Thames.[69]

In all of this, the sergeants were acting as part of a cohesive overall strategy applied by the crown to deal with the problems of the localities as it perceived them. That the crown was systematically applying many of its various manpower resources, of whom the sergeants were but one element, in an effort to maximize the achievement of its objectives, is suggested by the fact that so often, as has been seen in the cases above, the sergeants were commissioned alongside local men, such as the sheriffs or town bailiffs. In these cases the sergeants probably provided the king with optimum control, while the local men supplied local knowledge that the former lacked.[70] This sense of overarching method is confirmed if we think more broadly and look at what general function the sergeants were performing at this time. Evidently they were fulfilling what was essentially a police function, a necessary component in any campaign to restore order. Within the crown's overall strategy they thus satisfied a specific need. Other needs were met using other men. The second necessary component in the strategy – the judicial one – was performed through various commissions of inquiry, many with determining powers; in fact the strategy's main planks. These were

[67] For example Sayer Lorimer bailiff of Colchester.
[68] *CPR 1340–3*, pp. 95, 216, 276 and 305; *CFR 1337–47*, pp. 254–5.
[69] *CPR 1340–3*, pp. 388 and 439; *CPR 1343–5*, p. 92.
[70] As we have seen, this need for local knowledge was also manifested in the appointment of foreign sergeants at this time: see above.

100

overwhelmingly aimed in the same direction as the commissions issued to the sergeants – against corrupt officials and merchants – but dealt, of course, with the judicial not the policing side.[71] Like the sergeants, the men who typically headed them were directly connected with the king; men such as Robert Parving and William de Kilsby. In short, in pursuing an overall strategy for dealing with the shires, Edward used men close to him where possible in order to maximize his control, and directed those men to meet specific needs within his strategy. He used the sergeants to spearhead policing.

While this was true of policy in both Essex and Shropshire, the scale in each shire was quite different, and consequently so was the relative import-ance of the role played by the sergeants there. In Shropshire the commissions issued to Hanley represented the crown's main thrust against wool-related corruption, but in Essex – much more densely populated, coastal, and with many more merchants – numerous wool commissions were issued to men other than the sergeants. In Leicestershire the situation was different again; there the sergeants played no local role in the early 1340s. The crown's objectives in the county were atypical, though. Its overwhelming concern at this time was to deal not with officials and merchants so much as with the common criminality and social dislocation that had so bedevilled the shire since the late 1320s.[72] At this stage, then, it seems that the sergeants were being employed overwhelmingly against a specific element in disorder – the corruption that so preoccupied the king – rather than against disorder in general.

This changed in the second half of the 1340s. Once drawn into the localities by Edward's purge, the sergeants never really left them, though their engagement there did ebb and flow. Their initial flurry of activity continued until 1344, partly because the king sustained his campaign against officials and merchants, and partly because of the logistical demands made by the Breton campaigns. From that point, however, the crown rather retreated from the shires as it redirected its resources to war, withdrawing, for example, the commissions of inquiry that it had maintained there since late 1340. It is striking that it was in the face of this general withdrawal that the sergeants began to be regularly employed against wider disorder, and even more striking that their use in internal rule actually increased in the late 1340s at precisely the time that the crown's military commitments abroad were reaching their height. In 1345 Robert Monceux was commissioned with the sheriffs of Leicestershire and Northamptonshire to arrest certain disputants who had previously been pardoned but had re-offended, and in 1346 Walter

---

[71] PRO JUST 1/258; /260; /263–4; KB 9/22/1–2; *CPR 1340–3*, pp. 111–12, 204, 314, 317, 325, 359–60, 449, 547, 586, and 592; *CPR 1343–5*, pp. 68, 71, 98, 163, 281–2, 287 and 421.
[72] *CPR 1340–3*, pp. 102, 105–7, 111, 204, 540, and 543; *CPR 1343–5*, pp. 181 and 296.

de la Hay was ordered to enforce tax-collection throughout the Midlands.[73] Two commissions of some significance were issued to sergeants in the region in 1347. Firstly, Roger Archer and the sheriff of Flint were ordered by the Black Prince, who held palatinate powers in Flintshire and was clearly acting under his father's instructions, to 'execute a certain king's writ' in the county and imprison anyone who resisted its execution.[74] Secondly, Walter de Harwell, in a move singularly reminiscent of events in 1341,[75] was commissioned to arrest and bring to the Tower of London the collectors of the fifteenth and tenth in Shropshire, Sir Robert Corbet of Moreton and Sir John de Chetwynd, who had allegedly failed to hand over the taxes they had collected, as well as the earl of Arundel's deputy-sheriff in the shire, who had then failed to take them as ordered.[76] In February 1348 Thomas Wenlock and others were appointed to arrest certain outlaws in Shropshire, whom another deputy-sheriff had failed to take,[77] and in July William de Spalding was ordered to arrest James Lord Audley of Heighley, who had persistently neglected to appear before the king when summoned, and bring him to Edward in London. Revealingly, Spalding's commission stated that he had been appointed 'in case he [Audley] shall still refuse to obey a final summons sent to him in more peremptory terms'.[78]

Why did the way the sergeants were used thus shift, and why did their new and wider-ranging internal use increase in the late 1340s, just when the demands of foreign war were peaking? The change in the mid 1340s undoubtedly resulted from the suspension of Edward's campaign against officials and merchants. In the early 1340s that campaign had essentially dictated the way the sergeants were employed in the shires; they had been used overwhelmingly to satisfy its policing and enforcement needs. When it ended, therefore, those particular policing and enforcement requirements ended too. But Edward's purge had awakened the crown to the possibility of using the sergeants systematically in a police role as part of a wider strategy for maintaining internal order, one involving all the mechanisms it could employ in the shires. The benefit of using the sergeants in this way – in short, the control they provided – was obvious, and the crown was not simply going to give it up. So when it again became concerned about disorder in the counties it was inevitable that the sergeants would once more be used to enforce the settlement of that disorder, and this is what occurred in the second half of the 1340s.

What gave the sergeants' policing function a new focus at that time was a

[73] *CPR 1343–5*, pp. 582–3; *CPR 1345–8*, p. 100.
[74] *BPR*, I, 69.
[75] See the second commission granted to Walter de Hanley in Shropshire in 1341, above.
[76] *CPR 1345–8*, pp. 395–6.
[77] *CPR 1343–5*, p. 497; *CPR 1348–50*, pp. 64–5.
[78] *CPR 1348–50*, p. 172.

change in the crown's priorities when dealing with disorder. The demands of war, both military and financial, meant that the government still urgently needed to enforce tax-collection, and so the sergeants continued to be used for this, much as they had been in the early 1340s. Naturally, their use in this way increased in the late 1340s as the demands of war heightened. Where the shift came was in Edward's attitude towards criminality, especially criminality that, for whatever reason, seemed to him to threaten the crown and his people. While he had always taken the maintenance of order seriously, under sustained and immense military pressure he began in 1346 to view criminals of all kinds in the same way that in the early 1340s he had viewed corrupt officials and merchants: as enemies within who posed a threat to his great national enterprise – the war with Scotland and France – every bit as grave as that posed by his foe proper. Dealing with wider disorder therefore became central to his purposes in a way that it had not before, and this is why he began to use the sergeants against it. The process is symbolized by his unexampled use of the charge of treason, in the application of which the sergeants played a key enforcing role.[79]

In mid 1348 the Black Death forced a general reeling-in of governance, and although the sergeants continued to operate in the localities at this time, they did so at a reduced level. In 1349 William Walklate was commissioned to arrest and bring before the king and council tax-collectors in Essex and the North, and William de Spalding was ordered to find and take certain heiresses who had been abducted in the Midlands.[80] It was in the early 1350s that the sergeants re-appeared in the shires in numbers, which re-appearance bore clear parallels with their first burst of local activity in the early 1340s; for in the 1350s Edward conducted a second grand campaign to deal with disorder in the counties.[81] In accordance with the shift in his attitude that had occurred in the late 1340s, this campaign added wider criminality, especially oppressions by great lords and transgressions of the new economic legislation, to his earlier, more specific theme of official and merchant corruption. As before, its main planks were various commissions of inquiry and oyer and terminer,[82] this time led by the court of king's bench and even more systematic and sustained.[83] Again the sergeants performed a policing function, and did so in conjunction with local men. In 1351 William Walklate and a local man were commissioned to deal with wool-smugglers in Essex; in 1352 Roger Archer and John de Ellerton, along with the deputy-sheriff of Shropshire and others, were ordered to arrest various named rebels there; in

---

[79] *CPR 1345–8*, pp. 386–7; *CPR 1348–50*, pp. 590–1; Bellamy, *Law of Treason*, pp. 61–74.
[80] *CPR 1348–50*, p. 317.
[81] For this and what follows: Partington, 'Governance of Edward III'.
[82] Including commissions of the peace and labourers.
[83] KB 27/365–6; JUST 1/266–9; *CPR 1350–4*, pp. 28, 85–9, 161, 284, 287, 289, 332, 336, 449–50, 451–2, 455, 508–9, 512 and 519; *CPR 1354–8*, pp. 58–61, 66, 123–5, 162, 294, 385, 387–8, 449, 454, 548–51 and 613–14.

1353 Walter de Harwell and a local maritime specialist were commissioned to arrest smugglers and their vessels on the south coast; in 1354 John de Haddon received a commission to arrest an Essex chaplain, John Radcliff.[84]

In this period the sergeants were clearly providing the crown with local control where it had special concerns, much as they had done in the 1340s. Where the 1350s saw a change was in the balance between the sergeants and the other mechanisms that the king had at his disposal in the shires. By the 1350s new men and structures, in which Edward had real confidence, were emerging in the localities, and with their emergence some of the need for the sergeants to be deployed there faded. Whereas in the early 1340s, for example, Walter de Hanley had cut such a figure in Shropshire, in the early 1350s William de Shareshull, the chief justice of king's bench, Hugh de Aston, another justice of the central courts, and John de Delves, a rising local lawyer and administrator, stood out. The king's bench, which spearheaded the crown's judicial strategy at this time, was a structure in certain ways as close to Edward as the sergeants were. The latter did continue to play a unique role, however. Other men may have been commissioned to perform police functions without them, but one still has a sense that it was the sergeants who were sent in when there was a really serious problem of enforcement to be dealt with.

The early 1360s confirm this. At that time post-war demobilization met with the second outbreak of the Black Death to produce a real crisis of order that saw the sergeants again widely deployed in the shires.[85] Remarkably, in 1361 no fewer than nine sergeants, eight of whom seem to have been specially appointed for the purpose, were commissioned together to arrest malefactors throughout the south-east; in 1362 John de Ellerton was appointed along with the sheriffs of Leicestershire, Warwickshire and Shropshire to array archers for service in Ireland and to look into desertion by men previously arrayed; in 1364 Thomas Staple and two local men were commissioned on the Thames and the Essex coast to prosecute 'business very near the king's heart'.[86] As in earlier decades, the sergeants performed a police function within a broad royal strategy for dealing with disorder, a strategy again based on commissions of inquiry and oyer and terminer, and, as in the 1350s, led by the king's bench.[87]

The mid 1360s brought the only real respite from crisis that the reign experienced, and was marked by a reduction in crown intervention in the shires, to which the sergeants were no exception.[88] With the recommencement of war in 1369, however, they were reactivated in the localities, acting,

[84] *CPR 1350–4*, pp. 207 and 448; *CPR 1354–8*, p. 128; *CFR 1347–56*, p. 302.
[85] For this and what follows: Partington, 'Governance of Edward III'.
[86] *CPR 1358–61*, p. 584 and passim; *CPR 1361–4*, pp. 168, 534 and passim.
[87] KB 27/407–8; KB 27/411; KB 27/414–16; *CPR 1361–4*, pp. 63–6, 291–3, 366, 370, 372, 528–9 and 543.
[88] *CPR 1364–7*, passim.

as before, predominantly in a policing and enforcement role, and in connection with the organization of war.[89] They continued so to act until the end of Edward's rule. If we consider the 1360s and early 1370s together, the relationship between war and the incidence with which the sergeants were deployed in the shires is confirmed: war brought an increase in their local use, but not just in war-related matters.

Conclusion

The sergeants-at-arms were central to Edward's rule. In the 1330s he used them only lightly in governance. However, by late 1340 military failure in the Low Countries had convinced him that his purposes were being undone by corruption at home, and from that point he boosted their numbers and inserted them into the shires in force, in an effort to punish that corruption, deal with its consequences and prevent its repetition. He used them in conjunction with other confidants – other members of his household and certain royal clerks and justices – and local men, as part of a coherent and sophisticated governmental strategy that increasingly regarded the two sides of his kingship – defence and the maintenance of order – as an indivisible whole. As a consequence of this developing vision of rule, by the mid-1340s the sergeants, now consisting of a core of highly trusted permanent men augmented where necessary by temporary appointees, were being employed against all manner of disorder, not just the corruption that had drawn them into the counties in the first place. As the years passed their numbers rose and fell, but to the end of Edward's rule their application by the crown remained qualitatively the same.

Within the crown's overall strategy they performed a number of key functions. Specifically, they provided policing in support of the wider judicial system, military organization, and, where those two functions coalesced, effective action against recalcitrant merchants. More generally, they provided leadership and supervision of others (their personal retinues, fellow commissioners and locally-recruited support), especially in vital or technical areas, and supplied the crown with regular, up-to-date information about local developments. Most importantly, and this encompasses all of these functions, they provided enforcement. Moving quickly, and doubtless with surprise on their side,[90] they allowed Edward to reach directly into the shires to deal with those who stood in his way, or at least go around their incompetence or obstructionism. In the former case the sergeants typically brought transgressors back to London to face the king; in the latter they carried out orders that other officials had previously failed to execute. Even the mightiest local men

---

[89] *CPR 1370–4*, passim.
[90] Their control by, and accountability to, the king must have minimized the risk of their orders being leaked.

could not resist them: in Shropshire in the 1340s they arrested Sir Robert Corbet of Moreton, a knight of the first rank and holder of two castles in the county,[91] James Lord Audley, a middle-ranking baron whose main seat was Heighley Castle in Staffordshire, but who also held Red Castle in Shropshire,[92] and three close associates of the earl of Arundel, who quite dominated the region. This, together with the practical authority wielded in naval command by Walter de Hanley over his noble, nominal superiors, shows just how powerful the sergeants – men, it must be remembered, of very modest social standing – were. Whatever their physical might (which was evidently sufficient for their allotted tasks), their authority must have rested in their manifest closeness to the king and his purposes. This is suggested by the commissioning of temporary sergeants such as Bérard Mérignac, who were clearly awarded the title 'sergeant-at-arms' to facilitate their performance of specific tasks at specific times.[93] While the king's authority thus rendered the sergeants powerful, in return their practical action on the ground gave him power: in short, they ensured that his business in the counties was properly done, both explicitly, by acting there, and implicitly, as a retributive force that might be sent in should others fail.

It is revealing that Edward chose to use his bodyguard not only in support of war but also in support of justice, and still more revealing that he used them with such force against magnates and their followers. The arguments of the so-called 'law state-war state' historians have long been discredited,[94] but this undermines them still further, and perhaps even calls into question the widely accepted view that Edward's political success derived from the good relationship he built up with the nobility on the back of their mutual interest in war.[95] Finally, the apparent similarities between Edward's use of the sergeants and the use made of them by Richard II cannot go unnoticed, especially since that use provoked such divergent responses. If Edward's sergeants were such an effective political instrument because his authority stood emphatically behind them, then the fact that Richard's sergeants provoked such opposition emphasizes how differently contemporaries viewed their kingship and objectives. Richard's error was that he used, or over-used, his grandfather's mechanisms, without comprehending that it was the purpose to which they had been put – the common good – that had made them politically acceptable.

---

[91] Corbet's castles were Moreton Corbet and Wattlesborough. *CIPM*, XIV, 110.
[92] *CP*, I, 339.
[93] See above.
[94] W. M. Ormrod, *Political Life in Medieval England, 1300–1450* (Basingstoke, 1995) provides an excellent summary of the 'law state-war state' debate.
[95] For example M. McKisack, *The Fourteenth Century* (Oxford, 1959), pp. 253–7 and 269–71; W. M. Ormrod, *The Reign of Edward III: Crown and Political Society in England 1327–1377* (New Haven and London, 1990), pp. 18–19, 120 and 197–203; S. L. Waugh, *England in the Reign of Edward III* (Cambridge, 1991), pp. 230–6.

6

Sir Thomas Ughtred and the Edwardian Military Revolution

ANDREW AYTON

Among the men who shared the English triumph at Crécy there were few with better cause for satisfaction than the sub-marshal of Edward III's army, Sir Thomas Ughtred.[1] For this Yorkshireman, a man in his fifties, the events of 26 August 1346 represented the high point of a career marked by dramatic fluctuations of fortune. By 1346 Ughtred had borne arms for over thirty years, his career following the ups and downs – mainly downs – of the Scottish wars. He had fought at Bannockburn, when his retinue commander, William, Lord Latimer, was taken prisoner;[2] and he himself suffered the same fate at Byland in 1322, though only after a display of courage and skill with arms, which, as John Barbour recalled half a century later, brought him lasting renown.[3] In 1332 he accompanied Edward Balliol to Scotland and participated in the remarkable victory of the Disinherited at Dupplin Moor.[4] In October of the same year, a heroic stand against the Scots at Roxburgh Bridge added still further to his reputation.[5] Association with Balliol's cause was rewarded by land grants,[6] and ensured that Ughtred would serve in each of the Scottish campaigns from Halidon Hill until his appointment as keeper of the town of Perth in 1337. This was an important independent command, but also a poisoned chalice. Despite his best efforts, Ughtred's spell of duty at Perth was to be the most frustrating and ultimately humiliating experience of his life. It was concluded in August 1339 when

---

[1] Unless otherwise stated, all manuscript records cited in the footnotes are to be found at the Public Record Office, London.

[2] C 71/6, m. 3; C 81/1748, no. 77; *Rotuli Scotiae*, ed. D. Macpherson et al., 2 vols. (London, 1814), I, 130.

[3] 'He was renownyt for best of hand / Off a knycht off all Ingland': J. Barbour, *The Bruce*, ed. A. A. M. Duncan (Edinburgh, 1997), p. 689.

[4] *The Anonimalle Chronicle, 1307–1334*, ed. W. R. Childs and J. Taylor, Yorkshire Archaeological Society Record Series 147 (1991 for 1987), p. 146.

[5] *Anonimalle Chronicle, 1307–1334*, pp. 152–4; *Chronica monasterii de Melsa*, ed. E. A. Bond, 3 vols. (RS, 1866–8), II, 366.

[6] *Rotuli Scotiae*, I, 273–4.

he was forced, through shortage of supplies, to surrender the town to the Scots.[7] Suggestions were made that he had come to terms too readily, and in the autumn Ughtred's conduct at Perth was investigated in parliament; but, apparently proving as skilful with words as he had so often been with the sword, he succeeded in clearing his name.[8] Within a few months Ughtred was fighting in France, though it was perhaps characteristic of his career at that time that he missed the battle of Sluys (24 June 1340), only joining the English army in time to take part in Robert of Artois's unsuccessful attack on St Omer in late July.[9]

For several years Ughtred's life was both less eventful and more in keeping with what historians have regarded as the usual style of living of the county gentry. He was not involved in the expeditions to Brittany of 1342–3, nor was he summoned to the great council of April 1342 – perhaps the most surprising omission from the list of over a hundred laymen receiving a summons. The documentary evidence suggests that he divided his time between commissions of various kinds in Yorkshire and the pursuit of his own affairs. It was during this period, for example, that he secured a licence to crenellate two of his manors, whilst a carpenter's contract, a rare survival, offers a glimpse of Ughtred busily engaged in building work at another of his Yorkshire properties.[10] His first parliamentary summons came, somewhat out of the blue, in April 1344, and we must suspect that he was one of the numerous non-attendees of the June 1344 parliament.[11] During the following year, however, he was drawn back to the French war, serving with a company in the earl of Warwick's retinue in the abortive expedition to Sluys in July. Far more significant, and without doubt the climax of Ughtred's career, was the Crécy-Calais campaign. He is listed in the *Acta bellicosa* as one of the bannerets of the vanguard during the march across Normandy, whilst during the siege of Calais we catch sight of him in St Peter's church at the judgement in the court of chivalry case between Nicholas de Burnell and

---

[7] *The Anonimalle Chronicle, 1333–1381*, ed. V. H. Galbraith (Manchester, 1927), p. 14. John of Fordun gives the surrender date as 17 August: John of Fordun, *Scotichronicon*, ed. W. Goodall, 2 vols. (Edinburgh, 1759), II, 331. This is supported by a fragment of a garrison account (C 47/2/25, no. 20, alluded to in *CPR 1340–3*, p. 164), which shows pay ceasing on 16 August.

[8] *Foedera*, ed. T. Rymer, 4 vols. in 7 parts (London, 1816–69), II2, 1094. However, the financial aspects of Ughtred's term of duty at Perth were closely scrutinized upon Edward III's return from the siege of Tournai: *CCR 1341–3*, pp. 21, 33–4 and 116–17; *Rotuli Scotiae*, I, 607; E 159/117, *Recorda*, Easter term, mm. 183–183d.

[9] A. Murimuth, *Continuatio chronicarum*, ed. E. M. Thompson (RS, 1889), p. 108; *Chronica monasterii de Melsa*, III, 46.

[10] *CPR 1340–3*, p. 388; L. F. Salzman, *Building in England down to 1540*, 2nd edn (Oxford, 1967), Appendix D, document 1.

[11] *RDP*, IV, 552; J. S. Roskell, 'The Problem of the Attendance of the Lords in Medieval Parliaments', *BIHR* 29 (1956), 153–204 (pp. 166–7). Ughtred was not summoned again until November 1348.

Robert, Lord Morley.[12] In fact, as the more mundane administrative records show, he was Warwick's principal lieutenant and sub-marshal of the English army. This was a post demanding authority and administrative skill – a sure indication, therefore, of the standing that he had achieved in the military community.

For Ughtred, the most significant consequence of the Crécy-Calais campaign was that it brought him closer to the king. In March 1347, during the siege of Calais, Edward III granted him an annuity of £200 for life.[13] If the king intended to secure his services in the future, as surely he did, Ughtred did not disappoint his master. In December 1349, he was almost certainly at the king's side when Geoffrey de Charny's attempt to retake Calais by stealth was foiled. It is easy to imagine a man of Ughtred's predilections relishing such an escapade.[14] Ten years later Ughtred served at the head of a retinue in Edward III's great march to Reims and Paris. Although an outstanding feat for a man in his late sixties, Ughtred no doubt regarded it as nothing more than his duty, the service owed by a household banneret in receipt of robes as well as an annuity.[15] Be that as it may, during the 1350s and 1360s Ughtred was predominantly employed in the pursuance of less strenuous duties in England. He was regularly summoned to parliaments and great councils, and continued to act as commissioner and royal trouble-shooter in his home county. A few years before his death in 1365, he received a final and fitting reward from the king, when he was admitted to the Order of the Garter, occupying the stall left vacant by the death of Sir Henry d'Enne.[16] This was the ultimate accolade for a man of Ughtred's stamp and particularly appropriate for one of Edward III's companions at Crécy.

The period of Ughtred's remarkable career in arms, the years from Bannockburn to Brétigny, was remarkable too for the kingdom as a whole, witnessing the transformation of the English fighting machine and the consequent emergence of England as a front-rank military power. Whether this amounted to a military revolution, a localized one or part of a more general European phenomenon, is a problem that has engaged the attention of several historians in recent years.[17] For my part, 'Edwardian

[12] *The Life and Campaigns of the Black Prince,* ed. R. Barber (Woodbridge, 1986), p. 29; PRO 30/26/69, deposition no. 209.
[13] *CPR 1345–8,* p. 533.
[14] See below, Appendix, n. 11. For a recent account of this episode, see *The Book of Chivalry of Geoffrey de Charny,* ed. R. W. Kaeuper and E. Kennedy (Philadelphia, 1996), pp. 10–12.
[15] Robes for winter, 33 Edward III, and summer and winter, 34 Edward III: E 101/393/11, fol. 76r.
[16] *CP,* II, Appendix B, 535.
[17] Among them, Michael Prestwich and Clifford Rogers: for a brief discussion, with references, see A. Ayton, *Knights and Warhorses: Military Service and the English*

military revolution' seemed an altogether appropriate summary description of the changes that occurred in the structure and composition of armies, in the methods by which they were recruited, and in the ways in which they were employed, both strategically and tactically – particularly so, given the scale of these changes and the degree to which military performance had been improved and the reputation of English arms enhanced. That all this had occurred in so short a period of time appeared to clinch the argument.[18] However we choose to characterize the changes that occurred in the organization and conduct of war under the three Edwards, we must take care not to overlook the threads of continuity that undoubtedly existed.[19] Indeed, it is the contention of this paper that certain elements of continuity were of central importance to the elevation of English arms under Edward III.

To understand the Edwardian military revolution it is necessary to understand Edward III's armies, their organizational structures and the men who served in them. The most fundamental of the changes affecting the structure and composition of English armies at this time was the replacement of retinues of heavy cavalry and companies of arrayed infantry, recruited and functioning as separate contingents, by wholly mounted, 'mixed' retinues composed of men-at-arms and archers. The mixed retinue was frequently employed during the 1330s and gradually became dominant during the 1340s and 1350s. Such retinues were recruited and managed by captains who had contracted with the crown to supply a contingent for the army. From the mid-1340s, these contracts were increasingly likely to take the form of indentures of war; but the precise form of the agreement is less important than the make-up of the retinue, for a wholly mounted force of men-at-arms and archers offered maximum tactical and strategic flexibility.

These organizational developments stand out clearly in the army records, and particularly the pay rolls, just as the potency of English archery is shown unequivocally by the narrative sources. What is less immediately apparent is that there were important social dimensions to the Edwardian military revolution. One of these was that the rise of the mounted archer, rapidly replacing the infantry archer during the middle decades of the century, had a significant impact on the social profile of the military community. In a celebrated paper published in 1975, John Maddicott showed how the transition from foot soldiers to hobelars and mounted archers, from the 1290s to the 1330s, involved a four-fold increase in cost for local communities

Aristocracy under Edward III (Woodbridge, 1994, repr. 1999), 'Preface to the Paperback Edition', pp. ix–x.

[18] Ayton, *Knights and Warhorses*, chap. 1; A. Ayton, 'English Armies in the Fourteenth Century', in *Arms, Armies and Fortifications in the Hundred Years War*, ed. A. Curry and M. Hughes (Woodbridge, 1994), pp. 21–38.

[19] See, for example, Ayton, *Knights and Warhorses*, pp. 10–11 and 17.

providing manpower for shire levies.[20] Given that retinue-based mounted archers would usually provide their own equipment, the cost of providing horse and harness, which may have been in the region of £2, would naturally serve to restrict the size of the recruitment pool. It is tempting, therefore, to characterize Edwardian mounted archers as men of yeoman stock; images of Robin Hood and Chaucer's Knight's Yeoman are difficult to dispel. The reality was more complicated, though just how complicated will remain unclear until the fourteenth-century archer attracts an historian willing to tackle a challenging research project. For the present, it is difficult to avoid the conclusion that whilst the poorly equipped and undisciplined infantry of Edward I's reign were 'of villein status . . . the mounted archers are likely to have been drawn from the élite of village society'.[21]

Another social dimension of the Edwardian military revolution concerns the men-at-arms, the heavily armoured knights and esquires who could fight from the back of a warhorse or on foot as circumstances demanded. We may suspect that the social composition of this group was also undergoing change, as men who began their careers as mounted archers, 'men of small account' as Sir Thomas Gray called them, achieved elevation into the ranks of men-at-arms. Again, just how common such mobility was has yet to be established. More immediately apparent from an examination of the military records are marked elements of continuity in the heavy cavalry contingents of Edwardian armies. On one level, during the half century of campaigning before the start of Edward III's French war, we find the formation of traditions of service within gentry families, which, it may be suggested, when taken together amounted to the gradual forging of a military class. To gauge the significance of this process, it should be recalled, firstly, that Henry III's long reign had witnessed comparatively little warfare on a scale that could have involved the 'country gentry'; and secondly, that this social group, the gentry, was in the process of re-forming and stratifying during the early to mid thirteenth century, as knighthood became 'an increasingly exclusive club' and landed society gained recruits from 'the collaterals of knightly families, freeholding tenantry and townsmen'.[22] In these circumstances, the evolving gentry of the thirteenth century adopted the martial culture, the ethos and trappings, appropriate for the social elite, but without a

[20] J. R. Maddicott, 'The English Peasantry and the Demands of the Crown, 1294–1341', *PP Supplement* 1 (1975), 36–41.
[21] M. Prestwich, *Armies and Warfare in the Middle Ages: the English Experience* (New Haven and London, 1996), p. 143. For further comment, see P. Morgan, *War and Society in Medieval Cheshire, 1277–1403* (Manchester, 1987), pp. 37–41; and Ayton, *Knights and Warhorses*, pp. 15–16.
[22] P. R. Coss, *Lordship, Knighthood and Locality: a Study in English Society, c.1180– c.1280* (Cambridge, 1991), chap. 9; K. Faulkner, 'The Transformation of Knighthood in Early Thirteenth Century England', *EHR* 111 (1996), 1–23; P. Morgan, 'Making the English Gentry', *Thirteenth Century England V*, ed. P. R. Coss and S. D. Lloyd (Woodbridge, 1995), pp. 21–8.

foundation of actual military experience.[23] That experience was to be gained during the reign of Edward I, whose wars in Wales, France and Scotland provided plentiful opportunities for a real military role. Even allowing for the contribution of the royal household division,[24] the only way to raise as many as 3,000 men-at-arms (the probable number involved on the Falkirk campaign in 1298)[25] was through the heavy recruitment of the country gentry. This level of demand for knights and sergeants continued under Edward II. There were, for example, probably 2,500 men-at-arms at Bannockburn, whilst perhaps as many as 2,000 took part in the Scottish campaign of 1322. These are impressive figures, given that, for political reasons, part of the military community was unavailable to the king. The contours of this military service – the proportion of families contributing men, the geographical spread of recruitment, and the obligations, motivation and relationships underlying it – have yet to be explored in detail, and for the present we can do no more than offer preliminary, and sometimes tentative, observations on the evidence. It is clear that the nobility – captains of comital and baronial status – played a fundamentally important role in the recruitment of men-at-arms for the king's army, especially for campaigns in Scotland. High profile cases of magnates refusing to serve should not distract us from recognising the scale of the nobility's overall contribution, a good deal of it financed partly or wholly by the noblemen themselves.[26] As for the gentry, research as it stands at the moment suggests that the steady demand for heavy cavalry over the course of several decades created martial traditions at family level in all corners of the kingdom. For the gentry as a whole – not just the knightly elite – the Edwardian wars transformed an adopted military culture into a more vibrant one underpinned by collective experience and a shared mentality.

If the militarization of the gentry had begun under Edward I, it reached its peak under Edward III. The Scottish campaigns of the 1330s reinforced the developments of the previous decades, but Edward III's primary achievement in this regard was to secure the active involvement of his nobility and gentry in a continental war, for such an enterprise had proven anything but popular in the past. Whilst the appeal of the French war by the 1350s may occasion no surprise, we should not forget Edward's recruiting successes during the early years of the war, before the profit-making opportunities that it offered had become apparent. For each of the first three major campaigns –

[23] Morgan, 'Making the English Gentry', pp. 26–7.
[24] Prestwich, *Armies and Warfare*, pp. 38–41; cf. A. Ayton, 'Edward III and the English Aristocracy at the Beginning of the Hundred Years War', in *Armies, Chivalry and Warfare in Medieval Britain and France*, ed. M. Strickland (Stamford, 1998), pp. 173–206 (pp. 184–7).
[25] M. Prestwich, *Edward I* (London, 1988), p. 479.
[26] M. Prestwich, 'Cavalry Service in Early Fourteenth-Century England', in *War and Government in the Middle Ages*, ed. J. Gillingham and J. C. Holt (Woodbridge, 1984), pp. 147–58.

expeditions that he led in person – Edward secured the services of from 1,500 to 2,000 English men-at-arms.[27] The high-water mark was reached in 1346. A conservative estimate would assign to the army that landed at La Hougue and marched across northern France to Crécy at least 2,500 men-at-arms. In addition to the Crécy army, the English aristocracy were simultaneously involved in several other theatres of war. The earl of Derby had led an expeditionary force, which included 500 men-at-arms, to Aquitaine; there were further detachments in Brittany, Flanders, Ireland and elsewhere; and in the north of England, a few months after Crécy, the retinues of the northern magnates probably contributed in the region of 1,000 men to the army that came to blows with the Scots at Neville's Cross.[28] The following year, there may have been as many as 4,000 English knights and esquires outside Calais at the height of the siege. In 1346–7, therefore, the nobility and gentry of England were unquestionably performing the function of a military class.

In preparing for this major offensive on France in the mid-1340s the government had employed a degree of coercion in the form of a new military assessment based on landed wealth. We should not be surprised to find some opposition to it, for who in landed society would have welcomed a new form of military obligation? But as a consequence of it, many members of the gentry contributed personally, by proxy, or by fine to the king's triumphs in France. That they were prepared for such involvement can surely be attributed to what might be termed the martial conditioning that had been effected by several decades of warfare. In essence, the military mentality established during the wars of the first two Edwards fuelled the service of subsequent generations during the reign of the third. That king's reliance on the military traditions created during his predecessors' Scottish wars had further dimensions. The warrior lineages of many families must have had practical consequences. Most obvious, perhaps, was the accumulation of arms and armour. For example, the will of Sir Fulk de Pembridge (d.1325), which includes handsome bequests of military equipment to each of his four sons, testifies to a substantial family armoury.[29] Then there is the transmission of military expertise. It is easy to imagine a tyro man-at-arms being both instructed and inspired by the personal reminiscences and down-to-earth advice of an older generation of family and friends, men who had experienced campaigning at first hand.[30]

---

[27] Ayton, 'Edward III and the English Aristocracy', pp. 179–82.

[28] A. Ayton, 'The English Army and the Normandy Campaign of 1346', in *England and Normandy in the Middle Ages*, ed. D. Bates and A. Curry (London, 1994), pp. 253–68 (pp. 260, and sources cited there, and 263–8); M. Prestwich, 'The English at the Battle of Neville's Cross', in *The Battle of Neville's Cross, 1346*, ed. D. Rollason and M. Prestwich (Stamford, 1998), pp. 1–14 (pp. 6–7).

[29] BL Stowe Charter 622.

[30] Such discussion between old and young can occasionally be glimpsed in court of chivalry depositions, whilst the fullest record of paternal reminiscence is probably to be found in Sir Thomas Gray's *Scalacronica*.

Arriving at his first muster in the 1330s or 1340s, a young esquire would find an army bristling with veterans. It is difficult to overestimate the importance of such men and the fund of experience that they brought with them to England's military resurgence under Edward III. Long ago, J. E. Morris drew attention to the continuity of personnel in English armies from Halidon Hill to Crécy,[31] and it has now become a commonplace to argue that success in the French war was achieved by veterans of the Scottish campaigns. This can be demonstrated easily enough at the command level, and has been shown to be the case with subsets of personnel; but there has, as yet, been no published work establishing the extent of service continuity within the rank and file of Edward III's armies. Whilst this is not altogether surprising, given the volume, yet incompleteness, of the source materials and the nominal record linkage problems that such research entails, there can be little doubt that a prosopographical investigation of the military community would reveal a great deal about the workings of the Edwardian military revolution. That is a major research project, the completion of which lies some years in the future. The remainder of this paper will offer some thoughts on this subject from the perspective of the career – and the campaigning retinues – of a man who was at the centre of developments and who became one of Edward III's most redoubtable captains.

As the head of a knightly family based in Yorkshire, Sir Thomas Ughtred's involvement in the Edwardian wars, particularly those in Scotland, has a certain inevitability about it. He was the only son of Sir Robert Ughtred, who had fought regularly in the Anglo-Scottish wars of Edward I's reign, and who is listed among the Yorkshire knights on the Parliamentary Roll of Arms (*c.*1308).[32] But appearances can be deceptive, for the Ughtreds were actually one of those recently emergent gentry families who acquired for themselves a martial tradition during the Scottish wars. The thirteenth-century Ughtreds were prominent residents of Scarborough; one of their number was mayor of the town in 1260. However, the only Ughtred recorded in Kirkby's Inquest of 1284–5 was a minor landholder in the North Riding.[33] The foundations for the family's gentility were laid through a combination of inheritance and advantageous marriages. In 1291, Robert Ughtred and his brother, John, inherited the property of their uncle, Master Robert de Ughtred of Scarborough, dean of York. Robert had already married the heiress, Isabel de Steeton, whilst John's wife was Isabel, daughter of Sir John de Meaux of Gowthorpe.[34]

---

[31] J. E. Morris, 'The Archers at Crecy', *EHR* 12 (1897), 427–36 (p. 427).
[32] *Calendar of Documents Relating to Scotland*, V, ed. G. G. Simpson and J. D. Galbraith (Edinburgh, 1986), nos. 2109, 2306, 2344 and 2428; *Scotland in 1298*, ed. H. Gough (London, 1888), pp. 33 and 88; *A Roll of Arms of the Reign of Edward the Second*, ed. N. H. Nicolas (London, 1829), p. 61.
[33] Simon Ughtred: *Feudal Aids 1284–1431*, 6 vols. (London, 1899–1920), VI, 78 and 82.
[34] On the Ughtreds of Scarborough, including a brief biography of Sir Robert Ughtred,

During the 1290s and early 1300s, Robert methodically established his family's position within the Yorkshire gentry. He was taxer in 1294, sheriff in 1299 and knight of the shire in 1307. His status in the military community of the region was continually reinforced by regular appointments to commissions of array, and by personal military summonses.[35]

The process whereby the Ughtreds rose to join the ranks of the knightly families of Yorkshire may be traced, most illuminatingly, in the heraldic record. The Ughtred arms, *gules, on a cross patonce or, five mullets gules*, are first recorded on the Lord Marshal's Roll, which can be dated to *c*.1295.[36] The armorial records for Edward III's reign show that Sir Thomas Ughtred bore the same arms. Moreover, two of the most important rolls of arms from that reign, the Ashmolean Roll (*c*.1334) and Cotgrave's Ordinary (*c*.1340), suggest a close heraldic link between the Ughtreds and the Latimer family, whose arms were *gules, a cross patonce or*.[37] Here, it would seem, is a further example of that process of armorial dissemination, first noted by William Camden and subsequently investigated by, among others, J. H. Round, David Crouch and Peter Coss.[38] This is the process whereby the arms of a prominent noble family were adopted – and adapted – not only collaterally by kinsmen, but also by tenants, dependants and those from the same locality, a process that had been in progress throughout the thirteenth century. In the Ughtreds' particular case, the adoption of heraldic trappings appears to have been a close accompaniment to their rise to knightly status. There was a tenurial connection with the Latimers, as well as one based on shared locality, since

see *CP*, XII2, 156–8; also D. Crouch, 'Government and Oligarchy', in *Medieval Scarborough: Studies in Trade and Urban Life*, ed. D. Crouch and T. Pearson (Yorkshire Archaeological Society, Special Ser., 2001). For John Ughtred's property at the time of his death in 1298, see *CIPM*, III, no. 471.

[35] Military summons, 1296–1301; arrayer, 1301–8. *Parliamentary Writs and Writs of Military Summons*, ed. F. Palgrave, 2 vols. in 4 parts (London, 1827–34), I, 277, 312, 332, 356, 358, 360–2 and 370; II2, 375.

[36] *Rolls of Arms: Edward I (1272–1307)*, ed. G. J. Brault, 2 vols. (Woodbridge, 1997), I, 354 (no. 578); II, 428. The 'William' Ughtred on the Lord Marshal's Roll is evidently a transcription error. Also curious is Robert Ughtred's entry on the Parliamentary Roll, which has essentially the same arms but with the tinctures reversed: *Or, on a cross patonce gules, four mullets or*: *A Roll of Arms of the Reign of Edward the Second*, ed. Nicolas, p. 61.

[37] On the Ashmolean Roll, Sir Thomas Ughtred 'port les armes le Latimer a cynk moletz de goules': Oxford, Bodleian Library, MS Ashmole 15A. On Cotgrave's Ordinary, the section concerned with crosses patee is headed by the Latimer arms, immediately after which come those of Sir Thomas Ughtred: 'mesmes les armes, a cinq mulletts du champ sur le crois': *Rolls of Arms of the Reigns of Henry III and Edward III*, ed. N. H. Nicolas (London, 1829), p. 4. Cf. the arms as presented on Thomas Ughtred's seals, 1337–42: *Catalogue of Seals in the Public Record Office: Personal Seals*, ed. R. H. Ellis, 2 vols. (London, 1978–81), II, 108 (P2166–P2168).

[38] J. H. Round, *Geoffrey de Mandeville* (London, 1892), pp. 392–6; D. Crouch, *The Image of Aristocracy in Britain, 1000–1300* (London, 1992), pp. 233–5; P. Coss, *The Knight in Medieval England, 1000–1400* (Stroud, 1993), pp. 79–81.

the original heart of the Latimers' landholding interests lay in Scampston in the East Riding of Yorkshire.[39] But it was probably the benevolent patronage of William le Latimer (d.1304) – for example, at the time of the Ughtreds' inheritance of Master Robert of Scarborough's land in the early 1290s – that was the decisive consideration in Sir Robert Ughtred's mind when he adopted a variation of Latimer's arms, adding *five mullets gules* to the Latimers' *gules, a cross patonce or*.[40] This may well have occurred when Robert began his military career in the mid-1290s (which happens to be the likely date of the first documentary appearance of the Ughtred arms), and so we can assume with some confidence that these were the arms that Ughtred displayed when he served in Latimer's retinue in Scotland in 1301, and those that his son, Thomas, carried when he accompanied the next William le Latimer to Bannockburn.

As with so much relating to the Ughtreds, their heraldic experience is most instructive when it is contextualized. They were not, it seems, the only knightly family to adopt the cross patonce as a consequence of an association with the Latimers. Indeed, the Parliamentary Roll of Arms, which lists well over a thousand individuals, includes *at least* ten families, in addition to Latimer and Ughtred, for whom the blazon, combined with other evidence, suggests the use of the cross patonce, with different tinctures and charges.[41] Within the Yorkshire section of this roll of arms, the sequence of entries points to an association between the Latimers and at least four other families bearing a cross patonce: the Wards, the Samsons, and the Grindales, as well as the Ughtreds.[42] Turning to Cotgrave's Ordinary, in which the arms are arranged according to types of charge, we find that fourteen families are represented in the section concerned with crosses patée. That this section is headed by Latimer is significant, as is the fact that, apart from Ughtred, it includes only four of the families listed with crosses patonce on the Parliamentary Roll.[43] Although conclusive evidence for armorial dissemination is often elusive, it is not difficult to demonstrate connections between the Latimers and other knightly families who bore the cross patonce. Walter de

[39] Robert Ughtred held land in Burdale from William le Latimer in the early 1300s: *Feudal Aids*, VI, 158; *CIPM*, V, no. 204. For William le Latimer of Scampston (d.1268), see *CP*, VII, 460–1.

[40] Evidence of the Latimers' friendship for the Ughtreds: *CFR 1272–1307*, p. 284; *CFR 1307–1319*, pp. 122–3.

[41] 'Of the 29 crosses which the Parliamentary Roll blazons *patée*', those for twelve families (Latimer, Ughtred, Ward, Banbury, Colville, St George, Samson, Grindale, Goddard, Pulford, Banister and Aton) 'were certainly patonce', the others being either doubtful or known to be other forms of cross: H. S. London, 'Patee, Patonce and Formee', *Coat of Arms* 5/33 (1958), 358–64 (p. 361 n. 8); 5/34 (1958), 26–33.

[42] *A Roll of Arms of the Reign of Edward the Second*, ed. Nicolas, pp. 60–1.

[43] Latimer, Ughtred, Pulford, Banister, Sutton, Goldesbrough, Frevill, Ward, Bevercote, Lascelles de Worthorpe, Fanacourt, Colville, Percehay, Melton: *Rolls of Arms of the Reigns of Henry III and Edward III*, ed. Nicolas, pp. 4–5.

Percehay (*argent, a cross patonce gules*, sometimes differenced) was said to have lifted William le Latimer from the baptismal font of the church of St Andrew, Rillington (near Scampston) in 1330.[44] Scampston, moreover, was one of the elements in the tenurial relationship between Bartholomew de Fanacourt (*sable, a cross patonce argent, a bordure or*) and the Latimers.[45] This is not to suggest that all instances of the cross patonce, even in Yorkshire, should be related to the Latimers. It *was* a distinctive charge, but two other prominent thirteenth-century families with strong Yorkshire interests also bore it: the Forz, counts of Aumale and the Vescys.[46] Indeed, since the earliest records of the Latimer arms date from the 1260s and 1270s,[47] it may well be that the Latimers had themselves adapted the Aumale or Vescy arms. There can be no doubt that the Atons' arms in the early years of the fourteenth century – *gules, a cross patonce argent* – were derived from the Vescys, who had borne these very arms in the mid-thirteenth century but later changed to *or a cross sable*. Gilbert de Aton duly adopted the new Vescy arms upon his inheritance of their Yorkshire and Lincolnshire property in 1317.[48]

Changes of arms, whether (like the Atons) through inheritance or arising from disputes between men bearing the same or similar coats, must have been quite common during this period of armorial dissemination and adaptation. A number of cases involving the cross patonce group of families can be traced in the heraldic records. The Fanacourt arms in the mid-1290s were *sable, a cross patonce argent*, but by the 1320s a *bordure or* had been added, probably to distinguish them from the Pulford arms, which from about 1308 had been consistently recorded as *sable, a cross patonce argent*.[49] On the Ashmolean Roll we find Sir Walter Percehay bearing *argent, a cross patonce gules*, followed by Sir Henry de Colville of Cambridgeshire with 'les mesmes armes et sont en debat'. The outcome of the dispute (though not how it was resolved) is shown on Cotgrave's Ordinary, where the Colvilles are listed with the arms entire (as indeed they had been since the 1280s), whilst the Percehays bore the same arms but now differenced.[50] A third example brings

---

[44] *CIPM*, IX, no. 671.

[45] *CIPM*, VII, nos. 50 and 689.

[46] Forz, counts of Aumale: *gules, a cross patonce vair*: *Rolls of Arms: Henry III*, ed. T. D. Tremlett and H. S. London (London, 1967), pp. 43, 117 and 181; B. English, *The Lords of Holderness, 1086–1260* (Oxford, 1979), plates 5, 10 and 11. Vescy: *gules, a cross patonce argent*: *Rolls of Arms: Henry III*, pp. 17, 36, 43, 74 and 129.

[47] *Rolls of Arms: Edward I*, ed. Brault, II, 250–1. For the Latimers' rise to prominence in the mid thirteenth century, see *CP*, VII, 460–1.

[48] *Rolls of Arms: Edward I*, ed. Brault, II, 19 and 438; *CP*, I, 324–5; *English Mediaeval Rolls of Arms, vol. 1, 1244–1334*, ed. R. W. Mitchell (Peebles, 1983), 472.

[49] *Rolls of Arms: Edward I*, ed. Brault, II, 159 and 354; *English Mediaeval Rolls of Arms*, ed. Mitchell, pp. 394, 477 and 485; *Rolls of Arms of the Reigns of Henry III and Edward III*, ed. Nicolas, pp. 4–5.

[50] Bodleian, MS Ashmole 15A; *Rolls of Arms of the Reigns of Henry III and Edward III*, ed. Nicolas, p. 5; *Rolls of Arms: Edward I*, ed. Brault, II, 114–15.

us closer to the Ughtreds' armorial identity. In 1300 and 1304, the Wards of Givendale were recorded with the Latimer arms, differenced with *five mullets sable*. Perhaps because this coat resembled the Ughtreds' arms too closely, within a few years the Wards had changed to *azure, a cross patonce or*, with which arms they appeared on the Ashmolean Roll and in Cotgrave's Ordinary.[51] Sir Thomas Ughtred himself made a small change to his arms later in his career, for a seal, datable to 1342, shows his five mullets to be pierced, whilst the Antiquaries' Roll (*c*.1360) records that they were actually 'pierced vert'.[52]

What this analysis of the cross patonce group of knightly families appears to indicate is a process of armorial dissemination that was actually gathering pace during the late thirteenth and early fourteenth centuries, as new knightly families emerged and the Edwardian wars had the effect of militarizing the English gentry. Heraldry had a part to play in the forging of a military elite, and heraldic evidence can allow us glimpses of the processes at work.[53] We should not, of course, take too literally the apparent leap from the 200 or so armigerous Englishmen on Glover's Roll, datable to the 1250s, to the thousand plus that we find on the Parliamentary Roll. But what may well be significant is, firstly, the number – and it is not small – of knightly families listed on the rolls of arms of the 1330s and 1340s who do not figure on the Parliamentary Roll; and, secondly, that fourteenth-century rolls of arms show a heraldic world far more complex than that of the previous century. As Allen Barstow has observed: 'In earlier rolls the ordinary (or principal charge) is often the only element to be blazoned. When there is an ordinary, it is charged less than 10 per cent of the time. Between 1300 and 1350, on the contrary, roughly three in five of the ordinaries are either charged or separate a multiple charge.'[54]

At the time of his death in 1310, Sir Robert Ughtred held land in at least nine locations, principally in the East Riding and around York.[55] During the 1320s, 1330s and 1340s, Thomas consolidated this inheritance and extended it, including several acquisitions between York and Thirsk.[56] But that the

---

[51] *Rolls of Arms: Edward I*, ed. Brault, II, 447; *English Mediaeval Rolls of Arms*, ed. Mitchell, p. 473; *Rolls of Arms of the Reigns of Henry III and Edward III*, ed. Nicolas, p. 5.
[52] E 43/481; *Rolls of Arms: Edward I*, ed. Brault, II, 428.
[53] Including the evidence of seals: on the increased use of heraldic seals in the fourteenth century, see P. D. A. Harvey and A. McGuinness, *A Guide to British Medieval Seals* (London, 1996), pp. 55–7.
[54] A. M. Barstow, 'The Importance of the Ashmolean Roll of Arms for the Study of Medieval Blazon', *Antiquaries Journal* 54 (1974), 75–84 (p. 81).
[55] *CIPM*, V, no. 204; cf. for 1302–3, *Feudal Aids*, VI, 123–6, 149, 158 and 160. Also, *Percy Chartulary (1167–1377)*, ed. M. T. Martin, Surtees Society 117 (1911 for 1909), no. 396.
[56] *Yorkshire Deeds*, II, ed. W. Brown, Yorkshire Archaeological Society Record Series 50 (1914 for 1913), pp. 121–2 and 160–1; *Feet of Fines for the County of York, 1327–47*, ed. W. P. Baildon, Yorkshire Archaeological Society Record Series 42 (1910), pp. 20 and

East Riding and the neighbourhood of York were to remain the principal focuses of his estate was reinforced in 1332–3, when he acquired the manor of Kexby from his wife Margaret Burdon's family.[57] Ughtred set about developing this manor into a lordship centre. He was granted a licence to crenellate it in 1342 and, five years later, the right to hold a weekly market on Wednesdays and an Easter fair.[58] In short, Kexby became Ughtred's *caput honoris,* and in 1365 nearby Catton church was chosen as his final resting place.[59] Like his father before him, Thomas accepted the public responsibilities that were naturally connected with the lordship of land. He served as constable of the castles of Pickering and Scarborough in the early 1320s, was returned as knight of the shire for Yorkshire on several occasions (1320, 1330, 1332 and, possibly, 1344) and was appointed to numerous commissions,[60] though there must be a strong suspicion that he did not act on all of them.[61] However, above all, he was a warrior. Reaching manhood during the unstable years of Edward II's reign, Ughtred found the Anglo-Scottish wars an almost ever-present preoccupation, as indeed they were for many members of the knightly community north of the Trent. On the one hand, there was the exhilaration and hardships of campaigning in Scotland; on the other was the demanding and no doubt time-consuming task of arrayer, which brought Ughtred into regular contact with the menfolk of communities from all over Yorkshire.[62]

By the beginning of Edward III's French war, Ughtred had served a long apprenticeship in arms. He had fought at Bannockburn, Byland, Dupplin Moor and, almost certainly, Halidon Hill.[63] He epitomises, then, those Scottish war veterans who brought their experience and skills to the continental theatre of war. Did he play some part in the development of

---

179; *CPR 1343–5,* pp. 433 and 453; *CPR 1345–8,* p. 529; *CCharR 1341–1417,* p. 32; *Feudal Aids,* VI, 206, 214, 216, 234 and 248.

[57] *Feudal Aids,* VI, 173; *Yorkshire Feet of Fines, 1327–47,* p. 58. Margaret was the daughter of Brian Burdon and Isabel de Meaux, widow of John Ughtred (d.1298).

[58] *CPR 1340–3,* p. 388; *CPR 1345–8,* p. 527. He had been licensed to impark his woods at Kexby and elsewhere in 1334: *CPR 1334–8,* p. 36.

[59] He is addressed as 'dominus de Kexby' in 1354: *Foedera,* III1, 285. Thomas's burial is mentioned in his son's will: *Testamenta Eboracensia,* I, ed. J. Raine, Surtees Society 2 (1836), 242.

[60] See Ughtred's entry in the *CP,* XII2, 158–61.

[61] For example, appointed with two others to survey Scarborough castle in February 1342, he appears to have been absent from the inquisition, probably because he was busy tracking down deserters from the king's army: *CPR 1340–3,* p. 441; *CIM 1307–49,* no. 1805; *Rotuli Scotiae,* I, 622.

[62] *Rotuli Scotiae,* I, 196, 222–3, 383, 390, 393–4, 411–13, 479, 648–9, 657 and 762; *CPR 1321–4,* pp. 97, 131, 133, 192 and 274; *CPR 1324–7,* pp. 9, 54 and 79; *Foedera,* II1, 565; III1, 245.

[63] A few days after Halidon Hill, Ughtred was witness to a land grant at Berwick: *Yorkshire Deeds,* V, ed. C. T. Clay, Yorkshire Archaeological Society Record Series 69 (1926), p. 178.

English tactics during this period? There is, of course, no direct evidence that he did, though it would be easy to imagine the lessons that those who were present at Byland – when the English, although well positioned on a ridge, had been unable to resist frontal and outflanking assaults by the Scots[64] – might have carried to Dupplin Moor. It is equally uncertain whether his role in the dramatic events of July-August 1346 amounted to anything more than the performance of the routine administrative duties of the army's sub-marshal.[65] Although the chronicles praise him for skilful tactical handling of his contingent of English troops in the confused fighting outside St Omer in July 1340,[66] it cannot be denied that, on the eve of the Crécy campaign, he had less experience of the French war than many of Edward III's captains.

However, given that his career straddled a period during which English armies were fundamentally restructured, with the 'mixed' retinue emerging as the basic unit of recruitment, he was by necessity witness to the re-shaping of the military community and closely involved in the development of what were to become the distinctive English fighting methods of the French war. For example, he took part in Edward III's bold *chevauchée* into the Scottish Highlands in July 1336, an expedition which has been seen as a forerunner of the campaigning style that was to be used extensively in France. The fact that Ughtred led a separately accounting retinue from an early stage in his career[67] enables us to examine the organizational changes from the perspective of a regularly serving captain (see Appendix). Unfortunately, the data is not without interpretative problems: Ughtred's retinue illustrates how the contours of 'paid armies' are not always faithfully revealed in the pay records. Yet the evidence shows him at the head of companies composed of 'mixed' arms from as early as the later 1310s. Once hobelars had been replaced by mounted archers in the mid-1330s, we find Ughtred leading retinues of forty to fifty men, with men-at-arms and mounted archers in roughly equal proportions. The evidence of protections suggests that when serving in the retinue of the earl of Warwick in the summer of 1345 and, again, at Crécy in 1346, Ughtred had about twenty men-at-arms in his company.[68]

---

[64] Barbour, *The Bruce*, pp. 684–91, which conveniently includes extracts from other narrative sources.
[65] We see him testifying to the discharge of military obligations and to the performance of service by those seeking pardons: *Crecy and Calais from the Public Records*, ed. G. Wrottesley (London, 1898), pp. 167 and 181–2; *CPR 1345–8*, p. 488.
[66] Murimuth, *Continuatio chronicarum*, p. 108; *Chronica monasterii de Melsa*, III, 46.
[67] After serving at Bannockburn with William, Lord Latimer (see above, n. 2), Ughtred appears among those going to Scotland, without obvious connection to a captain, in 1315 and 1316 (C 71/8, m. 6; C 71/9, m. 7). In 1318 his name is grouped with two others (C 71/10, m. 10), which may indicate a small, independent company like that for which Ughtred certainly received pay during the siege of Berwick in 1319.
[68] In 1345, Ughtred's bill requesting protections lists 4 knights and 18 others, most of whom were probably combatant esquires: C 81/1741 no. 21; cf. C 76/20, m. 18. In 1346, a similar protection request lists 4 knights and 16 others: C 81/1741 no. 10; cf. *Crecy and Calais*, ed. Wrottesley, pp. 84, 86, 91, 96 and 173.

This is the number, along with twenty mounted archers, that he contracted to provide the king in 1347, and the number that he brought to the royal army in 1359. It was a respectable contingent for a banneret and clearly the size that he felt his personal resources could sustain.

As a captain, then, Ughtred was not a man to overreach himself. He never lost sight of practical realities, yet he could be unstintingly energetic as a public servant. Take, for example, his employment during 1336. He began the year as arrayer of Yorkshire archers, a post to which he brought much experience.[69] He was appointed Admiral of the Northern Fleet on 10 February and can be seen busying himself with the demands of the office, but was replaced in April, apparently to allow him to return to his duties as arrayer.[70] On 9 May he entered the king's pay with a retinue, having his warhorses appraised at Berwick on the 17th of the same month.[71] This spell of paid service, which included the celebrated raid into the Highlands, ended on 30 October. Two days later he was back in his home country, witnessing a charter at Stillingfleet in the East Riding.[72] By now it must have been clear to the king that there was more to Ughtred than a courageous knight with a strong right arm. He had emerged as a reliable and resourceful captain, bursting with energy. Who better, then, to take over command of Perth in the spring of 1337. The scale of the responsibility that Ughtred had been given was matched by the size of his personal retinue (see Appendix). This was to form the core of the garrison, which by some margin was the largest in Scotland.[73] Ughtred can have been under no illusion that he had accepted a tough assignment, for this was an exposed outpost, deep in hostile territory and dependent upon seaborne supplies carried up the Firth of Tay. In the indenture of 4 August 1338, by which his custody of the town was renewed, the good sense of an old hand in the Scottish wars is unmistakably revealed in a series of particularly detailed garrisoning and logistical provisions, which he had clearly insisted upon.[74] It must, therefore, have been all the more galling, when (as he bitterly observed in a letter to the king's council) none of the provisions of the indenture were observed and, as a consequence, Perth was on the point of being lost to the Scots.[75] Despite his pleas for help, the town fell 'pur default des vitailles' in August 1339. Ughtred's anger was aimed principally at his *vallettus* and companion in war, John de Gerwardby, who had been sent to the king's council to report on Perth's parlous state, but who, according to Ughtred, had acted in a treacherous and self-serving

---

[69] *Rotuli Scotiae*, I, 383, 390 and 393–4. Protection, dated 1 January 1336: C 71/15, m. 3.
[70] *Rotuli Scotiae*, I, 403–4 and 411–13.
[71] BL MS Cotton, Nero C VIII, fol. 240v; E 101/19/36, m. 2d.
[72] *The Register of William Melton, Archbishop of York, 1317–1340*, II, ed. D. B. Robinson, Canterbury and York Society 71 (1978), p. 178.
[73] BL MS Cotton, Nero C VIII, fol. 250v; E 101/388/5, m. 17.
[74] *CPR 1337–9*, p. 525.
[75] C 81/209, no. 10446.

fashion.[76] In fact, Ughtred appears to have been the victim of governmental complacency, combined with negligence and fraud by royal officials entrusted with the collection of supplies in Derbyshire, Nottinghamshire and Lincolnshire.[77] It is to his credit that the surrender terms of August 1339 preserved the lives and property of his men, but to be expelled from Scotland in such circumstances, *cum magno opprobrio*, as Fordun noted,[78] was a bitter pill to swallow. Did this setback in the north cause him to seek rehabilitation in the 'vasty fields of France'; or should we read into his attachment to Robert of Artois's retinue in the summer of 1340 the king's concern that there should be a steadying influence in that volatile Frenchman's company? Whichever interpretation is correct, the consequence was that an experienced captain whose land and interests lay north of the Trent was drawn into the French war at an early stage.

To what extent was Ughtred's example followed by the men who had fought with him in Scotland? Few of the captains of the northern military community served in France during the early years of the French war,[79] but what of the men who had ridden in Ughtred's retinue? It is something of an historiographical curiosity that the campaigning retinues of Edwardian captains of sub-comital rank have been so little investigated. Part of the explanation may lie in the unevenness of the sources, and it is certainly the case that the documentary materials for Ughtred's campaigning retinues are not abundant. There is but one muster roll (a horse inventory from 1336) and most of our information comes from documents related to the issue of letters of protection, which means that our data are not without interpretative problems.[80] In spite of this, and of the fact that only once, at Perth, did Ughtred's personal *comitiva* ever amount to more than a few dozen combatants, the names of a respectable number of his military associates can be recovered from the records. In all, there are more than 120 individuals on the list, with a few names for most of Ughtred's military expeditions. Some of these men were obviously non-combatants. In 1359, for example, we find a

---

[76] Gerwardby's double-dealing is manifest in the bargain that he struck with the government in March 1341 (*CCR 1341–3*, pp. 116–17; *CPR 1340–3*, p. 164). However, he vigorously denied Ughtred's charges and the dispute dragged on for years: E 159/117, Recorda, Easter term, mm. 181–2; *CCR 1346–9*, p. 211.

[77] D. Hughes, *A Study of Social and Constitutional Tendencies in the Early Years of Edward III* (London, 1915), pp. 205–7; *The 1341 Royal Inquest in Lincolnshire*, ed. B. W. McLane, Lincoln Record Society 78 (1987), nos. 57, 149, 743, 1050–1, 1064 and 1174. Gerwardby claimed that he had been told by the Treasurer in full council that 1,000 quarters of corn had already been shipped to Perth: E 159/117, mm. 181–181d.

[78] Fordun, *Scotichronicon*, p. 331.

[79] Ayton, *Knights and Warhorses*, pp. 246–7.

[80] For details of many of these documents, see the notes to Appendix 1. Unfortunately the surviving Perth garrison muster rolls cast no light on Ughtred's personal retinue. On enrolled protections and the documents requesting their issue, see Ayton, *Knights and Warhorses*, pp. 156–63.

cook and a chaplain among those receiving protections.[81] There may also be a few mounted archers and hobelars among the recipients of protections and pardons, but the great majority of the names are undoubtedly those of knights and esquires – the names behind the men-at-arms enumerated in the payrolls.

The most striking feature of the roll of Ughtred's military companions is its cohesion. Despite the incompleteness of the records, what we find is comparative stability of retinue composition. Thirty-four men served with Ughtred more than once, and of these nine are to be found on three or more occasions. If we exclude from consideration the twenty-one men who appear in his *comitiva* only in 1359–60 (this was very much a one-off occasion), we find that no fewer than a third of Ughtred's military associates (33%) served with him on at least two occasions. This is worthy of note since research on early Edwardian armies has shown that campaigning retinues were very unstable in composition: 'men would serve with a different lord on each campaign'.[82] Preliminary work on the armies of the second quarter of the century suggests that stability had become more common, and Ughtred's retinues seem to fit into this pattern. There is much continuity of personnel in Ughtred's retinues during the Scottish campaigns of the 1330s,[83] whilst as many as two-thirds of those who accompanied Ughtred to France in 1346 had been with him during the previous summer's expedition. But how much continuity was there from Scotland to the French war? Of the fourteen named men in Ughtred's company in 1340, four can be seen with him in an earlier campaign; and there may well have been more, for our knowledge of Ughtred's personal retinue at Perth is more than usually incomplete. Be that as it may, it is clear that in 1340 Ughtred set out to recruit a company of *local* men, men whom he knew; and there is every indication that he wanted experienced fighters. In addition to the aforementioned four, at least three others, including both knights, were Scottish war veterans, albeit with other captains.

Most of the men who served under Ughtred's command should probably be regarded as 'associates', rather than members of an affinity. There is little evidence of formal retaining ties. John de Gerwardby was described on one occasion as Ughtred's *vallettus* and on another, by Ughtred himself, as his *privatus*,[84] and theirs does appear to have been a close relationship, at least until the fall of Perth and the bitter recriminations that followed. There may

---

[81] C 76/38, m. 13.

[82] Prestwich, *Armies and Warfare*, pp. 44–5, which concedes, however, that retinues which were 'strongly regional in character' could provide rare exceptions.

[83] Of the fourteen men listed on his horse inventory in 1336, six had certainly served with him before, three of them on several occasions.

[84] E 101/20/19; E 159/117, m. 181. In a letter to the king's council, *c*.1350, Ughtred refers to his (unnamed) *vallet*, whom he had instructed to read out a royal order 'en pleyne counte' at York Castle: SC 8/162, no. 8089.

well have been some connection between Ughtred's enfeoffment, in September 1359, of Sir John de Meaux of a messuage in Petergate, York, and the latter's service in France under Ughtred's banner a few weeks later.[85] Those who served regularly with Ughtred – perhaps most conspicuously, the esquires, Robert de Boseville, John de Rouclif and William de Santon – may have been his retainers,[86] but it is quite possible that their service, and that of many others, was based on friendship, tenure or, simply, proximity. Family connections are altogether easier to identify. When, a matter of months after his father's death in 1310, his mother remarried, Ughtred began an association with the Roos family of Ingmanthorpe. He served with his step-father, Sir William de Roos, at Bannockburn,[87] and with his half-brother, Robert, at Dupplin Moor and elsewhere.[88] In fact, family relationships within a campaigning *comitiva* provided a form of cement that contributed to its cohesion. For example, Ughtred's little company of fourteen men-at-arms in 1336 included two Colvilles and two Longvills.[89] Having the same effect were the ties between Ughtred's knights and their *vadlets*, as we see in the *fiat* protection warrant for the abortive campaign of July 1345.[90]

Underlying the personal ties that held together the retinues which Ughtred took to war were shared regional origins, for the great majority of Ughtred's knights and esquires – and presumably the mounted archers as well – were from Yorkshire. That Ughtred would be accompanied by Yorkshiremen to Scotland is only to be expected. This occurred on a particularly large scale when, on 12 March 1337, Ughtred sailed from the port of Hull with 240 men, the core of the garrison that he was to have at Perth. It is no surprise to find many men with Yorkshire names among the hobelars and archers listed on the surviving muster rolls.[91] Given that the shires north of the Trent were

---

[85] Meaux's letter of protection and his enfeoffment licence were authorized from the port of embarkation, Sandwich, on 12 and 14 September respectively: C 76/38, m. 13; *CPR 1358–61*, p. 265. As we have seen, Ughtred was related by marriage to the Meaux family.

[86] As Ughtred's *scutifer*, Rouclif collected £50 on behalf of his master in 1338: E 372/184, m. 45.

[87] In William, Lord Latimer's retinue: C 71/6, m. 3. For Roos of Ingmanthorp, see *CP*, XI, 117–19.

[88] Aged 76, Sir Robert de Roos of Ingmanthorp stated in his deposition in the Scrope v. Grosvenor case, that he had been armed since Dupplin: *The Scrope and Grosvenor Controversy*, ed. N. H. Nicolas, 2 vols. (London, 1832), I, 105. An undated protection warrant lists Robert and Edmund de Roos in their elder half-brother's retinue (C 81/1741, m. 11). Edmund also served with Ughtred in 1336: E 101/19/36, m. 2d.

[89] E 101/19/36, m. 2d.

[90] C 81/1741, no. 21.

[91] An imperfect pay roll and muster list for hobelars and archers for the period from April 1337 until June 1338: E 101/612/37. A further, damaged muster roll of hobelars and mounted archers, *c*.1338: E 101/21/17. The only surviving roll of men-at-arms in the garrison lists the fifteen men in Sir Guy de Ferrers's retinue

generally not pressed for recruits for the French war, it is more interesting to find Yorkshiremen in the companies that Ughtred took to France. For example, the retinue that accompanied Ughtred in the summer of 1340, apparently sailing for France from Hull in ships provided by that port,[92] was as fully a company of Yorkshiremen – particularly East Yorkshiremen – as we can find at any time in Ughtred's service. Of course, the strongly regional character of Ughtred's campaigning retinues goes some way to explain the comparative stability of personnel that we noted earlier.[93] In fact, there was a greater level of stability than the simple comparison of Ughtred's campaign retinues would suggest, for the existence of a distinctive, Yorkshire-based regional military community, which supplied knights and esquires to a variety of captains, meant that the *comitiva* of a man like Ughtred might well be composed of men who knew each other and had fought together previously, even if they were serving with him for the first time. For example, of the newcomers to Ughtred's service in 1340, two – Sir John de Meaux and Peter de Nuttle – had served together in Thomas, Lord Wake's *comitiva* in 1337.[94] For the same campaign, William de Twyer returned to Ughtred's service after a spell in the retinue of John, Lord Mowbray.[95] Such localized and often temporary transfers of allegiance were encouraged to some degree by the presence in Yorkshire of a team of active (and probably fiercely competitive) captains; but what we are seeing is moderate 'shuffling' of what was essentially a cohesive pool of manpower.

If Ughtred's career offers an instructive case study of recruitment in the context of a regional military community, it is instructive too when we turn to consider the scale of rewards yielded by so long a career in arms. There is a hint of the booty that he may have accumulated in the reference, in his son's will, to a bedcover decorated with images of French noblemen and peasants;[96] but apart from the augmentation of self-esteem, such decorative items brought no lasting

---

during a four-month period in 1338: E 101/21/16. When Ughtred's custody of Perth was formally renewed by the crown on 4 August 1338, the indenture specifically stipulated that twenty of his men-at-arms should be Yorkshiremen. On the same day, orders were issued for the recruitment of these men, together with 120 hobelars and 240 archers, in Yorkshire. *CCR 1337–9*, p. 525; *Rotuli Scotiae*, I, 541 and 543.

[92] Order for three Hull ships to transport Ughtred and his men, dated 22 June 1340: *Rotuli Scotiae*, I, 596.

[93] Cf. Henry, Lord Percy (d.1352): despite growing territorial interests in Northumberland, he recruited heavily in his family's original landholding stronghold of Yorkshire, and the personnel of his retinues also exhibit a high degree of stability, particularly over short periods. For example, of his 55 men-at-arms in 1336, no fewer than 40 were again serving in his *comitiva* during the following year. E 101/19/36, m. 3; E 101/20/17, mm. 4, 5 and 9.

[94] E 101/20/17, m. 8d.

[95] E 101/20/17, m. 10d.

[96] *Testamenta Eboracensia*, I, 243.

benefit. Much the same can be said of Ughtred's temporary acquisitions in Scotland after Dupplin Moor. On 20 October 1332, Balliol granted him the forfeited lands of Sir John Stewart, principally the manor of Bunkle, Berwick-shire, but by March 1334 the barony of Bunkle was said to be waste due to the ravages of war.[97] It is no surprise, in the early to mid 1330s, to find Ughtred borrowing £100 from Archbishop Melton and (with his half-brother, Robert) 600 marks from William de Aton, in all likelihood to sustain his involvement in the Scottish war.[98] Despite regular feats of arms, there is no sign of windfalls, in the form of ransoms, coming Ughtred's way. Few prisoners were taken at Crécy, whilst Ughtred missed the battle of Neville's Cross, which proved so profitable for other members of the northern gentry.[99] Indeed, in this respect, Ughtred was ill favoured by the fortunes of war, for he was taken prisoner at the battle of Byland by Sir William Abernethy. In a remarkable letter written from captivity, Ughtred outlined the terms of his release and begged the king to assist with his deliverance from the Scots, since he feared *la malice* of Robert Bruce.[100] Whether moved by this, by Ughtred's heroics in the battle, or simply by the obligation due from the king to one of his household knights, Edward II granted him the custody of the manor of Bentley, Yorkshire, during the minority of the heir of Payn de Tibetot, to help meet the expense of his ransom.[101] The other dark chapter in Ughtred's career, the fall of Perth in 1339, also had serious financial consequences. In March 1341, a year and a half after the surrender, Ughtred was claiming over £1,800 in unpaid wages.[102] A captain had to be prepared for major losses, against which opportunities for gain, particularly in the Scottish theatre of war, were anything but abundant.

It has been observed, with some justification, that to gain access to the benefits of lordship was one of the most valuable of the potential profits of war. In Ughtred's case, associations with magnates do not seem to have been lucrative. There is no evidence of a formal connection with a northern magnate (not even one of the Latimers), whilst neither Edward Balliol, whom he served loyally for several years,[103] nor indeed Robert of Artois, with whom Ughtred was briefly associated in 1340, proved to be successful

[97] *Rotuli Scotiae*, I, 261 and 273–4.

[98] L. H. Butler, 'Archbishop Melton, his Neighbours and his Kinsmen, 1317–1340', *Journal of Ecclesiastical History* 2 (1951), pp. 54–67 (p. 61); *CCR, 1333–7*, p. 494.

[99] *Rotuli Scotiae*, I, 678 (list of prisoners and captors); cf. Thomas Samson's newsletter: *Battle of Neville's Cross*, ed. Rollason and Prestwich, pp. 134–7.

[100] SC 1/63, no. 178, calendared in *Calendar of Documents Relating to Scotland*, V, no. 684. The ransom was 500 marks and £20, but Ughtred had also to secure the release of Abernethy's *vallet*, Huchun de Rule.

[101] Granted on 12 February 1323, this was in effect a gift of 400 marks: *CFR 1319–27*, pp. 196–7; *Calendar of Documents Relating to Scotland*, III, no. 806. Ughtred was one of Edward II's household knights in 1322–3, though not it seems before or after this time. He received his fee, but not robes, during the period of his captivity: BL MS Stowe 553, fols. 65r, 66r, 102r, 105r and 108r.

[102] *Rotuli Scotiae*, I, 608–9.

[103] Ughtred was still working on Balliol's behalf in October 1335: *Foedera*, II2, 925.

patrons. For Ughtred, the greatest rewards came from the crown, though a formal relationship with Edward III was only slowly established. Edward II's grant of the custody of Bentley was confirmed by his son in January 1331, and in July 1338 Ughtred was granted in fee two parts of a messuage in York (and the third part in expectancy).[104] But throughout the first twenty years of Edward's reign, Ughtred's name is absent from the lists of household knights receiving fees and robes. Then, on 20 March 1347, after Crécy and during the siege of Calais, he was granted an annuity of £200 for life.[105] Although probably in part a reward for services rendered in the past, not least during the Crécy campaign, this grant cannot be detached from the immediate military situation outside Calais in the spring of 1347. The king was in need of reinforcements and acutely aware of the threat that a relief army would pose. (Philip VI had taken the Oriflamme at St-Denis on 18 March.) Accordingly, in an indenture dated 'devant Caleys', 1 April 1347, Ughtred contracted to serve for a year with twenty men-at-arms and twenty mounted archers, for which he would receive the usual terms of service, except that instead of *regard* he would draw his fee of £200 per annum.[106] The terms of the annuity were again modified by a further indenture of 28 November 1349, which laid down that Ughtred, attended by a retinue of the same proportions, would receive his £200 p.a. in wartime, but only the standard fee of a household banneret in time of peace.[107] This arrangement appears to have led to confusion at the exchequer, and in July 1357 it was decided that Ughtred should be allowed £200 per annum until 28 November 1349 and £100 per annum, plus robes, thereafter.[108] At Easter 1358 Ughtred made account according to this formula. Altogether, his claim came to £1,565 4s. 8½d., and some tidy accounting brought his actual receipts at the exchequer to within a few pounds of this figure (he was owed £6 11s. 4½d.).[109] However, Ughtred's particulars of account also show that although from late November 1349 his annuity was reduced to £100, he

---

[104] *CPR 1330–4*, p. 64; cf. *CPR 1334–8*, p. 239; *CPR 1338–40*, p. 104.

[105] *CPR 1345–8*, p. 533.

[106] E 101/25/33, m. 3, printed in N. B. Lewis, 'An Early Fourteenth-Century Contract for Military Service', *BIHR* 20 (1944), 111–18 (p. 118). The 'usual' terms of service included wages (paid quarterly), horse appraisal and *restauro equorum*, victuals and shipping for the troops. The king would provide Ughtred with a warhorse befitting his rank.

[107] For a full transcript of the indenture, see E 159/133, Recorda, Michaelmas term.

[108] *CPR 1358–61*, p. 430; E 159/133, Recorda, Michaelmas term.

[109] Ughtred's particulars: E 101/25/33, mm. 1–2. The account allowed £538 18s. ½d. for fees from 20 March 1347 until 28 November 1349. For the period from 28 November 1349 until 30 March 1359, £925 was allowed in fees and £101 6s. 8d. in robes. Although accounting at Easter 1358, his expenses account was carried a year into the future. This was apparently to bring his allowable expenses in line with his actual receipts from the exchequer. His actual receipts, as itemized, amounted to £1,500 in annuity payments and £58 13s. 4d. for robes.

was also allowed a number of additional payments for spells of service performed at the king's command during the following eight years. Towards the end of 1349, as we have seen, he served the king overseas with a retinue, probably participating in Edward III's chivalric escapade at Calais; and he was paid a supplementary fee, at a rate of £50 per quarter year, for service with his retinue during seven quarters from November 1349 to November 1357.[110]

Ughtred continued to draw his annuity until he died in 1365. It is tempting to view it as the only significant 'profit' to arise from his long military career. (A 'profit', it should be noted, gained not at the expense of the enemy, but from English taxpayers.)[111] Along with other royal grants during these years,[112] it provided some compensation for the costs that he had been incurring for many years as a captain and may well have fuelled his purchases of the manors of Coxwold, Yearsley and Thirkleby (all 15 to 20 miles to the north of York), and of property in Scarborough, during the 1350s and 1360s.[113] However, the annuity represented something more than a type of war profit: it may also be viewed as 'a stage in the "creation" of a peer'.[114] It was only after the grant of the annuity, in March 1347, that Ughtred was summoned regularly to parliaments and great councils. This in turn may be seen as part of a process whereby a valued royal servant was given increased authority – and responsibilities – in his home region. That Ughtred duly pursued these responsibilities with vigour cannot be doubted. Yet it would surely be a mistake to discount the connection between Ughtred's annuity and his role as a warrior. It had been granted as a retaining fee with a military purpose, and in 1359 it still functioned as such. In February of that year, he was ordered to array himself speedily for the king's continental expedition; and in the section of the Reims campaign pay roll concerned with Ughtred's retinue, we find that he was allowed wages, *restauro equorum* and shipping

[110] E 101/25/33: for 42 days service in late 1349 he was allowed £96 12s., whereas the stipulated rates of pay would produce a total of £100 16s. – one of several curious errors in these particulars. He received £350 for service with his retinue during seven separate quarters. Rather curiously, this section of the account has not been totalled.

[111] As Dr James Bothwell has shown, Ughtred's exchequer-based annuity involved assignments which were '"tailored" to be within [his] area of interest'; that is, they involved royal revenue sources from his home region of Yorkshire: J. S. Bothwell, '"Until he Receive the Equivalent in Land and Rent": the Use of Annuities as Endowment Patronage in the Reign of Edward III', *HR* 70 (1997), 146–69 (p. 158 n. 80).

[112] For example, in November 1349, wardship of the lands of John le Constable of Halsham during the minority of the heir, although this was to prove problematic: *CFR 1347–56*, pp. 182 and 281–2; *CIPM*, IX, no. 226; *CCR 1349–54*, pp. 318 and 357.

[113] *CCharR 1341–1417*, p. 141; C 81/360, no. 22470; *CPR 1361–4*, p. 96; *Feet of Fines for the County of York, 1347–77*, ed. W. P. Baildon, Yorkshire Archaeological Society Record Series 52 (1915 for 1914), p. 68; *CFR 1356–68*, pp. 93–4.

[114] Bothwell, '"Until he Receive the Equivalent in Land and Rent"', p. 148.

for his men, but not *regard*.[115] In Ughtred's case, *regard* – which may be interpreted as a bonus payment for the captain of a retinue, a contribution to his costs – had already been paid in the form of his annuity. For Ughtred, the real 'bonus' was to come shortly after the campaign, when he was admitted to the Order of the Garter. This, one suspects, was the 'elevation' that he regarded with greatest pride.

Ughtred's career coincided with a period of military revival in England in which elements of continuity within the military community, particularly among the gentle-born, played a crucial part. This paper has identified three such elements of continuity. First, it has been suggested that something resembling a military elite was forged from the nobility and gentry during the half-century of regular campaigning that preceded the Hundred Years War. Landed families, some of them only recently established, acquired military traditions founded upon service mainly in the Scottish wars. It is upon these traditions, which when taken together amounted to an abundant collective experience and a powerful shared mentality, that Edward III could draw in his continental adventures. Thus when we detect veterans of the Scottish campaigns of the 1330s fighting in France, what we are seeing is not simply experienced *individuals*, but men maintaining and building upon traditions of military participation established by their immediate forbears. The second area of continuity concerns the composition of retinues in English armies. Although more research is needed on this, initial indications suggest that the 'strikingly rapid turnover' of personnel that we find during the early fourteenth century was replaced by greater stability of retinue composition during the 1330s and 1340s. This may well have been one of the fundamental ways in which Edward III's armies differed from those of his predecessors, an important aspect of the transformation of English armies in the 1330s and 1340s contributing in some degree to the military successes of the period. Whilst more work is needed on these first two propositions, the third element of continuity is easier to substantiate: the role of 'old blood' in Edward III's military successes. Talk of an Edwardian military revolution naturally puts one in mind of 'new blood'; and some of the most notable of Edward III's successful lieutenants – Derby, Northampton and Warwick, for example – were, indeed, men of his generation. But it would be a mistake to present these younger men as the sole driving force behind the Edwardian military revolution. We should not forget the contribution of an older generation of veterans, men like Thomas Ughtred, whose careers spanned the period of crucial change from Bannockburn to Crécy and beyond. For every 'new man', like Thomas Dagworth, who rose to fame in France's regional theatres of war, there was an Oliver de Ingham and a John de Hardreshull. The length and variety of Ughtred's career is certainly unusual, but not unique. For example,

---

[115] *CCR 1354–60*, pp. 552–3; E 101/393/11, fol. 81v.

Robert de Morley, who first appears in the military records in the year after Bannockburn, led the English attack at Sluys, fought at Crécy and died during the course of the Reims campaign. Thomas Ughtred is but one of a whole generation of older captains who, in the early stages of Edward III's French war, embodied a service tradition stretching back to the 1310s and who had taken an active part in the transformation of armies and fighting methods between Bannockburn and Crécy. For such men as these, grey-beards in their fifties, the Crécy-Calais campaign represented the summit after a long climb, a triumph of tactics and elan, organization and endurance.

APPENDIX
Sir Thomas Ughtred's paid retinue, 1319–1360

1319	Siege of Berwick	4 men-at-arms[1] 44 hobelars
1322	Scotland & battle of Byland	4 men-at-arms[2] 20 hobelars
1333	Siege of Berwick & battle of Halidon Hill	no payroll[3]
1334–5	Scotland, Roxburgh campaign	34 mounted archers[4]

[1] According to the pay roll, Ughtred served, as a knight, with three *scutiferi* from 3 September until 22 September 1319, and then with two until 28th; he also had forty-four hobelars in his company from 30 August until 9 September, dropping to twenty-eight from 10 to 24 September (E 101/378/4, fols. 19r, 35v). There are enrolled protections, dated 20 July, for Ughtred and eleven men in his retinue (C 71/10, m. 3), somewhat more than the pay roll would have led us to expect.

[2] The pay roll states that Ughtred served, as a knight, with three *scutiferi* from 4 August until 12 September 1322, and then, after the Scottish campaign, with the same men, together with twenty hobelars, in defence of the Northumberland march, for 28 days from 5 October. Ughtred was captured by the Scots at Byland, but there is no mention of this event in the pay roll: BL MS Stowe 553, fol. 60v.

[3] Ughtred requested protections for himself, one other knight and four others, who appear to be esquires, which suggests a retinue somewhat larger than before: C 71/13, m. 20; C 81/1748, no. 52. No systematic pay records have survived for this expedition.

[4] The king's wages were provided for 34 mounted archers serving in Ughtred's retinue from 15 November 1334 until 17 January 1335: BL MS Cotton, Nero C VIII, fol. 253r. There is no record of pay being provided for men-at-arms, but we know that Ughtred requested protections for himself, three knights and nine others, most (if not all) of whom were combatant esquires: C 81/1741, m. 12, cf. C 71/14, mm. 11, 13. Although only three of these men have enrolled protections for the Roxburgh

1335	Scotland	12 mounted archers[5]
1336	Scotland	15 men-at-arms[6]
1337	Perth garrison	40 men-at-arms[7]
		100 hobelars
		100 archers
1340	Siege of Tournai & attack on St Omer	25 foot archers[8]

campaign, Ughtred's request is precisely datable, since the chancellor to whom it is addressed is 'Richard, bishop of Durham'. During the previous summer, Ughtred had secured protections (dated 3 July) for himself and fourteen men who were to serve in a defensive capacity in Scotland: *CPR 1330–4*, p. 556. Ughtred's men-at-arms in 1334 and 1335 were probably attached to Edward Balliol's affinity, which was financed by 'gifts' from Edward III, but not included in the army pay accounts: R. Nicholson, *Edward III and the Scots* (Oxford, 1965), pp. 177–9 and 201, Appendices III and IV.

[5] Wages were provided for twelve mounted archers (23 July until 7 October 1335), but no men-at-arms: BL MS Cotton, Nero C VIII, fol. 256r. There are enrolled protections for four men, all apparently knights or esquires, serving in Ughtred's retinue: C 71/15, mm. 26, 27 and 30.

[6] According to the pay roll (BL MS Cotton, Nero C VIII, fol. 240v), Ughtred served, as a banneret, with eleven men-at-arms (including two knights) from 9 May until 17 May 1336, when three further *scutiferi* arrived. The retinue remained in the king's pay until 30 October. A horse inventory for the retinue, drawn up on 17 May, lists only fourteen men, including Ughtred himself (E 101/19/36, m. 2d). The missing fifteenth man is probably John Donneur, who had a protection dated 4 May (the only man in the retinue to have one), but who appears to have missed the muster on 17 May (C 71/16, m. 26). Donneur served with Ughtred on at least one other occasion: C 81/1741, m. 19. The pay roll makes no mention of archers in Ughtred's retinue, though it is possible that a detachment of the shire levy actually served with him since one of the esquires listed in the inventory, William de Santon, was also one of the leaders of Yorkshire's contingent of mounted archers (BL MS Cotton, Nero C VIII, fol. 259v).

[7] Ughtred's personal retinue on 12 March 1337, the day that he left Hull for Perth (BL MS Cotton, Nero C VIII, fol. 250v). This was to be the core of a garrison with an overall strength of 100 men-at-arms, 100 hobelars, 100 *pedites armatos* and 200 archers (*Rotuli Scotiae*, I, 489). The pay rolls suggest fluctuations in garrison numbers: in March 1338, for example, Ughtred had a total of 115 men-at-arms, 240 hobelars and mounted archers and 140 foot archers under his command, including the retinues of Sir Henry de Haverington and Sir Guy de Ferrers (E 101/388/5, mm. 15 and 17). Ughtred's indenture with the crown, dated 4 August 1338, stipulated a wartime garrison of 200 men-at-arms, 200 hobelars and 400 archers, half of whom were to be mounted (*CCR 1337–9*, p. 525). Although a flow of orders were issued to recruit the required troops, the size of garrison, according to Ughtred's account for the period from May/June 1338 until 28 March 1339, was 5 knights, 71 esquires, 130 hobelars and 205 archers (E 372/184, m. 45). Apparently not included in these figures are the fifteen men-at-arms who served in Sir Guy de Ferrers's retinue from July until November 1338, and for whom Ferrers accounted separately (E 101/21/16).

[8] The army payroll has Ughtred at the head of a company of twenty-five foot archers (receiving pay from 10 July until 29 September: E 101/389/8, m. 14), yet the evidence of letters of protection shows that he served with a company of knights and esquires

APPENDIX (*cont.*)

1341–2	Scotland	8 hobelars[9]
		21 mounted archers
1347	Siege of Calais	20 men-at-arms[10]
		20 mounted archers
1349	[Calais]	27 men-at-arms[11]
		24 mounted archers
1359–60	Reims campaign	20 men-at-arms[12]
		20 mounted archers

(protections for fourteen men: C 76/15, m. 19; C 81/1750, no. 72) within the retinue of Robert of Artois (C 76/15, m. 20). Artois did not receive the king's wages in the usual way and so does not appear on the pay roll, but with nearly fifty of his men (not including Ughtred's company) receiving protections, we can be sure that his retinue was among the largest in Edward III's army.

[9] For Edward III's brief excursion into Scotland during Christmas 1341, Ughtred appears in the pay roll, once again, as the leader of a company of light troops, who were in pay from 19 December until 1 January 1342: E 36/204, fol. 104r. That he is not recorded as receiving wages for himself would suggest that, as on earlier occasions, he was actually serving under another magnate, who may or may not be included among the paid captains on the pay roll.

[10] Retained by Edward III (indenture, 1 April 1347): E 101/25/33, m. 3. Six of the men-at-arms were to be knights.

[11] Ughtred's retinue, which included six knights, received pay from 6 October until 8 December 1349 (E 101/25/33) for a spell of duty described merely as 'in the king's service overseas'. This was the time (according to the chronicles, the night of 31 December) of Geoffrey de Charny's unsuccessful attempt to retake Calais.

[12] The retinue was paid for service from 21 September 1359 until 31 May 1360. Ughtred, a banneret, was accompanied by five knights (E 101/393/11, fol. 81v) and about half of the men in his retinue are known by name: C 76/38, m. 13 (sixteen men, protections); *CPR 1358–61*, pp. 378, 391, 504 and 521 (six, pardons).

7

A Problem of Precedence: Edward III,
the Double Monarchy, and the Royal Style

W. M. ORMROD

Edward III's formal assumption on 26 January 1340 of the title of king of France represented surely the most momentous decision of his long and eventful reign.[1] Historians have long recognized that the claim marked a sea-change in Anglo-French relations, transforming the basis on which Edward sought to resolve the long-standing dispute over Plantagenet sovereignty in Aquitaine.[2] Much attention has also been paid to the juristic aspects of the French claim and to its use in English propaganda during the Hundred Years War.[3] The present study aims not to engage directly with the validity of the claim or with the way in which it was deployed in English diplomacy, but to establish how it evolved and was represented in the new royal style (the formal statement of the king's titles) adopted in the wake of the announcement of the double monarchy in 1340, and to explore some of the implications of the French royal title for mid-fourteenth-century English domestic politics.

There were two principal and overlapping ways in which the royal style was officially articulated in later medieval England. First, there was the heraldic representation of monarchy found in the royal coat of arms. This

---

[1] H. S. Lucas, *The Low Countries and the Hundred Years' War, 1326–1347* (Ann Arbor, 1929), pp. 364–5; J. Sumption, *The Hundred Years War*, in progress (London, 1990–), I, 302. The title was assumed on 26 January, but was asserted, implicitly, from the previous day by being dated from the beginning of Edward's new regnal year (25 January). I am indebted to Adrian Ailes, Joel Burden, Peter Rycraft and Craig Taylor for assistance and advice, and to the other contributors to this volume for their comments on an earlier version of this essay. Spellings of the royal style are standardized throughout.

[2] E. Déprez, *Les préliminaires de la Guerre de Cent Ans* (Paris, 1902), pp. 170–318; E. Perroy, *The Hundred Years War*, trans. W. B. Wells (London, 1951), pp. 95–108; G. Templeman, 'Edward III and the Beginnings of the Hundred Years War', *TRHS* 5th ser. 2 (1952), 69–88; J. Le Patourel, *Feudal Empires, Norman and Plantagenet* (London, 1984), chap. XI, XII, XIII, XV; J. Palmer, 'The War Aims of the Protagonists and the Negotiations for Peace', in *The Hundred Years War*, ed. K. Fowler (London, 1971), pp. 51–74.

[3] For further discussion of Edward III's use of propaganda, see A. K. McHardy, below.

visual statement of the king's claims was found in many different media, whether painted on banners, boards and walls, embroidered on cloth, engraved on gold and silver plate, or cast in the matrices of royal seals and coins. Recently, both Michael Michael and Adrian Ailes have worked on the significance of the new quartered arms of France and England adopted in 1340. They have shown that Edward's French mother Queen Isabelle, and possibly Edward himself, had already quartered the leopards of England with the *fleurs de lis* of France before that date, but had always given formal precedence to England by placing the leopards in what we read as the left-hand side of the upper level of the quartering (read heraldically, from the reverse, as the dexter) and subordinating the *fleurs de lis* to the right (the sinister). When Edward assumed the French royal title, however, he immediately altered this order of precedence, putting France in the dexter and England in the sinister. This symbolic ordering of the two monarchies within the royal arms remained unchanged for the rest of the reign, even during the period when Edward ceased to exercise the French title between 1360 and 1369.[4]

The second way in which the royal style was formally declared and disseminated was through text rather than through imagery: in the statements of the king's titles found in the legends (marginal inscriptions) on royal seals and coins; in the protocols (the opening addresses) of the formal documents issued in the king's name; and in the dating clauses of those documents, which after 1340 expressed Edward III's regnal year in both its English and French forms.[5] Seals and coins combined the visual with the

[4] M. Michael, 'The Little Land of England is Preferred before the Great Kingdom of France: The Quartering of the Royal Arms by Edward III', in *Studies in Medieval Art and Architecture Presented to Peter Lasko*, ed. D. Buckton and T. A. Heslop (Stroud, 1994), pp. 114–26; A. Ailes, 'Heraldry: Symbols of Politics and Propaganda' (forthcoming). Mr Ailes points out (personal communication) that Michael has misread the evidence for a reversal of the precedence under Henry IV. Geoffrey le Baker recorded a curious and perhaps garbled story in which Philip VI of France is supposed to have remonstrated with Edward III for relegating the great kingdom of France to a subordinate position below the 'little land of England': G. le Baker, *Chronicon Galfridi le Baker de Swynebroke*, ed. E. M. Thompson (Oxford, 1889), pp. 66–7. (The story is cited by Michael, 'Little Land of England', pp. 113–14, but only from what he calls the 'unsubstantiated' account of John Stowe.) Since Baker placed this in his account of events in 1340 (that is, after France had been promoted to the superior heraldic position), it may perhaps have been intended to suggest that, if Philip had previously grumbled about Edward's heraldic disparagement of the arms of France, the tables had now been turned and Edward, cunningly and brilliantly, had called Philip's bluff. For other French responses to Edward III's use of the fleurs de lis, see W. M. Hinkle, *The Fleurs de Lis of the Kings of France, 1285–1488* (Carbondale, Illinois, 1991), pp. 27–31. It is nice to notice that an apparently contemporary (and no doubt bored) English clerk practiced drawing the fleur de lis on the dorse of one of the treaty rolls: C 76/19, m. 3d.
[5] 25 January 1340 marked the beginning of Edward III's fourteenth year as king of England and his first as king of France. While Edward might have considered dating his reign in France from the death of Charles IV in 1328, he was presumably

textual, of course, by including both heraldic representations and statements of the royal style.[6] They might therefore be regarded as more powerful media for the expression of the king's authority and ambitions than the technical formulae embedded in documents: certainly, with the exception of Pierre Chaplais, few historians have given any more than passing consideration to the significance of protocols and dating clauses in the articulation of Edward III's double monarchy.[7] Two factors, however, suggest that this evidence is worthy of due consideration. First, as Elizabeth Danbury has shown, the most solemn instruments issuing from the royal chancery were written out in such a way as to allow the opening phrase – the royal style – to be embellished, decorated and illuminated: possibly the most famous example from the reign of Edward III is the highly illuminated deed by which the king granted the title of prince of Aquitaine to his eldest son, the Black Prince, in 1363.[8] This practice suggests that both the crown and the recipients of its favour regarded the standard formulae used in such documents certainly as having a relevance, and perhaps even as possessing a certain mantra-like quality that transcended its apparent predictability. Secondly, and significantly, the royal style deployed in protocols was not, in fact, stable, but was subject to change according to the king's aspirations and the context of the document in which it was expressed. Thus, as Chaplais has noted, the royal style used in the opening clauses of English royal documents issued between 1340 and 1360 permutated according to circumstances: if the business concerned relations with continental rulers and with Edward's putative subjects in France, the style gave precedence to France (*rex Francie et Anglie* . . .); but if it dealt with the government of England or with the king's affairs in Scotland and (normally) Gascony, it reversed the order to

---

constrained from doing so by an issue similar to that which was to dog the discussion of the succession in fifteenth-century England: that is, the need to recognize the validity of the acts that had been issued in the name of the king of France between 1328 and 1340.

[6] Space does not allow a discussion of the dynamic relationship between legend and iconography in seals and coins. For an instructive example precipitated by the change of royal style in 1259, see P. Binski, *Westminster Abbey and the Plantagenets: Kingship and the Representation of Power, 1200–1400* (London, 1995), pp. 84–6.

[7] P. Chaplais, 'English Diplomatic Documents to the End of Edward III's Reign', in *The Study of Medieval Records: Essays in Honour of Kathleen Major*, ed. D. A. Bullough and R. L. Storey (Oxford, 1971), pp. 22–56 (pp. 50–4); *EMDP*, I1, 154–5.

[8] E. Danbury, 'The Decoration and Illumination of Royal Charters in England, 1250–1509: An Introduction', in *England and Her Neighbours, 1066–1453*, ed. M. Jones and M. Vale (London, 1989), pp. 157–79; E. Danbury, 'English and French Artistic Propaganda during the Period of the Hundred Years War: Some Evidence from Royal Charters', in *Power, Culture and Religion in France c.1350–c.1550*, ed. C. Allmand (Woodbridge, 1989), pp. 75–97; E 30/1105, reproduced in *Foedera*, ed. T. Rymer, Record Commission edn, 3 vols. in 6 parts (London, 1816–30), III2, plate opp. p. 667, and in R. Barber, *Edward, Prince of Wales and Aquitaine* (London, 1978), plate 4.

prioritize England (*rex Anglie et Francie . . .*).[9] It is the primary intention of this study to provide a more detailed examination of the bureaucratic and political considerations that led to this notable but neglected compromise over precedence in the expression of Edward III's double monarchy.

Why could Edward not have simplified matters in and after 1340 by calling himself king of England in acts relating to his English subjects and king of France in those relating to the French? Had he been accepted as the Capetian heir and succeeded uncontested to the French throne on the death of his uncle, Charles IV, in 1328, then it might indeed have been possible for him to operate two independent secretariats on either side of the Channel: indeed, given his public declaration on assuming the name of king in France that the two realms were to remain separate entities, it could be argued that there was some constitutional obligation upon him to strive for this separation of titles.[10] This, admittedly, would have gone against general contemporary practice both in the federal monarchies of continental Europe and in the Plantagenet empire itself, where the tendency was to express the king's full title in all his dominions and either to operate from a single central secretariat or to impose careful restrictions on the delegated chanceries set up in certain of the dependencies.[11] The Normans and Angevins had shown a strong preference for building up a composite royal style asserted throughout their lands: even after the renunciation of the titles of duke of Normandy and count of Anjou in 1259, Henry III and his successors still called themselves 'king of England, lord of Ireland and duke of Aquitaine'.[12] Early in Edward III's reign, indeed (and perhaps as a reaction to the dismissal of Edward's formal claim to succeed his uncle of France in 1328), an English royal councillor had suggested a considerable elaboration of the king's style to include all his lesser titles, including lord of the Channel Islands and count of Ponthieu and Montreuil.[13] On the other hand, there had been no occasion between 1066 and 1340 when the Normans and Plantagenets had laid formal claim to another *kingdom* equal in status to England.[14] Consequently, whereas

---

[9] Chaplais, 'English Diplomatic Documents', pp. 50–4. The same point applies, by extension, to the order of precedence given to the two kingdoms in the dating clauses of all documents which expressed the calendar in regnal years.

[10] *SR*, I, 292.

[11] In the crown of Aragon, for example, there was a single chancery and royal archive for all parts of the federation, and the king's full title was exercised throughout his lands. P. E. Schramm, 'Der König von Aragon: Seine Stellung im Staatsrecht (1276–1410)', *Historisches Jahrbuch* 74 (1955), 99–123.

[12] P. Chaplais, *Essays in Medieval Diplomacy and Administration* (London, 1981), chap. I. For the complications arising from the grant of Aquitaine to Prince Edward in 1325, see *EMDP*, I1, 68–70.

[13] *EMDP*, I1, 154.

[14] Edward I had conveniently side-stepped the issue of the integration of Scotland into the royal style by treating its ruler, John Balliol, as a contumacious vassal, demoting it to the status of a 'land' and thereby effectively reducing it (as he had done with

the royal styles employed between 1066 and 1340 had been susceptible to arrangement in a reasonably straightforward hierarchy that preserved the precedence of the kingdom of England over the mere lordships, duchies and counties of the wider empire, the assumption and inclusion of another *royal* title in 1340 created a highly unusual challenge for the formal expression of Edward III's authority.[15]

Something of the complexity of that challenge is indicated by the series of experiments with royal diplomatic that occurred during the first six months of 1340. Since the king's departure for the continent in 1338, the privy seal and great seal had been kept in the household administration functioning at Edward's various bases in the Low Countries, and a substitute great seal had been left at home to provide the domestic administration with a means of authenticating chancery instruments tested by the regent, Prince Edward.[16] Both the great seals bore the legend *Edwardus Dei gratia rex Anglie dominus Hibernie et dux Aquitannie,* and it was this style that was used in the protocols of the charters and letters patent issued and enrolled in parallel sequence by the two writing offices down to the end of the regnal year on 24 January 1340.[17] When, on 8 February, the king's clerks took custody at Ghent of the

the principality of Wales) to a dominion of the English crown. R. R. Davies, *Domination and Conquest: The Experience of Ireland, Scotland and Wales 1100–1300* (Cambridge, 1990), p. 126.

[15] The only comparable case in the period 1066–1340 is that of the duchies of Normandy and Aquitaine, which were always placed in that order in the royal style (Chaplais, *Essays,* chap. I, p. 248). If justification for this ranking was ever needed, it would no doubt have been found in the fact that the king of England was duke of Normandy before he was duke of Aquitaine.

[16] T. F. Tout, *Chapters in the Administrative History of Mediaeval England,* 6 vols. (Manchester, 1920–33), III, 80–2.

[17] The identification of the successive great seals of Edward III is greatly complicated by the variety of numbering systems used by nineteenth-century sigillographers. The classification observed here is that used by W. de G. Birch, *Catalogue of Seals in the Department of Manuscripts in the British Museum,* 6 vols. (London, 1887–1900), I, 21–8, as favoured by T. A. Heslop, 'Seals of the Mid-Fourteenth Century', in *The Age of Chivalry: Art in Plantagenet England 1200–1400,* ed. J. Alexander and P. Binski (London, 1987), pp. 493–7 (pp. 493–5, catalogue entries nos. 670–2). The great seals in use in 1338–40 were the 'second' (which went abroad with the king) and the 'third' (which remained in England). See also (under a different numbering system) A. B. Wyon and A. Wyon, *The Great Seals of England* (London, 1887), pp. 29–31. The rolls recording charters and letters patent issued on the continent are C 66/200 (12 Edw III) (= *CPR 1338–40,* pp. 189–97) and C 66/201 (13 Edw III) (= *CPR 1338–40,* pp. 377–410). C 67/17 (= *CPR 1338–40,* pp. 370–6) is an additional roll of letters patent issued to the king's German and Netherlandish allies in 13 Edw III. Note that the ordering of the membranes in C 66/201 was incorrect when it was calendared, and the first and last membranes have since been reversed: those entries calendared as m. 1 in *CPR 1338–40,* pp. 408–9, are now on m. 27 and date January–February 1339; those calendared as m. 29 in *CPR 1338–40,* pp. 377–8, date to early 1340. This means that there is only one entry dating from after the assumption of the French title at the inception of the new regnal year 14 Edw III (English style), that for 27

new great and privy seals fashioned on the continent to accommodate the king's double royal style, *rex Francie et Anglie . . .*, they began to compile a new roll registering the instruments issued with the equivalent protocol.[18] Meanwhile, however, the domestic administration continued to issue and enroll its own instruments under the supplementary great seal in use since 1338 in the name of the 'king of England, lord of Ireland and duke of Aquitaine'.[19] This dual system was maintained until the king returned to England on 21 February, took the existing great seal out of use and distributed to the sheriffs impressions of the new great and privy seals adopted on the continent in order that the change of royal style might be advertised through the county courts.[20]

For a brief time between 26 January and 21 February 1340, therefore, it seems genuinely possible that two separate secretariats might have developed, one for documents simply in the name of the 'king of England' and one for instruments in the name of the 'king of France and England'. Insofar as it was led by administrative considerations, the decision *not* to pursue this line was no doubt coloured by the fact that the privy seal had already been changed on 8 February to accommodate the double title; since it (unlike the great seal) was not duplicated during royal absences, and provided the essential means of communication between the (temporary) continental and (permanent) domestic governments, there was no avoiding the infiltration of instruments bearing the style 'king of France and England' into England itself: writs using this formulation had been issued (and presumably despatched) from the continent on a regular basis between 8 and 21 February.[21] Similarly, the preference for a unified secretariat perhaps said something about the practical difficulties, already well appreciated in England, of separating two sets of inevitably overlapping business: the various series of specialized enrollments compiled by the chancery which took the name of the geographical areas to which they related – the Scotch, Gascon, Almain and French rolls – were not in fact exclusive records of business done by the king as ruler of those territories but included much material concerning the mobilization of the kingdom of England for military

February calendared in *CPR 1338–40*, p. 378. Reference to the original shows this entry to be highly exceptional, since the instrument in question was issued under the privy seal. Unfortunately the entry gives no indication of the royal style employed.

[18] Birch, *Catalogue of Seals*, I, 23–4 (the 'fourth' great seal); H. C. Maxwell-Lyte, *Historical Notes on the Use of the Great Seal of England* (London, 1926), p. 43; Tout, *Chapters*, V, 137–8. The new roll is C 67/18 (= *CPR 1374–7*, pp. 503–6).

[19] The use of this protocol in instruments issued in England between 8 and 21 February is proved by *Foedera*, II2, 1111; E 208/3, part 1, file 14 Edw III (passim); E 404/4/26, no. 2.

[20] *CCR 1339–41*, p. 457. The subordinate great seal was delivered to the king on 1 March: *Foedera*, II2, 1116.

[21] C 81/261/12554–7, 12558–60, 12562–73, 12576, 12578–9; E 404/4/26, nos. 3–4.

engagements in those war zones that might equally (and often did) appear on the main 'English' series of patent, close and fine rolls.[22] The fact that the government of Edward III never found a truly satisfactory method of separating the classification and archiving of its 'English' and 'French' business demonstrates the fundamentally ad hoc attitude that was inevitably taken towards a title – the Plantagenet claim to the French throne – that remained a mere aspiration: in fact, it was not until this aspiration was apparently fulfilled with Henry VI's accession to the thrones of both realms in 1422 that it was finally deemed necessary to create separate and permanent great seals and attendant writing offices for England and France.[23]

It is of some interest to the present discussion to notice that the resistance to the development of multiple seals and secretariats under Edward III happened to coincide with contemporary French chancery practice. The special bureaucratic circumstances that had obtained in 1338–40 were replicated when Edward III went to the Low Countries and/or France in mid-1340, 1342–3, 1345, 1346–7 and 1359–60: the king took both the great seal and the privy seal abroad and left a subordinate great seal for the use of the domestic administration in England.[24] (The subordinate great seal was not

---

[22] The point is demonstrated by numerous entries transcribed in *Foedera*, II–III, passim. Similarly, but vice versa, we may note that the chancery felt free to enroll instruments relating to international diplomacy on either the 'treaty' rolls (the modern term for the Almain and French rolls) or the close rolls.

[23] H. Jenkinson, 'The Great Seal of England: Deputed or Departmental Seals', *Archaeologia* 85 (1935), 293–340.

[24] Tout, *Chapters*, V, 18–19, 21–2; B. Wilkinson, *The Chancery under Edward III* (Manchester, 1929), p. 209. Special enrollments of the charters and letters patent sealed under the great seal during royal sojourns on the continent survive as: C 66/202 (July–November 1340) (= *CPR 1340–3*, pp. 114–17); C 67/28A (the so-called 'Brittany' roll, 1342–3) (uncalendared); C 66/215A (July 1345) (= *CPR 1374–7*, pp. 507–8); C 66/219 (the so-called 'Norman' roll, July 1346–January 1347) (= *CPR 1345–8*, pp. 473–517; G. Wrottesley, 'Crecy and Calais from the Public Records', *Collections for a History of Staffordshire* 18 [1897], 219–59), continued in the new regnal year as C 66/223 (the so-called 'Calais' roll, January–October 1347) (= *CPR 1345–8*, pp. 518–70; Wrottesley, 'Crecy and Calais', pp. 260–79). All of the instruments recorded in these enrollments were warranted *per ipsum regem*, signifying that it was unnecessary, when the privy seal and great seal were in the hands of the same keeper, for warrants under the former to be used to move the latter: see Tout, *Chapters*, III, 87, n. 1; III, 152, n. 3; III, 170, n. 2; VI, 125. In 1359–60 the system was rather different and more complicated. C 76/39, headed 'Rotulus Francie de anno regni regis Edwardi tertii post conquestum Anglie videlicet tricesimo tercio et Francie vicesimo editus post transfretum suum ad partes Francie', begins (m. 2) with a writ to the treasurer of Calais but is then given over to a transcription of the indenture of truce with the duke of Burgundy (mm. 2–1 = *Foedera*, III1, 473); the final entry (m. 1) is a later addition, warranted by the privy seal. The two documents now classified as C 76/41 and 43 seem originally to have been part of the same roll, though already separated when described by Rymer, who called them the 'Calais roll, 34 Edw III' and 'rot' de tract' pacis cum Franc'', respectively (*Foedera*, III1, 519, 550): this was clearly intended as a special roll to preserve diplomatic documents

the same as that used in 1338–40, but was a new one commissioned, along with another great seal for use by the king, prior to Edward's departure in June 1340. Both seals incorporated the new double royal title in the form *rex Francie et Anglie* . . . They were thereafter employed in this combination on every occasion of the king's formal absence until 1360.)[25] As in 1338–40, moreover, the chancellor and chancery remained at home; it was the keeper of the privy seal who accompanied the king to the continent and had custody of the great seal for the duration of the king's stay there. In contrast to the practice observed when the king was in England, when there were two separate writing offices for the great seal and privy seal, the secretariats set up by the keepers of the privy seal during these periods of royal residence abroad therefore operated a unified system, writing, sealing and issuing both great seal *and* privy seal instruments.[26] This latter practice directly mirrored

connected to the treaty of Brétigny. The roll now classified as C 76/42 also contains documents of October 1360 relating to the negotiations at Calais, but also has more routine instruments – pardons, safe-conducts, etc. – of the kind found on earlier rolls of charters and patents issued abroad. On this occasion, however, such instruments carry a variety of warranty notes, including 'by writ of privy seal'. This indicates that the writing office taken to the continent in 1359–60 observed rather different practices from its ad hoc predecessors.

[25] Birch, *Catalogue of Seals*, I, 24 (the 'fifth' [subordinate] and 'sixth' [principal] great seals); more accurate descriptions in Wyon and Wyon, *Great Seals*, pp. 33–6. The use of the phrase 'great seal of absence' to describe great seals used when the king was on the continent was criticized by H. Jenkinson, 'The Great Seal of England: Some Notes and Suggestions', *Antiquaries Journal* 16 (1936), 8–28 (pp. 17–27) on grounds relevant to the present discussion: namely, that it is a phrase adopted from French practice, where the 'absence' was not that of the king, but of the great seal. The phrase does, however, find favour with P. Chaplais, *Piers Gaveston: Edward II's Adoptive Brother* (Oxford, 1994), pp. 34–42. Given the similarity between the fifth and sixth great seals, it is not impossible that these were used interchangeably: indeed, the memoranda contained in *The Antient Kalendars and Inventories of the Treasury of His Majesty's Exchequer*, ed. F. Palgrave, 3 vols. (London, 1836), I, 157–8, 161, 168–9 and 188, suggest that it is perfectly possible that the seal used by the king on the continent was in fact his 'seal of absence' and that the seal remaining with the chancellor was the one in permanent usage in England. The matter demands further attention. It should also be noted that Tout, *Chapters*, III, 165–6, was in error in assuming that the privy seals created for regents might be called 'privy seals of absence': see Wilkinson, *Chancery*, pp. 209–10; W. M. Ormrod, 'Edward III's Government of England, c. 1346–1356' (unpublished D.Phil. dissertation, University of Oxford, 1984), pp. 107–8. One of the things that differentiated the privy seal from the great seal was that it could be taken abroad without a formal regency being appointed: Edward III took it with him on his journeys to France in 1331 (C81/181/4535, 4541) and to Calais in 1348 (*EMDP*, II, plate 21; *Foedera*, III1, 175); he also planned to take it with him to Calais in 1355 (Tout, *Chapters*, V, 34). It was also conventional for the king to take the privy seal with him on campaigns in Scotland: W. A. Morris, 'Introduction', in *The English Government at Work, 1327–1336*, ed. J. F. Willard et al., 3 vols. (Cambridge, MA, 1930–40), I, 3–81 (p. 64); Tout, *Chapters*, V, 9–10, 17 and 34.

[26] Tout, *Chapters*, III, 85 and 179.

the convention in France, where a single chancery was responsible for writing the documents issued under both royal seals, the great seal and the *sceau du secret*.[27] Moreover, when Edward III returned to England and re-instituted the separate writing offices, the close contact built upon between their staffs, and their more or less permanent location within the royal palace of Westminster, meant that they tended to work with a higher degree of co-ordination than ever before, sharing personnel and distributing responsibilities in a manner that made them in some respects almost indistinguishable.[28] For a short while in the early 1350s the privy seal took over from the chancery as the principal writing office for diplomatic documents.[29] And, in a striking parallel with fourteenth-century changes in the use of the French *sceau du secret*, the privy seal began increasingly from the 1340s to be employed not merely for the issue of letters close but also for drafting and sealing royal letters patent, operating in this respect as a direct substitute for the great seal.[30]

While there is admittedly no explicit evidence that these developments in the English royal secretariat were modeled consciously on French practice, two pieces of circumstantial evidence suggest that the connections may well have been more than mere coincidence. First, the great spurt of international diplomacy that preceded and accompanied the Hundred Years War gave the senior members of the royal secretariat much closer contact with their counterparts in the royal and princely chanceries not merely of France but also indeed of the Low Countries, Germany and the Iberian kingdoms, from all of which they seem to have picked up certain secretarial practices.[31] Secondly, it was under Edward III that the English royal writing offices first began to follow the recruitment stream observed by the French chancery and employ public notaries as senior members of the chancery and privy seal offices.[32] This in turn meant that certain technical conventions involving the

[27] R.-H. Bautier, 'Recherches sur la chancellerie royale au temps de Philippe VI', *Bibliothèque de l'Ecole des Chartes* 122 (1964), 89–176; 123 (1965), 313–459, describes how the tendency towards a separate office for the *sceau du secret* was resisted by Guillaume Flote, chancellor 1338–48, and provides an important discussion of the development of the *sceau nouveau* as a great seal of absence after 1338.
[28] W. M. Ormrod, 'Accountability and Collegiality: The English Royal Secretariat in the Mid-Fourteenth Century', in *Ecrit et pouvoir dans les chancelleries médiévales: espace français, espace anglais*, ed. K. Fianu and D. J. Guth (Louvain la Neuve, 1997), pp. 55–85 (pp. 64–76). This discussion disagrees with the longer-term trends noted by Tout, *Chapters*, V, 148–9.
[29] Chaplais, *Essays*, chap. XXII, pp. 173–4.
[30] For French practice, see O. Morel, *La grande chancellerie royale* (Paris, 1900), pp. 244–50; R. Cazelles, *Lettres closes: lettres 'de par le roi' de Philippe de Valois* (Paris, 1958), pp. 19–20. All but one of the letters patent discovered by Tout, *Chapters*, V, 128, nn. 1, 2, date from the period between the 1340s and the 1370s. For further examples from the same period, see *RP*, II, 196, no. 84; C 47/2/34, no. 15; C 47/3/32, no. 33; C 47/10/38, no. 33.
[31] Chaplais, 'English Diplomatic Documents', pp. 50–4.
[32] Chaplais, *Essays*, chap. XXII.

writing and checking of documents already well established in France were taken up, albeit sometimes only fleetingly, in English royal administration during the middle decades of the fourteenth century.[33] It is therefore very tempting to conclude that the inspiration and explanation for at least some of the changes in English royal diplomatic during the mid-fourteenth century was found in the context of Edward III's claim to the throne of France.

So much for bureaucratic considerations. The principal reason why it was deemed necessary to express the two royal titles in an apparently indissoluble combination in and after 1340 must, undeniably, lie in the international politics of Edward III's new style. Every student knows that the essential context to the assumption of the crown of France was a diplomatic one, arising from the conundrum facing the men of Flanders, who were inclined to support Edward's war against Philip VI for the recovery of Aquitaine but were not prepared to risk the recriminations that would result if they broke their own duty of homage to the crown of France.[34] By asserting his right to that crown,[35] Edward therefore provided the Flemish with the opportunity to release themselves from their obligations to the Valois monarchy and to join the anti-French alliance that he had been building up during the late 1330s in the Low Countries and Germany. Indeed, it was widely understood in England that Edward changed his arms and his seals specifically at the request of the Flemings, perhaps as a guarantee of his commitment to the new alliance thus formed.[36] That the title was part of a diplomatic and strategic re-positioning after the first, 'phony', phase of the Anglo-French war would certainly explain why the legends on

[33] See the discussion of the use of 'mentions of service' and 'mentions of clerks' in chancery and privy seal instruments in Ormrod, 'Accountability and Collegiality', pp. 66 and 70. The practice of the French chancery has in particular been suggested as an influence on the development of a new diplomatic form, the 'bill of privy seal', in 1349–50: E. Déprez, *Etudes de diplomatique anglaise* (Paris, 1908), pp. 56–64; R. L. Poole, 'Seals and Documents', *Proceedings of the British Academy* 9 (1919–20), 319–39 (pp. 337–8); Maxwell-Lyte, *Great Seal*, pp. 54–5; Ormrod, 'Accountability', pp. 71–2. One characteristic feature of the bill of privy seal, the placing of the impression of the seal on the face of the document, is echoed in the validation of petitions by the direct application of the privy seal: SC 8/228/11372–87; SC 8/247/12347; SC 8/332/15767.

[34] Lucas, *Low Countries*, pp. 328–74. For good recent re-statements of this classic position, see A. Curry, *The Hundred Years War* (Basingstoke, 1993), pp. 44–58; C. Barron, 'Introduction: England and the Low Countries', in *England and the Low Countries in the Late Middle Ages*, ed. C. Barron and N. Saul (Stroud, 1995), pp. 1–28 (pp. 2–5).

[35] *Foedera*, II2, 1107.

[36] For example, *Chronicles of the Reigns of Edward I and II*, ed. W. Stubbs, 2 vols. (RS, 1882–3), II, 148; *The Chronicle of Lanercost, 1272–1346*, trans. H. Maxwell (Glasgow, 1913), pp. 319–20; *Chronicon Galfridi le Baker de Swynebroke*, ed. E. M. Thompson (Oxford, 1889), p. 66.

the great and privy seals adopted on 8 February gave precedence to France, and why Edward's well-known letters patent to the people of France, issued on the same day and inviting them to offer allegiance to him as their rightful ruler, should have used the style *rex Francie et Anglie*.[37] In addition to sending the appropriate messages about his supposed scale of priorities, the hierarchy of titles thus declared would also indicate that Edward properly respected the political and moral superiority that the French monarchy claimed within the hierarchy of European kingdoms.[38]

The reason for retaining the English title within a scheme intended primarily for continental consumption still, however, requires some thought. One obvious explanation would be that Edward's new-found authority in France was, of course, only nominal: as the chronicler Jean le Bel commented, it was risking ridicule to claim to be the king of a country that one did not actually possess.[39] To be taken seriously either by his new 'subjects' in France or by the other rulers of Europe, it was therefore necessary that he should remind them that he was already an anointed king, even if only of a lesser realm: after all, neither Philip VI of France nor the pope, Benedict XII (who expressed himself vehemently opposed to Edward's new title), could deny that Edward was the legitimate ruler of England.[40] Another, rather neglected, explanation, however, may lie in the complications surrounding the constitutional status of the duchy of Aquitaine. The new seal cast on the continent early in 1340 expressed the king's title as *rex Francie et Anglie dominus Hibernie et dux Aquitannie* – the style which, incidentally, had been deployed on one earlier occasion prior to the formal assumption of the French title, in various special instruments issued by Edward III on 7 October 1337.[41] The protocols of instruments issued under this seal and its accompanying privy seal usually accorded with this deployment of the lesser titles to Ireland and Aquitaine, though sometimes the latter was dropped.[42] The new great seal and subordinate great seal put into commission for the king's absence in the summer of

---

[37] The letters patent were issued in both Latin and French: *Foedera*, II2, 1108–9 and 1111 (= *CPR 1374–7*, p. 505).

[38] J. Krynen, *L'empire du roi: Idées et croyances politiques en France, XIIIe–XVe siècle* (Paris, 1993), esp. pp. 345–414.

[39] *Chronique de Jean le Bel*, ed. J. Viard and E. Déprez, 2 vols. (Paris, 1904–5), I, 167–8, as noted by Le Patourel, *Feudal Empires*, chap. XII, p. 180.

[40] For the manner in which they addressed Edward after the assumption of the French title, see *Foedera*, II2, 1109–10, 1117, 1131–2. It is interesting to speculate as to whether Philip VI might have been tempted to follow a line of thinking concerning Edward III's possible bastardy and thus question his right to the throne of England: see C. Wood, *Joan of Arc and Richard III* (Oxford, 1988), pp. 12–28.

[41] Birch, *Catalogue of Seals*, I, 23–4; Wyon and Wyon, *Great Seals*, pp. 31–3; *Treaty Rolls 1337–9* (London, 1972), nos. 87–90 and 92–5; *EMDP*, I1, 154; Le Patourel, *Feudal Empires*, chap. XII, p. 180.

[42] C 81/261, passim; E 404/4/26, passim. The announcement of the new title to the people of France omitted Aquitaine from the protocol: *Foedera*, II2, 1108–9, 1111.

1340 then abandoned the separate title to Aquitaine altogether, in favour of the briefer style *rex Francie et Anglie et dominus Hibernie*.[43] Far from marginalizing the territories and issues that had caused the initial outbreak of war in 1337, this tacit assimilation of the duchy of Aquitaine into the jurisdiction of the French crown indicated that Edward was now, in theory, the automatic feudal suzerain of *all* the great fiefdoms of France.[44] However, as both the English and the Gascons were at pains to point out in the fourteenth century, the duchy of Gascony itself (as distinct from the larger and composite duchy of Aquitaine) was, despite the Treaty of Paris, an integral and inalienable part of the inheritance of the crown of *England*.[45] The amendments to the royal style suggested early in Edward III's reign had recognized this distinction by calling Edward both *dominus Vasconie* and *dux Aquitannie*: Gascony was to be treated as a lordship with the constitutional status equivalent to that of Ireland.[46] It is also to be noted that the seal of the seneschal of Gascony, used for all public instruments issued by the ducal administration in Aquitaine, was not changed after 1340 and continued to represent the king-duke's authority by his unquartered arms of the leopards of England, while (as noted above) royal instruments emanating from England relating to Gascon affairs generally expressed Edward III's dual monarchy in the form *rex Anglie et Francie*.[47] To articulate a truly transcendent and incontrovertible authority over *all* the provinces of his newly-acquired continental kingdom it may therefore have been necessary, ironically, for Edward III to use his English, as well as his French, royal title.

Thus far, then, our interpretation of the new royal style of 1340 depends on an understanding of the diplomatic context of the war and has the effect of reinforcing the conventional notion that it was a pragmatic response to the need for continental allies in a war intended primarily for the recovery of Aquitaine. There is, however, another way of reading the diplomatic of the

---

[43] Birch, *Catalogue of Seals*, I, 24–6; Wyon and Wyon, *Great Seals*, pp. 33–6.

[44] Curry, *Hundred Years War*, p. 58.

[45] P. Chaplais, 'English Arguments Concerning the Feudal Status of Aquitaine in the Fourteenth Century', *BIHR* 21 (1946–8), 203–13; Le Patourel, *Feudal Empires*, chap. XI; M. Vale, *The Angevin Legacy and the Hundred Years War, 1250–1340* (Oxford, 1990), pp. 60–3; J. J. N. Palmer, *England, France and Christendom, 1377–99* (London, 1972), pp. 36–40. The resulting anomalies in the status of the Gascons vis-à-vis England after the treaties of 1360 and 1420 are discussed by R. A. Griffiths, *King and Country: England and Wales in the Fifteenth Century* (London, 1991), pp. 33–54.

[46] *EMDP*, I1, 154.

[47] Chaplais, *Essays*, chap. VIII, p. 84; *EMDP*, I1, 154–5. Note, however, that the letters sent to Gascon nobles and communities in June 1340 rousing them to labour for the king's rights were addressed by Edward as *rex Francie et Anglie*: *Foedera*, II2, 1127–8. The heading to the Gascon roll for 14 Edw III gives only the English regnal year, though the note at the end of the roll provides both the English and French dates: C 61/52. For an indenture made by the seneschal of Gascony on 31 March 1340 in the name of 'the king of England, duke of Aquitaine', see *CPR 1340–3*, p. 115.

double monarchy: namely, from a domestic, English perspective. Just as Edward's credibility in France would rest in part on his existing and unchallenged status as a king in England, so would his expectations in the ensuing war only be fulfilled if his English subjects were persuaded to accept the consequences of his ambitions in France. It may therefore be that the assumption of a double royal title, rather than the alternative of employing parallel but separate styles in England and France, was driven as much by the attitudes of the domestic political community as it was by the demands of international diplomacy. This is certainly suggested by the more or less immediate adaptation of the royal style to accommodate domestic priorities and sensitivities.

The foregoing discussion has demonstrated that the style preferred in protocols on chancery instruments relating to English affairs changed with effect from the day of the king's return to England, 21 February 1340, the title *rex Francie et Anglie* being dropped in favour of *rex Anglie et Francie*. Given what has been argued about the operation of two separate chanceries observing different royal styles between 26 January and 21 February, it could be suggested that the change in the order of precedence accorded to the two kingdoms was occasioned primarily by the king's change of location: in other words, that the decision to dispense with the separate continental secretariat resolved into a temporary compromise that would employ only one great seal (whose legend gave precedence to France), but which would adapt the protocols of written instruments in order to have Edward as 'king of France and England' when on the continent and 'king of England and France' when in England.[48] This, however, is not what happened when Edward returned to the Low Countries in June 1340: it is from *this* point that we can properly date the practice of employing the style *rex Anglie et Francie* in all instruments relating to England and restricting the formulation *rex Francie et Anglie* to those concerning continental affairs.[49] As prominent

---

[48] This is supported by the fact that at least one chancery instrument relating to continental affairs issued during Edward's sojourn in England between February and June 1340, concerning the negotiations for the marriage of the Black Prince with the daughter of the duke of Brabant, did not accord with the norm indicated above for diplomatic documents but gave the king's English title precedence over the French: *Foedera*, II2, 1122 (= *CPR 1338–40*, p. 511).

[49] For privy seal writs despatched from the continent to the chancery and exchequer in England during this and subsequent royal expeditions, see: C 81/268–9, E 404/4/27 (June-November 1340): C 81/287–8 (1342–3), 305 (1345), 313–25 (1346–7), 380 (1359–May 1360), 385 (October 1360). The privy seal warrants deploying the style *rex Anglie, dominus Hibernie et Aquitannie* in C 81/380/24436, 24438, are in fact misplaced and belong to the period after Edward dropped the French title on 24 October 1360 (Foedera, III1, 514–18). C 81/385/24914 (15 October 1360) also drops the French title, but was probably made in retrospect since the resulting chancery instrument is dated 25 October (*CPR 1358–61*, p. 503, pardon to Robert Dyneley), after that style was officially set aside. The only significant exceptions to the ordering of the royal titles in privy seal writs for English business issued while the king was on the

examples we might cite the king's letter to the Westminster parliament, dated from Bruges on 9 July, in the name of the 'king of England and France', and his celebrated provocation of war addressed to Philip VI from Bruges on 26 July, whose sealing clause gave France precedence over England.[50]

While it is still perfectly possible to explain this new and permanent compromise in terms of the relationship between the privy seal operating on the continent and the chancery left at home in England,[51] it would be disingenuous if one failed to admit that these new diplomatic conventions also presumably owed at least something to the manner in which Edward's double title was received by the political elite within England. Remarkably, the king seems not to have informed his own subjects of the assumption of the French title until his return to England on 21 February, when he issued writs summoning parliament and (as noted above) distributed impressions of his new great and privy seals for display in the county courts.[52] The double monarchy was therefore presented to the political community (and even, perhaps, to the regency council itself) merely as a matter of record: indeed, the writs ordering the election of knights of the shire and representatives of the cities and towns made no allusion at all to the change – other, that is, than implicitly in the revised protocol, *rex Anglie et Francie*.[53] Edward's argument in defence of this *fait accompli* would, no doubt, have been that no-one other than he (and God) had the right to sanction, or to veto, his dynastic claim to the throne of France. But such high-handedness was in direct contradiction of the strategy he had adopted in 1337, when he had gone out of his way to seek parliamentary approval and consent for his projected war with Philip of

continent occur during his expedition into Burgundy in 1360: C 81/380/24446, 24448, 24458, 24459 (which all use the formula *rex Francie et Anglie . . .*). It is possible that this may be connected with the temporary employment of a local clerk.

[50] *Foedera*, II2, 1130, 1131.

[51] Since the chancery continued to write its protocols in the form observed since 21 February (*rex Anglie et Francie . . .*), those clerks responsible for drawing up the privy seal writs sent back to England as warrants to move the subordinate great seal may have been concerned lest their hitherto preferred form, *rex Francie et Anglie*, would produce confusion in the domestic government.

[52] *RDP*, IV, 515–18; *Foedera*, II2, 1115; *CCR 1339–41*, pp. 456–7. The only evidence produced by Le Patourel, *Feudal Empires*, chap. XII, p. 180, for the publication of the title in England was that drawn from the statute of 1340, discussed below, and cited by him from J. Froissart, *Oeuvres*, ed. Kervyn de Lettenhove, 25 vols. (Brussels, 1867–77), XVIII, 129–30. The inclusion of the letters patent to the people of France of 8 February in *Robert of Avesbury, De gestis mirabilibus regis Edwardi tertii*, ed. E. M. Thompson (RS, 1889), p. 309 (Latin) and *Calendar of Letter Books of the City of London*, ed. R. R. Sharpe, 11 vols. (London, 1899–1912), *Letter Book F*, p. 43 (French) indicates that this text circulated in England, but does not provide direct evidence that it was known there before the king's return: the London letter book places it between a letter from the king, dated from Sluys on 20 February, and the writ for elections to parliament, dated the day of the king's return (21 February): it is just possible, then, that a copy was sent home enclosed in the letter of 20 February.

[53] C 219/6, file 13A.

Valois.[54] Given that parliament had actually been in session at Westminster when the king announced his assumption of the French title at Ghent in January 1340,[55] the polity had particularly good grounds for complaining about the blatant lack of consultation over this change of strategy and for berating the king, if it was so inclined, for adopting a title so potentially injurious to the kingdom of England.

This implied hostility on the part of the English certainly provides the orthodox explanation for the discussions that took place in the parliament of March-May 1340 and which resulted in the celebrated statute guaranteeing the constitutional separation of the crowns of England and France:

> We ... will and grant and establish for us and for our heirs and successors, by assent of the prelates, earls, barons and commons of our realm of England . . . that our realm of England and the people of the same . . . shall not in any time to come be put in subjection or obedience to us, our heirs or successors, as kings of France . . .[56]

Considering the increasing restiveness of the parliaments of 1339–40 over Edward's outrageous fiscal demands to support an as yet unproductive war, it is easy to see why historians have sometimes assumed that this legislation represented a significant achievement on the part of those alarmed by the increasing grandiosity of the king's war aims and a major concession on the part of a ruler who had temporarily lost touch with political reality.[57] Yet there is also some suggestion that the statute represented a pre-emptive manoeuvre by the king specifically to offset such criticism of his diplomatic policy and to regain the support of an undeniably recalcitrant realm.[58] The personal summonses to the lords for the March parliament and the writs sent out to the sheriffs for the publication of the new seals announced that it was not the king's intention to prejudice the kingdom of England by assuming the title to the kingdom of France.[59] Insofar as this statement prefigured the

---

[54] E. B. Fryde, *Studies in Medieval Trade and Finance* (London, 1983), chap. V; G. L. Harriss, *King, Parliament and Public Finance in Medieval England to 1369* (Oxford, 1975), pp. 234, 316, and 372.

[55] *RP*, II, 107–11.

[56] *SR*, I, 292, as rendered in *English Historical Documents 1327–1485*, ed. A. R. Myers (London, 1969), p. 70.

[57] Fryde, *Essays*, chap. V; Tout, *Chapters*, III, 105–6; Sumption, *Hundred Years War*, I, 304–6; Curry, *Hundred Years War*, p. 59. Clifford Rogers has pointed out to me that the announcement of the double title issued in France implied that Edward would continue to use his English resources in pursuit of his French claim: *Foedera* II2, 1108–9, 111.

[58] It is interesting to notice that a special receiver and a special committee of auditors were established in this same parliament to deal with petitions from Flanders: *RP*, II, 112. This suggests that the king was quite prepared to exercise his rights as king of France in an English tribunal when pragmatism required.

[59] *RDP*, IV, 515–18; *CCR 1339–41*, pp. 456–7.

statute, it is possible that the latter was offered as a premeditated concession to parliament, rather than being wrung from the king against his will or better judgement. The admittedly laconic parliament roll states merely that the lords and commons requested a guarantee from the king that they would not be made subject to the crown of France: it provides no indication that the king's actual claim was either discussed or criticized.[60]

If we are correct in assuming that the royal style had real significance in the domestic politics of 1340, then the adaptation of that style after 21 February, from *rex Francie et Anglie* to *rex Anglie et Francie*, may therefore be seen as part of a concerted – and apparently successful – effort on the part of the king to offset both official and unofficial anxieties over the wisdom of his new claim. It is particularly interesting to notice that a number of private petitions processed during March 1340 specifically addressed Edward as 'king of England and France':[61] given that it was more usual simply to use the phrase 'our lord the king' in the address clauses of such documents, it is tempting to conclude that the petitioners and/or the chancery clerks who evidently advised them sought to make a statement about the official order of precedence recently adopted by the king in the expression of his double title. This would also provide a political (as distinct from a merely bureau-cratic) explanation for the perpetuation of the style 'king of England and France' in instruments relating to English affairs after the king's return to the continent in June. On the one hand, the legend on the great and privy seals preserved the original order of precedence, signalled also in the king's quartered arms, and represented his right to exercise the French royal title within England as well as on the continent: it is interesting in this respect to notice how, in the great seals used after June 1340, a hand of blessing issuing from clouds was placed before the opening of the legend, as a symbolic demonstration of divine blessing upon Edward III's title as *rex Francie et Anglie*.[62] On the other hand, the statute of 1340 and the protocols and sealing clauses used in great and privy seal instruments relating to English affairs after February (and more particularly June) 1340 provided an equally potent signal of Edward's commitment to rule England as a Plantagenet, rather than as a Capetian, king.

The pragmatism of this compromise, and its political acceptability to those in England who bore the burden of Edward III's wars, is suggested by the remarkable fluidity, not to say occasional inconsistency, found in the ex-pression of the royal style during the remainder of Edward III's reign. In terms of sigillography, the foregoing discussion indicates that while careful attention was paid to the arms and legend of the great and privy seals in 1340,

[60] *RP*, II, 112.
[61] C 81/262/12612, 12651, 12654, 12659, 12666–7, 12671, 12689.
[62] Birch, *Catalogue of Seals*, I, 24–6. For the significance of the title in obliging the realm of England to strive for the king's rights in France, see Harriss, *King, Parliament and Public Finance*, pp. 318–19.

there was no further change thereafter to adapt to the new diplomatic practices of the royal secretariat. It was only when the king dropped the title of king of France and assumed the sovereignty of Aquitaine under the terms of the treaty of Brétigny in 1360 that the legend on the new great and privy seals and the protocols of chancery and privy seal instruments once more came into line, in the revised form *rex Anglie dominus Hibernie et Aquitanniae*: even then, the royal arms continued to be represented as they had since 1340, with France taking precedence over England in the quartering.[63] Furthermore, the great seal, subordinate great seal and privy seal used during the period 1340–60 were not destroyed, as was the norm, but were deposited in the treasury of the exchequer in Westminster Abbey, whence they were removed and put back into commission as soon as the king resumed his title to France on the re-opening of war in 1369: the anomaly whereby seals bearing the legend *rex Francie et Anglie* were applied to instruments made in the name of the *rex Anglie et Francie* was thus restored, and continued down to the end of the reign and beyond.[64] It ought also to be noted that the attention lavished on the increasingly elaborate iconography of successive great (and, to a lesser extent, privy) seals both in 1340 and 1360 did not translate into a general reform of deputed and departmental seals used in the central administration and in the crown dependencies.[65] The deputed great seal in use in the English exchequer, for example, was not changed either at Edward III's accession to the English throne in 1327 or on his assumption of the French royal title in 1340: consequently, exchequer instruments issued between 1340 and 1360, and after 1369, observed the chancery formula *rex Anglie et Francie et dominus Hibernie* in their protocols, but were actually sealed with a seal bearing the legend *rex Anglie dominus Hibernie et dux Aquitanniae*.[66]

Given that it was very common during the later Middle Ages for deputed and departmental seals to be re-used from one reign to another over long

---

[63] Birch, *Catalogue of Seals*, I, 26–8 (the 'seventh' great seal); Wyon and Wyon, *Great Seals*, pp. 37–9; Maxwell-Lyte, *Historical Notes*, pp. 43–4; Tout, *Chapters*, V, 140–1. For the revised protocol used from 24 October 1360, see *Foedera*, III1, 519, 520–1, 524–5, 531, 533, 534–6, 537, 539, 542.

[64] Wyon and Wyon, *Great Seals*, pp. 35–6; Tout, *Chapters*, V, 141–2; *Antient Kalendars*, ed. Palgrave, I, 191; *Foedera*, III2, 868. There was much debate in the nineteenth century as to whether Edward III used a great seal with the legend *rex Anglie et Francie*: this was refuted by Wyon and Wyon, *Great Seals*, pp. 40–1.

[65] Heslop, 'Seals of the Mid-Fourteenth Century', pp. 494–5, catalogue nos. 670–2; Tout, *Chapters*, V, 136–42.

[66] For the use of Edward II's exchequer seal under Edward III, see C. L. Kingsford, 'On Some Ancient Deeds and Seals belonging to Lord De L'Isle and Dudley', *Archaeologia* 65 (1913), 251–68 (pp. 257–8). An impression of this seal is illustrated in Jenkinson, 'Deputed or Departmental Seals', plate LXXXIV (opp. p. 298). For letters patent issued under this seal bearing the protocol *rex Anglie et Francie et dominus Hibernie*, see E 43/645.

periods of time, it could perhaps be argued that these and other similar discrepancies simply did not matter to contemporaries, who were careless or oblivious of the exact form and deeper meanings of the royal style.[67] But the suggestion already made about the continued use of exclusively 'English' heraldry on the (unchanged) seal of the seneschal of Gascony after 1340 suggests that the departmental and colonial secretariats may have been aware that they, unlike the English chancery, only enjoyed competence in their own relevant political units of the Plantagenet federation, and did not therefore need to accommodate the king's 'foreign' title to the kingdom of France within the legends of their seals. That this position might also have appealed to the recipients of instruments under those seals is further suggested by the changes in the legends on English coins after 1340. Whereas the established denomination of the penny continued to bear the simple style *Edwardus rex Anglie*, the crown took advantage of the currency reforms of 1343–51 to introduce the new legend, *rex Anglie et Francie et dominus Hibernie*, both on the new silver coins, the groat and half-groat, and on the new, high-denomination, gold currency. In the manner of the royal seals, this style was appropriately modified, according to the diplomatic situation, in 1360 and 1369.[68] This discrepancy of styles may suggest a kind of recognition that a denomination already in circulation before 1340 and intended specifically for English usage (the penny) need not, and perhaps ought not, to be altered, whereas new denominations – and particularly the gold coins, which were intended primarily for international trade – could appropriately bear the full range of the king's titles as they were expressed within his kingdom of England.

That these elements of inconsistency were not mere carelessness but arose from the very flexibility of Edward III's claims in France and the manner of their representation within his various dominions is also suggested by the pragmatic usage of the king's subsidiary titles in instruments relating to other

---

[67] It may be that the new deputed great seals made for the king's bench and common pleas in 1344 bore the legend *rex Anglie et Francie* (and were, therefore, like the great seal itself, put into storage in 1360–9): *Foedera*, III2, 868; B. Wilkinson, 'The Seals of the Two Benches under Edward III', *EHR* 42 (1927), 397–401 (p. 399). Contrary to the suggestion that recipients of royal letters were careless of form, we may note the concern of contemporaries to have royal instruments re-issued under the current great seal: for a pertinent example, see *English Gilds*, ed. T. Smith, Early English Text Society 40 (London, 1870), p. 227 and n.

[68] H. B. Earle Fox and J. S. Shirley-Fox, 'Numismatic History of the Reigns of Edward I, II and III', *British Numismatic Journal* 1st s. 10 (1913), 95–123; L. A. Lawrence, *The Coinage of Edward III from 1351* (Oxford, 1937); W. J. W. Potter, 'The Silver Coinage of Edward III from 1351', *Numismatic Chronicle* 6th s. 20 (1960), 137–81; 7th s. 2 (1962), 203–24. The additional iconographic elements included in the gold currency – the quartered royal arms and the image of the king aboard a ship of war – certainly say much for the potential use of these coins in expressing and disseminating Edward III's explicit challenge to the Valois regime: B. Cook, 'English Coinage under Edward III', in *Age of Chivalry*, ed. Alexander and Binski, pp. 490–3 (catalogue nos. 660–8).

parts of his real or theoretical dominions. The decision not to adopt the recommendation made early in Edward's reign and include all the king's lesser titles within the standard royal style meant that instruments relating to particular parts of his empire sometimes deviated from the chancery's norms and deployed a relevant 'local' usage. This was regular practice before 1340 within the established areas of Plantagenet jurisdiction: it is found, for example, in instruments relating to the county of Ponthieu.[69] It was natural, therefore, that it should be deployed over a wider geographical area when the king sought alliances within the kingdom of France. In November 1339 he used the title of count of Toulouse in order to secure the allegiance of certain dissidents of that region against Philip VI; and in the 1350s he more famously exercised the title of 'duke of Normandy' in various instruments concerning Godfrey Harcourt and other Norman lords who had defected from the Valois regime and were making common cause with Edward against John II.[70] As John le Patourel argued, such variations of style signalled Edward III's sympathy with regional sensitivities in France and were therefore a necessary part of the so-called 'provincial strategy' operated through alliances in Flanders, Brittany, Normandy and elsewhere.[71]

One of the most interesting examples of the impact of this phenomenon upon royal diplomatic and the royal style is provided by the town of Calais, captured by the English in 1347.[72] Jurisdictionally, the town lay within the county of Artois, part of the dominions of the duke of Burgundy: in granting Calais a charter in 1347, Edward was acting as king of France and feudal suzerain of the immediate lord of the town. In theory, the situation was transformed by the treaty of Brétigny, which at once deprived Edward of the French royal title and gave him sovereignty over Calais, together with the adjoining territories of Marck and Guînes. It still remained uncertain, however, as to how his authority might be articulated locally. There is some suggestion that the local administration sought to represented him as count of Guînes. There is other evidence, from the series of deputed seals put into commission in the 1360s, that Calais, Marck and Guînes might have been jurisdictionally assimilated into the county of Ponthieu, which Edward ruled by hereditary right and also acquired in full sovereignty under the terms of the 1360 settlement.[73] The re-opening of the war

---

[69] *EMDP*, I1, 154.

[70] C. Johnson, 'An Act of Edward III as Count of Toulouse', in *Essays in History Presented to R. L. Poole*, ed. H. W. C. Davis (Oxford, 1927), pp. 399–404; J. Le Patourel, 'Edouard III, "roi de France et duc de Normandie"', *Révue historique du droit français et étranger* 4th s. 31 (1953), 317–18; W. M. Ormrod, 'England, Normandy and the Beginnings of the Hundred Years War, 1259–1360', in *England and Normandy in the Middle Ages*, ed. D. Bates and A. Curry (London, 1994), pp. 197–213 (p. 205).

[71] Le Patourel, *Feudal Empires*, chap. XI, XII, XV.

[72] For what follows, see Le Patourel, *Feudal Empires*, chap. XIV.

[73] For the existence of a great seal for 'the sovereignty of Ponthieu, Guînes, Marck and Calais', see *Antient Kalendars*, ed. Palgrave, I, 193; S. B. Storey-Challenger, *L'administration anglaise du Ponthieu, 1361–1369* (Abbeville, 1975), p. 102.

in 1369 seems to have put a stop to such experiments, and the burgesses of Calais (as distinct from the English colonists there) reverted to calling Edward 'king of France and England' in recognition of the fact that incontrovertible sovereignty could only now be claimed again through the active exercise of the French title.[74] These shifts in the constitutional status and political identity of Calais suggest a willingness on the part of the English crown to adapt the manner of its claim to jurisdiction there in such a way that not only ensured the town's preservation as a crucial element in English military and economic organization but also gave at least some consideration to its historical and cultural identity as part of northern France.

If this particular case reinforces the main line of the argument outlined above, then it becomes apparent that the employment of the royal style within England during and after 1340 also has interesting things to tell us about the way in which Edward III managed to make the French claim acceptable and attractive to the domestic political community. Both the king and his people clearly enjoyed elaborate titles. The chancery was assiduous in addressing the kings of the Iberian peninsula, for example, by their full panoply of titles: the king of Castile was styled 'king of Castile, Leon, Toledo, Galicia, Cordova, Murcia, Jaen and Algarves and count of Molina'.[75] It was under Edward III that the king's subjects also began to elaborate the opening clauses of their petitions to apostrophize the king with phrases such as 'our most gracious and most redoubted lord'.[76] Some continued in the manner of the petitions of early 1340 quoted above and deviated from the normal diplomatic to style Edward as 'king of England and France'.[77] One petitioner in 1360 even went so far as to address him as 'the mightiest king of all the world'.[78] It is hardly surprising, given the complexity of the arrangements worked out for the formal statements of the royal style after 1340, that both the king's clerks and the king's subjects sometimes made mistakes.[79] The use of two regnal years, one for England and one for France, was a particular trial in this respect, resulting in errors being made even in such an important document as the roll of proceedings of the great council of September 1353.[80] Despite these

---

[74] For example, SC 8/177/8814.

[75] *Foedera*, II2, 1207, 1226, 1232–3; III1, 19–20, 21, 25, 27, etc.

[76] For datable variations on this theme see SC 8/227/11344 (1373); SC 8/227/11342 (1376); SC 8/246/12286 (1353); SC 8/247/12303 (1356); SC 8/247/12313 (1361); SC 8/247/12332 (1375). The significance of this new elaboration is discussed by N. Saul, 'Richard II and the Vocabulary of Kingship', *EHR* 110 (1995), 854–77 (p. 858).

[77] C 81/341/20564 (1349); SC 8/178/8867 (1354); SC 8/246/12279 (1351).

[78] SC 8/247/12318. I owe this reference to Dr Anthony Verduyn.

[79] *EMDP*, I1, 155.

[80] *RP*, II, 246 (checked against the original), where the regnal date is twice given as 28 Edw III (England) and 15 Edw III (France): it ought to have been expressed as 14 Edw III (France). It is to be remarked that after the re-assertion of the French title in 1369, the headings to the parliament rolls expressed the regnal date only in its

complications, however, the royal secretariat held firm throughout the periods 1340–60 and 1369–77 to the clear distinction established between those instruments issued by the 'king of France and England' and those made in the name of the 'king of England and France'. That France was included, and given formal precedence, in the protocols and dating clauses of diplomatic proceedings with the Valois regime could perhaps be said to represent little more than the maintenance of an increasingly untenable position, rather as (in a different context) the English crown had stubbornly continued to treat Scotland as a 'land' and to deny the existence of the Bruce monarchy between 1306 and 1328.[81] In this sense, Richard II's increasing tendency to place England before France in diplomatic as well as domestic business, and Henry IV's decision to reverse the title on the great seal to read *rex Anglie et Francie*, were a belated and open acknowledgment of the fact that the claim to France had become merely a token gesture, preserved within the royal style merely to save face and to provide a residual diplomatic bargaining position.[82] In another sense, however, the very persistence of these stylistic formulae through the long periods of war and truce under Edward III provided a message to the king's English subjects about the legitimacy of his double monarchy and, through their manipulation into forms of precedence acceptable to this domestic audience, helped to convince the king's subjects that their own support of this double monarchy was both appropriate and positively beneficial for the kingdom of England.[83]

English form. In 1345 a clerk endorsed a petition with a note 'ceste bille fust io onande par le roi le viij iour de Septembre l'an du regne le roi de France . . .', and then, realizing his mistake in placing France before England, continued, '. . . et d'Engleterre cest assavoir d'Angleterre xix et France vj . . .': SC 8/207/10317.

[81] M. Prestwich, 'England and Scotland during the Wars of Independence', in *England and Her Neighbours*, ed. Jones and Vale, pp. 181–97.

[82] Chaplais, 'English Diplomatic Documents', pp. 50–1; Michael, 'Little Land of England', p. 123. It was still, however, considered necessary to assert the title *rex Francie et Anglie* in documents referring specifically to the king's rights in France: for the deployment of Edward III's great seal for this purpose, for example in 1420, and the adoption of a special seal bearing the title *rex Francie et Anglie* for a similar reason under Edward IV, see Jenkinson, 'Deputed or Departmental Seals', pp. 310–13. For more on Edward III's claim to the French throne, see Craig Taylor, below.

[83] Discussion of the impact of the double monarchy on English domestic politics requires more space than is allowed here, but an instructive contrast may be drawn between the propaganda statements of the origins and aims of the French war made in 1337 (which represented it as a feudal dispute) and 1346 (which emphasized the dynastic dispute): *English Historical Documents 1327–1485*, ed. Myers, pp. 62–3; *Foedera*, III1, 72–3. For further discussion, see W. M. Ormrod, 'The Double Monarchy of Edward III', *Medieval History* 13 (1991), 68–80 (pp. 76–7); W. M. Ormrod, 'The Domestic Response to the Hundred Years War', in *Arms, Armies and Fortifications in the Hundred Years War*, ed. A. Curry and M. Hughes (Woodbridge, 1994), pp. 83–101 (pp. 99–101).

8

Edward III and the Plantagenet Claim to the French Throne

CRAIG TAYLOR

The title of King of France was one of England's stage properties . . . No one dreamed of justifying it: it was part of the succession. (Edouard Perroy)[1]

In 1340, Edward III officially laid claim to the French throne and thereby transformed his struggle with Philip VI, the Valois king of France, from a feudal squabble between liege lord and vassal into a war between two contenders for the royal succession. In practice, this claim to the throne remained a secondary goal for the English during the Hundred Years War, at core a bargaining tool in their negotiations for an expansion of their continental empire and an end to French sovereignty over those lands.[2] Moreover it enabled Edward III to defend alliances with enemies of the French crown such as Lewis of Bavaria and the Flemings, who were in turn able to pose as supporters of the true king of France against the Valois usurpers: the Flemings informed Benedict XII that they could not be excommunicated for breaking their oaths to the crown because Edward was the rightful king of France.[3] This Machiavellian manipulation of Edward's claim to the French throne for ulterior ends has led many historians to dismiss the

---

[1] E. Perroy, *The Hundred Years War* (London, 1951), p. 213. Perroy also described the dynastic issue as 'preposterous' in 'Franco-English Relations, 1350–1400', *History* 21 (1936–7), 148–54 (p. 154). I am very grateful to Norma Aubertin-Potter, James Bothwell, Peter Lewis and Mark Ormrod for their help and advice. My particular thanks go to Ralph Giesey for allowing me to see his notes on the English legal brief used at Avignon in 1344: he will be pleased to see that this text has a much wider manuscript history and significance than his preliminary work on the eighteenth-century French transcription in Paris, Bibliothèque Nationale, MS Moreau 699 revealed. I intend to examine the complete body of unpublished materials relating to Edward III's claim to the French throne in a future publication.

[2] J. Le Patourel, *Feudal Empires: Norman and Plantagenet* (London, 1984), chap. XII; J. J. N. Palmer, 'The War Aims of the Protagonists and the Negotiations for Peace', in *The Hundred Years War*, ed. K. Fowler (London, 1971), pp. 51–74.

[3] H. S. Lucas, *The Low Countries and the Hundred Years War, 1326–47* (Ann Arbor, 1927), pp. 328–74.

actual legal foundations of that title, influenced also by the pervasive notion that the Salic Law confined the royal succession in France to males in direct line and hence barred Edward from inheriting a claim through his mother, Isabelle.[4] This myth was firmly established by the anonymous French treatise *Pour ce que plusieurs* (1464) when it was published in conjunction with Claude de Seyssel's *La grande monarchie de France* in 1507, 1541 and 1557: the anonymous author even claimed that Edward III had publicly accepted that Philip of Valois was rightful heir to the French throne because of the Salic Law.[5] Yet in reality this was an otiose Frankish law concerning private inheritance that could have no direct bearing on the royal succession; moreover, it is clear that the Salic Law was not used by official Valois writers until around 1413, when Jean de Montreuil added a marginal note to a text that he had originally composed in 1406.[6] Little is known about the arguments actually used to justify the Valois succession during the reigns of Philip VI and Jean II but English lawyers were certainly able to present a powerful defence of the Plantagenet claim to the French throne in a range of documents, particularly a lengthy legal opinion and summary credence used by English diplomats sent to Avignon in 1340 and 1344.[7] These materials demonstrate that, at least from a legal standpoint, Edward III was able to mount an effective challenge to Philip of Valois' accession to the French throne.

On 1 February 1328, Charles IV, king of France and last son of Philip the Fair, died. Given the precedents set in 1316 and 1322, there was no question that either of his daughters (one of whom was born posthumously) might succeed to the French throne and so there were three contenders for the throne. Edward III, king of England, was the nearest male heir as the son of Charles

---

[4] See, e.g., *The Poems of Laurence Minot, 1333–1352*, ed. R. H. Osberg (Kalamazoo, Mich., 1996), p. 67, n. 45; A. G. Rigg, 'John of Bridlington's Prophecy: a New Look', *Speculum* 63 (1988), 596–613 (pp. 608–10).

[5] J. M. Potter, 'The Development and Significance of the Salic Law of the French', *EHR* 52 (1937), 235–53 (pp. 249–50). *Pour ce que plusieurs* was also published in Rouen in 1488 and 1522.

[6] N. Pons and E. Ornato, 'Qui est l'auteur de la chronique latine de Charles VI, dite du religieux de Saint Denis?', *Bibliothèque de l'Ecole des Chartes* 134 (1976), 91–3. Montreuil's work influenced a series of official Valois writers, mainly based in the *chambre des comptes*. See my forthcoming article, '*La vraye loy des François*: the Salic Law and the Plantagenet Claim to the French Throne'.

[7] For the English materials, see footnote 16 below. A number of writers in the entourage of Charles V addressed the question including, most prominently, Nicole Oresme: 'Maistre Nicole Oresme, *Le livre de politiques d'Aristote*', ed. A. D. Menut, *Transactions of the American Philosophical Society* 60 (1970), 155b–156a (book II, chap. 23); *Le songe du vergier: édité d'après le manuscrit Royal 19 C IV de la British Library*, ed. M. Schnerb-Liévre, 2 vols. (Paris, 1982), I, chap. 142; *Somnium viridarii*, ed. M. Schnerb-Liévre, 2 vols. (Paris, 1993–7), I, chap. 186. The issue was also raised briefly by François de Meyronnes, Thomas Waleys and Raoul de Presles in their commentaries on St Augustine's *De civitate dei*.

IV's sister, Isabelle, but the nearest heirs in direct male line were two cousins, Philip of Valois and Philip of Evreux. Unfortunately, little is known of the arguments used by Edward III's proctors at the assembly of notables which met to determine the situation, or indeed of the wider discussion of the royal succession during that meeting. But there can be little doubt that Philip of Valois was chosen as king for political rather than legal reasons. He had already been appointed regent upon the death of Charles IV and offered the greatest hope for stability for the country; not only did he have a clear power base and political support in France, but he was also twenty years older than the teenage Edward III and the latter was still very much under the control of Isabelle and Mortimer.[8] Yet Edward did not immediately renounce his claim to the throne: on 28 March he wrote to the seneschal of Gascony and the constable of Bordeaux, indicating his continued desire to recover 'our rights and our inheritances' and on 16 May, he instructed the bishops of Worcester and Chichester to put forward his claim as rightful heir to the French crown. But Philip VI's victory over the Flemish rebels left the English without sufficient support to prosecute Edward's claim and so he paid homage to the new French king at Amiens on 6 June 1329.[9]

According to a number of French chronicles, Edward III was encouraged to resurrect the claim to the French throne in 1337 by Robert of Artois, who was taking refuge against Philip VI at the English court. Yet the decision to lay claim to the crown must be seen within a wider context of deteriorating Anglo-French relations, affected not just by the English protection of Robert of Artois but also piracy in the Channel, tensions in Aquitaine and French interference in Scotland.[10] A royal council held in the Tower of London on 23 January 1337 discussed the king's right to the French throne, advising the king to seek peace with Philip VI, strengthen his own fleet and secure aid from friends against the unjust occupation of the French realm.[11] Yet after Philip VI's efforts to confiscate the duchy of Aquitaine began in May, Edward made an alliance

---

[8] P. Viollet, 'Comment les femmes ont été exclues, en France, de la succession à la couronne', *Mémoires de l'Académie des inscriptions et belles-lettres* 34 (1895), 125–78; E. Déprez, *Les préliminaires de la Guerre de Cent Ans: la papauté, la France et l'Angleterre, 1328–1342* (Paris, 1902), pp. 27–37; R. Cazelles, *La société politique et la crise de la royauté sous Philippe de Valois* (Paris, 1958), pp. 35–73.

[9] *Foedera*, ed. T. Rymer, 3rd edn (The Hague, 1739), II3, 9, 13 and 27.

[10] The Artois story appears in Jean le Bel, Geoffrey le Baker and Jean de Venette, and may have originated in the poem, the Vow of the Heron. Déprez, *Les préliminaires de la Guerre de Cent Ans*, pp. 224–6. Also see H. Jenkins, *Papal Efforts for Peace Under Benedict XII, 1334–42* (Philadelphia, 1933); J. Campbell, 'England, Scotland and the Hundred Years War', in *Europe in the Late Middle Ages*, ed. J. R. Hale, J. R. L. Highfield and B. Smalley (London, 1965), pp. 184–216 (pp. 184–91); and M. G. A. Vale, *The Origins of the Hundred Years War: the Angevin Legacy, 1250–1340* (Oxford, 1990), pp. 244–65.

[11] R. M. Haines, *Archbishop John Stratford: Political Revolutionary and Champion of the Liberties of the English Church, ca. 1275/80–1348* (Toronto, 1986), pp. 244–5.

against the French with Lewis of Bavaria and then issued letters patent on 7 October, styling himself 'king of France and England'.[12] Benedict XII persuaded both sides to accept a series of truces, but on 6 May 1338 Edward revoked his promise to the papal nuncios not to invade France and subsequently crossed to Antwerp where, on 22 July 1338, he revoked the procurations given to his ambassadors to negotiate with Philip of Valois: Edward expressed concern lest these documents be taken as a recognition that Philip was the legitimate ruler of France. When the English king was persuaded to send further envoys in November 1338 and in July 1339, their instructions did not refer to Philip as king of France, but rather as the 'one who called himself king of France'.[13] In a letter addressed to Boniface very shortly afterwards, Edward cited his natural right to defend himself against flagrant injustices, including Philip of Valois' usurpation of the French throne, the invasion and attempted confiscation of Aquitaine, and the French alliance with the Scottish vassals of the English crown.[14] Six months later, the Plantagenet claim to the French throne took centre stage when Edward officially assumed the title of king of France on 25 January 1340.[15]

English lawyers quickly produced a credence defending the Plantagenet claim to the French throne and William Bateman, dean of Lincoln, John Offord, archdeacon of Ely, and John Thoresby, canon of Southwell, then delivered this document to Benedict XII in November 1340. This sealed schedule, shorn of all legal citations, offered an abbreviated version of a much fuller 'factum' which was subsequently used by Bateman, Offord and the English delegation that attended the conference at Avignon in October and November 1344; these envoys carried a dossier that included not just the 'factum' itself, but also a genealogical account of the descendants of Philip IV, an abbreviated copy of Edward's homage to Philip VI in 1329 and a copy of the credence originally presented to Benedict XII in 1340. This dossier was published over a century ago by Kervyn de Lettenhove, drawing upon an eighteenth-century French transcription of the earliest English manuscript, itself dating from the end of the fourteenth century. Unfortunately Lettenhove suppressed all but two of the legal citations in the text, along with a number of key passages from the original document, and it is therefore perhaps not surprising that historians have paid almost no attention to this important material.[16]

---

[12] *EMDP*, I1, 154–5. For more detail on this, see W. M. Ormrod, above.
[13] *Foedera*, II4, 29–30, 39 and 49, and Jenkins, *Papal Efforts for Peace under Benedict XII*, pp. 31–69.
[14] The letter, dated 16 July 1339, also sought to justify Edward's alliance with Lewis of Bavaria, and was cited by both Adam Murimuth and Robert of Avesbury. *Adae Murimuth, continuatio chronicarum. Robertus de Avesbury, De gestis mirabilus regis Edwardi tertii*, ed. E. M. Thompson (London, 1889), pp. 91–100 and 303.
[15] From that point until 24 October 1360, Edward was usually styled *rex Anglie et Francie* in documents relating to domestic affairs and Scotland, and *rex Francie et Anglie* in relations with continental rulers. *EMDP*, I1, 154–5; Ormrod, above.
[16] The complete dossier from the 1344 conference, along with English accounts of the

The English case rested upon the central contention that Edward III was the nearest male heir of Charles IV, king of France: Edward was the nephew of the last Capetian king, and hence a kinsman in the second degree, while Philip of Valois was the cousin of Charles VI and thus related in the third degree. The English lawyers certainly accepted that women could not inherit the French throne because otherwise the daughters of the last three Capetian kings, not to mention Edward's mother, Isabelle, would have held a superior claim to the crown to the English king.[17] But why should the principle that women were incapable of inheriting the French throne affect Edward? The crucial issue was that:

> If it is said by this edict that a woman cannot succeed in the kingdom of France, it can be said that this will not hurt the son unless express mention is made of him.[18]

Yet when the public assembly first rejected the claim of Jeanne de France to inherit from her father in February 1317, they could have said nothing about males claiming through the female line because that possibility simply did not arise then. As the genealogies contained in the English memorandum demonstrated, Jeanne had had no son at the time when her father and brother died in close succession.[19] Similarly when Philip V died in 1322, none of his daughters had sons; the eldest girl was married to Eudes, duke of Burgundy, but their son 'Robert had died before his grandfather, king Philip, himself died'.[20] In short, the question of cognate succession did not arise until Charles IV died in 1328 leaving a proximate male heir whose claim came through a woman for the very first time. Thus the English lawyers emphasised that the exclusion of women

---

meeting and various letters, is preserved in BL MS Cotton Cleopatra E ii, and an eighteenth-century transcription, [Paris,] B[ibliothèque] N[ationale,] MS Moreau 699, and was edited in Jean Froissart, *Chroniques*, ed. Kervyn de Lettenhove, 25 vols. (Brussels, 1867–77), XVIII, 235–56. The credence originally presented to Benedict XII in November 1340 also appears in Vatican, Archivio Segreto Vaticano, Reg. Vat. 135, fols. 112v–115r, edited in *Benoît XII (1334–1342): lettres closes et patentes*, ed. Vidal (Paris, 1935), fascicule IV, number 2982. Pierre Chaplais has combined the original credence with the fuller legal opinion in *EMDP*, I2, 438–52.

[17] The summary document presented to the pope simply stated that '[mulier] juris hereditarii regni Francie non est capax': *EMDP*, I2, 451. In 1389, English diplomats cited the Salic Law to emphasise that the exclusion of women from the French royal succession could not therefore extend to males claiming through women. The French replied: 'par lestatut que vueullent alleguer les gens du roy dAngleterre qui est en la loy salique, la terre doit venir au sexe masculin qui est la ligne masculine en excluant la ligne femenine, tant les femmes comme les masles qui delles seroient descenduz.' BN MS Nouvelle Acquisition Française 6215, fol. 28v.

[18] *EMDP*, I2, 440: 'Item si dicatur quod statutum est super hoc editum quod mulier in regno Francie non succedat, dici potest quod hoc non nocebit filio, nisi de eo expressa fiat mencio.'

[19] *EMDP*, I2, 448–9 and 451. Jeanne's son Charles was not born until 1332.

[20] *EMDP*, I2, 449 and 451–2.

from the French royal succession was a recent development, a statutory
enactment of the assemblies that met between 1316 and 1322, which could
not have ruled against cognate succession.[21] Edward's lawyers initially stated
that the exclusion of women from the royal succession was established 'by
custom or statute' (*consuetudine vel statuto*), but subsequently described it as
'this custom, if it ought to be called a custom' and then 'the established and
lawfully prescribed custom in the kingdom of France'. The crucial issue was
that this law did not derive its authority from long-standing practice, but rather
from the specific decisions of the assemblies that met between 1316 and 1322.[22]

Thus the English argued that there could have been no French law barring
cognates from the royal succession when Edward laid claim to the throne in
1328, because 'a custom does not extend to more than is directly prescribed by
it'. Thus the only authority capable of resolving the debate was Roman law: the
'*Libri feudorum* holds expressly that in cases about which custom does not
speak expressly, recourse is had to written law.'[23] But, according to the English,
Roman law did permit the son of a daughter to be admitted to the succession of
the lord: in the parlance of the fifteenth-century Valois writers, she could act as
a *pont et planche* through which her son could inherit the throne. Women were
excluded from the royal succession just as in Roman Law; they were not
allowed to exercise guardianship (*tutela*) or to hold civil or public offices.[24] But
why should this incapacity extend to their sons? After all, *Digest*. 5.1.12 offered
a crucial commentary on the exclusion of women from public offices:

> By nature the deaf, the mute, the insane, and minors, because they are
> wanting in judgment; . . . by custom women and slaves, not because they do

---

[21] *EMDP*, I2, 445: 'Preterea statutum illud editum fuit post nativitatem dicti Edwardi,
ejus matre tunc et adhuc superstite.'

[22] *EMDP*, I2, 439, 440 and 449: 'mulier non poterit neque debet, obstante consuetudine
in regno Francie approbata et legitime prescripta, admitti ad obtinendum jure
successorio dictum regnum.' Custom was generally regarded as long-standing
practice that became prescriptive through official legal recognition, though it is
important to note that many French lawyers did accept that a single act might be
enough to establish a custom if it genuinely expressed the consent of the people.
L. Waelkens, *La théorie de la coutume chez Jacques de Révigny. Edition et analyse de sa
répétition sur la loi 'De quibus'* (D. 1, 3, 32) (Leiden, 1984), pp. 262–72.

[23] *EMDP*, I2, 440: 'Consuetudo enim ad plus non extenditur quam in quo prescribitur,
Digest. 43.19.1.5, et habetur expresse in *Libri feudorum*. 2.1.1, ubi dicit quod, in casu ubi
consuetudo expresse non loquitur, ad jus scriptum recurritur, set de jure scripto filius
filie ad successionem admittitur, ergo et rex Anglie ad successionem in regno Francie'.

[24] *EMDP*, I2, 443: '. . . de jure civili digestorum mulier non est apta persona ut tutele
officio fungatur, quia virile munus est et ultra sexus feminee infirmitatis tale
officium est', citing *Digest*. 26.1.18 ('foeminae tutores dari non possunt, quia id
munus masculorum est'); *Digest*. 26.2.26 ('Iure nostro tutela communium liberorum
matri, testamento patris frustra mandatur est'); *Digest*. 50.17.2 ('Foeminae ab
omnibus officiis civilibus vel publicis remotae sunt'); *Codex*. 5.35.1 ('Tutelam
administrare, virile munus est, & ultra sexum foeminae infirmitatis tale officium
est').

not have judgment, but because it is received that they do not administer civil offices.[25]

Thus women were excluded from judicial offices solely because of received custom and not because they lacked the natural aptitude to make sound judgment. The relevance to the case at hand was clear: the custom excluding a woman from the French royal succession was not based upon her inherent incapacity to rule and so could not prejudice the rights of her son to rule. Perhaps more importantly, in AD 543, the emperor Justinian had issued the edict, *Novel* 118, which swept away the differences between agnates and cognates: he declared that the right to be a guardian did pass through a woman to her son if he were the nearest male relative of the ward.[26] Thus the English lawyers argued that:

> The governance of the realm compromises the supreme guardianship of the realm, along with the dignity or office of adjudication . . . To the exercise of which tutelage, granted the incapacity of a woman who is the sister of the defunct . . ., her son, the nearest consanguine heir to the defunct king should be preferred in succession to the defunct to whomsoever is more remote in grade of consanguinity, even if he be an agnate, since the difference between agnates and cognates has been voided by *Novel* 118.[27]

In short, the English case was that the Roman custom preventing women from exercising guardianship and civil or public offices had to be construed in a strictly limited fashion, and thus could have no effect upon her son's right to such duties: 'this custom, if it ought to be called a custom, affects only the person of the mother and not the son'.[28]

In summary, the English did not challenge the notion that there was a law

---

[25] *Digest.* 5.1.12: '.. ne sint iudices, quidam natura, quidam moribus. Natura, ut surdus, mutus, & perpetuo furiosus, & impubes, quia judicio carent . . . Moribus, foeminae, & servi, non quia non habent iudicium, sed quia receptus est, ut civilibus officiis non fungantur'.

[26] *Novel* 118 was confirmed by *Novel* 127 in AD 548. W. W. Buckland, *A Text-book of Roman Law from Augustus to Justinian*, rev. P. Stein (Cambridge, 1963), pp. 142–50 and 367–75; B. Nicholas, *An Introduction to Roman Law* (Oxford, 1962), pp. 237–8 and 243–51.

[27] *EMDP*, I2, 443–4: 'Regimen etenim regni tutelam suppreman regni continet cum dignitate seu offico judicandi, *Decret. Grat.* II, 23.5.23 ubi dicitur: Regnum est proprie facere judicium. Ad quam tutelam exercendam, licet mulier soror defuncti sit inhabilis, *Digest.* 5.1.12 et nota in glossa ordinaria *Codex.* 5.4.23.4 super verbo "dignitatem", filius tamen ejus, videlicet defuncti regis, consanguineus proximus consanguineo quocumque ipsius defuncti in gradu consanguinitatis remociori existenti, licet agnatus fuerit, preferetur, cum, quantum ad successionem pertinet, sit omnino inter agnatos et cognatos differencia vacuata, in eadem autentica, *Novel.* 118.4. Mulieres etenim dignitatem cum administracione habere non possunt ut in glosa, *Codex.* 5.4.23.4, super verbo "dignitatem".'

[28] *EMDP*, I2, 440: 'Praeterea hec consuetudo, si consuetudo dici debeat, inficit tantum personam matris et non filii.'

against female succession to the French throne but rejected the further claim that there was a special French law that extended this prohibition to cognates. The proper authority to determine the validity of Edward's claim in 1328 was written law, and at the very least this offered conflicting authorities because of the actions of Justinian who had wiped away the distinction between agnates and cognates in AD 543. Of course, the Valois diplomats also noted that Edward had publicly accepted the superiority of Philip VI's claim to the French throne by paying liege homage to the new king for the duchies of Aquitaine and Ponthieu. But in response, the English lawyers cited the fact that Edward had been a minor at the time that he had paid homage to Philip and hence could not have lost any of his rights. Roman law provided a host of rules supporting the protection of minors, and customary law was equally firm on this matter: no span of years could prevent a rightful legal heir from recovering an estate of which he had been cheated as a minor. Moreover they noted that when Edward had paid homage in 1329, he had expressly stated that he was not thereby harming any of his hereditary rights or renouncing his claim to the French throne.[29] Thus the dossier carried by the English diplomats in 1340 and 1344 may not have provided a conclusive defence of the Plantagenet title to the French throne, but it certainly presented a significant legal challenge to Philip of Valois.

What precise role did this dossier play in the negotiations and in the wider field of English propaganda?[30] Clearly the primary function of the dossier was as a work of reference for William Bateman, John Offord and the English envoys to Avignon in 1344, for whom the Plantagenet claim had become the most crucial weapon in their armoury.[31] Clement VI tried to persuade them to set aside the dynastic question and instead focus upon the tensions arising from the status of the king of England as a vassal of the French crown. But the English diplomats declared that:

> . . . the previous peace made in Gascony [in 1327] was agreed in order to resolve the disagreements first arising over the lands within the duchy between the king of France as suzerain on the one hand and the duke of Guyenne as his vassal on the other. But this present treaty ought to be made between our lord the king on the one hand and his adversary on the other, in order to resolve, with God's grace, the war and the tensions that have arisen between them due to and because of the realm of France and the crown.[32]

[29] *EMDP*, I2, 445–7 and 449–51.
[30] For further discussion of Edward III's use of propaganda, see A. K. McHardy, below.
[31] The course of the negotiations between 22 October and 29 November is set out in the English journal of the conference, together with the letters that they sent to Edward III and members of the government, printed in Froissart, *Chroniques*, XVIII, 202–56, and also see E. Déprez, 'La conférence d'Avignon (1344)', in *Essays in Medieval History Presented to T. F. Tout*, ed. A. G. Little and F. M. Powicke (Manchester, 1925), pp. 301–20.
[32] Froissart, *Chroniques*, XVIII, 222: '. . . la dite pees faite en Gascoygne fuist faite pur

The cardinals mediating between the two sides proposed that Edward give up his lands in France, but could not suggest suitable compensation for Aquitaine: Philip VI could hardly afford to buy Aquitaine, the lands of the Hospitallers in England were not sufficient to balance such losses and Scotland could hardly serve as compensation given that it was already subject to the English crown. Thus the English diplomats were able to reject these attempts to find a compromise, along with the proposal that Edward grant the duchy to one of his sons who could then hold the duchy under the suzerainty of Philip VI and his heirs: if such a plan had been adopted, Edward would have lost his rights to Aquitaine, but, more importantly, it would have implicitly denied Edward's rightful claim to be king of France. In other words, even though the English diplomats emphasised their willingness to seek a negotiated peace, they clung to the dynastic claim which presented an insuperable obstacle to attempts to find a settlement. Ultimately, the only solution acceptable to the English diplomats was that Edward III hold Aquitaine as an allod, free from the lordship and interference of the French crown: this *bonum initium* to the negotiations presumably represented their price for Edward III's renunciation of his claim to the French throne. But the cardinals rejected this proposal because Aquitaine could not be separated from the French crown, despite English claims that it had originally been an independent allod.[33]

It was common practice for both French and English envoys to make use of complex legal opinions during high-level negotiations, particularly during meetings before the papacy or cardinals. Philip Martel and Raymond de la Ferrière had advised Edward I on the debate over Aquitaine, and in 1369, two legal opinions by John de Legnano and Richard Saliceto, doctors of Bologna, were used by the French to justify their abandonment of the treaty of Brétigny (1360).[34] In 1344, the English diplomats were almost

apeiser les dissentions primerement meues par occasion des terres de la duchee entre le roi de France comme seignur cheveteyn d'une part et le duk de Guyenne come son vassal d'autre part; mes ceste tretee en present se doit faire entre nostre seigneur le roi que hore est de une part et son dit adversaire d'autre part, pur apeser, se Dieu plest, la guerre et les dissentions meues entre eux par occasion et cause du roialme de France et de la corone.'

33 Froissart, *Chroniques*, XVIII, 242–3 and 248. For the development of the English case that Guyenne was originally an allod, see H. Rothwell, 'Edward I's Case against Philip the Fair over Gascony', *EHR* 42 (1927), 572–82; P. Chaplais, 'English Arguments Concerning the Feudal Status of Aquitaine in the Fourteenth Century', *BIHR* 21 (1946–8), 203–13. For the importance of this debate in the wider development of concepts of inalienability in France, see my forthcoming article, *'Lez pierres precieuses de la couronne:* English Territorial Claims and the Development of the Concept of Inalienability'.

34 *EMDP*, I2, 422–30 and P. Chaplais, 'Some Documents Regarding the Fulfilment and Interpretation of the Treaty of Brétigny (1361–1369): II. The Opinions of the Doctors of Bologna on the Sovereignty of Aquitaine (1369): a Source of the *Songe du vergier'*, *Camden Miscellany XIX*, Camden 3rd s. 80 (1952), pp. 51–78. Various legal opinions

certainly using the lengthy legal opinion themselves, while the brief summary document, originally given to Benedict XII in November 1340, presumably served as a simple position paper for distribution to the pope and perhaps also the cardinals.[35] Thus the principal function of the dossier was to equip the diplomats with the necessary materials with which to defend Edward's rights. For example, the cardinals twice observed that Edward III had paid homage to Philip of Valois and thereby recognised his right to the French crown. In reply, the English cited the arguments contained in their legal brief, particularly the fact that the ceremony of homage at Amiens in 1329 could have not prejudiced the rights of their king.[36] In this context, it is important to note that the dossier made frequent reference to the principle of just war: for example, it noted that the king of France did not recognise any superior in temporal affairs and hence that there was no suitable authority to rule on the dispute between Edward and Philip of Valois, which inevitably meant that the 'Querelle' would have to be settled on the battlefield.[37] Thus the diplomats were armed with the material not just to press the dynastic claim as a lever through which to secure an independent Aquitaine, but perhaps more importantly to provide a public justification for the resort to war. The papacy was not likely to support the Plantagenet claim to the French throne: in a letter addressed to Edward in March 1340, Benedict indicated his clear support for the Valois title, influenced particularly by the French argument that if cognates could succeed to the French throne, then Charles of Navarre, grandson of Louis X, had a superior claim to Edward III.[38] Thus the English position at Avignon in 1344 was that 'it is not for us to offer suggestions for peace, but only to put forward our demand for the kingdom and to listen to the proposals that he [Clement VI] may put to us as mediator'.[39] They must have calculated that, at the very least, a stalemate at the conference would demonstrate the

---

were comissioned on the treaty of Troyes (1420); see, e.g., *EMDP*, I2, 636–47 and T. M. Izbicki, 'The Canonists and the Treaty of Troyes', in *Proceedings of the Fifth International Congress of Medieval Canon Law 1976* (Vatican, 1980), pp. 425–34. This piece has been heavily revised in an unpublished article by Professor Izbicki and Dr Margaret Harvey.

[35] See footnote 16 above.

[36] Froissart, *Chroniques*, XVIII, 241–2 and 246–7.

[37] *EMDP*, I2, 441: 'videtur quod rex Anglie possit manu militari procedere, cum aliud remedium non supersit. Quamvis enim in negocio privatorum non est manu militari procedendum, quia aliud ibi superest remedium eciam in execucione superioris auctoritate faciendum, secus hic, pro quo facit lex cum sua glosa, ff. *De rei vendicacione*, l. *Qui restituere* (*Digest.* 6.1.68). Et pro recuperacione rerum temporalium licitum est ad arma recurrere, C. *Unde vi*, l. I (Codex. 8.4.1).'

[38] *Foedera*, II4, 70.

[39] Froissart, *Chroniques*, XVIII, 222: 'a nous ne apartint pas montrer voye quelconque de pes, mes tant seulement esteer en nostre dite demaunde du roialme et oyer les voyes queles il mesmes nous vorroit monstrer come mediatour.'

ineffectiveness of the Pope and thus enable future diplomacy to be conducted without the interference of the papacy.[40]

But how far were the materials developed by the English lawyers used as wider propaganda? There is little evidence for the circulation of either the complex legal opinion or even the abbreviated summary document outside of official circles during the reign of Edward III. Adam Murimuth clearly had access to official documents emanating from the royal council, particularly relating to negotiations with the papacy, including Edward's letter to Benedict XII, dated 16 July 1339. This letter, which also appears in other chronicles, covered a wide range of ground but made very limited use of the technical, legal arguments developed by Bateman, Offord and the English lawyers.[41] Robert of Avesbury made use of a manifesto issued by Edward III on 8 February 1340, which also appears in the London letter books; this document again referred to Edward's position as king and natural lord of France, and to the Valois usurpation as a breach of divine law, but went little further in exploring the legal issues surrounding the dynastic claim.[42] Other chroniclers provided even less information: Knighton could not even provide an accurate account of the genealogical basis for Edward's claim to the French throne.[43] Turning to different sources, at least two writers had no knowledge of the case developed by Edward's lawyers and instead adopted entirely different arguments. The anonymous author of *An Invective against France* (1346) invoked a legendary dream in which the heirless Charles the Fat, great-grandson of Charlemagne, met his uncle Lothar and his cousin Louis, and was told by them to allow the throne to pass to Louis' grandson through his daughter Ermengard. The commentary upon the prophecies of John of Bridlington (1362–64) cited the Biblical story of Numbers 27 where Moses upheld the right of the daughters of Salphad to inherit from their father in the absence of male heirs, a precedent that actually worked against Edward III's official position and which the French were easily able to reject by citing the distinction between private inheritance and public property. Both texts cited a story that a French king, either Hugh Capet or Philip the Fair, had barred women from the royal succession out of shame at his own lowly origins and accession to the throne as the husband of a genuine princess.[44]

---

[40] The conference at Avignon had been delayed by negotiations over the precise status of the pope: it was agreed that Clement would act in a private capacity as arbitrator rather than as a judge, imposing a solution upon the two sides by his own authority. But the English were concerned that Clement VI was partial towards the French and were also involved in a heated debate over papal provision of benefices in England to foreigners. Déprez, 'La conférence d'Avignon (1344)', pp. 302–04.

[41] See footnote 14 above.

[42] *Adae Murimuth continuatio chronicarum Robertus de Avesbury de gestis mirabilus regis Edwardi tertii*, p. 309; *Calendar of Letter Books of the City of London*, ed. R. R. Sharpe, 11 vols. (London, 1899–1912), *Letter Book F*, p. 43 (French).

[43] *Knighton's Chronicle, 1337–1396*, ed. G. H. Martin (Oxford, 1995), p. 16.

[44] *Political Poems and Songs Relating to English History Composed During the Period from*

It is hardly surprising that contemporary sources had such limited knowledge of the legal basis of Edward's claim to the French throne, given that this hardly featured in official propaganda aimed at a wider audience. In general, such material focussed upon the need to defend the realm and also the rights of the king, rather than the legal basis for those rights.[45] Edward III probably did not inform his own subjects about the momentous decision to lay claim to the French crown until the writs for parliament were issued on 21 February 1340; even these simply used the title *Rex Anglie et Francie* without providing any discussion of the new title, and there is no indication that the claim was discussed in any detail in the subsequent parliament.[46] He made no attempt to set out a detailed justification for his claim to the French throne even for a continental audience. In his manifesto distributed across France on 8 February 1340, he preferred to present himself as the leader of an 'alternative government', playing very carefully upon the political sensibilities of the French: he promised to provide justice for all men and respect the privileges and liberties of everyone, especially the Church; to respect the customs and laws that had been in force since the time of that great king St Louis; to be guided by the counsel of the great magnates; to avoid unlawful taxation and the manipulation of currency. The threat posed by these documents is testified to by Philip VI's proclamation two weeks later, ordering his officials in Amiens to punish those in possession of this 'false, deceitful, treasonous and malicious' letter as traitors and to tear down copies from church doors and public squares.[47] That the English were hitting a raw nerve is shown by the rare hints about public attitudes, particularly in

the Accession of Edward III to That of Richard III, ed. T. Wright, 2 vols. (RS, 1859–61), I, 34–5 and 206–7, and see A. G. Rigg, 'The Legend of Hugh Capet: the English Tradition', in *The Centre and its Compass: Studies in Medieval Literature in Honour of Professor J. L. Legerle*, ed. R. A. Jaylon *et al.* (Kalamazoo, MI, 1993), pp. 389–406, together with G. Mombello, 'Une hypothèse sur l'origine d'une légende: Hugues Capet fils d'un boucher', in *Pratiques de la culture écrits en France au XVe siècle: Actes du colloque internationales de CNRS* (Louvain, 1995), pp. 179–90.

[45] Most famously, the French plans for an invasion of England, seized at Caen, were read out in the churchyard of St Paul's by the archbishop of Canterbury and in Parliament in 1346. *Adae Murimuth, continuatio chronicarum, Robertus de Avesbury, De gestis mirabilus Edwardi Tertii*, pp. 205, 211; *RP*, II, 158–9.

[46] English concerns focussed less upon the legal niceties of the title to the French throne than the fiscal and constitutional consequences of the claim, expressed in the famous statute establishing that 'our realm of England . . . shall not in any time to come be put in subjection or obedience to us, nor our heirs or successors as kings of France'. *SR*, I, 292, as translated in *English Historical Documents, 1327–1485*, ed. A. R. Myers (London, 1969), p. 70. See W. M. Ormrod, above.

[47] *Foedera*, II4, 66–7, translated in *English Historical Documents, 1327–1485*, pp. 66–7, and A. Guesnon, 'Documents inédits sur l'invasion anglaise et les Etats au temps de Philippe VI et Jean le Bon', *Bulletin historique et philologique* (1898), pp. 218–22. For the circulation of Edward's letter inside England, see footnote 42.

letters of remission. In 1353, Jehan de Lions declared that Edward III was the rightful king of France because he could cure scrofula; his refusal to retract this statement led to a six year stay in the royal prison at Les Andelys. In December 1363 Benoît Taquet, inhabitant of the Somme town of Saint-Valéry, declared that he would prefer the kings of England or Navarre to rule because then there would be less destruction and pillage.[48] Ultimately, the beleaguered inhabitants of France cared more about the ability of the king to bring peace and security, than the legal niceties of his claim to the throne: as a medieval proverb said, 'Whoever keeps the peace, controls the territory.'[49]

Thus the importance of the case presented by the English memorandum in 1344 lies less in its influence over official propaganda than its use by English diplomats throughout the Hundred Years War. Copies of the legal opinion appear in the dossiers composed by Bishop Thomas Bekynton in the 1440s containing the complete range of materials used by English diplomats in the middle of the fifteenth century, and William Worcester also possessed a copy of the document originally sent to Benedict XII in November 1340. Bekynton was almost certainly building on earlier collections of materials used by English diplomats, and the implication is that the materials developed by Edward III's lawyers were used by English officials and diplomats through-out the course of the war: these documents certainly set out a powerful case in support of the Plantagenet title.[50] This in turn may shed some light on the decision by the fifteenth-century defenders of the Valois monarchy to adopt the Salic Law. According to Jean de Montreuil, an active participant in Anglo-French negotiations, and Jean Juvénal des Ursins, the English were claiming that the custom excluding Edward III had been created in 1328, solely to defeat his claim to the French throne.[51] By giving this custom precise form as the Salic Law, the Valois writers were able to deny this centrepiece of the English case. As *Pour ce que plusieurs* explained in the most detailed discussion of the origins of the Salic Law, this ancient authority was originally

[48] J. Hoareau-Dodinau, 'Les fondements des preferences dynastiques au XIVe siècle d'aprés quelques lettres de rémission', in *La France Anglaise au moyen âge: Actes du IIIe Congrès National des Sociétés Savantes (Poitiers, 1986)* (Paris, 1988), pp. 113–21.

[49] 'Qui tient la paix, il tient le pays', cited in P. S. Lewis, 'La "France Anglaise" vue de la France Française', in *La France Anglaise au moyen âge*, pp. 31–9 (pp. 31–3).

[50] The credence presented to Benedict XII in November 1340 appears in BL MS Cotton Tiberius B XII, fols. 13v–19r, in BL MS Harley 861, fols. 8v–14r, and in BL MS Harley 4763, fols. 10v–17v. This document, renamed *De jure hereditario regis Angliae in regnum Franciae*, appears in London, Royal College of Arms, MS Arundel 48, fols. 155r–158r, a collection of materials belonging to Sir John Fastolf and William Worcester, and was edited in *Liber niger scaccarii*, ed. T. Hearne (London, 1774), II, 534–41.

[51] Jean de Montreuil, *Opera. II: L'oeuvre historique et polémique*, ed. N. Grévy-Pons, E. Ornato and G. Ouy (Turin, 1975), pp. 164 and 326; Jean Juvénal des Ursins, *Les écrits politiques de Jean Juvénal des Ursins*, 3 vols., ed. P. S. Lewis (Paris, 1978–93), II, 41.

commissioned by the first king of France, Pharamond, and was written by four wise men, Usogast, Bosogast, Salagast and Wisogast; it was later confirmed and added to by other kings including, most famously, Charlemagne.[52] Thus, thanks to the Salic Law, Montreuil was able to assert that the law was 'made and confirmed . . . such a long time ago that there is no memory of anything else, either in writing or any other fashion', and Jean Juvénal could declare that the antiquity of the Salic Law disproved the English claim that 'this constitution was specifically created during the time of King Philip because of the situation that arose then'.[53] Clearly these writers adopted the Salic Law for a variety of reasons, not least of which were their own nascent humanistic interests which encouraged them to seek the historical context for the custom governing the royal succession, and also contemporary royal interest in Charlemagne.[54] But it seems likely that they were influenced by the pressure exerted by English diplomats, using the materials originally developed by Edward III's lawyers.[55]

In conclusion, there can be no question that Edward III placed a higher priority upon the acquisition of sovereignty over Aquitaine and other lands in France than his claim to the French throne. Yet English lawyers did develop a powerful case in defence of this Plantagenet title, casting further doubt upon the assumption of previous historians such as Perroy and Déprez that the claim was 'un artifice politique, un engin de guerre savamment machiné', merely designed to win public support in England for the war.[56] In practice, it would always be difficult for Edward to challenge an anointed, elected ruler St Bridget of Sweden said in October 1348 that Edward might have the rightful claim to the French throne but as Philip of Valois had been elected king, he should remain in place for the rest of his life, to be succeeded by Edward.[57] But the legal issues surrounding the French royal succession

---

[52] Montreuil, *Opera*, II, 132, 168, 209, 226, 274 and 326; Jean Juvénal, *Les écrits politiques*, I, 156, 159–60 and 345, and II, 20–2; *Pour ce que plusieurs* in BN MS Français 5058, fols. 4v–5r.

[53] Montreuil, *Opera*, II, 166–7 and 272–3; Jean Juvénal, *Les écrits politiques*, I, 159.

[54] As discussed in Taylor, 'La vraye loy des François'.

[55] Sarah Hanley has argued that the English claim to the French throne was 'a popular theme invented by French propagandists' and that the Salic Law was really deployed as a weapon against the defence of women offered by Christine de Pizan in the *Livre de la cité des dames*: see, e.g., S. Hanley, 'Identity Politics and Rulership in France: Female Political Place and the Fraudulent Salic Law in Christine de Pizan and Jean de Montreuil', in *Changing Identities in Early Modern France*, ed. M. Wolfe (Durham, NC, 1997), pp. 78–94. For a critique of this position, see my forthcoming article, '*Le royaume ne peut tumber en fille*: the Salic Law and French Queenship', in *Capetian Queenship*, ed. K. Nolan and J. C. Parsons.

[56] Déprez also declared 'Qu'Edouard ait cru de bonne foi à la légitimité de ses prétentions, c'est chose douteuse'. Déprez, *Les préliminaires de la Guerre de Cent Ans*, pp. 234–6.

[57] E. Colledge, '*Epistola solitarii ad reges*: Alphonse of Pecha as Organizer of Brigittine

were certainly not clear, and the materials developed by English diplomats demonstrate that one should not take Edward's claim lightly. Moreover, as Jean le Bel observed, Edward risked ridicule by presenting himself as king of a country that he did not possess; and according to Froissart, the English king initially delayed laying claim to the French throne because he would incur great dishonour if he failed to take action to secure his rights if Philip VI refused to give up the crown.[58] Sir John Fastolf expressed similar sentiments in the context of the Anglo-French negotiations under Henry VI: if the king were to abandon his claim to the French throne as part of a peace deal, then it might appear that 'the king nor his noble pregenitours had, nor have, no righte in the corone of Fraunce, and that all there werres and conquest hathe be but usurpacion and tirannie'.[59] Thus it is perhaps not surprising that in 1354 and 1360, it was the English who ultimately stepped back from deals that involved the renunciation of this claim to the French throne.[60]

and Urbanist Propaganda', *Mediaeval Studies* 18 (1956), 32–3. The same problem stood in the way of Richard duke of York's claim to the English throne in 1460, and the identical solution was employed in the Act of Accord (*RP*, V, 375–9), itself modelled on the Treaty of Troyes by which Charles VI 'adopted' Henry V as his heir.

[58] Le Patourel, *Feudal Empires*, chap. XII; *English Historical Documents, 1327–1485*, pp. 60–1; *Chronique de Jean le Bel*, ed. J. Viard and E. Déprez, 2 vols. (Paris, 1904–5), I, 167–8.

[59] *Letters and Papers Illustrative of the Wars of the English in France During the Reign of Henry VI*, ed. J. Stevenson, 3 vols. RS 22 (London, 1861–4), II, 576.

[60] F. Bock, 'Some New Documents Illustrating the Early Years of the Hundred Years War (1353–1356)', *Bulletin of the John Rylands Library* 15 (1931), 60–99 (pp. 84–99); Chaplais, 'Documents Regarding the Fulfilment and Interpretation of the Treaty of Brétigny', pp. 5–50.

9

Some Reflections on Edward III's Use of Propaganda

A. K. McHARDY

'Edward III, like Mrs Thatcher, needed a good war.'[1] Edward, of course, ended up fighting more wars than he really needed, but the assertion focuses on a basic element in his kingship whose aim was the restoration of royal authority and prestige. In this policy, public relations and image-building were central tools, and they have attracted a large literature.[2]

Yet although this reign was an important one in the history of public relations, image-making and political point-scoring, Edward's record as a propagandist was mixed. It is true that the king's military achievements were publicized by the use of newsletters, some of which have survived embedded in chronicles.[3] Edward also became skilled at manipulating both parliament and the convocation of Canterbury province. In the case of the latter there were occasions when he sent war heroes to address the assembly when seeking exceptional tax grants. Thus, in 1356, he dispatched Sir Walter

---

[1] An examination question proposed at the University of Birmingham but voted down by spoilsport colleagues. I am grateful to Julia Barrow for this inside information.

[2] See C. Shenton, 'The English Court and the Restoration of Royal Prestige, 1327–1345' (unpublished D.Phil. dissertation, University of Oxford, 1995). There is a vast literature on the fine and applied arts at this time, but on the links between culture and propaganda see A. K. McHardy, 'Culture and Propaganda in the English Cause during the Hundred Years War', in *Proceedings of the 18th International Congress of Historical Sciences* (Montreal, 1995), pp. 328–30. Especially useful in the writing of this were E. Danbury, 'English and French Artistic Propaganda during the Period of the Hundred Years War: Some Evidence from Royal Charters', in *Power, Culture and Religion in France c.1350–1550*, ed. C. T. Allmand (Woodbridge, 1989), pp. 75–98; and W. M. Hinkle, *The Fleurs de Lis of the Kings of France, 1285–1488* (Carbondale, Illinois, 1991).

[3] A number of these were helpfully identified by the editors of the Record Commission edition of *Foedera*, ed. T. Rymer, Record Commission edn, 3 vols. in 6 parts (London, 1816–30): e.g., II2, 1094, 1096–7. Other references are given in A. Gransden, *Historical Writing in England, c.1307 to the Early Sixteenth Century* (London, 1982), p. 601, and see now, *Knighton's Chronicle 1337–1396*, ed. and trans. G. Martin (Oxford, 1995), pp. xxii–xxiv.

Manny to argue in favour of a sexennial tenth, though this resulted in the grant only of a biennial tenth; the grant of the triennial tenth in 1371 was achieved only by the personal intervention of the Black Prince after persuasion by Gaunt and others had failed.[4]

On the other hand, aspects of his propaganda effort appear haphazard and amateurish when contrasted with some continental kings. Unlike the kings of Aragon he neither preached to meetings of parliament nor wrote chronicles himself;[5] and unlike his French rivals he did not sponsor the writing of an official chronicle.[6] Though, as we shall see, some of the documents he sponsored were sophisticated, he never achieved the levels of subtlety and insidiousness generated by some of the Valois propaganda.[7] Even some of his information dissemination made less impact than we would have supposed. When in 1337, for example, Edward issued a manifesto explaining the cause of the French war, this was copied into the register of the Archbishop of York, William Melton,[8] but otherwise made no impact on ecclesiastical records (though who knows what the lost register of archbishop Stratford contained).[9] The other point at which we might have expected precise information and opinion-forming to be evident was in publicising the reasons for Edward's claim to the French throne.[10] Yet here again the evidence is scarce; it made no impact on episcopal registers, those excellent barometers of political pressure; not even in the register of Robert Wyville of Salisbury, Queen Isabelle's former chaplain, is there any mention. Such slight evidence as survives is lacking in uniformity. We might, for example, have expected copies of the family tree showing the king's claim through his mother, Queen Isabelle, to have been widely distributed, but yet few have come to light, and these show no standard pattern.[11]

---

[4] J. R. L. Highfield, 'The Relations between the Church the English Crown from the Death of Archbishop Stratford to the Opening of the Great Schism' (unpublished D.Phil. dissertation, University of Oxford, 1951), I, 240–4.

[5] S. F. Cawsey, 'Royal Eloquence, Royal Propaganda and the Use of the Sermon in the Medieval Crown of Aragon, c.1200–1410', *Journal of Ecclesiastical History* 50 (1999), 442–63. James the Conqueror either wrote or inspired a chronicle, while Pedro the Ceremonious certainly composed one. *Dictionary of the Middle Ages*, ed. J. R. Strayer, 13 vols. (New York, 1982–9), I, 413 and 417. Thanks are due to Michael C. E. Jones for help with this point.

[6] 'Why medieval England failed to produce official history on the lines of the *Grandes Chroniques* in France is a question not easily answered.' J. Taylor, 'Richard II in the Chronicles', in *Richard II: The Art of Kingship*, ed. A. Goodman and J. Gillespie (Oxford, 1999), pp. 15–35.

[7] A. Gransden, 'The alleged rape by Edward III of the countess of Salisbury', *EHR* 87 (1972), 333–44.

[8] *The Register of William Melton Archbishop of York 1317–1340*, ed. R. M. T. Hill, Canterbury & York Society 76 (1988), III, 157.

[9] It was stolen in an act of highway robbery in 1402. A. K. McHardy, 'The Loss of Archbishop Stratford's Register', *HR* 70 (1997), 337–41.

[10] For more on Edward III's claim to the French throne, see Craig Taylor and W. M. Ormrod respectively, above.

[11] An interesting contrast is to be found between the family tree of the French royal

It was a different matter when it came to enlisting heavenly help and terrestrial support for particular military enterprises. Here Edward could utilize a well-established mechanism, for the link between liturgy and royalty was an old one; prayers for the king were a part of daily worship in the late Anglo-Saxon period.[12] From the late thirteenth century, when memoranda sections begin to appear in bishops' registers, and when the crown was making increasing and insistent demands upon its people – it is probably no coincidence that the two occurred simultaneously – we can observe the English Church throwing its weight behind royal enterprises by organising special liturgical efforts. During the early fourteenth century the saying of prayers for the crown became commonplace, and the biographer of Walter Reynolds, the archbishop of Canterbury from 1305 to 1334, has been able to identify ninety-four occasions when such prayers were said.[13] Admittedly, some of these were essentially personal in character; a number of requests for prayers at this time were for the souls of the recently deceased, whether kings (there were nine requests for Edward I, three for Edward II, one for Philip IV), or such notables as Joan, countess of Gloucester, and Piers Gaveston. But others were for such political causes as peace between the king and his barons (1312) or for expeditions to Scotland (1314, 1317, 1319). A notable feature of these early examples is their international character; both Edward I and Edward II had requested the general chapters of the Dominican and Franciscan friars, at their meetings in European cities, to say special prayers. Conversely, popes ordered English prelates to organize special prayers for members of the royal family, or for international peace.

Edward III thus was heir to a well-established tradition when he sought divine help for his military and political enterprises. The events and circumstances of his reign both modified and developed this tradition. The modification was the loss of an international element in the saying of prayers for any of the king's concerns. Requests to the Dominicans' chapter-general meeting at Dijon in 1333, to the Franciscans convening at Assisi in 1334, and again to the Dominicans assembled at London in 1335, were the last of a tradition. All these were for prayers for the royal family, not for any political purpose.[14] With the ending of this international dimension references to a distinctive role for the mendicants become scarcer. It was rarely that separate

family in Leeds, Brotherton Library, Brotherton MS 29 fol. 2v, which places Queen Isabelle at the centre, with that printed in *Adae Murimuth, Continuatio chronicarum. Robertus de Avesbury, De gestis mirabilibus regis Edwardi tertii*, ed. E. M. Thompson (RS, 1889), p. 100, which places her at the left-hand side.

[12] For some discussion of the tradition see A. K. McHardy, 'Religious Ritual and Political Persuasion: The Case of England in the Hundred Years War', *International Journal of Moral and Social Studies* 3 (1988), 41–57.

[13] For what follows see J. Robert Wright, *The Church and the English Crown 1305–1334: A Study Based on the Register of Archbishop Walter Reynolds* (Toronto, 1980), appendix 11, pp. 348–60.

[14] *CCR 1333–7*, pp. 97, 294, and 486.

mandates to the religious orders asking for prayers for political or military purposes were recorded, those of 1 June 1355 and 8 May 1375 being exceptions.[15] In spring 1346, however, a very long and detailed statement of the king's position with respect to France and his war there was addressed to the prior provincial of the Dominicans, and to the prior and convent of St Augustine's, the Austin friars' house in London. No action was requested, and this very detailed exposition of the king's policy was what we would now call a briefing paper. The assumption must be that the recipients would publicize the king's arguments, through sermons, and in their capacity as confessors and personal advisors.[16]

In general, however, separate mandates addressed to mendicants were replaced by, and subsumed in, orders transmitted through diocesan machinery. Edward found it natural, when seeking to raise popular awareness of his needs and successes, to turn to the bishops, those obliging, all-purpose workhorses of the realm, who had such a crucial role as the links between the crown and the localities. It was they who summoned the clergy of their dioceses to meetings of convocation, meetings whose main aim was the voting of taxes, as well as attending themselves; they performed the same functions in respect of parliament, where they gave assent and advice; as wealthy individuals they were asked to give loans to the king; and, when royal cash-flow problems became pressing, they were ordered to convene meetings of their diocesan clergy in order to persuade them to advance the dates of tax payments. A bishop of Hereford might also be commanded to supply a score of Welshmen for a forthcoming expedition.[17] In all these roles they obeyed the royal will and propagated the arguments of royal aims and necessity.

They also performed a unique function in organising special liturgical efforts in support of the crown, especially for success in foreign warfare. This essay examines the way that information was diffused and public opinion mobilized in support of the king's military ventures, in such a way that the widest possible audience was reached. Just how widely transmitted such information and opinions were we may see from the instructions issued on numerous occasions for the holding of special services in support of the king,

---

[15] In 1355 the same request for prayers as was made to the archbishop of Canterbury was also sent to the provincial of the Dominicans, Augustin friars and Carmelites, to the Franciscans' minister, the Dominican priors of Oxford, Canterbury and York, as well as to the chancellors and proctors of both universities (*CCR 1354–60*, p. 210); in 1375 the request was again sent separately to the four main orders of mendicants (*CCR 1374–7*, p. 224).

[16] 15 March: *CCR 1346–9*, pp. 57–8.

[17] *The Register of John de Trillek, Bishop of Hereford (A.D. 1344–1361)*, ed. J. H. Parry, Cantilupe Society, V (1910–11), pp. 166–7 (convocation), 260, 310 (parliament), 295 (council), 298 (loan), 267–71, 277–9, 294–5 (anticipation of taxes), and 241–2 (Welshmen, 'without prejudice to any rights of the prince of Wales'; this order was later countermanded).

for these were typically to be held 'in the cathedral church and in all parochial, collegiate and conventual churches', and the instructions were addressed to the 'cathedral dean and to all abbots and priors, all rectors, vicars, and parish priests'. This was a wider target audience than the county courts, and a very much wider audience than parliament. And though sheriffs played a part in disseminating information,[18] it was the church which was uniquely able to contact the 'grass roots' level of the king's subjects by means of a chain of command which reached into every parish and religious house.

The part played by these special services in forming public opinion has been insufficiently recognized. Their study opens interesting lines of enquiry, and reminds us that the people of the fourteenth century had an outlook different from ours; 'that the Middle Ages were not *us* in fancy dress'.[19] The special devotions organized by the church on the crown's behalf in this reign were numerous, including as they did petitions for good weather, for the cessation of plague, for the health and (after death) for the souls of members of the royal family.[20] The mechanisms for organising such efforts were various: a writ might be sent to all the bishops; or they might be approached through the good offices of the two archbishops (the archbishop of Canterbury distributed his commands *via* the bishop of London, the 'dean of the province'); sometimes bishops seem to have used their own initiative.

Whoever was giving the orders, a mixture of liturgical elements was always specified, some being asked for more than others. Prayers always headed the list of the efforts requested; next, in many cases, came masses. Preaching and processions were regularly demanded by royal writs. Less frequently mentioned were vigils, almsgiving, or the vaguer 'other works of piety', or 'other divine offices'. Bishops sometimes ordered bells to be rung. Each of these must be examined in turn.

Prayers for success and of thanksgiving were the most commonly-requested elements, and long ago Dr Hewitt suggested that these may have been said in English.[21] No evidence to support this hypothesis has been found and, on reflection, this would have been unlikely. Latin was the proper language in which to address the Almighty; even the layman William

---

[18] E.g., the letter close issued on 21 August 1337 to the sheriffs, on the subject of the French war, and ordering proclamations to be made on this, was only one of a number of publicity measures undertaken. *Foedera*, II2, 989. Other examples are collected in *Foedera*, II2, 964, 990, and 994–5.

[19] As J. L. Carr put it, *The Harpole Report* (London, 1972), chap. 21.

[20] The list in the Appendix is confined to services for political and military causes. Prayers were also organized for the souls of the duke of Clarence (1368), Queen Philippa (1369), the earl of Warwick (1369) and the prince of Wales (1376): [Lincoln,] L[incolnshire] A[rchives] O[ffice,] Reg. 12 (John Buckingham: Memoranda), fols. 62v, 81v, 82v, 133.

[21] H. J. Hewitt, *The Organization of War under Edward III* (Manchester, 1966), p. 163. This stimulating book has been the starting-point for all my investigations.

Ramsbury, who in 1389 was accused of saying a Lollard mass, had simply used the rite of Sarum, and excised those parts which he found repugnant.[22] There was not even the need to write special prayers for these occasions. Bishops, faced with extra demands on their time, did what most administrators do in like circumstance: they reached for the precedent book, and they found in the well-established liturgy, and in the archives of their predecessors, material sufficient for their needs. There is one possible exception, when a bishop prescribed prayers which *may* have been original, though the fact that his registrar did not bother to record these suggests otherwise.[23]

When the prayers and other words to be used are precisely described (which is in the minority of cases) they are often found to consist of the most basic and well known, namely the Lord's Prayer and Hail Mary. The advantage of these was that the laity could join in, and even obtain merit for saying them in private, if they could not attend the special services.[24] In other cases the instructions were aimed at the clergy, with details of psalms to be sung,[25] versicles to be used, and the collect, secret and post communion prayers specified for the saying of masses. Investigation shows that, when these instructions are identifiable, they were either prescribing words in a widely recognized form (e.g. the prayers from votive masses) or that had been included in instructions previously issued.[26] Thus the very detailed mandates drawn up by Robert Wyville of Salisbury in 1335 and 1342 turn out, upon inspection, to be greatly indebted to a bull ordering special prayers promulgated by pope John XXII in 1328, and conveniently recorded in the register of Roger Martival, Wyville's predecessor.[27] Similarly precise, though

[22] A. Hudson, 'A Lollard Mass', *Journal of Theological Studies* n.s. 23 (1972), 407–19, reprinted in A. Hudson, *Lollards and their Books* (London, 1985), chap. 7.

[23] Simon Montacute in 1334. *Register of Simon de Montacute Bishop of Worcester 1334–1337*, ed. R. M. Haines, Worcestershire Historical Society n.s. 15 (1996), p. 210. Montacute was then newly promoted to the episcopal bench, and was not long out of Oxford.

[24] In 1346 Archbishop Stratford granted thirty days' indulgence to those who, living too far from their parish church to attend the special ceremonies, yet said the *Pater Noster* and *Ave Maria* five times. *Register of John de Trillek*, ed. Parry, pp. 273–4.

[25] In 1367 Simon Langham ordered the seven penitential psalms, and litanies, to be used in the thanksgiving services for the Black Prince's victory in Spain (Nájera). *Diocesis Cantuariensis: Registrum Simonis de Langham*, ed. A. C. Wood, Canterbury & York Society 51 (1956), p. 162. In 1370 Bishop Buckingham of Lincoln ordered the saying of the seven penitential psalms and of the fifteen gradual psalms: LAO Reg. 12, fol. 96v.

[26] This subject is more fully examined in A. K. McHardy, 'Liturgy and Propaganda in the Diocese of Lincoln during the Hundred Years War', *Studies in Church History* 18 (1982), 215–28.

[27] Wiltshire Record Office, Register of Robert Wyville, fols. 21v, 75v; *The Register of Roger Martival bishop of Salisbury 1315–1330, V: Divers Letters*, ed. C. R. Elrington, Canterbury & York Society 58 (1972), p. 591. All the elements ordered were of easily identifiable conventional form.

less elaborate, instructions were issued on occasion by Archbishop Langham, and by John Buckingham of Lincoln.[28] These instructions gave little scope for individual initiative, yet some bishops injected a local angle into their commands. In York, for example, there was a tradition of addressing prayers not only to God, the Blessed Virgin Mary, and the apostles Peter and Paul but also to St William the Confessor, both Archbishops Melton and Zouche invoking this local saint.[29] John Trillek of Hereford ordered prayers to be addressed to the patron saints Ethelbert, king and martyr, and Thomas, confessor and pontiff,[30] while at Winchester in 1369, William of Wykeham ordered prayers to be addressed not only to God, the Blessed Virgin Mary and the Apostles Peter and Paul, but also to 'Saints Ethelwold, Swithun, Birinus and Hedde [Hedda] our patrons'.[31]

Processions were the other effort repeatedly demanded, and since they were of two types, they could suit all occasions. Thus penitential processions were appropriate when seeking divine favour for an enterprise at its outset, festival processions when there was something to celebrate. The use of processions, like well-known prayers, was psychologically shrewd, for it meant that the whole community could join in; everyone could feel that they had a part to play and so were drawn in to the support of the ceremonies, and the objects for which they were held. Processions also quite clearly appealed to bishops, and it is in their instructions for these that we get rare glimpses of their individual enthusiasms. Thus Archbishop Melton of York was an activist who, on 14 April 1333, wrote to the dean of the Christianity of York commanding him to join the archbishop in a procession on the forthcoming Friday (16 April) which would start from the priory of Holy Trinity, Micklegate, and end at St Mary's Abbey. We may compare this with a similar effort organized by Melton in 1319, when, again starting from Holy Trinity, the procession had ended at the Minster.[32] Two newly-promoted bishops also specified very visible processions. In 1334 Simon Montacute of Worcester enjoined all rectors, vicars, parish priests and religious 'to process round their churches, weather permitting, otherwise inside them', while in spring 1346 William Edington of Winchester ordered special services '. . . on market-days, going around the church or through the market-place, as weather permits'.[33]

[28] *Registrum Simonis de Langham*, ed. Wood, pp. 151–2; LAO Reg. 12, fol. 96v.
[29] *The Register of William Melton Archbishop of York 1317–1340, III: Divers Letters*, ed. R. M. T. Hill, Canterbury & York Society 76 (1988), pp. 118–19; York, Borthwick Institute of Historical Research, Reg. 10 (William Zouche, 1), fol. 257.
[30] Ethelbert (d.794) king of the East Angles, and Thomas (Cantilupe) of Hereford (d.1282). D. H. Farmer, *The Oxford Dictionary of Saints* (Oxford, 1978), pp. 137 and 379–80; *Register of John de Trillek*, ed. Parry, p. 78.
[31] *Wykeham's Register*, ed. T. F. Kirby, Hampshire Record Society (1899), II, 89–90.
[32] *Register of William Melton III*, ed. Hill, pp. 118–19; Wright, *Church and Crown*, p. 354.
[33] *Register of Simon de Montacute*, ed. Haines, p. 210; *The Register of William Edington Bishop of Winchester 1346–1366 Part I*, ed. S. F. Hockey, Hampshire Record Society 7 (1986), p. 8.

On the other hand, John Buckingham of Lincoln was a great believer in the spiritual benefits of bare feet. In 1363 he had impressed observers by walking barefoot from the episcopal manor of Nettleham, some three miles outside the city of Lincoln, to his enthronement, and in 1370, when directing the means to be used to seek peace, he ordered clergy and laity alike to make their processions barefoot.[34] This was the only time that he did so, and perhaps reflected his concern at the renewal of the French war, for in his days as keeper of the privy seal, he had been closely involved in the making of the treaty of Brétigny. His arms were painted on the Calais chest, after all.[35] Such public processions, as well as the ringing of bells, which was sometimes enjoined, would have alerted those not actually taking part to the existence of such ceremonies.[36]

The masses which were ordered to be said were probably votive masses, and it was for this reason that the great majority of mandates ordered these special efforts to be made on workdays, usually Wednesdays and Fridays (*quartis et sextis feriis*). This was because on *ferias* (as opposed to feast days and Sundays), a votive mass could be substituted for the mass of the day. The votive masses, which included those for peace, for the king, for sinners, for penitents, and in time of war, offered plenty of choice to the celebrant wishing to combine patriotism and spirituality.[37]

It is when we come to examine how the command to provide sermons was obeyed that we encounter uncertainty. Compared with the saying of prayers and masses, and the making of processions, they demanded much more effort on the part of the clergy. And while it is true that sermons were not specified in every command, each special occasion compelled the clergy to make at least a short 'presentation' by way of drumming up support for the forthcoming ceremonies. We have seen that the prayers and processions were of common form; must we assume that, in complete contrast, commands to preach threw the clergy of England into a frenzy of composition? It is true that this war stimulated some of the most distinguished preachers to write sermons, but what of those many parishes, and religious houses, which did not have a FitzRalph[38] or a Brinton[39] to hand? The answer may well lie in the writs which were issued by the chancery to order such efforts. The more

---

[34] LAO Lincoln Dean and Chapter Muniments, A/2/3, fol. 43v; LAO Reg. 12, fols. 96v–97.

[35] The chest in which the treaty was kept still survives in the PRO (E 30/153 case) and is illustrated and described in C. Jenning, *Early Chests in Wood and Iron*, PRO Museum Pamphlets 7 (1974), p. 8.

[36] Bell-ringing was ordered by Wyville of Salisbury for the Black Prince's expedition to Spain in 1367. Wiltshire Record Office, Reg. Wyville, fol. 228v.

[37] *The Sarum Missal*, ed. J. Wickham Legg (Oxford, 1916), e.g. pp. 395–412.

[38] K. Walsh, *A Fourteenth-Century Scholar and Primate: Richard FitzRalph in Oxford, Avignon and Armagh* (Oxford, 1981), pp. 223, 228–9 and nn. 230, 251.

[39] *The Sermons of Thomas Brinton Bishop of Rochester (1373–1389)*, ed. M. A. Devlin, Camden 3rd s. 85 (1954), esp. pp. 49–54.

these commands are examined, the more skilful are they seen to be. They were resonant with biblical and liturgical language (rather than employing direct quotations),[40] and above all they conveyed a sense of importance and sonority, especially by using the rhetorical device known to literary critics as *amplificatio*, making the same point in several ways, usually three, to reinforce the effect.[41] This rhetorical device was used repeatedly in these writs, which are entirely different in character from the workaday demands for action and money with which bishops and their clerks were bombarded.

One good example, which must represent this whole genre, is the writ *Ad hoc in terris*, issued from York on 23 October 1334, whose translation is printed *in extenso* in Professor Haines' edition of Montacute's Worcester register.

> The king complains of the pride, fury and wickedness of the Scots, their violation of fealty and homage, their traitorous waging of war against the king and his allies, and the many evils they have committed. . . . To prevent further evils, by the counsel of his parliament at Westminster he is proceeding to Scotland for the defence of his lands and of the realm of England.

After explaining that, for the success of his Scottish campaign, the king was trusting 'more to assistance from above than to earthly power, more to the prayers of the faithful than to bands of armed men', the writ went on to request the bishop to commend the king and his army to the prayers and other merits of his subjects, 'instructing the clergy and people, secular and religious, so that the Lord of all dominion, placated by their prayers and merits, may pour out his blessing so as to provide a successful advance [*progressum*], a favourable campaign [*aggressum*] and a glorious return [*regressum*]'. This would bring 'glory to Him, esteem to the king, benefit and solace to his subjects, and peace and quiet to the Church and the whole realm . . .'[42]

Contemporaries clearly recognized that these writs were something special, very different from the usual royal commands: in bishops' registers they were always copied into the memoranda sections, never among the writs. It is, in fact, somewhat remarkable that they were registered at all, for their currency was of limited length, and unlike, the commands of courts,

---

[40] Thus the writ of 12 August 1342, known as *Terribilis in judiciis*, contains such near-quotations as *Qui digne flagellat filios quo diligit*; cf. Ecclesiasticus, 30.1, *Qui diligit filium suum adsiduat illi flagella*. That of 28 February 1346 contains *ambulantes in umbrae mortis medio consolantur*; cf. Psalm 22. 4, *si ambulavero in medio umbrae mortis non timebo*.

[41] For most modern readers the most well-known use of this device is probably in the Authorized Version of St John's Gospel, 1, v.13, '. . . which were born, not of blood, nor of the will of the flesh, nor of the will of man, but of God'.

[42] *Register of Simon Montacute*, ed. Haines, p. 209.

they demanded no return, and there were no penalties for non-compliance. In character they resemble commands which prelates themselves issued on this subject, in those cases where no royal authority is apparent. Good examples are the mandate of Archbishop Melton of York, dated 5 April 1333, an elaborate composition full of rhetorical devices, and Simon Langham's order for thanksgiving for Prince Edward's victory in Spain in 1367. The latter combines lofty sentiments with a long exposition of the reasons for English involvement in Castilian affairs, and constitutes in effect a briefing paper.[43] In 1370 William of Wykeham employed theological argument and biblical language in an effort to stimulate the enthusiasm of his reluctant subjects.[44]

Why did the crown's servants go to such trouble over commands whose usefulness would be confined to a limited time-span? How can we explain the heady mixture of patriotic and religious fervour, a call to action which cost nothing but which brought everlasting benefits, expressed in language carefully crafted by masters in the art of Latin prose composition? The suggestion made here is that these writs were intended to form the basis of sermons or homilies which would be preached on these occasions. The ceremonies must have been surrounded by a good deal of explanation: they were announced in church on Sundays and feast-days to encourage attendance,[45] and the sermons would have been strongly political in character. Though the part played by the sheriffs in promoting royal policy was important, it was in the writs which set in motion the making of special services that the king's case is put with greatest force and passion, exhibiting as many do a powerful invective and racial prejudice.[46]

The fact that these mandates were written and recorded in Latin is no indication of the language of the sermons which the crown requested, which were certainly in English; the aim, after all, was for maximum impact within the nation.[47] The language of record is not the same as the language of use,[48] and common sense, coupled with references to the

[43] *Register of William Melton III*, ed. Hill, pp. 118–19; *Registrum Langham*, ed. Wood, pp. 161–3.
[44] *Wykeham's Register*, ed. Kirby, II, 105 and 108–9.
[45] Richard de Bury of Durham ordered the publicising of these special ceremonies on Sundays and feast days. *Registrum Palatinum Dunelmense*, ed. T. D. Hardy (RS, 1875), III, 500. A similar instruction is found in Simon Langham's provincial mandate of 5 February 1367 to order prayers for the Prince of Wales's expedition to Spain. *Registrum Langham*, ed. Wood, pp. 151–2.
[46] The writ of 26 February 1346 is especially precise about the misdeeds of Philip de Valois and his intentions. It is printed in full in *The Register of Ralph of Shrewsbury Bishop of Bath and Wells 1329–1363*, ed. T. S. Holmes, 2 vols., Somerset Record Society 9, 10 (1895–6), II, 527.
[47] For the wide distinction between the language in which sermons were preached and in which they were recorded, see G. R. Owst, *Preaching in Medieval England* (Cambridge, 1926), pp. 223–7.
[48] A good example is Michael Northburgh's letter describing the landing at La Hogue

inaccessibility of Latin,[49] suggests that the vernacular was used. These explanations may have been strongly political, but they were not necessarily devoid of moral and spiritual content. Two theological subjects call for special mention. One is the desire for peace; the other is the call to repentance.

The object of many, if not all, requests for prayers in support of war was said to be 'peace', and the mandates to make such intercessions are invariably indicated in episcopal registers by the margin-flag: *Ad orandum pro pace*. Such a petition sits awkwardly in documents whose language is full of hatred, of descriptions of violence or treachery, and expressions of hope for revenge. It would be wrong, however, to be cynical about the insistence that peace was the aim, while making war; rather what these mandates demonstrate is the persistence and pervasiveness of St Augustine's perception of peace as man's ultimate aim. Even the most cursory observation of humanity, said Augustine, reveals that:

> . . . there is no man who does not wish for peace. Indeed, even when men choose war, their only wish is for victory; which shows that their desire in fighting is for peace with glory. For what is victory but the conquest of the opposing side? And when this is achieved, there will be peace. Even wars, then, are waged with peace as their object, even when they are waged by those who are concerned to exercise their warlike prowess. . . . Hence it is an established fact that peace is the desired end of war.[50]

The repeatedly-stressed necessity for repentance on the part of those performing and participating in such rituals is linked to the question of their effectiveness. Was all this effort worthwhile? In considering this we must remember that the target 'audience' of the liturgical efforts was not man, but God. Valuable as their effect on the political community may have been, their main intention was to solicit divine favour. Those wishing to judge the efficacy of such ceremonies had only to look at the early years of Edward's reign. There is no evidence that special prayers were requested for his first campaign, to Scotland in 1327, a campaign which was an abject

and the capture of Caen. It was written in Anglo-Norman and one version in that language was copied into the register of Bishop Trillek of Hereford (*Register of John de Trillek*, ed. Parry, pp. 280–1), and in another into the chronicle of Robert de Avesbury: *Adae Murimuth, Continuatio chronicarum. Robertus de Avesbury, De gestis mirabilibus regis Edwardi tertii*, ed. E. M. Thompson (RS, 1889), pp. 358–60. It was translated into Latin and appeared in that language in versions by Adam Murimuth, *ibid.*, pp. 212–13, and *Knighton's Chronicle*, ed. Martin, pp. 54–5.
[49] For examples of lack of Latinity, even among the religious, see *Register of Hamo de Hethe of Rochester Diocese, A. D. 1319–1352*, ed. C. Johnson, 2 vols., Canterbury & York Society 48, 49 (1948), II, 818 and 875.
[50] Augustine, *City of God*, trans. Henry Bettenson (Harmondsworth, 1972), Book XIX, chap. 12, p. 866.

failure.[51] The omission was rectified in 1333 when on 23 April the bishops of England were asked to arrange special services for the Scottish expedition of that year. The result was military success. The link between liturgical endeavour and military victory was thus established and for nearly thirty years these services were largely beneficial.

There was a strong link in men's minds between repentance of sin and living well – morally speaking – which led to divine favour. And divine favour was manifested in military success. A contemporary poem implored God not to take vengeance on English sins just as an army was going to France, and a few lines later asked for peace, 'and war after, if we are miscreants'.[52] This link between spiritual virtue and military success was reinforced during this period by the requests for prayers, both of petition and thanksgiving, discussed here. The commands of the crown, of archbishops and bishops all made the same point: to be effective the liturgical practices had to be performed by people who were in spiritual good standing, and that meant those who repented their sins.[53] For them, too, a reward was offered: the grant of forty days' indulgence to those taking part in these ceremonies was almost universal. But what about the times when these special prayers were unanswered? Contemporaries were naturally quick to point out incompetence and corruption in their fellow-men when they thought they detected such flaws, but the connection between moral virtue, divine approbation, and military success was so strongly imbued in the public mind that there was a feeling of hurt and puzzlement when divine goodwill was apparently withdrawn in the 1370s and 1380s.

When we turn to investigate the response of Edward III's subjects to these prayers, we are faced by the problem of lack of vital information. Were the commands really executed with the thoroughness demanded? Were special services attended with enthusiasm? Did they attract universal support, or were they the preserve of particular groups? What they demanded from the king's subjects was effort, rather than money. Yet because the special liturgical practices were usually to take place on working days they surely had economic implications for the laity, and perhaps this made them especially attractive to economically marginal groups: the old and the underemployed. This would have been a way for such groups to make a valued contribution to the war effort, and of drawing them into national life. The prayers of the poor were considered

---

[51] The Franciscans, however, were requested to make special prayers for Edward, his mother and siblings, at the general chapter at Perpignan. Wright, *Church and English Crown*, pp. 359–60.

[52] Brotherton MS 29, fol. 4v.

[53] A good example of the link between puritanical behaviour and divine favour was the insistence of Archbishop Simon Islip, OSB, that Sunday should last a full twenty-four hours, from vespers to vespers, and that no markets or fairs should take place then, while prayers were said for the success of the king and his army. Otford, 14 August 1359; see *Register of William Edington*, ed. Hockey, II, 49.

particularly precious, and time was one resource which marginal groups always have in plenty.[54]

The attitude of Edward's subjects towards these special liturgical efforts is by no means clear, just as it is now impossible for us to judge precisely the attractiveness of the periods of remission offered by the Church to participants. It seems reasonable to suppose that popular enthusiasm was affected by the length of time over which the prayers, processions and preachings took place, yet the sources are silent about the duration of each 'campaign' of intercession. This suggests that their length may have been such a matter of routine that no instructions were necessary. We can infer from the mandates only that the effort was to continue for two weeks or more, but the failure of mandates to specify a time-limit is baffling. A suggestion may, however, be offered. In archiepiscopal mandates which demand certification by their recipients the date for doing so is a considerable time ahead. Thus, in 1333, when Simon Meopham ordered prayers for the Scottish war on 23 April he ordered a certificate of action taken to be returned by his bishops by 29 July, an interval of ninety-eight days; while in 1367 Langham's mandate for action to the bishop of London was dated 5 February; the certificate of compliance to be returned by 3 May, a period of eighty-eight days.[55] The deadlines for returning certificates were set far further ahead than, for example, the certificates of action and information required by royal writs.[56] This raises the possibility that in each case the date given for the certificate concerning special prayers marked the end of that liturgical episode. This plausible suggestion must remain a speculation.

The evidence for the popular attitude to these rites is largely negative; there is no evidence that the calls to make such liturgical efforts provoked the widespread apathy which they were to do in the fifteenth century.[57] There is, though, one piece of evidence exceptional to this. On 5 February 1370 William of Wykeham wrote to the archdeacons within Winchester diocese to invigorate the petitionary efforts of his flock in the face of an imminent invasion. The lesson of scripture, he said, teaches that:

> while Moses the bringer of law, the leader of the people of Israel, poured out devout prayers of supplication before the face of the Most High, that same people conquered their enemies; and when he ceased to pray, his

---

[54] In 1412 Henry IV asked for twice-weekly ceremonies on working days during harvest, an impractical request, as Archbishop Arundel pointed out. *The Register of Robert Hallum bishop of Salisbury 1407–17*, ed. J. M. Horn, Canterbury & York Society 72 (1982), p. 151. The contribution which the retired and other unwaged persons can make to the community is now recognized in parts of the USA by the concept of 'time dollars'.

[55] LAO Reg. 5 (Burghersh, Memoranda), fols. 466–7; *Reg. Langham*, ed. Wood, pp. 151–2.

[56] *Royal Writs Addressed to the Bishop of Lincoln 1363–1398*, ed. A. K. McHardy, Canterbury & York Society 86 (1997), passim, but good examples are nos. 198, 213, 216.

[57] Negligence and torpor were reactions to mandates for prayers for Henry V; LAO Reg. 15 (Philip Repingdon, Memoranda), fols. 189–189v, 200.

people were vanquished. . . . We, indeed, learning how much the dangers of war and of the invasions of our external enemies who are preparing to attack, invade and crush the borders of the realm of England, as much by land as by sea, with no small multitude of ships and of armed men, have ordered and caused processions to be made and celebrated and other devout prayers to be said and continued in all monasteries, churches and other sacred places of our diocese of Winchester, granting certain indulgences to those doing and saying, in the spirit of humility, those masses, processions and prayers. But alas! it greatly distresses the depths of our heart [to learn] that the clergy and people subject to us are now slacking off from these masses, processions and prayers which, while they made them, brought defence from on High. Therefore, in order to revive from all slackness sufficient masses and processions to the praise of the divine name so dormant in our diocese, we firmly enjoin you, in virtue of obedience and order you that etc., with grant of forty days' indulgence.[58]

Three days later, a letter in similar vein to the prior of Winchester was yet more rhetorical in style and biblical in language. Wykeham referred back to his previous mandate to organize prayers, which was dated 16 April 1369, and ordered the resumption of petitions that God would strengthen, restore and confirm the peace of the kingdom. 'Do not desist from this praying until we order you otherwise by our special letters', he concluded.[59] The unique nature of these letters among the material examined prompts some comment. Wykeham was a relatively recent recruit to the episcopal bench (he was consecrated in October 1367) who may have been acting through excessive zeal; he may have expected unusually strenuous efforts from the monks of his cathedral priory; and the resumption of war in 1369 may have been received with less enthusiasm than earlier phases of conflict, especially by the denizens of Hampshire whose coast was vulnerable to attack.[60]

It is by considering the years before 1360 that we can make a surer answer to the question: if God was impressed by these prayers, were men? In other words, how effective were these and other measures in promoting support for the king's foreign wars? We are so used to thinking of Edward III as a king who was successful and popular during his reign, and a hero to subsequent generations, that it seems almost impertinent to ask this question.[61] In the search for the elusive 'public opinion' in the years from 1333 to 1360, our conclusions must be largely negative: in this reign there was no general uprising against royal policy. Yet such an episode may have come

---

[58] *Wykeham's Register*, ed. Kirby, II, 105.
[59] *Wykeham's Register*, ed. Kirby, II, 108–9. The biblical language, *oracio justorum assidua*, is an echo of James, 5. 16, *deprecatio justi adsidua*.
[60] Cf. the hostility encountered by the bishop of Lincoln when trying to array his clergy for home defence purposes in 1369. LAO Reg. 12, fol. 77.
[61] See the approving comments quoted by W. M. Ormrod, 'The Personal Religion of Edward III', *Speculum* 64 (1989), 849–77 (p. 850); D. A. L. Morgan, 'The Political After-Life of Edward III: The Apotheosis of a Warmonger', *EHR* 112 (1997), 856–81.

dangerously close. A poem of complaint, the *Song against the King's Taxes*, now dated to the period 1337–40, or even more precisely to 1338–9, contains the warning that the oppressed peasantry would rise in rebellion if only they had a leader:

> Je me doute, s'ils ussent chief, quod vellent levare.
> Saepe facit stultas gentes vacuata facultas.[62]

We might argue that this threat was simply a conventional poetic device. Yet Archbishop Melton, writing to his suffragans in exactly this period, was also concerned at the unpopularity of royal taxation, for, after ordering processions to be made, he continued, 'Clergy and people should be urged to bear kindly and charitably the various tallages and other impositions which the king made through necessity, not in malice or presumption.' The command, dated 10 April 1338, was also unusual in specifying that processions should be made on four feast-days, when congregations would be larger.[63] Recent work draws attention to the criticisms made of Edward and his friends by the Northumberland knight Sir Thomas Gray: Gray deplored the comital creations of 1337, accused Edward of treating the 1338–9 Flanders campaign as an excuse for jousting and high living, and he despised tournaments which were mere social occasions and excuses for display. Similarly, the author of the *Anonimalle Chronicle* commented sourly on the wasteful costs of a grand tournament held at Windsor in 1343.[64] A cautious attitude to royal ambitions is also seen in a poem contained in a manuscript associated with St Mary's, York. This has the wish for peace as its main theme, even while the king is abroad fighting, and it ends with a plea for safe borders and an end to burning and hostile incursions – which suggests a north-country outlook.[65] None of this is quite sufficient to suggest a north-south divide in public opinion, yet it should perhaps warn us against thinking that the king enjoyed

---

[62] Wright's full translation reads: 'Such tribute can in no manner last long; Out of emptiness who can give, or touch anything with his hands. People are reduced to such ill plight, that they can give no more; I fear, if they had a leader, they would rise in rebellion. Loss of property often makes people fools.' *Thomas Wright's Political Songs of England: From the Reign of John to that of Edward II*, ed. P. Coss (Cambridge, 1996), pp. 185–6, and, for the revised dating, pp. liii–liv and notes. For a discussion of this type of poetry see J. R. Maddicott, 'Poems of Social Protest in Early Fourteenth-Century England', in *England in the Fourteenth Century: Proceedings of the 1985 Harlaxton Symposium*, ed. W. M. Ormrod (Woodbridge, 1986), pp. 130–44.

[63] *The Register of John Kirkby Bishop of Carlisle 1332–1352*, ed. R. L. Storey, Canterbury & York Society 79 (1993), I, 82–3. This is not included in Melton's own register.

[64] I am grateful to Andy King for sending me, in advance of publication, a copy of his paper, 'A Helm with a Crest of Gold: The Order of Chivalry in Thomas Gray's *Scalacronica*', from which these references are taken. For Gray's famous comment on the 1337 earldoms, see Given-Wilson and Prestwich above, 'Introduction'.

[65] Brotherton MS 29, fol. 4v.

the same reputation in all parts of the country, just as we would recognize that his prestige was not constant.

Though we can point to some shortcomings in English propaganda of the period, we can, conversely, turn to good examples of even greater success, that is, to instances in which the king was lauded, not by his own efforts, but by those of his supporters: what we might call advertising at second hand. Traditionally, this has been seen as an essential role of the chroniclers,[66] but I suggest that visual examples, which would have had a much wider public, are also worth investigation. Three will be cited here.

The largest and most spectacular of these examples is the great east window in what is now Gloucester cathedral, the former Benedictine abbey of St Peter. The body of the king's father was buried in the abbey church, having been brought from Berkeley Castle, as the house's historian tells us, by the fearless abbot Thoky when the cowardly abbots of Bristol, Kingswood and Malmesbury feared to receive it because of their terror of Roger Mortimer, Queen Isabelle and their accomplices. The gifts of the faithful who flocked to the royal tomb enabled the abbey to complete the rebuilding of St Andrew's aisle within six years, doubtless to the delight of Thoky's successor John Wigmore (1329–37), a connoisseur 'who greatly delighted in divers arts'.[67]

It is surprising that the abbey's chronicler, who was conscientious in recording both building works and notable benefactions, made no reference to the new east window, whose size alone makes it remarkable.[68] It was probably the largest window in England at the time of its construction, and even now only the great east window of York minster (1405) surpasses it. Though vandalism, injudicious cleaning, and the building of the Lady Chapel in the later fifteenth century now detract from its original appearance the window is still an important source for the polity of Edward III's reign. Under elaborate canopies are six angels. Below them are the Virgin and Christ in majesty flanked by the apostles. At the lowest heavenly level are fourteen intercessory saints. The highest rank on earth now consists of fourteen lords spiritual. However, Jill Kerr suggests that the two regal figures which have been erroneously relocated among the apostles probably represent the kings Osric and Edward II, both buried in the church, and were

<hr/>

[66] See Gransden, *Historical Writing in England II*, chap. 3 and 4; *Knighton's Chronicle*, ed. Martin, pp. xxvi–xxvii.
[67] *Historia et Cartularium Monasterii Gloucestriae*, ed. W. H. Hart (RS, 1863), II, 44 and 46. The profitability of royal tombs, regardless of the individual's character, was not new. In 1183 the corpse of Henry, 'the young king', was seized by the citizens of Le Mans while being transported for burial at Rouen, in the expectation that it would bring profit to the town. *Gesta Regis Henrici Secundi*, ed. W. Stubbs (RS, 1867), I, 301 and 303–4.
[68] For what follows see J. Kerr, 'The East Window of Gloucester Cathedral', *Medieval Art and Architecture at Gloucester and Tewkesbury*, British Archaeological Association Conference Transactions 7 (1985 for 1981), pp. 116–29.

originally in the central place of honour in this line. Most interesting, for our purpose, is the lowest earthly level, the lords temporal, kings and nobles, represented by their shields of arms.

It is this section which has given the window its nickname of the 'Crécy Window', since most of those depicted fought in the battle; the rest later joined in the siege of Calais. However, as Kerr says, the surviving shields could equally be a roll of fighters in Edward's Scottish wars. For our purpose the significant point is surely that king and nobility are represented as a group which made plain to all the fellowship which existed between them. In the absence of documentary evidence the dating of the window must be done on stylistic grounds, and the armour of the figure of St George indicates the decade 1350–60 as most likely. By that time Edward himself was taking little interest himself in the tomb of his father and its surroundings, but in 1353, as W. M. Ormrod has discovered, he sent his sons to Gloucester 'to pay their respects to their deceased grandfather',[69] and it is tempting to place the completion of the east window at this time.

Two further examples of 'secondary propaganda' may be briefly noted. The first is a window in the Lincolnshire church of Haydour, which, though it lacks the royal arms, does depict the fashionable royal and political saints of Edward the Confessor (complete with the spurious shield of arms later popularized by Richard II), George and Edmund. The donor was a member of the family of Scrope of Masham, perhaps Henry Lord Scope, as Richard Marks suggests, but doubtless with the approval of Master Geoffrey Scrope, prebendary of Haydour-cum-Walton for nearly fifty years, and, as such, rector of the church and patron of the vicarage. On stylistic grounds this has been dated to about 1360.[70]

Shortly after this window was installed, John Buckingham became bishop of Lincoln (1363) and this former royal servant, whose last office had been keeper of the privy seal (1360–3) remodelled the north front of Vicars' Court in his cathedral close, which he adorned with the arms of himself, of his first patron Thomas Beauchamp I, earl of Warwick (through whose presentation he entered crown service), and of his royal master. The royal arms, depicting English leopards quartered with French lilies, offered a reminder of Edward III's overseas pretension to anyone passing through the close of Lincoln. They still do. Equally impressive, though, was surely the depiction of solidarity and comradeship between king, magnate, and a clerical servant of obscure origins who won the trust of them both.

Many other such examples of the royal arms must surely have existed

---

[69] Ormrod, 'Personal Religion', p. 871.

[70] R. Marks, *Stained Glass in England during the Middle Ages* (Toronto, 1993), p. 169, and n. 14 in which he thanks Penny Dawson for providing donor evidence for this window, but cites no documentary reference. For Master Geoffrey Le Scrope as prebendary, see John Le Neve, *Fasti Ecclesiae Anglicanae 1300–1541* (London, 1962), I, 68.

which were open to the public gaze. Stained glass was probably one of the most important media, since Richard Marks informs us that '[the] inclusion of the royal arms was almost *de rigeur* in domestic glass'. Whatever Edward's political aims or military achievements, the quartering of French and English arms reminded everyone who saw them, even in peaceful settings, that he was a king who was successful in war, who had restored English pride and made himself feared by his enemies.

We may conclude on a different note, however, by suggesting that the greatest legacy of Edward III's propaganda was not artistic, but linguistic. During the fourteenth century, Latin was the language of administration and salvation, French the language, of (among other things)[71] upper-class and high-status leisure. What about the standing of English? Three English language scholars have recently discussed the changing position of this language in the trilingual world of the later Middle Ages, each arguing that their own field of interest was crucial in the development of the vernacular. Professor Turville-Petre has examined the emergence of English as a literary medium in the half-century from 1290, and shown its increasing acceptability to an upper class and educated audience. English became socially respectable, in part because of political events which led to an interest in English history, and which provoked a literature of complaint and comment. This theory addresses the interests of a socially restricted group, and focuses, perforce, on a small number of manuscripts.[72]

By contrast, Professor Hudson has advanced the case for the Lollards who, a century later than Professor Turville-Petre's literary audience, made English the language of their Bible and of their theological discourse, the most solemn of subjects. This shocked the orthodox establishment, which considered that only Latin was suitable for such matters.[73] Though social exclusivity was not a charge which could be laid to the Lollards, the fact that this soon became a persecuted sect, which attracted legal penalties and which 'went underground' in the early fifteenth century, must raise some doubt as to its influence on the use of English among the population as a whole.

In contrast to the claims made for members of a persecuted heretical group, Professors Richardson and Fisher champion the name of Henry V. For them, the turning-point in the story of the language came in August 1417 when Henry changed to using English for his correspondence. This

---

[71] From about 1330 French almost entirely replaced Latin as the language of legislation.

[72] T. Turville-Petre, *England the Nation: Language, Literature, and National Identity, 1290–1340* (Oxford, 1996).

[73] A. Hudson, 'Lollardy: the English Heresy?', *Studies in Church History* 18 (1982), 261–84; reprinted in Hudson, *Lollards and their Books*, chap. 9.

new policy greatly enhanced the position of the vernacular and led rapidly to standardization as the prestige of 'chancery English' became recognized.[74]

Study of the methods used by Edward III to publicize his military aims and successes suggests a different conclusion. The need to provide propaganda in favour of foreign warfare introduced, for the first time and on a large scale, the use of English into churches, for we are talking about a period when sermons were rare (they must have been non-existent in many parishes). The use of English for political purposes, yet within church buildings, as an essential element of patriotic services, was, it may be argued, more important than any literary purpose. It was both all-embracing and highly influential, for these patriotic explanations had the blessing of the twin establishments of Church and crown. It can surely be no coincidence that the later fourteenth century saw a great flowering of writing in the English language, a language whose status had been raised by its association with liturgical endeavours of a propagandist nature. Thus the secular had invaded 'sacred space' through language, as surely, and more influentially, than the hanging of arms and armour and the installation of 'patriotic' windows in churches; and this was with the aim of winning support for the defence of south-west France – a place as remote to many subjects of the third Edward as the south Atlantic was to many subjects of the second Elizabeth some 650 years later.

[74] J. H. Fisher, M. Richardson and J. L. Fisher, *An Anthology of Chancery English* (Knoxville, Tenn., 1984), introduction and references.

APPENDIX
Prayers for success in war

1. 1333. For the king and his army proceeding against the wickedness of the Scots; York (5 & 14 April): Melton III, 118–19; 15 May, Lincoln: Reg. 5 (Burghersh, Memoranda), fol. 465v.

2. 23 April 1333 (writ), *CCR 1333–7*, p. 107. For the king's expedition against the Scots. 23 April (archbishop's mandate); 30 April (forward by bishop of London); 25 May (received by bishop of Lincoln); executed, 10 July; certificate, 29 July, Lincoln: Reg. 5, fols. 466–467.

3. 23 October 1334 (writ). For success in the Scottish war, *CCR 1333–7*, p. 347; execution, 28 October 1334, Lincoln: Reg. 5 (Burghersh, Memoranda), fol. 485v; Worcester: Montacute, 209–10.

4. 28 June 1335 (writ). For good success against the scoundrelly Scots; execution on 5 July 1335, York: Melton III, 142 and Lincoln: Reg. 5, fol. 503; on 12 July 1335, Worcester: Montacute, 248–9; and 18 July 1335, Salisbury: Reg. Wyville, fol. 21v.

5. 19 August 1336 (archbishop's mandate). For success against the Scots; execution, 27 August 1336, Worcester: Montacute, 232–3.

6. 2 June 1337 (archbishop's mandate), 12 June 1337 (forward by bishop of London). For the king proceeding to reprimand the obstinate malice of the Scots; Bath and Wells: Shrewsbury I, 305–6.

7. 28 March 1338 (writ). For the safety of the king and his army campaigning abroad in defence of his rights; execution 10 April 1338, Carlisle: Kirkby I, 82–3.

8. 15 August 1339 (writ). For the success of the king's expedition to France; Worcester: Bransford, 286–7.

9. 28 June 1340 (writ). To publicize and give thanks for the naval victory of 24 June [Sluys]; execution 12 July 1340. Worcester: Bransford, 290. Also contained in Rochester: Hethe II, 652, Carlisle: Kirkby I, 110 (but with no notes of execution).

10. 12 August 1342 (writ) (cf. 20 August 1342, *CCR 1341–3*, p. 650.) For the king's expedition to France and for the army sent against the Scots; executions on 29 August 1342, Salisbury: Reg. Wyville, fol. 75v; 31 August

1342, Durham (Bury): *Reg. Pal. Dunelm.* III, 499–500; 3 October 1342, Lincoln: Reg. 7 (Bek, Memoranda), fols. 3v–4.

11. 15 June 1345 (writ). For the king's intended expedition against Philip of Valois; execution on 23 June 1345; York: Reg. Zouche, fol. 257; certificate of execution, 11 September 1345, Worcester: Bransford, 315.

12. 26/27/28 February 1346. (27 Feb., *CCR 1346–9*, p. 45). For the king's success in war which the breaking of the truce by Philip of Valois compels him to renew. 4 March 1346 (archbishop's mandate), 12 March 1346 (bishop of London); execution on 16 March 1346, Winchester: Edington I, 7–8; undated, Hereford: Trillek, 264–6, 273–4; Bath and Wells: Shrewsbury I, 526–7.

13. 3 August 1346 (writ), *CCR 1346–9*, p. 145. To publicize the successful landing at La Hogue, and the capture of the town of Caen. Executions on 9 August 1346, Winchester: Edington II, 3; 11 August 1346, Hereford: Trillek, 77–8. Also contained in Carlisle: Kirkby I, 173 and Worcester: Bransford, 321 (no notes of execution).

14. 20 August 1346. Indulgences granted to those who contribute to the poor brothers of the hospital of St Oswald at Worcester, and who pray for the good estate of the Church, realm and for the success of the king's expedition; Hereford: Trillek, 77–8.

15. 12 January 1350. To give thanks for the king's victory over the treacherous French; Hereford: Trillek, 149–50; Bath and Wells: Shrewsbury II, 602 (undated).

16. 10 August 1350 (writ), *CCR 1349–54*, p. 266; 20 August 1350 (archbishop's mandate); 1 September 1350 (forward by bishop of London); execution, 10 October 1350. For the king about to set off to counter the wickedness of the Spanish; Bath and Wells: Shrewsbury II, 643.

17. 1 June 1355 (writ), *CCR 1354–60*, p. 210. For the king and his aims, with an explanation of the reason for the failure of the recent peace negotiations: French recalcitrance.

18. 19 December 1355. For the expedition of the king, prince of Wales, and the duke of Lancaster; Lincoln: Reg. 8 (Gynewell, Memoranda), fol. 76.

19. 1 June 1356 (writ). For the king, duke of Lancaster and the army: after the concord signed at Calais peace is still in danger; execution, 24 June 1356, *ibid.*, fols. 65–65v; undated, Winchester: Edington II, 42.

20. 10 October 1356 (writ), *CCR 1354–60*, p. 334. Thanksgiving for the victory of the prince of Wales over the French army near Poitiers when king John de Valois was taken prisoner; execution, undated, Winchester: Edington II, 43.

21. 12 August 1359 (writ), *CCR 1354–60*, p. 645; 14 August 1359 (archbishop's mandate); 16 August 1359 (forward by bishop of London). For the expedition of the king and the prince of Wales and their army; execution, 24 September 1359, Winchester: Edington II, 49.

22. 29 May 1363. For the prince of Wales' expedition to Aquitaine; Winchester: Edington II, 56.

23. August/September 1366. Success in wars and for the cessation of the plague; Lincoln: Reg. 12 (Buckingham, Memoranda), fol. 34v.

24. 5 February 1367 (archbishop's mandate); 11 February 1367 (London). For the king and the prince of Wales; execution, 24 April 1367, *ibid.*, fol. 41; execution, undated, Salisbury: Reg. Wyville, fol. 228v.

25. 16 April 1369. For peace and tranquillity, and against the dangers of the invading enemy, Winchester: Wykeham's Register II, 89–90.

26. 28 April 1369, archbishop's mandate. For peace, the king and the prince of Wales, against the plague, and for the queen, the duke of Lancaster and the earl of Cambridge; execution: 15 May 1369, Lincoln: Reg. 12, fol. 71; received 20 June 1369 (no date of execution), Winchester: Wykeham's Register II, 82–8.

27. 23 August 1370. For peace; Lincoln: Reg. 12, fol. 96v.

28. 5 May 1372. For peace, for the king, prince of Wales, the duke of Lancaster and the king's other sons. *ibid.*, fol. 107.

29. 11 August 1372 (writ), *CCR 1360–4*, p. 460. For protection against the expected Spanish invasion.

30. 16 June 1373 (writ), *CCR 1370–4*, p. 563. For the success of the planned expedition of the king's son John king of Castile and Leon and other nobles to recover the king's rights in France.

31. 20 August 1374 (writ). For the prosperity and peace of the realm; execution, 4 September 1374, Lincoln: Reg. 12, fol. 125; 9 September 1374, Winchester: Wykeham's Register II, 218.

32. 8 May 1375 (writ) *CCR 1374–7*, p. 224. For the expedition of Edmund earl of Cambridge and John duke of Brittany whom the king is sending overseas to preserve the rights of his kingdom; execution, 25 May 1375, Lincoln: Reg. 12, fol. 128.

33. 27 October 1376, archbishop's mandate. For peace. Execution, 14 November 1376, Winchester: Wykeham's Register II, 265.

10

The Anglo-French Peace Negotiations of 1354–1360 Reconsidered

CLIFFORD J. ROGERS

According to the terms of the Treaty of Brétigny, which was sealed on 8 May 1360, Edward III was to be given full, sovereign rule over Guienne, Saintonge, the Angoumois, Poitou, the Limousin, Périgord, the Agenais, Rouergue, Guare, Bigorre and Quercy, as well as Calais, Guînes, and the surrounding areas, and on top of these lands he was to receive the almost unimaginably huge sum of 3,000,000 gold *écus*, or £500,000. The French, furthermore, agreed to abandon their troublesome old alliance with the Scots. In exchange, Edward was to cancel his own alliance with the Flemings, abandon his claim to the French throne, and agree to a perpetual peace and alliance with Valois France.[1] Surprisingly enough, the current orthodoxy holds that these terms represented a major defeat for Edward III, one which he accepted only because of the threat of imminent military disaster. It seems to me, however, that this interpretation, put forward most elaborately by John Le Patourel but also found in the works of Kenneth Fowler, Edouard Perroy, Philippe Contamine and others, is wrong on both counts: the treaty was in fact a triumph for King Edward rather than a surrender, and the campaign of 1359–1360 was hardly the military failure often described.[2]

To decide whether the terms of the Treaty of Brétigny represent a strategic success or a strategic failure, it is necessary to review the history of English war-aims and peace negotiations over the preceding quarter century. One reason for the misinterpretation of the peace of 1360 is a number of misreadings of the terms of earlier, unimplemented agreements. Let us begin with the English objectives. Edward III began his war with France with three basic aims: to end French interference in his subjugation of Scotland; to end the meddling of the Valois royal administration in his government of his French territories, especially Guienne, by persuading the

---

[1] The Treaty of Brétigny is printed in *Foedera*, ed. T. Rymer (The Hague, 1740), III1, 202–9. For more about Edward III's claim to the French throne, see articles by W. M. Ormrod and C. Taylor, above.

[2] The views of these historians are quoted below, passim.

Clifford J. Rogers

French to acknowledge that he held them as allods (that is, in sovereignty, not as a vassal's fiefs); and to regain the lands occupied by Charles of Valois in 1324 which by the treaties of 1326 and 1329 were supposed to be returned to the Plantagenets but which, by the outbreak of the war in 1337, it had become clear that the French did not intend to hand over. Of course, in 1340 Edward also formally laid claim to the crown of France, a claim resting on the fact that in 1328 he had been the nearest male relative of King Charles IV on that monarch's death, thus raising the stakes of the conflict considerably. The terms of King Edward's instructions to his negotiators, however, show pretty clearly that (as the best-informed chroniclers also indicate) this step was taken more as a means to achieving his initial ends than as a fundamental change in his aims themselves. By assuming the title of king of France, he gained the support of Flanders, and made it possible for French opponents of the Valois to switch to the Plantagenet side without unambiguously committing treason against the French crown. Edward, however, constantly proclaimed his willingness to accept a reasonable and honourable peace whenever it should be offered to him, and his internal diplomatic documents indicate that in practice this meant that he was generally willing to give up his claim to the French throne in exchange for Valois acknowledgment of his claim to sovereignty over Aquitaine and suzerainty over Scotland. That was the fundamental issue of principle; the exact size of the French territories over which Edward would gain sovereignty was subject to negotiation, and his demands in that area waxed and waned with his military fortunes (though he was never prepared to accept any *less* French land than his ancestors had ruled as dukes of Aquitaine).

Edward was asking a great deal of the French, and all he was offering in return was peace and the retraction of his claim to the crown. Thus, before he could get what he wanted, he had to make the damage inflicted by his war, and the risk posed by his claim to the crown, greater than the sacrifice he demanded; those conditions could only be fulfilled if he were clearly winning the war. As long as the French had a hope of victory, they would never consent to the dismemberment of their kingdom.[3]

The first big step towards eliminating the Valois hopes for victory was the battle of Crécy. Although this victory has often been described as strategically barren, that assessment is seriously in error.[4] The measure of the strategic success of a battle is the degree to which it moves one closer to achieving one's political objectives, and Crécy came very close to pushing the French into accepting Edward's war aims. As Jean Froissart observed, after Crécy the French were 'much weakened in honour, strength and counsel'; their subsequent failure to prevent the capture of Calais, Poitiers, St. Jean-

[3] Cf. C. von Clausewitz, *Vom Kriege*, ed. W. Hahlweg (Bonn, 1952), p. 92 (Bk 1, chap. 1, no. 4).
[4] E.g. J. Sumption, *The Hundred Years War*, in progress (London, 1990–), I, 532; E. Perroy, *The Hundred Years War* (New York, 1965), p. 120.

d'Angély, Châteauneuf and Lusignan highlighted their weakness.[5] It is only with this in mind that it is possible to understand the negotiation of the Treaty of Guînes, the first of the three draft treaties which preceded the Brétigny agreement, in 1353–4 – otherwise this becomes, as J. J. N. Palmer considered it, 'the most mysterious episode of the whole war'.[6] The terms of this draft treaty, which was concluded on 6 April 1354, were the basis of all subsequent negotiations up through 1360. They gave Edward all his original war aims and more: in addition to an end to the Franco-Scottish alliance and sovereignty over the duchy of Aquitaine, he was also to receive the counties of Poitou, Touraine, Anjou, Maine, Ponthieu and Limoges, and the Calais pale, all as allodial possessions without obligation for homage.[7] Although this agreement was accepted by the French diplomatic team charged with peace negotiations, and brought before Pope Innocent VI for final confirmation at the end of 1354, it was not ratified. Historians have often suggested that the English were responsible for the failure of the treaty. According to Le Patourel:

> There is no direct evidence to show which side was responsible for this breakdown; most English chroniclers blame the French, but Knighton, whose information may ultimately have come from Henry of Lancaster, the leader of the English delegation, says that Lancaster refused specifically to give up Edward's claim and title to the kingdom of France. Such a stand would have wrecked the treaty at once; and . . . it may be that he came to Avignon with no intention of ratifying.[8]

Le Patourel makes this point in the course of a general argument that Edward III's claim to the French crown was meant more seriously than usually believed, and that his ultimate acceptance (at Brétigny) of anything less – even a third of France held in full sovereignty, a free hand in Scotland, and a huge ransom – was a 'surrender' which could only have been forced on the English king by a military defeat. By this same logic, Kenneth Fowler

---

[5] J. Froissart, *Oeuvres*, ed. Kervyn de Lettenhove, 25 vols. (Brussels, 1867–77), V, 64–5.

[6] J. J. N. Palmer, 'The War Aims of the Protagonists and the Negotiations for Peace', in *The Hundred Years War*, ed. K. Fowler (London, 1971), pp. 51–73 (p. 58).

[7] The draft Treaty of Guînes is transcribed in F. Bock, 'Some New Documents Illustrating the Early Years of the Hundred Years' War', *Bulletin of the John Rylands Library* 15 (1931), pp. 60–99 (Appendix II).

[8] J. Le Patourel, 'Edward III and the Kingdom of France', *History* 43 (1958), 173–89 (p. 177). Cf., more recently and more definitely, M. Prestwich, *The Three Edwards: War and the State in England 1272–1377* (London, 1980), p. 179: 'The English refused to ratify an agreement reached at Guines in 1353, which would have given Edward extensive lands in France in full sovereignty. It is probable that at the last minute they refused to abandon the claim to the French throne, since they were tempted to reopen the war with the aid of a new ally, the maverick Charles, King of Navarre.' The most elaborate discussion, which takes the same general stance, is in K. Fowler, *The King's Lieutenant: Henry of Grosmont, First Duke of Lancaster, 1310–1361* (London, 1969), pp. 111–46.

concludes that at Guînes, '[i]t was the English, not the French, who had been brought to a surrender'.[9]

If it had indeed been the English who blocked the completion of the Treaty of Guînes, that would certainly be a strong indication that Edward's war-aims in 1354–5 went far beyond what they had been at the beginning of the war; that a sovereign greater Aquitaine and an end to French interference in Scotland were no longer enough for him; and that the terms ultimately agreed on at Brétigny did indeed indicate something of a defeat, since by that treaty he would then be accepting what he had deemed insufficient in 1354–5. That, however, seems rather an improbable proposition on the face of it – one would expect that, if anything, the English would demand *more*, not *less*, from the French after crushing their royal army for a second time at Poitiers, capturing Jean II there, and watching French society buckle and nearly crumble under the subsequent assaults of Etienne Marcel's proto-revolution, the ravages of the *routiers*, and the Jacquerie.

I contend, however, that Edward's war-aims were quite consistent between 1353 and 1360, and that what he got at Brétigny was more or less what he had been seeking throughout this period (with the exception, perhaps, of the interval between the rejection of the Second Treaty of London and Black Monday in 1360). He would have been quite happy in 1354–5 to accept the terms negotiated at Guînes, and even to make conces-sions in the interpretation of them, provided that he did not give up any of the lands his ancestors had held as Dukes of Aquitaine. Thus, as Fowler acknowledges, 'Edward was anxious to hurry up the proceedings' leading to the ratification of the treaty (which would be rather odd if he did in fact view the agreement as a 'surrender').[10] Thus, Edward's ambassadors were in fact given clear and explicit power to renounce his claim to the French throne in exchange for the sought-after resolution of matters relating to Aquitaine and Scotland.[11]

Why would he try to expedite the final negotiations if he did not intend to ratify them? Why would he give his ambassadors powers he did not intend for them to use? Reasons can be found to answer these questions, and Fowler and Le Patourel try do to so, but their answers are quite hypothetical. They might be justified in their speculations were they simply making an effort to explain *why* something that clearly did happen, happened, but their argu-ments are far from sufficient to justify discarding the overwhelming pre-ponderance – indeed the unanimity – of the evidence which indicates that it was in fact the French, not the English, who refused to ratify the Treaty of Guînes. Even before Lancaster's peace embassy arrived at Avignon, there

[9] *King's Lieutenant*, pp. 129 (quotation) and 143. Fowler later softens his assertion, saying it was 'a profitable peace – not a complete surrender – but a compromise on good terms'.
[10] *King's Lieutenant*, p. 132.
[11] Bock, 'Documents', pp. 76–7 and 94–6. Cf. also pp. 98–9 and *Foedera*, III1, 100–2.

were signs that the French would not hold to their agreement. One of the English proctors at the curia, Gérard du Puy, wrote to Edward III that there were rumours that the men who had negotiated for Jean II at Guînes had since fallen from favour, and that some, therefore, 'were not as eager for the peace as previously.' The English diplomat added that he and his colleagues still hoped that, with Lancaster's arrival, a good peace could be made, but warned the king to prepare for war in case it could not.[12] This document is especially important because it was an internal communication, clearly not influenced by any propagandistic desire to shift the blame for the future collapse of the agreement onto the French.[13] According to Lancaster himself, by April 1355 Guy's fears had proven fully justified, for at the end of that month the duke sent a messenger to explain to the emperor 'how the treaty of peace failed by the default of the French, all the articles agreed and sworn by the councils of the two [kings] and recorded before the pope notwithstanding'.[14]

Edward III too stated quite clearly, in a letter to the archbishops and bishops of England explaining the reasons for the resumption of the war, that it was the Valois ambassadors who had broken faith and rejected the treaty agreed upon at Guînes.[15] Even more importantly, he also blamed the duplicity of the French for the failure of the peace in a letter to Pope Innocent VI.[16] If it had really been the English who refused to ratify the negotiated peace, it would have been most foolish to blame the other side in a letter to one of the few people who would have known the full truth of the matter. There are no comparable French documents which accuse the English of a refusal to implement the agreed-upon terms. English chroniclers say the Valois diplomats broke the deal by withdrawing their offer to surrender sovereignty over the ceded territories; the French chroniclers neither deny this nor say the English were unwilling to keep their side of the arrangement.[17] In fact, there is no contemporary source that indicates it was the

[12] *EMDP*, I1, 297 ('nont mie si grand desir de la pais come devant.').

[13] Note also that it was written well before the meetings between Lancaster and Charles the Bad at Avignon.

[14] *EMDP*, I1, 298.

[15] *Foedera*, III1, 109 ('juxta formam dictae Concordiae, fide mediâ mutuò roboratae, misissemus, bonâ fide, ad praesentiam Domini Summi Pontificis, pro Confirmatione dictae Concordiae, solempnes Nuncios, paratos, quantum ad nos attinet, facere quae sic fuerant Concordata, Pars adversa, Vulpinâ Calliditate, Unum Agens & Aliud Similans . . . mittens in dolo Nuncios ad dictum Dominum Summum Pontificem . . . Qui . . . in Elatione Spiritûs, cum Violatione Fidei, dictam habere Concordiam recusârunt.') Similarly, Sir Walter Mauny, acting as the king's prolocutor, explained to Parliament how 'apres le dit Tretee [de Guînes] ens certeins pointz ent acordez, nostre Seign' le Roi . . . envoia le Duc de Lancastr'. . . pur acomplir & finalment parfournir en presence nostre dit Seint Piere les choses issint devant tretes, queles ne y purroient prendre esploit solonc le dit acort, pur defaut & coupe trove de la par son dit Adversair.' *RP*, II, 264.

[16] *Foedera*, III1, 122; also Delachenal, *Histoire de Charles V*, 5 vols. (Paris, 1909–31), I, 92 n. 3.

[17] *Chronicon Galfridi le Baker de Swynbroke*, ed. E. M. Thompson (Oxford, 1889), pp. 123–5;

English who backed out of the terms agreed at Guînes, for even the passage from Knighton cited by Le Patourel, when read carefully, sets the responsibility for the failure to ratify the proposed peace firmly on the Valois. Knighton actually says it was the *French* ambassadors who 'repudiated the articles to which they had assented and agreed at Calais [that is, at Guînes]', and refused peace 'unless they could have it just as they wished'. Lancaster's statement that Edward would not abandon the arms of France was specifically a *response* to French demands that he do so *and do homage to the king of France for Gascony*. Thus, it was a French demand, not an English one, which 'wrecked the treaty at once'. Indeed, after Lancaster refused to accept the French demands which violated the terms of the Guînes agreement, he went on to add 'that if they wanted to accept any other reasonable way of peace, the king of England, as a lover of peace, fully desired it'.[18]

Why, then, did the French change their policy and decide not to ratify the agreement? The most likely explanation is simply that King Jean had been persuaded that, before accepting defeat – for that *is* what the Treaty of Guînes would have meant for the Valois – he should risk one more attempt to defeat Edward III's armies in battle, and thus redeem both the military and political situation at a blow. In 1356, at Poitiers, he had his chance, but was once again defeated by the Plantagenets, and this time, what is more, he was himself captured and led into prison in England.[19]

see also *Chronica Johannis de Reading et Anonymi Cantuariensis, 1346–1367*, ed. J. Tait (Manchester, 1914), p. 116 ('per fraudem Francorum'); Robert of Avesbury, *De gestis mirabilis regis Edwardi tertii*, ed. E. M. Thompson (RS, 1889), p. 421 ('nuncii praedicti Francigeni ipsam pacis formam negarunt omnino'); *Anonimalle Chronicle 1333–1381*, ed. V. H. Galbraith (Manchester, 1927), pp. 31–2. The author of the *Récits d'un bourgeois de Valenciennes*, ed. Kervyn de Lettenhove (Louvain, 1877), pp. 273–4, does claim that the peace failed because of 'les grandes et excessives demandes que le conseil du roy d'Engleterre faisoit', but does not say what they were, and makes no reference to the Guînes agreement having already been reached, so the 'great and excessive claims' made may well be the demand for sovereignty over Aquitaine. Thus, his statement is not inconsistent with the hypothesis that, as the English chroniclers say, the treaty fell through when the French backed out of their commitment to concede sovereignty over the lands to be transferred.

[18] *Knighton's Chronicle, 1337–1396*, ed. and trans. G. Martin (Oxford, 1995), pp. 126–7: 'ambassiatores Franciae . . . dedixerunt cunctos articulos ad quos assensum prebuerant et conuenerant apud Calesiam. Et sub breui eloquio, nullam concordiam amplecti uolebant nisi ad suam propriam uoluntatem. Et dixerunt se paratos et satis potentes ad tuendam partem suam contra Anglicos cunctis diebus seculi et sic abinuicem recesserunt. Nam primo pecierunt Franci quod rex Anglie omitteret arma Francie. Item quod rex Anglie faceret homagium regi Francie pro Vasconia. Respondit dux Lancastrie . . .'; 'Quod si aliam uiam pacis racionabilem capere uellent, rex Anglie tanquam pacis amator amplecti desiderat.' The translation of the first phrase is Martin's.

[19] For the Poitiers campaign, see C. J. Rogers, *War Cruel and Sharp: English Strategy under Edward III, 1327–1360* (Woodbridge, 2000).

Having made his bid to reverse the military situation and instead only worsened it, the French king immediately began to seek a new peace treaty along the lines of the Treaty of Guînes, but with the addition of a large cash sum payable to Edward III for his personal ransom. The outlines of such an agreement were accepted by both sides as early as March of 1357,[20] but it took until May of 1358 before the details were sufficiently worked out that a new draft treaty could be drawn up: this is the document known as the First Treaty of London.

As Le Patourel read this agreement, it was far less favourable for the French than the Treaty of Guînes. Its territorial terms were comparable: the Plantagenet was to receive sovereignty over Aquitaine, Saintonge, Angoumois, Poitou, Limousin, Quercy, Périgord, Bigorre, Guare and the Agenais, along with Ponthieu, Guînes and the Calais Pale. Suzerainty over Brittany, however, was now also to go to King Edward. In addition, moreover, King Jean was to pay an unprecedentedly huge ransom of 4,000,000 écus (£666,667), which for comparison's sake was approximately twenty years' worth of the 'ordinary' revenues of the English crown.[21] And, even more significant, all of this was to be given to the English merely in exchange for the release of Jean II; the two major concessions granted by Edward III under the terms of the 1354 Guînes agreement, peace and the retraction of his claim to the throne, were supposedly not dealt with in the 1358 document, which was thus a mere 'ransom treaty'.[22]

Le Patourel, whose views have been widely accepted on this matter,[23] is simply wrong on this latter crucial point. There is every reason to be confident that the agreement summarized in the draft of the First Treaty of

[20] Edward III's December 1356 instructions to Prince Edward concerning the negotiations are published in Bock, 'Documents', pp. 98–9; initial agreement was reached on 18 March 1357 (*Chronique des règnes de Jean II et Charles V*, ed. R. Delachenal [Paris, 1910], p. 107); on 29 May 1357, the Pope wrote to express his pleasure that peace was 'quasi concordata' (*Foedera*, III1, 140). See also *Knighton's Chronicle*, p. 158. Although little is known of this initial draft agreement, it must have included both the sovereignty concession and the breaking of the Franco-Scottish alliance, for otherwise (as the instructions of December 1356 make fairly clear) it would not have been termed a 'peace'.

[21] The figure of twenty years is very rough; the revenues varied substantially from year to year, and furthermore different totals for 'ordinary' revenues are reached depending on exactly which sources are comprised within that term. G. L. Harriss, *King, Parliament and Public Finance* (Oxford, 1975), pp. 523–6; R. W. Kaeuper, *War, Justice and Public Order* (Oxford, 1988), p. 62; K. Fowler, 'Truces', in *The Hundred Years War*, ed. Fowler, pp. 184–215 (pp. 204–5). Looked at another way, £666,667 was probably greater than the sum total of all the coinage in circulation in England at that time. S. L. Waugh, *England in the Reign of Edward III* (Cambridge, 1991), p. 80.

[22] J. Le Patourel, 'The Treaty of Bretigny, 1360', *TRHS* 5th ser. 10 (1960), 19–39 (pp. 24–6).

[23] E.g. by Fowler, *King's Lieutenant*, pp. 197–8, 210; P. Contamine, *La guerre de cent ans* (Paris, 1972), pp. 44–5. Le Patourel is still accepted as the authority on the draft treaties leading up to Brétigny. See *Knighton's Chronicle* (Oxford, 1995), p. 163 n. 3.

London did indeed retain those two key concessions by the Plantagenets. First of all, it simply makes no sense that Jean would abandon the formula which in all past and future negotiations was an obvious quid pro quo – Valois renunciation of their claim to sovereignty over part of France in exchange for Plantagenet renunciation of their claim to sovereignty over all of it – or that he would make any such massive transfer of territory without gaining in return an end to the war, which by 1358, after Crécy, Poitiers, the Jacquerie, and the ravages of the *routiers*, his country desperately needed. If he were to do so without securing a promise of peace, he would simply be placing in his enemy's hands all the means necessary to complete the destruction of the Valois monarchy in the next phase of the fighting. 'Sense', however, is in the mind of the observer, so I will not rely on that assertion to make my case; instead, I will turn to the document itself.

First of all, this *was* clearly a full peace agreement. The document is entitled 'La trattié et la parlaunce de la *paix*', not the 'trattié et la parlaunce de la raunsoun' or 'de la trewes',[24] and it furthermore specifies that once the French abandon their Scottish alliance and complete the other terms of the agreement, 'final and perpetual peace, accord, friendship and alliance will be established between the kings and the realms of France and England'.[25] In addition, although Le Patourel claims that 'the English chroniclers speak of this agreement . . . as though it were concerned simply with King John's ransom',[26] in fact the most accurate chronicle notice of the treaty, that of the Anonymous of Canterbury, lists the concessions to be made by the French then says: 'and thus [Jean] would hold the country of France in peace.'[27]

Second, on the matter of the exchange of sovereignties, the draft treaty is (as Le Patourel recognized) quite unambiguously clear that greater Aquitaine was to be held by Edward and his heirs 'perpetually, fully, and freely . . . as sovereign lords . . . and as neighbours to the kings and realm of France, without recognizing or making any obedience, homage, sovereignty, resort or subjection, and without doing any service to the crown or the kings of

[24] See the First Treaty of London in R. Delachenal, *Histoire de Charles V*, II, 405. Palmer, 'War Aims', also points this out. Cf. the 1356 negotiating instructions (Bock, 'Documents', pp. 98–9), clauses 4 and 5, for a clear distinction between 'paix' (which requires the 'libertee' of Edward's French lands and also must include the sacrifice of the Scots) and 'trewes' (which does not): 'Item que en le tretee de *pees*, les Escotz soient de tout oustez, et en cas qils purront estre oustez hors des *trewes*, tant vaudroit le plus . . .' [emphases added].

[25] First Treaty of London in Delachenal, *Charles V*, II, 407: 'Et aussi le dit adversaire et toute la partie de Ffrance seu departiront de tout de les alliances q'ils ount avec les Escotz desore en avant, et adonqes serront faites accordz et paix finales et perpetuels alliances et amistiez entre les roys et les roialmes de Ffrance et d'Engleterre'.

[26] 'Treaty of Bretigny', p. 25.

[27] *Chronica Johannis de Reading et Anonymi Cantuariensis*, p. 208: 'et sic terram Francie in pacem teneret.'

France'.[28] As to the renunciation of Edward's claim to the throne of France, it is true that the draft which survives does not include a specific clause on this subject, but nonetheless such a renunciation *is* everywhere clearly implicit in the document. Although King Jean is referred to merely as 'the adversary of France' in the treaty, the text repeatedly speaks of his heirs as future kings of France, a title never accorded in the document, despite the draft's English origin, to Edward or his heirs.[29] Furthermore, the treaty explicitly called for Edward's protégés John of Montfort and Philip of Navarre – who had both already done homage to Edward as king of France for their French lands – to do homage to Jean after the settlement of the peace, which also clearly indicates that the agreement involved acknowledgment of the Valois claim to the French throne.[30] Finally, the already-mentioned provision that 'friendship and alliance will be established between the kings [note the plural] . . . of France and England' makes no sense at all unless it is understood that Edward III intended to drop his claim to *be* king of France as well as king of England.[31] Indeed, the chronicler Matteo Villani reports that when the two kings spoke in public of the peace, Edward went beyond merely agreeing to *accept* Jean's rule in France: he even promised to use all his force to 'restore the king of France to lordship in his realm'.[32]

It is also worth noting that Le Patourel was also mistaken about the First Treaty's disposition of the Breton question. As mentioned above, he says that the treaty included 'the stipulation that, whatever the outcome [of the dispute between Montfort and Blois] the sovereignty of Brittany should remain with the king of England' – a major concession to the English not found in the agreement of 1353–4.[33] In fact, however, the agreement of 1358 envisioned that the homage due for Brittany *would* eventually go to the king of France – just as the Guînes agreement implicitly did, since it did not list Brittany as among the lands to be transferred to Edward's control. What the First Treaty actually calls for is an elaborate process by which the competing claims of John of Montfort and Charles de Blois would be resolved either by arbitration or by gauge of battle. If either side declined to participate in the process or accept its outcome, both kings would support the other side. Edward would continue to exercise sovereignty over Brittany (or at least as much of it as was

---

[28] First Treaty of London in Delachenal, *Charles V*, II, 405–6.

[29] E.g.: 'Et aussi rendra et baillera le dit adversaire pour lui et *pour toutes ses heirs rois de Ffrance* . . . au dit nostre seigneur le roi et à ses heirs rois d'Engleterre.' Delachenal, *Charles V*, II, 405.

[30] First Treaty of London in Delachenal, *Charles V*, II, 410–11. For Philip's homage to Edward 'come a Roy de France & Duc de Normandie', see *Foedera*, III1, 128.

[31] The text quoted above offers another similar implication of Edward's renunciation of his claim to the throne of France when it speaks of him holding Aquitaine as a neighbour to the king of France; if he were maintaining his claim he would thus be a neighbour to himself.

[32] Matteo Villani, *Cronica*, ed. G. Porta, 2 vols. (Parma, 1995), II, 200–1.

[33] Le Patourel, 'Treaty of Bretigny', p. 24.

currently held by Montfortian partisans) only *until* final peace was reached between the two sides.[34]

Thus, in sum, the First Treaty of London was closely comparable to the Treaty of Guînes, except that a huge cash ransom for King Jean's release had been added. Considering how much worse the French situation was in 1358 than it had been in 1354, it is easy to see why the reaction to this generous agreement in the French capital was very positive.[35]

Despite the warm reception of the First Treaty in Paris, it was never implemented. It has been asserted that this was because Edward 'seiz[ed] the opportunity afforded by [the] increased internal difficulties [of the French kingdom] to tear up the treaty and press for an even more generous settlement'.[36] In fact, however, it was again *the French* who failed on all counts to meet the terms of the agreement. They failed to raise the first instalment of the ransom on time; they failed to provide the specified hostages who were to be held to guarantee the execution of the treaty; and they failed to persuade the pope to make certain concessions which Edward was demanding as part of the peace settlement.[37] The fact that Edward

---

[34] First Treaty of London in Delachenal, *Charles V*, II, 410–11. 'Mais toutes voies, *tanqes* la paix soit fait finale entre les dites parties . . . le hommage du dit Mountfort et la soveraineté de Bretaingne et de quant qe le dit Mountfort ou autres de par luy y tiegnent au present demourront au Roi d'Engleterre. . . .' [emphasis added]. Once the dispute over Brittany was resolved, Montfort, regardless of what happened concerning Brittany, was to receive again his county of Montfort, for which he was to do homage to the king of France. Of course, Edward had been acting as king of France when he accepted Montfort's homage, and Brittany was not among the territories which by the treaty were to be removed from the kingdom of France, so it was natural that whichever claimant ultimately kept the duchy would do so as a vassal of the Valois, since the treaty required Edward to renounce his title to the crown of France.

[35] *Chronique des règnes de Jean II et Charles V*, p. 144: 'Le quel traictié plot moult aus diz duc [de Normandie] et conseilliers, si comme ilz disoient.'

[36] Palmer, 'War Aims', p. 59 (cf. p. 62); Fowler, *King's Lieutenant*, p. 198, agrees that the First Treaty (which he considers a mere ransom treaty) failed 'apparently on Edward's initiative'.

[37] Jean le Bel, *Chronique de Jean le Bel*, ed. J. Viard and E. Déprez, 2 vols. (Paris, 1904–5), II, 287, heads his chapter on the invasion as follows: 'Comment le paix des II roys de France et d'Angleterre fut acordée et seellée par eulx mesmement, *mais les Françoys ne la voulurent garder*; si s'apresta le roy d'Angleterre de venir derechief en France' [emphasis added]. Similarly, T. Walsingham, *Historia Anglicana*, ed. H. T. Riley, 2 vols. (RS, 1863–4), p. 284: 'Ad habendam ergo majorem securitatem istius summae [the ransom] solvendae, postulatum ex parte Regis Angliae habere potentiores et valentiores personas regni Franciae in obsidatum; sed huic petitioni noluerunt Gallici consentire, quamobrem vicesimo die Novembris responsum est Francis, ut se defendant et praeparent ad bellandum.' Equally, we have no evidence that Edward III made much effort to resuscitate the treaty. Knighton, however, does say that the French brought 1,200,000 marks (£800,000, more than the total amount of the ransom; perhaps an error for 120,000 marks) to London, but Edward refused to accept it because the money was not accompanied by the stipulated hostages

waited two full months past the first instalment's due-date of November 1 before he began to make any military preparations suggests that he was not as eager to see the treaty's demise as has usually been assumed.[38]

The First Treaty of London, had it been implemented, would have met Edward's war aims; since it was not implemented, it did not meet his war aims. He thus had the choice of re-negotiating a more generous treaty which would have been easier for the French to fulfil, or resuming the war. Given that the realm of France was on the edge of a deep abyss in the autumn of 1358, and also that the First Treaty was already quite generous, Edward had no reason to make additional concessions to the Valois. Instead, he chose to resume the war.

His design for the new campaign, probably from the start, involved an effort to capture the city of Reims, where he could be anointed with the holy oil of St Remy and re-crowned as king of France. There were two ways the regent, Prince Charles, could be expected to respond to a threat to Reims – the capture of which would quite likely lead to the fall of the Valois dynasty, which was already on the ropes, and so to his disinheritance. First, he might be pressured into re-negotiating *and implementing* a new peace treaty, in which case Edward would get what he wanted. Second, Charles might be pressured into a desperate attempt to save the situation by risking yet

(*Knighton's Chronicle*, pp. 160–2). This is an interesting tale, and the latter part sounds credible, but it is hard to imagine a shipment of 120,000 marks (much less 1,200,000) which left no record in English or French archives. Had this occurred as described by Knighton, there should at least have been appropriate safe-conducts issued, which (from Rymer) does not seem to have been done. Knighton's credibility on this whole issue is further lessened by his story of a French messenger captured bearing letters of the king of France stating that he never intended to surrender a single foot of his lands to Edward. Had this been true, it would doubtless have found its way into Edward's propaganda and his justifications for resuming the war; furthermore, it is hard to credit such duplicity on Jean II's part, who seems to have been very sincere in his desire to make peace (*Knighton's Chronicle*, p. 163). It is possible that Knighton was confused by a report that the French king brought 1,000,000 *sterlings* (i.e. pence, or about £4,166) with him to London in 1357. BL MS Sloane 560, fol. 59v. Even if Knighton were correct about the 1,200,000 marks, however, it would still be true that the French rather than the English broke the treaty (in a serious, not a trivial way) by failing to provide the stipulated hostages. See also Delachenal, *Charles V*, II, 72. The importance of the issue of papal affairs (renunciation of the Church's claim to suzerainty over and tribute from England, and the end of the curia's interference in the administration of royal justice against 'criminal churchmen' in England) should not be under-estimated. See T. Gray, *Scalacronica*, ed. J. Stevenson (Edinburgh, 1836), p. 177; Delachenal, *Charles V*, II, 64 and 400–407 (letter of Jean II); Froissart, *Oeuvres*, XVIII, 429; *Chronica Johannis de Reading et Anonymi Cantuariensis*, pp. 129–30; J. Aberth, *Criminal Churchmen in the Age of Edward III: The Case of Bishop Thomas de Lisle* (University Park, Penn., 1996), passim and p. 171.

[38] The first order for bows and arrows to be sent to the Tower was issued January 2; commissions of array were appointed only on January 12. *Foedera* (Record Commission edn), III1, 414–16.

another major battle – which Edward doubtless calculated would lead to yet another major defeat for the French. After three such, it is unlikely that the Valois would have been able to mount any further resistance. Again, Edward would emerge the winner. If the French did neither of these, and Reims did fall, Edward would be in an excellent position.

The latter two of these three possibilities, indeed, held out the chance of Edward gaining even more than he had gained by the First Treaty – that is, of gaining de facto the French throne which he had long claimed – and without the worry that the French might yet again make and then break another deal (as, from the English perspective at least, they had so often done before). Thus, once military preparations had begun, and as the situation of the Valois monarchy was getting worse and worse thanks mainly to the ravages of the free companies and Edward's *routiers*, Edward was not especially anxious to make a new peace agreement on the Guînes model. King Jean, on the other hand, was most eager to come to an accord and prevent the attack on the coronation city.

Ultimately, in a face-to-face meeting between the two monarchs from which the usual diplomats and counsellors were largely excluded, Jean did manage to persuade Edward to accept a new peace offer. This new arrangement, the Second Treaty of London, is universally depicted by modern historians as 'clearly impossible', 'extravagant', even 'preposterous'. Indeed, some have argued that Edward's acceptance was a 'grim farce' not even meant as a 'sincere proposal for peace' – that he accepted the treaty only because he anticipated a propaganda victory in the inevitable French rejection of it, or else that he intended it merely as a Hitlerian prelude to gobbling up the whole kingdom.[39]

---

[39] Le Patourel, 'Treaty of Bretigny', pp. 20 and 30; Delachenal, *Charles V*, II, 80 ('ne pouvait-il [le traité] obtenir l'approbation de personne'); R. Barber, *Edward, Prince of Wales and Aquitaine* (London, 1978), p. 158; K. Fowler, *The Age of Plantagenet and Valois* (New York, 1967), p. 61 ('so preposterous that it is difficult to believe that it was ever intended seriously'); Fowler, *King's Lieutenant*, p. 198; Le Patourel, 'Edward III and the Kingdom of France', pp. 177–8 ('if one tries to visualize what France would have been like [shorn of all her western and northern provinces] if the treaty had been carried into effect, it is difficult to believe that it represents a sincere proposal for peace on Edward's part or, if it does, then his price for a promise to renounce his claim – a promise unsupported by any security – was the kingdom virtually delivered into his hands'). Cf. the summation of this argument in Palmer, 'War Aims', p. 60, incorporating a quotation from Le Patourel, 'Treaty of Bretigny', p. 29: 'As for the Second Treaty of London (24 March 1359), its terms were so extravagant that Edward could not possibly have intended to stop there: "Did anyone seriously suppose that these territorial provisions could be carried out, or, if they were, that the rump of the kingdom of France could have survived as an independent state?"' At least one contemporary chronicler, however, agreed in part: Matteo Villani thought that Edward had agreed knowing in his heart that the treaty was impossible, but thinking that when it failed he could blame the French for the rupture of the peace. *Cronica*, II, 293–4.

It is true that the Second Treaty was more favourable to Edward than the First Treaty had been, for it added Normandy, Brittany, Maine, Touraine and Anjou to the territories to be handed over to English sovereignty: it promised, in other words, to restore Henry II's old Angevin Empire to Plantagenet rule. It seems to me, however, that if the First Treaty is viewed (as these historians do see it) as 'reasonable and moderate', then the Second Treaty is not so extravagant. Normandy and Brittany were in 1359 already de facto largely lost to Valois rule, between the Navarrese and the English garrisons and *routiers*, and Maine, Touraine and Anjou had been included in the lands to be given up in the Treaty of Guînes in 1354, *before* the battle of Poitiers, the Jacquerie, the Parisian revolt, and the Navarrese war. Furthermore, the increase in the territory to be transferred was at least partially balanced by significant concessions by Edward III (a fact which previous historians seem not to have noted). First, and most importantly, the Second Treaty called, essentially, for a reduction of King Jean's ransom from 4,000,000 to 3,000,000 *écus*, a very substantial reduction when one considers that the difference of 1,000,000 *écus* was the equivalent of £166,000, twenty times the annual revenues produced by the estates of Henry of Grosmont, duke of Lancaster, earl of Derby, Lincoln and Leicester, and lord of extensive Welsh lands, the greatest magnate in England.[40] A further obligation of 1,000,000 *écus* was to serve as a bond for the prompt payment of the first three millions. Second, the 3,000,000 *écus* were to cover the ransoms not only of King Jean, but also of all King Edward's other French prisoners, including at least Philip the Bold, Jacques de Bourbon, and the counts of Sancerre, Auxerre, Vendôme, Longueville, Eu and Joigny, among others (a concession perhaps worth upwards of £50,000).[41]

---

[40] Fowler, *King's Lieutenant*, p. 172. Note that twenty times the annual revenues of an estate would have been a fairly typical purchase price. The acquisition of the Dauphiné, for another point of comparison, cost Philip VI and Jean II only about 400,000 *écus* in total (including sums paid in life-rents). Delachenal, *Histoire de Charles V*, I, 30 and 34–5.

[41] The king paid £20,000 (160,000 *écus*) to the prince of Wales for just Philip the Bold, the count of Sancerre, and the lord of Craon, and probably could have made a profit on the transaction. Among the other prisoners whose ransoms would apparently have been included by this provision are Marshal d'Audrehem, the lords of Derval and of Aubigny (for whom the king paid 2,500 marks), the counts of Tancarville, Ventadour, Dammartin, and Saarbrücken, and probably the bishop of Le Mans; there may have been many others. This list is based on H. J. Hewitt, *The Black Prince's Expedition, 1355–57* (Manchester, 1958), pp. 158–9 and *Foedera*, III2, 27 (dealing with the equivalent provision in the Treaty of Brétigny). Since the treaty clause simply speaks of 'des autres prisons françois', it is quite possible that it was intended to cover *all* the unransomed prisoners of the Poitiers campaign, even those whom the king had not already acquired, with the presumption that he would be responsible for compensating their captors. In that case, those covered by the provision would also include the archbishop of Sens (who eventually brought 48,000 *écus* ransom for the earl of Warwick), Marshal Boucicaut, the counts of Vaudemont, Nassau, and Roucy, etc.

Finally, as already noted above, the key issue was the surrender of sovereignty; the precise extent of the land transfer was secondary to this matter of principle.

Thus, in sum, while the terms of the Second Treaty were indeed harsher than those of the First Treaty, the difference – the additional lands net of the reduced ransoms – was not quite as radical as usually claimed. Furthermore, though the Estates did in the end reject the Second Treaty as 'neither acceptable nor feasible', that does not mean that its terms were 'clearly impossible' or that its rejection was inevitable: in fact, at least according to the strictly contemporary chronicler Jean le Bel, the Estates debated ratification for a long time without reaching any accord on the subject; some considered it too harmful to the realm of France to accept, but others were ready for peace even at the high cost demanded.[42] Nor is it likely that Edward viewed the treaty's rejection as inevitable, considering the chronicles' reports of his anger at hearing what he himself termed the 'troublesome and urgent news' of the French failure to ratify it, and the lack of military preparations undertaken between its negotiation and its rejection by the Estates.[43]

Many of those who decline to take the Second Treaty of London seriously do so because of what seems to be another misreading of the document itself. Le Patourel (and the other historians who have followed him on this point) interpreted the repayment schedule provided in the treaty as requiring the payment of a full 3,000,000 *écus* of the ransom by August first of 1359.[44] This would indeed have been quite impossible to accomplish, so if that had been what was demanded in the treaty, the interpretation of the Second Treaty as a bogus propaganda ploy might well have been justified. That is not, however, what the document says; nor, for that matter, does the treaty even call for the three million to be paid by 24 June 1360, which is how Roland Delachenal interpreted it in his magnificent history of Charles V.[45]

This is quite an important point, so let me begin by quoting the original French of the treaty:

> le Roy françoiz pour le raençon et delivrance de sa personne et des autres prisons françoiz paiera au dit Roy d'Engleterre ou à ses hoirs ou aianz cause de lui quatre millions de deniers d'or al escu, chascun au pris de XL deniers d'esterlins, dont accordé est que le dit Roy françoiz paiera en la cité de Londres III millions des diz escus qui sont VC mille livres d'esterlins,

---

[42] According to Jean le Bel, *Chronique*, II, 289: 'quant ilz eurent bien longuement conseillié, *si ne furent ilz pas d'acord*, car ladite paix sembloit aux *aucuns* trop grieve' [emphasis added].

[43] Anger: *Chronica Johannis de Reading et Anonymi Cantuariensis*, p. 132; cf. Jean le Bel, *Chronique*, II, 289–90; Froissart, *Oeuvres*, VI, 271. 'Nova ardua et urgenta': C 67/37, m. 16 (and see also Delachenal, *Charles V*, II, 141n). Resumption of military preparations: C 67/37, mm. 14–16.

[44] Le Patourel, 'Treaty of Bretigny', pp. 29–30; Fowler, *King's Lieutenant*, p. 198; Barber, *Edward, Prince of Wales*, p. 158; also implicitly in Contamine, *Guerre de cent ans*, p. 45.

[45] Delachenal, *Charles V*, II, 81.

desquiex il paiera dedens le premier jour d'aoust prochain avenir cent mille
livres d'esterlins [au] moins d'or ou d'argent à la value, et le demourant aux
termes qui seront accordés entre les conssaux des deus roys dedens la feste
de la Nativité-Saint-Jehan-Baptiste dèsore prochain ensuivant, et du quart
million rendra lors le roy d'Angleterre au roy françois, tant qu'il li devra
souffire.[46]

The claim that the treaty demanded the payment of the full 3,000,000 by
1 August is thus not supportable, apparently having been caused by the
reader skipping over the phrase 'desquiex . . . cent mille livres d'esterlins'.
Delachenal's reading, on the other hand, is not without basis. He is evidently
taking the 'dedens la feste de la Nativité-Saint-Jehan-Baptiste dèsore prochain ensuivant' to mean 'by the feast of St John next following [after the
payment of the initial 600,000]' and to refer to the verb 'paiera' rather than to
'qui seront accordés'. This reading cannot be correct, however. First, it is
preferable to attach the 'dedens' phrase to the closest future verb phrase, 'qui
seront accordés', rather than the more distant 'paiera'. Second, Delachenal's
reading ignores the word 'dèsore', meaning 'from *now*'.[47] Thus, if the 'dedens'
phrase did refer to 'shall pay' rather than 'shall be agreed upon', the clause
would require the payment of £100,000 by 1 *August* 1359 and of the
'remainder' of the 3,000,000 by 24 *June* 1359 – five weeks *earlier* – which
obviously makes no sense.

Thus, I think, the proper translation must be:

> For his deliverance and the ransom of his person and of the other French
> prisoners, the French king shall pay to the said king of England or to his
> heirs, or to his designees, four million gold *écus*, each worth 40d. sterling; of
> which it is agreed that the said French king will pay in the city of London
> 3,000,000 *écus* (which make 500,000 pounds sterling); of these, he will pay at
> least 100,000 pounds sterling, or the equivalent value in gold or silver, by
> the upcoming first of August [1359]; and the remainder at terms to be
> agreed upon, by the time of the 24th of June next [when the truce specified
> in the draft treaty was to expire], between the councils of the two kings. The
> fourth million, as much as shall still be owing, shall then [after the payment
> of the 3,000,000] be released to the king of France by the king of England.

Since these payment terms are not unreasonable or obviously infeasible, and
since they do represent a de facto reduction of the ransom by 1,000,000 *écus*,
to partially counterbalance the additional French territories to be handed
over [relative to the First Treaty], there is no sufficient reason to presume that

---

[46] From the copy printed in Froissart, *Oeuvres*, XVIII, 424, with corrections based on
Delachenal, *Charles V*, II, 81–2n. Unfortunately, Delachenal's note giving the text of
this clause from a better manuscript than the one transcribed in Froissart ends with
an ellipsis after the phrase 'avenir cent mille livres d'esterlins'.

[47] A. J. Greimas, *Dictionnaire de l'ancien français*, 2nd edn (Paris, 1968), s.v. 'desor,
desore, desores'.

the Second Treaty was indeed preposterous, nor that it was one 'to which no one could have agreed'.

After the rejection of the treaty of May 1359, Edward resumed his preparations for war. By the late autumn of 1359, he landed at Calais with one of the largest English expeditionary armies assembled during the Hundred Years War. This army marched unopposed into Champagne, besieged Reims unsuccessfully through the winter, then advanced south-east to the borders of Burgundy – one of the few remaining areas of France never to have felt the scourge of an English *chevauchée*. The Burgundians bought off King Edward with a ransom large enough to cover a substantial portion of his wage bill for the campaign and an implicit promise that their duke would support Edward's coronation if the English could garner the support of the majority of the peers of France.[48]

In March and early April of 1360, still without meeting any active opposition from the Valois, the English army laid waste to the area south-east and south of Paris, right up to the gates of the capital, which was packed to bursting with pitiful refugees from the countryside all around. The regent, Prince Charles, still declined to give battle to Edward's army, however. Instead he sent peace messengers to try to arrange a new treaty, probably on terms similar to those of the First Treaty of London, but he found the English unwilling to moderate their demands. Edward planned to continue his *chevauchée* to his base in Brittany, leaving garrisons behind him, as Froissart explains, 'to harry and make war on the realm of France, and so torment and beat down the cities and good towns of France that they would willingly accept him [as king]'.[49] His intent was then, at harvest time, when it would be easy to feed his troops, to come back with a refreshed army and mount a sustained siege of Paris – which, after another six months of semi-blockade by the *routiers*, the capital would be in poor shape to resist.[50] There was little the French could do to stop this plan from succeeding, so it is not surprising that Edward showed no disposition to compromise with Charles' negotiators.

And yet, within a few weeks of his arrival before Paris, Edward did agree to the Treaty of Brétigny, which was indeed a compromise (at least relative to the Second Treaty of London). Normandy, Brittany, Maine, Anjou and Touraine were dropped from the territories to be ceded to England, with only the county of Rouergue added to counterbalance a small part of that concession, and the obligation for the bond of 1,000,000 *écus* was also dropped, leaving the ransom figure at a simple 3,000,000 *écus*. Why did the Plantagenet so reduce his demands?

[48] For details of the campaign, see Rogers, *War Cruel and Sharp*.
[49] Froissart, *Oeuvres*, VI, 279.
[50] Froissart, *Oeuvres*, VI, 279.

As we have already seen, the historians who have followed Le Patourel's interpretation exaggerated the severity of both the First Treaty of London (failing to recognize that it was indeed a true peace treaty which envisioned Edward's abandoning his claim to the French throne, and mistakenly believing that it called for the English to retain suzerainty over Brittany) and the Second Treaty (not noting the reduction of the ransom from 4,000,000 *écus* to 3,000,000 *écus* plus a bond of 1,000,000 *écus* or the inclusion of the other French prisoners' ransoms within that reduced sum, and even suggesting that the concessions offered by Edward in this agreement, notably the release of his claim to the throne, were insincere). Thus, they saw the Treaty of Brétigny as more of a retreat by the English than it actually was, especially in relation to the First Treaty. Historians from J. E. Morris and Edouard Perroy to Kenneth Fowler have explained this retreat by Edward III by describing the 1359–60 campaign as 'a hopeless failure', 'a lamentable escapade', a 'failure of strategy' that 'achieved nothing', and so on.[51] Philippe Contamine claims that the Plantagenet king accepted the Treaty of Brétigny 'only to avoid a military disaster, which he had believed to be imminent'.[52] Le Patourel went so far as to call the campaign a 'great victory' for the Dauphin's battle-avoiding strategy and to describe the treaty itself as 'the measure of [Edward III's] fear, his disillusion, and the growing strength of the French government'. 'It was the French, then,' he adds, 'who were victorious at Brétigny' and 'the treaty of Brétigny-Calais registers Edward's defeat.'[53]

Although there is a grain of truth to these evaluations, they are overall highly misleading. The campaign of 1359–60 was not exactly a defeat for Edward III, and still less was it a victory for the Dauphin.[54] Yes, lack of supplies had forced the English to leave Paris after 'merely' burning all the villages and farms surrounding the capital city – but the fact remains that there was an unchallenged English army laying waste to the heart of France, not a French army besieging Westminster or ravaging Middlesex. There is no evidence whatsoever that the English were faced with 'imminent disaster';[55]

---

[51] J. E. Morris, *The Welsh Wars of Edward I* (Oxford, 1901), pp. 129–30; Perroy, *Hundred Years War*, p. 138; Fowler, *King's Lieutenant*, pp. 209–11.

[52] Contamine, *Guerre de cent ans*, p. 47.

[53] Le Patourel, 'Edward III and the Kingdom of France', p. 189 (cf. pp. 177–8); Le Patourel, 'Treaty of Bretigny', pp. 32 and 33. J. M. Tourneur-Aumont, similarly, says the Treaty of Brétigny 'was a retraction, an avowal of weakness': *La Bataille de Poitiers (1356) et la construction de la France* (Paris, 1940), p. 390.

[54] Compare Jean le Bel's rubric: 'Vous pouez cy veoir quelles marches du royaume de France le roy d'Angleterre gasta et raenchonna et combien de temps il y demoura sans estre empeschyé.' *Chronique*, II, 305; cf. 311–12. Consider also Froissart, *Oeuvres*, VI, 271–2 and 279–80.

[55] Le Patourel, 'Treaty of Bretigny', p. 32. He gives no citation in support of this claim. Contamine supports his identical view with a reference to the *Chronique des quatre premiers Valois (1327–1393)*, ed. S. Luce (Paris, 1862), p. 117 (as well as to Le Patourel), but that chronicle actually says only that his army was 'half-starved' and that Edward was about to be compelled to leave France because of his lack of

Clifford J. Rogers

on the contrary, it is hard to see how the French posed much threat even to the small and isolated garrisons which Edward had left scattered behind him like caltrops (many of which the French were unable to recover by force even after the conclusion of the treaty, having instead to buy out the occupying *routiers* with large cash payments), much less to his main force.[56] Indeed, some in England believed that the garrisons could within a short time have completed the conquest of France for King Edward, if he had been willing to let them.[57]

It is difficult to see how the Dauphin could have stopped Edward from, at a minimum, plundering the as-yet unspoiled regions of Anjou and Maine and then returning to the Ile de France in the autumn. The best that Charles' Fabian strategy could accomplish was a stalemate, and it would be a stalemate almost unbearably painful for France to maintain, if it could be maintained at all.[58] The economy was collapsing, people were afraid to work the lands, and famine seemed imminent. As Froissart explained, wise men in the French court 'worried that [France] could not bear such burdens much longer' and 'would be in excessively great peril' if the war continued for the summer.[59] The demonstration of the sorry fate in store for the French if they

supplies – a statement also supported by *Knighton's Chronicle*, p. 181, which says that after Black Monday 'oportuit necessario redire uersus Angliam'. Other sources dispute this, however (e.g. Jean le Bel, *Chronique*, II, 312; Villani, *Cronica*, II, 408), and in fact the army did not starve during the more than three weeks between Black Monday and the sealing of the peace, despite the logistic difficulties of staying relatively stationary. In any case, even if Edward had been forced for supply reasons to move into relatively untouched Beauce, Maine and Anjou, or even all the way to his bases in Brittany, that would not quite qualify as a 'désastre militaire'. Contamine, *Guerre de cent ans*, p. 47.

[56] P. Chaplais, 'Some Documents Regarding the Fulfilment and Interpretation of the Treaty of Brétigny (1361–1369)', *Camden Miscellany XIX*, Camden 3rd s. 80 (1952), pp. 18–19 and 42–45; cf. Jean le Bel, *Chronique*, II, 304.

[57] *Anonimalle Chronicle*, p. 49. Because of the peace, many captains gave up their strongholds in accordance with Edward's orders, 'a graunt perde et damage al roy Dengleterre et a ses heirs pur toutz iours, qare bien pres toute la communalte de Frauns fuist en subieccion et raunsoun a eux et si purroient les ditz captayns od lour gentz deinz brieff [temps] avoir conquis la roialme de Frauns al oeps le roy Dengleterre et ses heirs sil les voldroit avoir soeffre.' Cf. Froissart, *Oeuvres*, VI, 95: the regent earlier worried that 'par tels gens se poioit perdre li royaulme de France dont il estoit hoirs'. See also Froissart, *Oeuvres*, VI, 271–2 and 279–80.

[58] Froissart, *Oeuvres*, VI, 279: 'Adont estoient en Paris li dus de Normendie [etc.] qui imaginoient bien le voiage dou roy d'Engleterre, et comment il et ses gens fouloient et apovrissoient le royaulme de France, et que ce ne se pooit longement tenir, ne souffrir, car les rentes des signeurs et des églises se perdoient généraument partout.' Note also Jean's own statement that one reason for accepting the Treaty of Brétigny was the probability that the future would be worse for the French than the present. A. Bardonnet, *Procès-verbal de l'delivrance à Jean Chandos, commissaire du roi d'Angleterre, des places françaises abandonnées par le traité de Brétigny* (Niort, 1867), p. 136. Cf. also the *Chronique Normande du XIVe siècle*, ed. A. and E. Molinier (Paris, 1882), p. 149 and n. 8.

[59] Froissart, *Oeuvres*, VI, 271–2: 'li dis royaummes estoit durement blechiés et grevés

210

continued to resist the English which the 1359–60 campaign provided
explains why the Treaty of Brétigny was, to a great extent at least, actually
implemented, unlike the First Treaty of London which it otherwise closely
resembled, and to that extent it was a success.[60] The Treaty of Brétigny did
not give the Plantagenet everything he had hoped for, but it *did* give
everything he had sought at the beginning of his war with France, and
much more besides. To call it a defeat is comparable to arguing that the
Germans 'lost' the war of 1870–1 because the peace terms negotiated by
Bismarck were less exacting than those sought by Moltke – except of course
that no one in Germany remotely contemplated imposing conditions comparable to what Jean II, the dauphin, and the Estates agreed to surrender to
Edward III. Weigh Alsace-Lorraine against Calais, Guînes, Saintonge, the
Angoumois, Poitou, the Limousin, Périgord, the Agenais, Gaure, Bigorre,
Quercy and Rouergue – a full third of the French kingdom – and it becomes
evident just what sort of 'overwhelming defeat'[61] (to use Le Patourel's words)
the English had suffered in 1359–60.

If Edward was not facing the 'desperate' military position which Le
Patourel describes,[62] then it might well be asked why he should have
accepted a treaty that was admittedly less favourable to him than either of
the Treaties of London (albeit closer to them than previous historians have
thought, and only slightly less favourable than the First Treaty of London).
Edward's own contemporaries explained his renewed willingness to
compromise as the result of a religious experience. On April 13 – 'Black
Monday', as the Monday after Easter Monday was for centuries after
known in England in commemoration of this event – the English army
was struck by a sudden and fearsome hailstorm, one so severe that many
horses and men in the English army perished in the cold. 'It seemed the

---

de cief en qor, se doubtoient que il ne peuist longement porter si grant fès, car on ne
pooit aller en nulle marce dou royaumme de France qu'il n'y euist Englès ou
Navarrois qui constraindoient si les bonnes villes, que nulle marchandise n'y pooit
aller, ne venir, et ossi le plat pays que les terres demoroient en ries et les vignes à
labourer, par quoy grant famine et grant chiereté de temps y apparoient.' Froissart,
Oeuvres, VI, 280: 'il veoient le royaulme de France en si povre estat et si grevé que en
trop grant péril il estoit, se il attendoient encores un esté.'

[60] If, as Lancaster said, the English might 'lose in a day more than we have conquered
in twenty years', that could only happen if the regent chose to risk a major battle,
and that would equally carry the chance for Edward to gain in a day what twenty
years had not yet enabled him to win: the success of his bid for the crown. The
Plantagenet was accepting a great and certain triumph in exchange for an even
greater but uncertain possibility, a fact which reflects well on the 47-year-old king's
wisdom.

[61] Le Patourel, 'Edward III and the Kingdom of France', p. 178: 'If, a year later, Edward
was prepared to give up his claim and his title for considerably less territory [than
provided by the Second Treaty of London], this was due to the overwhelming
defeat he had suffered in the winter of 1359–60.'

[62] Le Patourel, 'Edward III and the Kingdom of France', p. 179.

heavens would crack,' wrote one chronicler, 'and the earth open and swallow everything up.'[63]

According to Froissart, Edward's response to the hailstorm was, 'as he has since confessed,' to 'turn himself towards the church of Our Lady at Chartres, and religiously [vow] to the Virgin . . . that he would accept the terms of peace'.[64] There is no reason to doubt the chronicle's testimony: had not the king always said he was willing to accept any just and reasonable offer in order to end the war?[65] And had he not already admitted, in 1358, that the provisions of the First Treaty of London were sufficient to allow him to make peace with honour? What clearer sign from Heaven could he ask for to tell him to do so?

In the past, Edward had often proclaimed that his victories were signs of divine favour. He had, furthermore, sometimes acted in ways which are most difficult to understand if one does not credit the sincerity of his belief that God was on his side, the clearest case being his intention in early June of 1340 to sail without delay to attack a vastly superior French fleet at Sluys, even against the strong advice of his chancellor and his two admirals.[66] The only reason I can see *not* to accept this explanation of Edward's behaviour is the *a priori* assumption that he would not make such a strategic decision based on anything but rational calculation of the strategic balances. I reject that assumption on two grounds. First, it is absurd to deny that medieval people in general did believe in God, did believe in direct divine intervention in human affairs, and did believe in his use of signs and portents, and it seems inordinately cynical to presume that kings were any different in that regard. It is of course impossible to know with full certainty how sincere King Edward's practice of religion was, but the most careful study of his beliefs concluded that 'Edward III was utterly conventional and predictable in his

---

[63] Froissart, *Oeuvres*, VI, 273: 'il sambloit que li chiels deuist s'en partir, et li tierre ouvrir et tout engloutir'.

[64] Froissart, *Oeuvres*, VI, 282: 'adont regarda li rois d'Engleterre devers l'église Nostre-Dame de Chartres, et se rendi et voa dévotement à Nostre-Dame, et prommist, sicom il dist et confessa depuis, que il s'acorderoit à le pais.'

[65] Most recently just as he left Paris: 'Le count de Tankiruille enueint hors de la cite en le houre, requist tretice du counsail le dit roy Dengleter, qe ly fust respoundu qe lour dit seignour prendroit toutdiz resoun toutez houres.' *Scalacronica*, p. 193. A particularly significant statement to this effect (given its audience) is the one he made in a private communication to the prince of Wales in 1342 during his expedition to Brittany: Avesbury, *Gestis*, p. 341; see also his letter to the Emperor of November 1356, *Foedera*, III1, 131; and *Knighton's Chronicle*, p. 126. Finally, Jean le Bel says that, on receiving word of the Estates' rejection of the Second Treaty, Edward proclaimed 'sy hault que chascun le pouoit bien ouïr que avant ce que l'aoust fust passé, il vendroit si poissaument ou royaume de France *qu'il y demourroit tant qu'il avroit fin de guerre ou paix à son honneur*' [emphasis added]. *Chronique*, II, 289–90. Cf. *Chronica Johannis de Reading et Anonymi Cantuariensis*, p. 133; Froissart, *Oeuvres*, VI, 271.

[66] See Rogers, *War Cruel and Sharp*, for details.

personal devotions. All the evidence suggests a simple, practical and rather old-fashioned view of Christianity. . . . His personal piety was based on an unquestioning belief in the intercessory role of saints . . .' Furthermore: 'In the king's personal society of saints, Mary ranked particularly high.'[67] The second reason to accept this explanation for Edward's change of heart is that, as I have argued above, there was nothing in his strategic situation to compel him to moderate his peace terms: the storm had not done that much damage to his army,[68] and the regent was no threat.

To conclude: the Treaty of Brétigny was in fact a triumph for Edward III, for it finally gave him de facto what he had gone to war for in 1337 – a free hand in Scotland, an end to French interference in Gascony, and restoration of the lands promised to him in 1329 – and furthermore gave him extensive additional lands and a huge sum of cash. The French had agreed to similar terms twice before, in 1354 and 1358, but in both instances had failed to implement them. The campaign of 1359–60 was enough of a success that it compelled the Valois to make the transfers of territory, hostages, and cash (the initial instalments, at least) actually happen. On the other hand, the Treaty of Brétigny was a step back from the hard terms of the Second Treaty of London (though not as big a step as often believed); the explanation for this, however, is not 'imminent military disaster', but a religious experience which convinced Edward to return to the framework of a peace which he had often before accepted as just, rather than stubbornly insisting on the some-what greedy terms of May 1359. The final treaty was still, however, the worst humiliation ever inflicted on the kingdom of France, and arguably the most impressive military success ever secured by an English monarch.[69]

[67] W. M. Ormrod, 'The Personal Religion of Edward III', *Speculum* 64 (1989), 849–77 (pp. 853–4, 857).
[68] Walsingham, *Historia Anglicana*, I, 289.
[69] The only competition I can think of is the Treaty of Troyes, but that agreement, unlike Brétigny, was never acknowledged in much of France.

11

Isabelle of France, Anglo-French Diplomacy and Cultural Exchange in the Late 1350s

MICHAEL BENNETT

In the middle decades of the fourteenth century, England occupied centre stage in international diplomacy and culture. The English victories of the 1340s held the promise of a new golden age for Britain. Edward III, the new Arthur, celebrated his triumph with a magnificent series of feasts and tournaments and the founding of a new chivalric order, the Order of the Garter. The ravages of the Black Death must have cast a pall over the celebrations, but the victory at Poitiers in 1356 appeared to reaffirm the inauguration of a new Britain. King Jean of France and many other noblemen were made captive and brought as prisoners to England, where King David of Scotland, captured at Neville's Cross a decade earlier, still remained in captivity. From 1357 to 1360, England was thus not only the focus of international diplomacy, but also very much the centre of international court culture. The festivities between autumn 1357 and spring 1358 were especially splendid. The cycle began with a tournament at Smithfield which was attended by the kings of England, France and Scotland as well as by noblemen and knights from all three kingdoms. There was a great feast at Marlborough at Christmas before the court moved on for a courtly and chivalric extravaganza at Bristol at Epiphany. They were merely the prelude, though, to the festivities held around St George's Day at Windsor. They certainly impressed King Jean of France who reputedly observed, all too aware that his ransom provided the English king an almost inexhaustible source of credit, that he had never seen such expenditure without payment of gold and silver.[1] He also noted in a letter to the townsmen of Nimes the attendance of three queens: Edward III's wife Queen Philippa, Edward's sister the queen of Scotland and – a ghost from the past – Edward's mother Isabelle of France.[2]

The presence of Isabelle of France, the queen mother, is especially worthy

---

[1] *Chronica Johannis de Reading et Anonymi Cantuarensis 1346–1367*, ed. J. Tait (Manchester, 1914), p. 130.
[2] R. Delachenal, *Histoire de Charles V*, 5 vols. (Paris, 1909–31), II, 65–6, n. 3.

of note. In a number of sources and histories it is assumed that after the coup of 1330 she was in disgrace, or at least rusticated, at Castle Rising in Norfolk.[3] A close analysis of the sources does reveal, however, that in the 1340s she remained in contact with her son, and appeared at a number of court functions.[4] Her presence at Windsor in April 1358 is documented by the accounts of her household which cover the period from Michaelmas 1357 until shortly after her death in August 1358. The household accounts, extant as BL MS Cotton Galba E XIV, have been curiously neglected. They were a matter of extensive report by E. A. Bond in the mid-nineteenth century.[5] Through Bond they were known to early French historians, including the duc d'Aumale in the 1850s, and R. Delachenal, the author of the five-volume *Histoire de Charles V*.[6] Hilda Johnstone was aware of the manuscript, but there is no evidence that she consulted it.[7] Despite its relevance to their concerns, it has not been used in recent studies of Edward III or of the late medieval household.[8] One factor which may explain the neglect of this remarkable set of accounts is the curious fact that it is not listed in the catalogues of Cotton Manuscripts, including the master catalogue at St Pancras. The listing of the Cotton MSS Galba E series ends tantalisingly with 'E XIII'. It is likely that Bond had the manuscript in his possession at the time that some assistant put together the catalogue.[9]

Isabelle's accounts not only document an important public role for the queen mother but also offer rare insights on court life in the late 1350s. The sources for the politics, diplomacy and cultural patronage of Edward III at this time are otherwise surprisingly exiguous. The chancery records contain little useful information, and the exchequer records are especially disappoint-

---

[3] A. Strickland, *Lives of the Queens of England from the Norman Conquest* (London, 1842), II, 287–92; H. Johnstone, 'Isabelle, the She-Wolf of France', *History* n.s. 21 (1936–7), 208–18.

[4] See J. Vale, *Edward III and Chivalry: Chivalric Society and its Context 1270–1350* (Woodbridge, 1982), pp. 50 and 129, n. 129.

[5] E. A. Bond, 'Notices of the Last Days of Isabelle, Queen of Edward the Second, Drawn from an Account of the Expenses of Her Household', *Archaeologia* 35 (1859), 453–69.

[6] *Notes et Documents relatifs à Jean, Roi de France, et à sa captivité en Angleterre*, ed. duc d'Aumale (Philobiblon Society, 1855), pp. 33 and 34n; R. Delachenal, *Histoire de Charles V*, 5 vols. (Paris, 1909–31).

[7] Johnstone, 'Isabelle, the She-Wolf of France', 208–18.

[8] E.g. Vale, *Edward III and Chivalry*; K. Mertes, *The English Noble Household 1250–1600: Good Governance and Politic Rule* (Oxford, 1988); C. M. Woolgar, *The Great Household in Late Medieval England* (New Haven, 1999).

[9] Notwithstanding its obscurity, the manuscript is not entirely unknown. F. D. Blackley, 'Isabelle of France, Queen of England 1308–58, and the Late Medieval Cult of the Dead', *Canadian Journal of History* 15 (1980), 23–49, used it as the starting-point for an examination of Isabelle's funeral and other observances after her death. On a recent visit to the British Library I found Martha Carlin working on it. I would like to thank Professor Carlin for sharing some of her notes with me.

ing. The chamber and wardrobe accounts which document expenditure on feasts and tournaments in earlier decades are wholly lacking. If it were not for the brief notices in a number of chronicles, the festivities associated with England's triumph at Poitiers and the captivity of Jean of France might have been left entirely to the historical imagination. Of course, Isabelle's accounts cannot begin to remedy this defect, but they offer some compensation. To add to their value, there survive exchequer accounts inventorising her property on her death in 1358. Coincidentally, there survive three other sets of household accounts from this time, namely the account of the cofferer of the household of Queen Philippa for 1357–8, some fragmentary accounts relating to the household of her daughter-in-law Elizabeth countess of Ulster, the wife of Lionel of Antwerp, for the period 1356–9, and the accounts of the captive King Jean from Christmas 1358 until his return to France in 1360.[10] One feature of the accounts of the countess of Ulster which has long been noted is the earliest reference to Geoffrey Chaucer. To reveal a little more fully the world in which the young poet found himself at the threshold of his career is a further good reason for focusing on Edward III's court in the late 1350s.

The prince of Wales and his French captives, including King Jean, left Bordeaux on 11 April 1357, and arrived at Plymouth on 5 May.[11] The *Anonimalle Chronicle* gives the impression of a stately progress across the countryside. Edward III and other English magnates met up with them at various points along the road. There were some elaborate diversions, as when the cavalcade passed by a forest and was accosted by some five hundred men dressed in green coats and mantles as if they were robbers or outlaws. The prince explained to King Jean that they were foresters who were accustomed to dress in this manner.[12] On 24 May the cavalcade entered London across London Bridge. According to Froissart, King Jean rode on a white steed, while the prince of Wales followed on a black hackney.[13] The mayor and

[10] Manchester, John Rylands University Library, Latin MS 236 is the account of the cofferer of Queen Philippa, April 1357–8. BL Additional MS 18,632, fols. 2 and 101 are fragments from household accounts of the countess of Ulster. They are transcribed by E. A. Bond, 'Chaucer as Page in the Household of the Countess of Ulster' in *The Chaucer Society: Life Records of Chaucer* (London, 1886), III, 97–113. Accounts of expenditure by King Jean of France are published as *Notes et Documents relatifs à Jean, Roi de France, et à sa captivité en Angleterre*; and *Comptes de L'Argenterie des Rois de France au xive siècle*, ed. L. Douët-D'Arcq (Paris, 1851).
[11] *Chronica Johannis de Reading et Anonymi Cantuarensis*, p. 126; *Knighton's Chronicle 1337–1396*, ed. G. H. Martin (Oxford, 1995), pp. 150–1; Delachenal, *Histoire de Charles V*, II, 54. According to Froissart, the party came through Kent, spending nights at Canterbury, Rochester and Dartford: Froissart, *Chronicles*, ed. Johnes, I, 234. It is conceivable that the party first landed at Plymouth, and then went by sea to Sandwich or Dover.
[12] *The Anonimalle Chronicle, 1333–81*, ed. V. H. Galbraith (Manchester, 1927), pp. 40–1.
[13] Froissart, *Chronicles*, ed. Johnes, I, 234.

aldermen rode out to meet the captive king, and a thousand citizens, arrayed in their guild livery, escorted him through streets festooned with bows, arrows and weapons of all kinds.[14] With the king of Scotland still lodged in the Tower of London, King Jean was given as his residence the splendid Savoy palace, built by Henry Grosmont, duke of Lancaster.[15] According to a northern chronicle, all the nobles of the realm were invited to a great banquet in Westminster 'to honour the great splendour of royalty never seen before in England'. Edward III sat at the centre of the high table, with King Jean on his right and King David on his left.[16] In June Edward withdrew briefly to Woodstock, where he was based around 15–16 June.[17]

On 20 June Peter, archbishop of Rouen, cardinal priest of the Basilica of the Twelve Apostles, arrived in haste from France to seek a confirmation of the truce which had been agreed at Bordeaux. He was followed soon afterwards by the papal legates, Talleyrand de Périgord, cardinal bishop of Albano, and Nicholas Capocci, cardinal priest of St Vitalis, who were to negotiate the return of the French king and a general peace. On 3 July they were met outside London by Prince Edward and the archbishop of Canterbury, who then escorted him to the king at Westminster. Finding him seated on his throne, with imperial trappings and a lion-like countenance, the cardinals prostrated themselves in adoration.[18] In August the king held a great feast in their honour, and received a formal embassy from France.[19] There was good will and magnanimity on both sides, and negotiation proceeded in an amicable fashion. In autumn 1357 there was a grand tournament at Smithfield, distinguished by the presence of the kings of England, France and Scotland. King Jean was invited to Windsor where he was able to indulge his passion for the hunt.[20] Meanwhile, after a decade in captivity in England, King David was allowed to return to Scotland on parole.[21] The French seem to have looked forward to King Jean's early release. At the beginning of 1358 the French emissaries returned to Paris in an optimistic mood.

[14] *Knighton's Chronicle*, pp. 150–1; Delachenal, *Histoire de Charles V*, II, 54 and n.
[15] Knighton, noting that the two kings were prisoners at the same time, stated that the French king was at Windsor while the Scottish king was at the Tower of London. *Knighton's Chronicle*, pp. 152–3.
[16] *The Kirkstall Abbey Chronicles*, ed. J. Taylor, Thoresby Society 42 (1952), p. 62.
[17] CPR 1354–8, pp. 563 and 567.
[18] *Knighton's Chronicle*, pp. 150–3. Letters of protection were issued on 3 June for the cardinal bishop of Albano and the cardinal priest of St Vitalis to come to England. Like letters for the cardinal priest of the Basilica of the Twelve Apostles, who arrived first and clearly in haste, were issued only on 15 June. CPR 1354–8, pp. 566–7.
[19] R. Barber, *Edward, Prince of Wales and Aquitaine: A Biography of the Black Prince* (1978), p. 156.
[20] According to Froissart, King Jean went to Windsor shortly after the visit of the cardinals: Froissart, *Chronicles*, ed. Johnes, I, 234. Knighton likewise implies that King Jean was at Windsor around this time: *Knighton's Chronicle*, pp. 152–3.
[21] King David was back at Berwick by Michaelmas: *Knighton's Chronicle*, pp. 156–7.

Over the summer of 1357 Queen Isabelle presumably shared in the general excitement associated with the arrival in England of the captive King Jean. It is not known whether she was present at his reception in London in 24 May, but it may be significant that her steward, John atte Legh, was knighted at her request and granted an annuity around this time.[22] The surviving household accounts begin in October 1357, at which time she was setting out from Hertford on pilgrimage to Canterbury. It is tempting to imagine that her main motive for travel was to meet her Valois cousin and other French nobles. Isabelle's pilgrimage naturally took her through the capital, and on her return on 26 October she entertained Edward III, Queen Philippa and the prince of Wales in her London house.[23] There is no record of her meeting with King Jean of France, but she must have made contact with him around this time, if indeed she had not done so earlier. On 10 December, when she was back at Hertford castle, there is record of a payment made to a French man who came on an errand from King Jean in London. The errand was an interesting one. It was with regard to the loan of two books. They were French romances, namely the Holy Grail and Sir Lancelot.[24] Queen Isabelle's interest in and ownership of French romances is well-attested by earlier borrowings from the royal collection and by the books listed in the inventory on her death. The books she lent to the French king have hitherto not been noted. Given Isabelle's notorious adultery with Roger Mortimer, her ownership of a romance of Sir Lancelot seems especially noteworthy. If she identified with Queen Guinevere, she was not too embarrassed to acknowledge it.

From this time Queen Isabelle remained in contact with King Jean and regularly entertained prominent members of his entourage. She was joined in this activity by two close confidantes who were themselves regular visitors to Hertford: Jeanne, dowager countess of Warren, and Marie, dowager countess of Pembroke. Though of English royal descent on their mothers' side, both ladies had French fathers. Jeanne was the daughter of the count of Bar, while Marie was the daughter of Guy de Chatillon, comte de St Pol. On 16 November Queen Isabelle was visited by the captal de Buche, the Gascon warlord who had served with distinction on the English side at Poitiers.[25] On the following day she received Jacques de Bourbon, comte de la Marche.[26] Later in the month, she was hostess to the comte de Tancarville, another

---

[22] On 29 May Edward III granted him an annuity of £40 on taking the order of knighthood at Queen Isabelle's request: *CPR 1354–8*, p. 580.

[23] BL MS Cotton, Galba E. XIV, fol. 49v.

[24] BL MS Cotton, Galba E. XIV, fol. 50r.

[25] BL MS Cotton, Galba E. XIV, fol. 4r.

[26] BL MS Cotton, Galba E. XIV, fol. 4r. The account refers to the count 'de la Marche'. Bond believed that it was the earl of March, the grandson of Isabelle's lover, but it is most likely Jacques de Bourbon, comte de la Marche. Otherwise styled the comte de Ponthieu, he was a grandson of Louis IX. *Notes et Documents relatifs à Jean, Roi de France, et à sa captivité en Angleterre*, p. 11.

prisoner of war, who came on the 28th in the company of the earl of Salisbury.[27] She was certainly feeling drawn to her French roots. On 1 December she paid for masses for the soul of her father, Philip IV of France, in the five parish churches of Hertford, the convent and hospital at Hertford, and the Franciscan friary at Ware. Of course, this observance may have been a long-established practice, but another payment on this day – a gift to Jean Dardell, a Franciscan friar from France – might well indicate that she had been reminded of the anniversary.[28] By mid-December when she received a visit from Hankyn de Oreby, the French king of arms, the stage was probably being set for the arrival of Arnauld sire d'Audrehem, marshal of France, and Regnaut sire d'Aubigny, seneschal of Toulouse, on Christmas Eve.[29]

Edward III held his Christmas court at Marlborough. Queen Philippa, her youngest son Thomas of Woodstock, her two daughters, and the daughter of the duke of Brittany, were at Bristol during Advent. On St Nicholas's eve gifts were given to boys singing carols in the presence of the prince and princesses.[30] The royal family came together for Christmas at Marlborough, where there were seasonal jousts and revels. The accounts of the countess of Ulster record expenditure on dress for the occasion.[31] The court then returned to Bristol for the feast of the Circumcision.[32] On the feast of Epiphany Edward, Philippa and their children attended a great mass in the queen's chapel at Bristol.[33] According to the continuator of the *Eulogium historiarum*, the highlight of the festivities was a tournament held at night-time with a magnificence never before seen.[34] From Hertford, Queen Isabelle kept in touch with her son and his family. Payments were made to messengers taking letters to Marlborough and Bristol, and to servants taking and bringing New Year's gifts.[35]

Queen Isabelle shared her Christmas with the marshal d'Audrehem. On Epiphany she received handsome New Year gifts from the king of France as well as her son and daughter-in-law. Isabelle's accounts, which are full of payments to minstrels, both English and French, indicate that there was festive cheer at the court of the winter queen. Yet it may well be that she was playing a role in sustaining the peace process which was facing heavy weather in the parliament held at Westminster in February. Two French lords who returned to Hertford were the comte de Tancarville, who stayed

[27] BL MS Cotton, Galba E. XIV, fol. 5r. Jean de Melun II, comte de Tancarville, grand chamberlain of France d.1382.
[28] BL MS Cotton, Galba E. XIV, fol. 33r.
[29] BL MS Cotton, Galba E. XIV, fol. 7r.
[30] John Rylands University Library, Latin MS 236, fol. 3r.
[31] *Chaucer Life Records*, Part III, ed. E. A. Bond and W. D. Selby (1886).
[32] *Eulogium historiarum sive temporis*, ed. F. S. Haydon, 3 vols. (RS, 1858), III, 227.
[33] John Rylands University Library, Latin MS 236, fol. 2v.
[34] *Eulogium historiarum*, III, 227.
[35] BL MS Cotton, Galba E. XIV, fol. 50v.

with her several days at the end of January and early February,[36] and the marshal d'Audrehem, who stayed over at Hertford on 21–22 March.[37] On the 21st the marshal was accompanied by the archbishop of Sens. In welcoming to her table two of the key negotiators on the French side, Isabelle may have been doing no more than fulfilling the obligations of hospitality. Her castle was conveniently positioned between London and King's Langley, where Edward was based for much of the spring.[38] Nonetheless it remains very probable that her position was an intermediary in more than a merely topographical sense.

When Edward III left King's Langley in mid-April, the queen mother likewise set out for London. Assisted by the countess of Pembroke, she entertained the marshal d'Audrehem in the capital on the 17th and the 18th. On the 17th they were joined by John Winwick, keeper of the privy seal, and the man largely responsible for the conduct of English diplomacy at this time. On the 18th Jacques de Bourbon, comte de la Marche and de Ponthieu, made up the numbers. The queen mother's stay in London concluded on the 19th with a meeting with the key English stakeholders. She dined with chief clerical ministers – the chancellor, the treasurer and Winwick – and afterwards received her son, the prince of Wales, and Henry, duke of Lancaster. Along with all the other notables, she then set out for Windsor for the St George's Day celebrations. En route she entertained the comte de Tancarville at Sheen.[39]

The Garter Feast of 1358 was a major diplomatic and cultural event. Earlier in the year Edward had proclaimed a great tournament, offering safe-conduct to all foreign knights who wished to compete.[40] Edward was clearly seeking to make Windsor a new Camelot. Through the 1340s and 1350s a major building programme was underway, and by 1358 the new St George's chapel at least was complete. Queen Isabelle made offerings there. The festivities were well-attended. King Jean of France was the guest of honour. The duke of Brabant led a distinguished company of foreign lords, including many Gascons, who had been stirred by the prospect of pageantry and prowess. Edward III, his five sons, and his cousin, Henry of Lancaster, were naturally in attendance. While King David of Scotland was back in his kingdom, attempting to raise his ransom, his queen, Isabelle's daughter, made her way south for the occasion. The French king was greatly impressed by the extravagance of the proceedings, not least since most of it was paid for by the exchange of tallies. The continuator of the *Eulogium historiarum* claimed

---

[36] BL MS Cotton, Galba E. XIV, fols. 9v–10r.
[37] BL MS Cotton, Galba E. XIV, fol. 13r.
[38] Patents were dated at King's Langley from 1 March until 10 April: *CPR 1358–61*, pp. 33–5. Queen Philippa gave alms in adoration of the cross at Langley on the 30th: John Rylands University Library, Latin MS 236, fol. 2v.
[39] BL MS Cotton, Galba E. XIV, fol. 15r.
[40] *Knighton's Chronicle*, pp. 158–9.

that they were tournaments such as had not been seen since the time of King Arthur, while Knighton simply confessed that the splendour of the occasion was beyond his powers to relate.[41] The tournaments which followed the feast were called by Roger Mortimer, earl of March.[42] Queen Isabelle's sentiments at seeing her lover's grandson lead the field must be left to the imagination.

It was during the festivities at Windsor that Edward III, with suitable theatricality, assured the king of France of his disposition to come to terms. The main problem envisioned at this stage was with respect to the papal curia at Avignon. Given her meeting with key players the previous week, it is possible that Queen Isabelle made a significant contribution to the peace process. Ten years earlier the French court had proposed her as a mediator between the two kingdoms, and Isabelle seems to have continued to make it her business to be informed of political developments on both sides of the Channel. Over the winter of 1357–8, for example, the activities of her grand-nephew Charles, king of Navarre, provided a clear focus of interest. A thorn in the side of the French government, Charles had been in custody in a castle in Artois since the middle of 1356, but on the night of 8 November he was sprung from prison. After declaring his own title to the French crown at Amiens, he proceeded to demand admittance to the city of Paris.[43] What is remarkable is that Isabelle received a report of Charles's liberation as early as 10 November from a courier of the countess of Pembroke.[44] That Isabelle's interest in Charles's fate was not idle is indicated by a payment on 10 December to a messenger who confirmed the report of Charles's escape, and by payments on the 20th and the 26th to messengers bringing letters respectively from Charles's brother Philippe of Navarre, and then from Charles himself.[45]

If the eminent people she entertained in London at this time are any guide, Queen Isabelle played a role in the process by which Edward's assurances were translated into a reasonable settlement. On 1 May she received the king, and on the following day the king, the prince of Wales and the earl of March. On the 3rd she entertained the marshal d'Audrehem and other French magnates, while on the 4th it was the comte de Tancarville's turn. On the 5th she dined with the marshal d'Audrehem, and the pair were joined after dinner by other French noblemen and the chancellor of England.[46] Still, Isabelle seems to have been excluded from the final diplomacy, which appears to have taken place at Windsor. On 10 May she received news of the agreement reached between the kings of England and France from three separate sources: John Winwick, Queen Philippa, and the marshal d'Audrehem. In her

[41] *Eulogium historiarum*, III, 227; *Knighton's Chronicle*, pp. 158–9.
[42] Barber, *Black Prince*, p. 155.
[43] Delachenal, *Histoire de Charles V*, I, 323–5.
[44] BL MS Cotton, Galba E. XIV, fol. 50r.
[45] BL MS Cotton, Galba E. XIV, fol. 50r.
[46] BL MS Cotton, Galba E. XIV, fol. 16r.

enthusiasm she gave no less than 10 marks each to the two English messengers, and 40s. to the marshal's squire.[47] In the evening Winwick joined her for dinner, presumably bringing her a blow-by-blow account of the final round of negotiations. On the 11th she dined with Queen Philippa, on the 12th hosted a banquet for the two cardinals, the archbishop of Sens and other French noblemen, and on the 13th entertained King Jean of France.[48]

Isabelle's accounts do more than provide a new perspective on the pageantry and diplomacy of 1357–8, they offer valuable insight into the domestic life of a lady of considerable wealth and power. They reveal her friendships, and her acts of piety. During the period of the account Isabelle went twice on pilgrimage to Canterbury, firstly in November 1357 and then in June 1358. If the first occasion may have arisen from an urge to savour some of the excitement brought to the capital by the arrival of so many distinguished French lords, the second may well have been by way of a thanksgiving for the accord reached between the kings of England and France. Isabelle was certainly generous in her benefactions. While the household accounts contain a record of many offerings at churches, including at Canterbury, the inventory of her goods after her death reveal an even grander level of gift-giving. She seems to have been in the habit of offering pieces of gold cloth to the altars of the churches she visited on special occasions. To mark her visits to Canterbury, in October 1357 and June 1358, she gave on each occasion pieces worth over £2 to both Christ Church and St Augustine's. Indeed on the latter occasion she gave extra pieces on behalf of her daughter, the queen of Scotland, who was in her company.[49]

Finally, it is Isabelle's cultural patronage that merits some attention. Isabelle's longstanding interest in secular literature is well-established. Even in the midst of the political upheavals of 1327 the young queen mother can be found borrowing chivalric romances from the royal collection.[50] The inventory of her goods at her death in 1358 includes books on King Arthur, Tristram and Isolda, Sir Perceval and Sir Gawain.[51] Since the books relating to the Holy Grail and Sir Lancelot which she received from the French king in 1357 do not appear in the inventory, it may be that her collection was even more extensive. The evidence is that Isabelle's books were still valued and in use. Several were given to Edward III, and others to her daughter the queen of Scotland. Through her cultural patronage and the loan of her books, Queen Isabelle played at least some modest role in the maintenance and dissemination of French literature in England. The countesses of Warren and Pembroke, who likewise seem to have maintained their French connections, may have shared this sense of cultural mission. Yet the

---

[47] BL MS Cotton, Galba E. XIV, fol. 52r.
[48] BL MS Cotton, Galba E. XIV, fols. 16v–17r.
[49] E 101/393/4, fols. 7r–v.
[50] Vale, *Edward III and Chivalry*, pp. 49–50.
[51] E 101/393/4, fol. 8r.

queen mother and her friends cannot be regarded as culturally isolated in mid-fourteenth-century England. The English royal court was still decidedly francophone. Even if he felt uncomfortable doing so, Henry of Grosmont, duke of Lancaster, wrote in French. In fact the events of the 1340s and 1350s, which had so stirred the chivalric imagination, probably served to reinvigorate a courtly and chivalric culture whose medium was still predominantly French. Edward's court at Windsor in 1358 must be regarded in some wise as the cultural capital of the francophone world. There was a literal sense in which this was at least partly true. Among the booty brought back from France were a great number of books. If King Jean was forced to borrow from Queen Isabelle, it was perhaps because he could not afford to buy back the books that had slipped into the hands of his captors. There are a number of interesting book migrations, like the French bible captured at Poitiers that William Montagu, earl of Salisbury acquired for 100 marks. When, in the 1380s, the duc de Berri compiled a romance relating to Melusine for his sister, he had to borrow a book from the earl of Salisbury.[52]

It must not be thought, though, that Queen Isabelle disdained local English culture. Her accounts are full of gifts to minstrels performing on feast days and other occasions, including one minstrel who was performing, busker-like, in the vault of Christ Church, Canterbury.[53] She made generous gifts to minstrels of the king, the prince of Wales, the earl of March, the earl of Salisbury, the countess of Ulster, and indeed to some minstrels of the king of France and duke of Brabant.[54] One of the most remarkable items in the account is a payment to Walter Hert, one of the queen's viol-players, going to London at Lent to a school of minstrelsy.[55] This world of cultural patronage, spanning and mediating between the English and French courts, and between the world of romance-reading and minstrelsy, is the world in which Geoffrey Chaucer first appears in the historical record as a page in the household of the countess of Ulster, who indeed, perhaps with Chaucer in tow, not only attended all the great feasts of this remarkable year, but also, on occasion, dined with Queen Isabelle at Hertford castle.

Queen Isabelle appears to have been in poor health from early in 1358. On 12 March she paid master Lawrence, surgeon, 60s. for unspecified medical treatment.[56] She seems to have been active enough in spring and early summer, but after her pilgrimage in June she returned to Hertford. On 12 July Edward III made a formal visit, seemingly his last.[57] A few days later her daughter the Queen of Scots came to visit.[58] In August there was a crisis.

---

[52] BL MS Royal, 19 D II; BL MS Royal, 18 B II.
[53] BL MS Cotton, Galba E. XIV, fol. 32r.
[54] BL MS Cotton, Galba E. XIV, fols. 49v–52v.
[55] BL MS Cotton, Galba E. XIV, fol. 51v.
[56] BL MS Cotton, Galba E. XIV, fol. 51v.
[57] BL MS Cotton, Galba E. XIV, fol. 21r.
[58] BL MS Cotton, Galba E. XIV, fol. 21r.

Messengers were sent, firstly, to seek out a physician, Mr Simon de Bredon, in London and then to an unnamed physician in Canterbury.[59] In her extremity she was accompanied by her daughter, and by the countesses of Pembroke and Warren. The countess of Ulster and John Winwick likewise visited her in her last days.[60] According to the continuator of the *Eulogium historiarum*, she desired the physician to purge her, which he did, but she was not able to bear it, and died the following day, the feast of SS Timothy and Simphorien.[61] The household accounts confirm her date of death as 22 August.[62] She had originally planned to be buried in Westminster Abbey, but in the end chose burial with the Franciscans in London.[63] According to an early, but doubtful, tradition, it was at the Greyfriars that the remains of Roger Mortimer had been laid to rest.[64] In 1358, though, it was her special devotion to the Franciscans, not to the memory of her paramour, that was noted by the chroniclers. As the Kirkstall Abbey chronicler wrote, 'the venerable queen always appeared as the particular mother and protector of the Friars Minor while she lived here on earth'.[65] On 20 November orders were issued to the authorities in London for cleaning of refuse and filth from the streets for the arrival of the queen mother's body through Bishopsgate and Aldgate.[66] Her burial in the chapel of the Franciscans on 27 November was attended by the king, the archbishop of Canterbury and other members of the royal family, including the countess of Ulster and, perhaps, her page Geoffrey Chaucer.[67]

---

[59] BL MS Cotton, Galba E. XIV, fols. 41r–v.
[60] BL MS Cotton, Galba E. XIV, fol. 24r.
[61] *Eulogium historiarum*, III, 227.
[62] BL MS Cotton, Galba MS E. XIV, fol. 24r.
[63] *Chronica Johannis de Reading et Anonymi Cantuarensis*, pp. 128–9.
[64] Blackley, 'Isabelle of France and the Cult of the Dead', p. 28.
[65] *The Kirkstall Abbey Chronicles*, p. 62.
[66] *CCR 1354–60*, p. 484.
[67] *Eulogium historiarum*, III, 227; *Chaucer Life Records*, Part III, ed. Bond and Selby.

INDEX

YORK MEDIEVAL PRESS: PUBLICATIONS

God's Words, Women's Voices: The Discernment of Spirits in the Writing of Late-Medieval Women Visionaries, Rosalynn Voaden (1999)

Pilgrimage Explored, ed. J. Stopford (1999)

Piety, Fraternity and Power: Religious Gilds in Late Medieval Yorkshire 1389–1547, David J. F. Crouch (2000)

Courts and Regions in Medieval Europe, ed. Sarah Rees Jones, Richard Marks and A. J. Minnis (2000)

Treasure in the Medieval West, ed. Elizabeth M. Tyler (2000)

Nunneries, Learning and Spirituality in Late Medieval English Society: The Dominican Priory of Dartford, Paul Lee (2000)

Problem of Labour in Fourteenth-Century England, ed. James Bothwell, P. J. P. Goldberg and W. M. Ormrod (2000)

New Directions in Later Medieval Manuscript Studies: Essays from the 1998 Harvard Conference, ed. Derek Pearsall (2000)

Prophecy and Public Affairs in Later Medieval England, Lesley A. Coote (2000)

Cistercians, Heresy and Crusade in Occitania, 1145–1229: Preaching in the Lord's Vineyard, Beverly Mayne Kienzle (2001)

Guilds and the Parish Community in Late Medieval East Anglia c.1470–1550, Ken Farnhill (2001)

York Studies in Medieval Theology

I *Medieval Theology and the Natural Body*, ed. Peter Biller and A. J. Minnis (1997)

II *Handling Sin: Confession in the Middle Ages*, ed. Peter Biller and A. J. Minnis (1998)

York Manuscripts Conferences

Manuscripts and Readers in Fifteenth-Century England: The Literary Implications of Manuscript Study, ed. Derek Pearsall (1983) [Proceedings of the 1981 York Manuscripts Conference]

Manuscripts and Texts: Editorial Problems in Later Middle English Literature, ed. Derek Pearsall (1987) [Proceedings of the 1985 York Manuscripts Conference]

Latin and Vernacular: Studies in Late-Medieval Texts and Manuscripts, ed. A. J. Minnis (1989) [Proceedings of the 1987 York Manuscripts Conference]

Regionalism in Late-Medieval Manuscripts and Texts: Essays celebrating the publication of 'A Linguistic Atlas of Late Mediaeval English', ed. Felicity Riddy (1991) [Proceedings of the 1989 York Manuscripts Conference]

Late-Medieval Religious Texts and their Transmission: Essays in Honour of A. I. Doyle, ed. A. J. Minnis (1994) [Proceedings of the 1991 York Manuscripts Conference]

Prestige, Authority and Power in Late Medieval Manuscripts and Texts, ed. Felicity Riddy (2000) [Proceedings of the 1994 York Manuscripts Conference]

Middle English Poetry: Texts and Traditions. Essays in Honour of Derek Pearsall, ed. A. J. Minnis [Proceedings of the 1997 York Manuscripts Conference]